100
YEARS OF
MUSIC

100

YEARS OF

MUSIC

After Beethoven and Wagner

Third Edition

GERALD
ABRAHAM

Aldine Transaction
A Division of Transaction Publishers
New Brunswick (U.S.A.) and London (U.K.)

Library of Congress Catalog Number: 2008002001
ISBN: 978-0-202-36194-9
Printed in the United States of America

Library of Congress Cataloging-in-Publication Data

Abraham, Gerald, 1904-1988.
    One hundred years of music : after Beethoven and Wagner /
Gerald Abraham.—3rd ed.
        p. cm.
    Originally published: Chicago : Aldine, A hundred years of music, 1964.
    Includes bibliographical references (p.   ) and index.
    ISBN 978-0-202-36194-9
    1. Music—19th century—History and criticism. 2. Music—20th
century—History and criticism. I. Abraham, Gerald, 1904-1988.
    Hundred years of music. II. Title. III. Title: 100 years of music.

ML196.A3 2008
780.9'034—dc22   2008002001

CONTENTS

PREFACE

A CENTURY is an arbitrary period, and a century measured backward from the late nineteen-thirties is not obviously less so than any other century. But, as it happens, the early eighteen-thirties saw the opening of the careers of a number of composers—Chopin, Liszt, Berlioz, Schumann—who brought a new note into music. By general agreement we call that note "romanticism," and during the hundred years that followed, romanticism blossomed, became overblown, and began to run to seed, leaving only the rather barren stalks of neo-classicism. This book might well be sub-titled "The Triumph, Decline, and Fall of Musical Romanticism."

My approach to the period has been that of the historian of musical style rather than that of the æsthetic critic. (The two methods are necessarily very different.) For the most part I have been content to leave the throwing of brickbats and bouquets to others better qualified than I am to distribute them. Any that may have slipped out of my hand have done so accidentally.

But I realize that the historian is exposed to dangers that the critic of æsthetics can easily avoid. For one thing he is obliged to consider each composer's contribution to the development of art instead of his contribution to the sum of art. In reducing the chaos of facts to some sort of order, he is obliged to draw firm lines at the end of tendencies that actually faded out gradually and imperceptibly, to group composers as "schools" when in truth no such schools existed (even the celebrated Russian "mighty handful," almost a legendary model of a school, really consisted of five markedly different personalities with widely different artistic aims), to show the making of artistic history as a stream, whereas it actually consists of innumerable ripples on a great lake, each set of ripples—large or small—radiating from every individual composer. The historian traces the influence of one composer on another—it is a necessary and most fascinating occupation—but in doing so he gives an entirely false

7

impression of progress and development, of Weber preparing the way for Wagner, Wagner for Strauss, whereas Weber should be considered as an individual, self-contained artistic entity, Wagner as another. "Absolument il y a progrès et relativement il n'y en a pas," as Amiel said. "Les circonstances s'améliorent, le mérite ne grandit pas." Still these lines of artistic genealogy should mislead none but sciolists and the very innocent.

The central position of any book on the music of the last hundred years must inevitably be occupied by Wagner. Not because Wagner was the finest creative musical intelligence of the last hundred years—he quite probably was not—but because his work bulks far bigger than any other single contribution to the musical history of the period. I must repeat that the last thing I have attempted is æsthetic valuation of composers with allocation of space according to value.

Nor have I tried to catalogue names and works. The names of many talented minor composers, particularly contemporary ones, have been omitted. Even important works by major composers have not been referred to where reference would add nothing but a title to the course of the narrative. (This should be useful to reviewers; I know from personal experience how satisfying it is to draw attention to the fact that "Mr. So-and-so does not even mention Hässlichberg's masterly Trio for piccolo, trombone and side-drum.")

In order to correct the historical perspective, I have included a "prelude" and three "interludes," giving rough sketches of general conditions in the musical world at intervals of thirty years. An occasional glance at the chronology at the end will also help. And as the reader's sense of chronology is very apt to get confused when a number of simultaneous streams of development have to be described, I have inserted the date of composition or performance (both if they are widely separated) of each work at the first mention of it. I trust the usefulness of this liberal sprinkling of dates will more than compensate for any slight annoyance they may cause the reader.

The same may be said of my constant detailed references to specific passages. The ideal course would have been to use a music-type example in each case. But not only is the ordinary music-type quotation too short to suit my purpose; the use of even brief examples on the necessary scale would have made the cost of production prohibitive. On the other hand, it seems to me useless to talk "in the air," without giving chapter and verse. I have therefore tried to make everything clear to the reader who has no scores at his elbow for reference, but at the same time have told him where to look for confirmation or example if he wants it.

PREFACE TO THE SECOND EDITION

I HAVE taken advantage of this second edition to revise a few judgments, add and correct information on a number of points, enlarge the bibliography, and generally bring the book up to date.

G. A.

February, 1949

PREFACE TO THE THIRD EDITION

THIS third edition incorporates some corrections of fact, further enlarges the bibliography and chronology, and adds some comment on developments in musical techniques in the fourteen years since the last revision. But the musical judgments have not been revised. It is now twenty-five years since the book first appeared, so that the title is now a considerable understatement of its scope, and in those twenty-five years my opinions of this, that or the other composer or work have naturally undergone some modification—though, in no case, I think, fundamental change. But I have not tried to register these modifications in revising the book.

G. A.

May, 1963

I

AFTER BEETHOVEN

PRELUDE: MUSIC IN THE EIGHTEEN-THIRTIES

IT is generally too hastily assumed that the history of music is
simply the history of musical composition. To a great extent it
is that, of course; just as the history of literature consists mainly
of a record of the achievements of great writers. But musical
composition depends much more directly and obviously than
literary composition on mere circumstance. The literary man
may swim on a broad stream of general tendencies and he may
swim into favour on a current of fashion, but his work is not, like
the composer's, largely conditioned by hard practical surroundings. For one thing, the composer can never—unless he happens
to be a virtuoso—communicate directly with his public. The
very texture of his operas, his orchestral music, will be limited
by the technical ability of the performers he is likely to have at
his disposal. Even by their constitution: in the days when two
timpani were the normal number in the orchestra, to ask for
six was to ask for trouble. Unless choral singing flourishes in his
country, it will not occur to a composer to write elaborate choral
works. In a country that does not care enough about opera to
support state and municipal opera-houses, the man who writes
operas is either an heroic optimist or an unpractical fool, and
(even more to the point) he is unlikely to have had enough practical experience of the stage to turn out a work that will succeed
in other countries. Again: publication of music is a very different
matter from publication of a book. To get your music published
is only half the battle. The public can get to know your work,
other than piano pieces or songs, only through performance. When
the days of patronage were over, as they were after the first few
years of the nineteenth century, the only way to get your music
performed in public was to arrange a concert at your own expense,
as we read of Berlioz doing, or to interest a concert-giving organization in your work. The indifference, conservatism or even, in some
cases, almost complete lack of concert-giving societies is an obstacle

11

unknown to the literary man; it is a very potent force in the musical world. The musical innovator who dares to disregard social and material conditions risks far more than his literary colleague.

Before discussing the actual musical production of a hundred years ago, therefore, I shall make a brief sketch of the general musical conditions in which it was produced. The music of the eighteen-thirties and 'forties can be properly understood only if one understands the state of musical culture in which it was composed.

In two invaluable chapters of the first volume of his *Life of Richard Wagner*[1] ("The State of Music in Germany" and "The Status of the Musician"), Ernest Newman has summed up the results of careful research into the state of German music during the first three or four decades of the nineteenth century. He calls as his witnesses Spohr, Berlioz, Wagner, Lortzing, and English visitors such as Chorley and Edward Holmes, and the sum of their testimony will astonish the reader who thinks of nineteenth-century Germany as a musician's paradise, the most musical country in Europe (which perhaps, after all, it was).

Schumann, in the introduction to his *Gesammelte Schriften*, looking back twenty years, says:[2] "It cannot be said that musical conditions in Germany at that time [in 1833–34] were very pleasing. Rossini ruled the stage, Herz and Hünten almost exclusively the pianoforte. . . . True, Mendelssohn's star was in the ascendant, and wonderful things were being heard of a Pole, one Chopin, but it was not till later that these exercised a more lasting influence." Home music-making flourished; opera appeared to flourish—with innumerable petty Court opera-houses, municipal opera-houses as at Leipzig, and touring companies all over the country; nearly every town had some sort of concert-giving organization. But the general standard of performance was low. Newman concludes that "in all but two or three of the largest German cities the orchestral and vocal material and technique must have been quite inadequate for the performance of anything but the simplest works. . . . We need not be surprised to learn that audiences found Beethoven's symphonies incomprehensible when they were played, as they were at the Gewandhaus concerts in Leipzig in Wagner's youth, by an orchestra of about thirty, without a conductor, such leading as there was being given by the first violin."

[1] Cassell, 1933.   [2] Niecks's translation.

Even in Vienna "as late as 1837, while concerts were frequent enough, there was no concert orchestra of more than third-rate quality. Concerts indeed had to suffer for the benefit of the Opera: no public concerts could be given in the evening, while private concerts were not allowed to be publicly advertised." The orchestra of the famous Gesellschaft der Musikfreunde consisted mainly of amateurs and even the "friends of music" followed the example of similar societies all over Europe in giving their audiences "symphonies without tears"—with songs sandwiched between the movements.[1] It was not until 1842 that Otto Nicolai, composer of *Die lustigen Weiber von Windsor* and conductor of the Vienna Opera, gave the Viennese adequately rehearsed orchestral concerts.

Mendelssohn's command of the Gewandhaus concerts from 1835 to 1843 had done the same for Leipzig a little earlier. Until his advent orchestral works at the Gewandhaus "were not conducted at all;[2] they were simply played through under the leadership of the principal first violin. . . . The principal classical pieces which presented no particular technical difficulties were regularly given every winter; the execution was smooth and precise; and the members of the orchestra evidently enjoyed the annual recurrence of their familiar favourites." But in the case of Beethoven's Ninth Symphony the result was so "utterly confused and bewildering" that the young Wagner "lost courage and gave up the study of Beethoven for a time." Even in 1836, when Mendelssohn was in charge, Sterndale Bennett noted in his diary that "the overture to *Oberon* was not so well played as I have heard it in London." As for the Leipzig opera orchestra, Bennett considered it "*rather* more musician-like than our orchestras in England, though it is far inferior in *force* and spirit."

And the adventurous orchestral composer's troubles were not confined to defective orchestral technique and conductors who still directed from a first violin part. The average "full orchestra" of the 'thirties and 'forties was less than half the full orchestra of to-day. Berlioz tells us that the Frankfurt orchestra in 1842

[1] When Beethoven's Choral Symphony was played at the Paris Conservatoire in 1832 and 1834, half was given at the beginning and the rest at the end of the concert. At the Gewandhaus in 1826 it had been played under a "conductor" who had never seen the score.

[2] Wagner: *On Conducting* (Dannreuther's translation slightly adapted).

consisted of 8 first violins, 8 seconds, 4 violas, 5 'cellos, 4 basses, 2 flutes, 2 oboes, 2 clarinets, 2 bassoons, 4 horns, 2 trumpets, 3 trombones, and timpani—not a bad little force—and adds that "such a body of 47 musicians is to be found, with trifling differences, in all the smaller German towns." But he was trying to impress his friends in France. We know that in 1843, the year before Liszt became musical director at Weimar, the orchestra there consisted of only 35 players, though it was considerably augmented for Berlioz's visit. When Liszt gave *Lohengrin* there in 1850, *Lohengrin* with its famous divided strings, he had only 5 first violins, 6 seconds, 3 violas, 4 'cellos, 3 basses, 2 flutes, 2 oboes, 2 clarinets, 2 bassoons, 4 horns, 2 trumpets, 1 trombone, 1 tuba and 1 timpanist. In other words, the orchestras were constituted to tackle the compositions of twenty or thirty years earlier and hopelessly inadequate for the new orchestral writing of Berlioz and Wagner. We learn from Berlioz that few German orchestras possessed a harp, much less two harps (except at Berlin), and that hardly any had a cor anglais;[1] on the other hand, the new valve brass instruments were winning a footing in German orchestras, he notes. At Mannheim, where there was "a very intelligent little orchestra," he was unable to give the finale of *Harold en Italie* "because the trombones were manifestly incapable of playing their part." As for timpanists with what we to-day should consider just reasonably efficient technique, Berlioz declared: "I know of only three in all Europe, besides M. Poussard of the Paris Opera."

The economic condition of the composer in Germany, indeed all over Europe, was incredibly bad. The days of aristocratic patronage were over. Even if he held an official post, a musician was miserably underpaid. Unless he happened to be a virtuoso performer like Chopin or Liszt or Paganini, he was liable to starve as Lortzing did, Lortzing who composed *Czar und Zimmermann*, one of the most successful of all German comic operas. Royalties and performing rights were practically non-existent; inadequate copyright laws made the composer an easy prey for pirates. But, since Beethoven, the musician *was* beginning to be

---

[1] Weimar had neither harp nor cor anglais, he says. Even at Leipzig "the cor anglais was so dilapidated, and so extraordinarily out of tune, that notwithstanding the talent of the artist who played it, we were obliged to substitute the first clarinet."

treated as something a little better than a hired servant. It was only in the aristocratic houses of London that, as Liszt complained, "artists of the first rank, such as Moscheles, Rubini, Lafont, Pasta, Malibran, and others are forced to enter by the service stairs," and, when they reached the drawing-room, were separated from the guests by a cord stretched across the room.

If conditions were bad in Germany, they were worse in other parts of Europe. In Italy the only kind of music that existed at all was opera. Italian opera was organized, in so far as it was organized at all, on lines very different from those in Germany. In most of the smaller towns scratch companies were gathered by *entrepreneurs*, often wealthy amateurs, whose custom it was to commission new operas from composers of repute. The composer would come to the town, be handed a wretched libretto by the hack attached to the theatre, study the voices of the company, and "compose" his music often in two or three weeks, not seldom cobbling it up from bits of earlier works. He got his money and if his opera proved successful he might have it produced elsewhere; if it failed, he could still use the material in a fresh work—for it seldom got into print. It was in these conditions that Donizetti, Bellini and Rossini did most of their work; remembering them, it becomes easier to understand how Donizetti managed to produce between sixty and seventy operas in a period of thirty years. As for the artistic standard aimed at in these works, it is characteristic that the second act of an *opera seria* invariably contained one or two numbers significantly called *arie del sorbetto* (literally, "ice cream arias") during which refreshments were handed round, arias to which no one, except perhaps a few enthusiasts in the pit, listened and which were sometimes even written by another composer. Aiming so low, it is almost incredible that composers should have achieved things as fine as *Il Barbiere, Norma* and *Don Pasquale*.

Italian conditions were naturally at their best at La Scala, Milan, and the San Carlo, Naples. What they were like at the San Carlo in 1831 we learn again from Berlioz:[1] "In comparison

---

[1] All my quotations from Berlioz's *Memoirs* are taken from the Holmes translation revised by Ernest Newman (New York, 1935). In spite of his notorious inaccuracies and exaggerations, we may accept Berlioz as a reliable witness on these points; there is plenty of corroborative testimony.

with the orchestras I had heard (in Italy), this one seemed to me excellent. There is nothing to fear from the wind instruments; the violins play fairly well, and the violoncellos are harmonious, though too few. Even the kind of music which the Italian orchestras usually play does not justify their always having fewer violoncellos than double basses. I must protest against the disagreeable noise which the conductor makes by striking his desk with his bow; but I am assured that but for this some of the players would find it difficult to keep time. . . . The chorus is hopelessly weak; and a composer who writes for the San Carlo says it is very difficult, indeed, almost impossible, to get choruses in the ordinary four parts decently performed. The sopranos cannot sing apart from the tenors, and it is almost always necessary to write for them at the octave." As for opera manners, Berlioz went to hear Donizetti's *L'elisir d'amore* at the Cannobiano, Milan, and "found the theatre full of people talking at the top of their voices, with their backs to the stage." But talking at the opera and at concerts seems to have been then a common practice all over Europe. Schumann, a couple of years before Berlioz's visit, wrote that "music in Italy is hardly to be tolerated; you have no idea of the slovenliness and, at the same time, the spirit with which they fiddle through everything."[1]

Italian musicians took Italian standards of performance to other parts of Europe. Russia, for instance, was hopelessly Italian-ridden at this period. A Venetian, Catterino Cavos, was Director of the Italian and Russian Opera in Petersburg from 1799 to 1840 and enjoyed a high reputation as a conductor. But we read in Glinka's *Memoirs* that Cavos "took no notice of nuances; *pp*, in particular, was practically non-existent and was taken as a sort of *mf*. He was likewise incapable of hitting on the right tempo; he always took things either a little too slowly or too quickly." As for the orchestra of the Imperial Russian Opera: "It was good, but not altogether satisfactory. The second violins were far worse than the firsts, the violas too few, the basses not all good; of the wind, not all the horns were accurate—nor some of the second wind players. On the other hand there were some good artists among the first violins, four or five excellent 'cellists; of the wind, the clarinettist Bender distinguished himself by unusual fullness of tone, while the

[1] Letter to Wieck (November 6th, 1829) (Niecks's translation).

flautist Soussmann was undoubtedly one of the best artists (if not actually the best) in Europe." There was no school of music in the whole of Russia, and only one concert-giving society, the Petersburg Philharmonic.

Opera in France and England was in no better state. England got the cream of the foreign opera soloists because she was willing to pay for them. Her best orchestral players were foreigners too. French opera seems to have been more self-supporting. In both countries the execrable taste of the public is evident from the success in Paris of Castilblaze's notorious "adaptation" of *Der Freischütz* as *Robin des bois* and by the fact that when "a new grand opera, called *The Seraglio*" was given at Covent Garden in 1827, the music was "arranged and adapted from Mozart's celebrated opera, with additional arias, etc. composed by Mr. Kramer." Costa added parts for bass drum, ophicleide and trombone with impunity to Mozart's opera scores in London, and similar tricks were commonly played in Paris.

In France, almost as much as in Italy, a composer had to succeed at opera to succeed at all. The English composer did not succeed because he did not exist, except parochially. The chief glories of English music a hundred years ago were the pallidly tuneful operas of Balfe and Bishop[1] and the solid, stolid church music of the two Wesleys, Samuel and Samuel Sebastian. The youthful Sterndale Bennett was producing his early overtures *Parisina* (1834) and *The Naiades* (1836), rich with a promise never fulfilled. John Field, who shares with Francesco Pollini the honour of initiating the modern style of writing for the piano, made one solitary reappearance in London in 1832, playing his E flat Concerto at a Philharmonic concert, then wandered about Europe drinking himself to death, and died in Moscow in 1837, while that other lost Englishman, Henry Hugo Pierson, the great might-have-been of British music, did not begin to attract attention till the early 'forties.

[1] High hopes were raised in 1834 by the success of John Barnett's *Mountain Sylph*, the production of which was hailed as opening "a new period for music in this country, from which is to be dated the establishment of an English dramatic school." That school got considerable encouragement during the next decade; yet who to-day knows even the score of a single work by Barnett, Loder or Macfarren? Its crowning masterpieces were Balfe's *Bohemian Girl* (1843) and Vincent Wallace's *Maritana* (1845).

The Society of British Musicians, founded with high hopes in 1834 by a group of enthusiastic young men including Sterndale Bennett, Macfarren and J. W. Davison (then a promising youth known to his friends as "Overture Jim," afterwards famous as critic of *The Times*), began by producing orchestral works by themselves and other rising hopes of British music, such as Thomas Mudie, and soon degenerated, *faute de repertoire*, into an ordinary chamber music society playing works of all nations and periods. As for the Philharmonic Society, not yet Royal, practically the only British musicians whose works it performed during the 'thirties were Bishop, Sterndale Bennett and—Cipriani Potter.

The list of novelties produced by the Philharmonic Society during the 'thirties shows fairly accurately the general mental background of the cultured English musician a hundred years ago. It includes symphonies by Mendelssohn, Moscheles, Potter, Spohr, Maurer, Lachner and Onslow (the last an Englishman only by descent), the *William Tell* and *Fingal's Cave* overtures, Sterndale Bennett's overtures and concertos, Beethoven's Violin Concerto, concertos by Mendelssohn, Herz and Moscheles. The Society gave eight concerts a season, the season's subscription being four guineas, though admission to a single concert cost a guinea. The orchestra of about seventy "was as remarkable for vigour as for want of finish and up to the season of 1846 [when Costa was appointed permanent conductor] was directed by a leader, the first violin, as well as by a conductor, who was frequently changed, the leading and conducting being not infrequently at cross-purposes."[1] The Philharmonic shared the Hanover Square Rooms with the Society for Ancient Concerts, equally fashionable and equally expensive, conducted by Bishop. The middle-class public had to be content with the cheaper concerts of the Sacred Harmonic Society, with its mainly Handelian repertoire, at Exeter Hall.

The backbone of French orchestral music at this period was the Société des Concerts du Conservatoire, founded by Habeneck in 1828 and conducted by him for twenty years. Habeneck deserves credit for introducing Beethoven's symphonies in Paris in the teeth of fierce opposition from the conservatives and the

[1] Henry Davison: *From Mendelssohn to Wagner (Memoirs of J. W. Davison)*. William Reeves, 1912.

Rossini-ists. But the testimony differs as to the value of his interpretations of Beethoven. Wagner tells us[1] that Habeneck's reading of the Ninth Symphony in 1839 opened his eyes. "I came to understand the value of *correct* execution and the secret of a good performance. The orchestra had learned to look for *melody* in every bar . . . and the orchestra made that melody *sing*." Habeneck, he goes on to say, was "not a conductor of special genius" but he was possessed of infinite patience. On the other hand, Berlioz accuses Habeneck of "correcting" Beethoven's scoring and says that he conducted not from a full score but from a first violin part—a common practice at that period, especially in France. And Glinka[2] says that the Conservatoire Orchestra[3] "sometimes, particularly in difficult passages, had recourse to snuff-boxes and pocket handkerchiefs. . . . Moreover the wind—particularly the horns and clarinets—sometimes 'squawked'." He considered Habeneck's reading of the *Pastoral* Symphony so "ultra-pretentious" as to be unrecognizable (i.e., apparently, with all the lights and shades exaggerated) and complained, "On m'a escamoté la symphonie."

It seems that the works of Beethoven's maturity were really understood by few musicians during the first decade or so after his death (in 1827), the works of his last period by none. It was not till 1853 that even Wagner "first got to know the C sharp minor Quartet really intimately" through the playing of the Maurin-Chevillard Quartet in Paris, "for now its melody was made clear to me for the first time."[4] The last great Quartets were long generally regarded as incomprehensible. But chamber music was then an essentially German form of art. It was played everywhere, except in France and Italy, but composed by few non-German musicians.

I. ROMANTIC MUSIC: ITS SPIRIT AND FORMS

Musical historians have universally agreed to call the 'thirties and 'forties of the last century "The Romantic Period." Then they proceed to define romanticism and promptly fall out.

[1] *On Conducting.* [2] *Memoirs.*
[3] Including the conductor, according to a famous passage in Berlioz's *Memoirs* (Chapter XLVI).
[4] *Mein Leben.*

Romanticism is admittedly a good deal easier to recognize than to define, but for the sake of clearness we may as well accept the ruling, such as it is, of the two men with whom the discrimination between "classical" and "romantic" actually originated. "The distinction between classical and romantic poetry came originally from Schiller and myself," Goethe told Eckermann.[1] "I laid down the maxim of objective treatment in poetry, and would allow no other; but Schiller, who worked quite in the subjective way, deemed his own fashion right, and to defend himself against me, wrote the treatise upon *Naïve and Sentimental Poetry*. He proved to me that I, against my will, was romantic, and that my *Iphigenia*, through the predominance of sentiment, was by no means so classical and so much in the antique spirit as some people supposed. The Schlegels took up this idea, and carried it further, so that it has now been diffused over the whole world; and everybody talks about classicism and romanticism— of which nobody thought fifty years ago."

Now if "romantic music" means nothing more than "music impregnated with subjective sentiment" it had certainly appeared long before the eighteen-thirties. But if we qualify the Goethe-Schiller definition by the recollection of Walter Pater's remark that "the essence of romanticism is the blending of strangeness with the beautiful" and Heine's observation that romantic art deals much in symbolism, we shall have, not a flawless definition certainly, but a sufficiently clear and accurate working idea.

As a matter of fact the musical "romantic movement" was due not so much to increasingly subjective tendencies among nineteenth-century musicians as to their wider culture. There is very little evidence that even Beethoven was a well-read man but he certainly had a wider general culture than any of the earlier great masters. But Liszt, Berlioz, Schumann and Wagner were not only widely read; they mixed with literary and artistic people. They not only mixed with literary men; they were literary men themselves. And it is significant that Chopin, who was a bad writer and hated even letter-writing, was the least "literary" of all the romantic composers despite his intimate links with literary circles in Paris. The literary and pictorial

[1] J. P. Eckermann: *Conversations with Goethe* (entry of March 21st, 1830). (Quoted in John Oxenford's translation.)

tendencies characteristic of romantic music in general should not be regarded, as they commonly are, as a phase or consequence of romanticism. Just the reverse. It was the literary tendencies of the composers that made them romantics, for wherever they looked in contemporary literature they found romantic literature.

A few names and dates will make this clear and show how literary romanticism preceded the musical movement. The conscious founders of romanticism were four Germans: the Schlegels, A. W. (1767–1845) and F. (1772–1829), Tieck (1773–1853) and Novalis (1772–1801). (Lamartine (1790–1869), the originator of the French romantic movement, came along a little later.) The writers who exercised the greatest influence on the romantic composers of the 'thirties were probably Jean Paul Richter (1763–1825), E. T. A. Hoffmann (1776–1822), Walter Scott (1771–1832), Byron (1788–1824), Chamisso (1781–1838) and Eichendorff (1788–1857), all men of an earlier generation, men who had not affected their own musical contemporaries because those contemporaries were not particularly interested in literature. Weber, who alone had literary leanings and was personally acquainted with Tieck and Hoffmann, was the first definitely romantic composer, while his chief rival in the field of German romantic opera—Spohr—was also sufficiently interested in writing to produce an autobiography. But although all German romantic opera was stamped as such by the choice of romantic subjects—*Freischütz, Oberon,* Spohr's *Berggeist* and *Alchymist,* Marschner's *Vampyr, Templer und Jüdin* and *Hans Heiling*— Weber alone caught much of the real spirit of these subjects and successfully expressed it in his music, though Marschner excelled in the cultivation of one notable romantic malady: love of the macabre.

On the other hand it has been suggested that in at least one case musical romanticism gave an impetus to literature. Harold Nicolson[1] conceives that the Parisian success in 1824 of *Robin des Bois,* Castilblaze's "adaptation" of *Der Freischütz,* was one of the factors that "convinced Hugo that the Parisians were ready for something exciting, something explosive. . . ." French romanticism certainly ripened later than the German variety; the preface to *Oliver Cromwell,* proclaiming that "the object of modern art is not beauty but life," was published in 1827,

[1] Article "Victor Hugo" in the *Encyclopædia Britannica.*

Hernani produced in 1830—and Berlioz's *Symphonie fantastique* was being composed just between those two dates.

We have already seen that composers were romantic because they were literary, not literary because they were romantic. Even their tendency to frank programme-music was not a specially romantic trait. Berlioz's printing of an extended descriptive programme to his *Symphonie fantastique* (as distinct from the mere indicative titles occasionally printed by Beethoven and earlier composers) almost certainly originated in the example of his master at the Conservatoire, J. F. Lesueur, whose compositions were "written in accordance with a *plan raisonné,* which plan or programme was printed for the benefit of the audience."[1] Indeed, the romanticism of the Symphony as a whole is commonly exaggerated. The general conception is intensely, wildly romantic, but the principal subject of the first movement, the famous *idée fixe* that pervades the whole work, is as naïve (in the Schillerian sense) and objective—that is, classical—as a musical theme possibly can be. This vein of classicism runs through not only this Symphony but most of the other wildly romantic works of Berlioz's younger days and it actually predominated in his make-up as he grew older. Indeed, all the romantic composers of the period possessed certain classical traits, just as even the sturdiest classicists were tinged with romanticism.

And romanticism itself, this new, strange, symbolistic, emotional element in music, expressing "not beauty but life," took diverse forms. Berlioz revelled, as we learn from his life and from his prose, in the picturesque side of romanticism—in the scenery of *Rob Roy, Waverley* and *Childe Harold,* in banditry and opium-dreams and unhappy love. These provided him with the literary *données* of his early compositions. But when they had done that he had finished with them. The general conception was romantic; the actual music, as we have just seen, was frequently not. The "orgy" in *Harold en Italie* was nothing like as wild, even for 1834, as Berlioz gave it out to be and presumably supposed it to be; the brigands are about as alarming as Mr. Tupman at Mrs. Leo Hunter's famous breakfast. The *Symphonie fantastique,* nominally a partially autobiographical work, is singularly free from subjective emotion. How could it be otherwise, seeing that two of its movements, the "Ball" and

[1] Dannreuther: *Oxford History of Music* (Vol. VI).

the "Witches' Sabbath," were almost certainly written originally for a *Faust* ballet, while a third, the "March to the Scaffold"—possibly the "Scène aux champs" as well—was first intended for an unfinished opera, *Les Francs Juges*? Even the *idée fixe* was borrowed from the cantata *Herminie* of 1828. We may safely say that if there had been no romantic movement in literature in the late 'twenties and the early 'thirties Berlioz would not have been attracted even to romantic subjects. Unfortunately the romantic side of Berlioz bulks far too large in popular imagination. Mention the *Requiem* (1837) and everyone thinks of the romantically conceived *Tuba mirum*, with its four additional brass bands; never of the beautiful *Requiem et Kyrie*.

Schumann, on the other hand, was saturated with literature. It is true that he sometimes attached the literary titles to his piano pieces after they were written.[1] But that has very little to do with the case. He was profoundly introspective and his music, particularly his early music, is consequently profoundly subjective. His mind was saturated with literary rhythms and images, the characters and prose style of Hoffmann and Jean Paul, the verses of Heine and Chamisso and Eichendorff. He was the first musician who can be said to have actually relived his poet's experience—in the Heine songs in particular. From literature he draws a little band of figures—Hoffmann's Kreisler, the Florestan and Eusebius of his own *Neue Zeitschrift* articles, the "poet" of the *Dichterliebe*—who people his brooding mind as so many embodiments of his own personality. He even plays with the fiction that they write his music (the F sharp minor Sonata, the *Davidsbündlertänze*, the *Kreisleriana*).

Chopin is almost equally introspective and subjective, much more limited mentally than Schumann, hardly interested in other people's music at all (whereas Schumann was keenly interested in it), quite uninfluenced by literature, except in his Ballades, which are supposed to have been inspired by certain of Mickiewicz's poems. Chopin's mind remains a far greater enigma than Berlioz's or Schumann's or even Liszt's. He seems so straightforward, so commonplace, yet at the same time so subtly intelligent. But it was a limited mind; it played around

[1] This is true of *Carnaval* and the *Kinderszenen* at any rate. See Schumann's letters to Moscheles (August 23rd, 1837) and Dorn (September 5th, 1839).

only three main subjects, his own morbid emotions, the fate of Poland, and the wonderful, unexploited sonorities of the piano.

Liszt had six times Chopin's intellect and barely three-quarters of his musical fertility. And so, despite his apparent superficiality, he cuts a bigger, not greater, figure in the pages of history. As through-and-through a romantic as Schumann, he was a sort of inverted Schumann. Whereas Schumann absorbed literary images into his mind and made them his own, Liszt projected himself into the world of literature and art that surrounded him and lived intensely in that. A quotation from *Childe Harold* prefixed to his piano piece *Les Cloches de Genève* (1835–36) is curiously revealing:

> "I live not in myself, but I become
> Portion of that around me."

Comparatively little of his music seems to have sprung *spontaneously* from his inmost depths. His creative imagination usually took fire from some outside contact, generally from literature. His major orchestral works were inspired by Goethe, Lenau, Dante, Tasso, Victor Hugo, Lamartine, Byron, Shakespeare and Schiller. Sometimes he found stimuli in paintings (e.g., Kaulbach's "Battle of the Huns," Raphael's "Sposalizio," and Andrea Orcagna's frescoes, "The Triumph of Death," in the Campo Santo at Pisa); often in other music—for instance, in plainsong melodies—which frequently gave his musical imagination starting-points for excursions into quite other worlds. Even the operatic fantasias—"those prodigious fantasies which few pianists can play and fewer understand," as Bernard Shaw once justly described them—above all the masterly one on *Don Giovanni* (1841), are far from being the mere flashy pot-pourris they are assumed to be by those who have never heard a note of them. They may not be great music but they do exemplify one of Liszt's most striking qualities: the creative power of his exuberant imagination when given one or two "external" themes to play upon. At the same time, that quotation from *Childe Harold* tells only part of the truth about Liszt. Though he had this peculiar tendency to identify himself with his surroundings, he did not weakly lose himself in them. Quite the contrary; if his music is a record of extraordinarily varied and largely external experience, the record is expressed in intensely personal terms.

From the point of view of musical style, Liszt is one of the most individual composers who have ever lived. He owed a little to Chopin (e.g., his chromatic harmony and the slow *cantabile* type of melody found in the Piano Sonata and the two Concertos), a little (like Chopin himself) to Italian opera, less to Beethoven, Berlioz and Meyerbeer, and very much less than is commonly supposed—certainly no more than Brahms—to the music of the Hungarian gypsies. No composer has been less indebted to his predecessors, and none more thoroughly pilfered by his successors.

If Wagner was the highest peak of the musical romantic movement, Liszt sums up most completely all that was most characteristic of it. It is not only that he was later chronologically, his earliest really important compositions dating from the end of the 'forties when Chopin was dead and Berlioz and Schumann had already sobered down into more or less classical styles. His music, like his life, overflows with an exuberance peculiarly characteristic of nineteenth-century romanticism. The actual stuff of his music is exuberant as that of Berlioz's never is; the contrast with Schumann's reticence and Chopin's polished restraint is even more striking. Liszt loved to squeeze the last drop of emotion out of both art and life, equally from a chord or orchestral effect and from a love-affair or religious ecstasy. It is often darkly hinted that Liszt's exuberance is all pose, animated by no real creative impulse; that there is no living personality behind it; that his work is a showy façade concealing a soulless void. No more specious slander has ever been spoken of a musician. But it is true that the façade of Liszt's music matters immensely; in that, as in every other respect, the music is a perfect projection of the man himself. Liszt's private life was as public as that of the proverbial goldfish. And he lived it with such a frank zest that it certainly never occurred to him to be ashamed of it, any more than it occurred to him that his music might overstep the boundary dividing healthy exuberance from mere vulgarity.

In Liszt's symphonic poems we see how far literary influences had affected both the outer structure and the inner texture of music. As we shall see later, it is nonsense to assert that their forms are conditioned by their literary programmes. Nevertheless, the symphonic poem of the 'fifties is much further from the early programme symphonies of the 'thirties than the programme symphony was from the symphonies of Beethoven.

Beethoven himself had begun the breaking up of the "perfect" symphonic form (essentially the highest possible evolution of the pure dance and song forms) achieved by Mozart and by himself in his Second, Third, Fourth, Seventh and Eighth Symphonies. Just as the first movements of the Third and Fifth Symphonies set a new standard of musical logic, of symphonic thought (if you will, of musical organism), so the Fifth Symphony provided a totally new conception of "symphony" as a whole. It not only went a little further than the *Eroica* in its suggestion of an implied emotional programme underlying the whole scheme; the various movements are actually physically linked by the relationship of the *fortissimo* horn theme in the scherzo to the opening of the first movement, by the scherzo passing without a break into the finale, and by the finale harking back unexpectedly to the scherzo.[1] In the Sixth, the *Pastoral*, written at the same time as the Fifth, we have frankly programmatic titles to each movement and an extra movement, the storm, inserted to make the programme more effective. And the choral finale of the Ninth (1824) smashes the old instrumental conception of symphony to smithereens. After that, anything could be done.[2] Even Spohr, who disliked the Choral Symphony and had a poor opinion of Beethoven in general, called his Fourth Symphony (1832) *Die Weihe der Töne*, and followed it with a *Historical* Symphony (1839), its movements dated respectively 1720, 1780, 1810 and 1840, a Symphony for Double Orchestra, *Irdisches und Göttliches im Menschenleben* (1841) and a *Seasons* Symphony (1850).[3] As we shall see later even the composers with more

---

[1] There was a precedent in Haydn (Symphony No. 46 in B major), though it is very doubtful whether Beethoven knew it; the nineteenth-century romanticists certainly did not.

[2] Here, again, the credit must go to Beethoven, though he was not actually the first to introduce a choral movement in a symphony. He was anticipated by Peter von Winter (1755–1825) in his *Battle Symphony*, among others.

[3] *The Consecration of Sounds*, based on a poem by Karl Pfeiffer, was laid out in four movements: (1) *Largo:* Unbroken silence of Nature before the creation of sound. *Allegro:* Subsequent active life; sounds of

classical leanings—Mendelssohn and the later Schumann—were acutely conscious that Beethoven had thrust the symphony on to new paths which they must willy-nilly follow. They disagreed from the programme symphonists only as to which new path it was to be.

Of the programme symphonists, of course, Berlioz stands far above the rest equally in artistic achievement and historical importance. Spohr's music is dead. So are *Le Désert* (1844), *Christophe Colomb* (1847) and the other "ode-symphonies" of Félicien David—who, in any case, was little more than an imitator of Berlioz.[1] Berlioz is as alive to-day as he was a hundred years ago.

As early as February, 1829, Berlioz had thought of writing "a descriptive symphony of *Faust*." When he did put together his first symphony, the *Fantastique*, the next year, his whole method of approach showed how broadly he defined the word "symphony." He, in fact, anticipated Mahler's famous definition: "Mir heisst Symphonie mit allen Mitteln der vorhandenen Technik mir eine Welt aufbauen"—"the building up of a world, using every available technical means." As a matter of fact, Berlioz might have defined the *Symphonie fantastique* as "an excuse for using up a lot of available material," for that is what the truly fantastic programme, with its ultra-romantic opium-eating lover, actually was. He had three or four orchestral pieces, from the derelict *Faust* ballet of 1828 and the *Francs Juges* opera, on his hands; cast about for some central literary idea to bind them together; and, having found it, composed the first movement and revised and rearranged the remainder to

---

Nature; tumult of the elements (with much frank tone-painting). (2) Cradle song; dance; serenade. (3) Martial music; departure for battle; feelings of those left behind; return of the victors; thanksgiving. (4) Funeral music; comfort in tears. The *Historical* Symphony has movements imitating various styles. In the *Earthly and Divine in Human Life*, the divine element is represented by a body of eleven solo instruments, while the full orchestra depicts the earthly; there are three movements: (1) Childhood, (2) The Time of the Passions, (3) Triumph of the Divine. *The Seasons*, rejecting the obvious, is in two main parts: Winter—transition to Spring—Spring and Summer—transition to Autumn—Autumn. But Spohr's music is of no great value for its own sake and he exercised little or no influence on the historical development of the symphony.

[1] The still earlier programme symphonies of Dittersdorf (1739–99) are in a rather different category.

fit into the scheme. (In the case of the "Marche au supplice" we know that he simply altered the final cadence of his *Francs Juges* march, added the *idée fixe* on the clarinet, brought down his G minor guillotine, and wrote nine additional bars of G major triads.) One's first reflection is that Beethoven would never have thought of sticking several unrelated pieces of music together and calling them a symphony; one's second that the result, at any rate, is just as much a symphony as Beethoven's *Pastoral*, no more and no less. Berlioz's programme is slightly more elaborate than Beethoven's; on the other hand the appearance of the *idée fixe* in every movement caught the fancy of even non-programmatic symphonists, such as Schumann and Dvořák, who conceived that even an abstract symphony might be bound together by the use of a motto-theme recurring in every movement.

We have already seen that the romantic element in the *Fantastique* lay principally in the literary conception and we must now consider to what extent literary ideas conditioned the actual musical texture. They certainly had very little influence on the general outline of the work; but for the interpolation of the waltz, and the substitution of a march for a scherzo, the general layout is perfectly normal. As for the first movement, the most important of every symphony, Berlioz cast his "rêveries et passions" in the shape of a perfectly comprehensible modification of classical "first movement form." The slow introduction is Beethovenian and the exposition of the *allegro*—the melodic line of its first thirty-two bars (after the transition chords) taken note for note from *Herminie*—is perfectly normal, even with double bar and repeat; moreover, the theme of the *largo* is woven into the *allegro*, which Beethoven had never thought of doing. It is only the development and recapitulation that could puzzle the blindest of school-analysts. All that happens, however, is that the recapitulation is an organic continuation of the development, with the second group of themes *not* in the tonic and placed before the first subject instead of after it. In other words, Berlioz, like Beethoven, conceived form as an organic thing, not as a mechanical affair of rule-of-thumb. For the rest, one notes that the music as a whole is just what a very clever but immature young man who had just gone mad about Beethoven might have been expected to write.

Nor, as wholes, are the other movements of the Symphony conditioned by the programme, though the finale is admittedly literary (probably suggested by the Brocken scene in Goethe's *Faust*). The one great literary blot on the work is the macabre touch of the guillotine at the end of the march; it is as comic as most of the romantic extravagances of those days, and there is no musical justification for it; it merely spoils a thrilling movement. On the other hand, the distant thunder at the end of the slow movement is justified symphonically; to repeat a passage with an expected oboe reply replaced by timpani chords was musically a stroke of genius.

Harold en Italie, composed in 1834, is written more or less on the same formula as the *Fantastique* but leans more to the old classical conception of a symphony. The solo viola "impersonating" Harold himself, a characteristically romantic idea, hardly complicates the problem of form. This time there are only the conventional four movements: "Harold aux montagnes: Scènes de mélancolie, de bonheur et de joie" (normal introduction and *allegro*), "Marche de pèlerins, chantant la prière du soir" (an *allegretto*, obviously suggested by the corresponding movement in Beethoven's Seventh),[1] "Sérénade d'un montagnard des Abruzzes à sa maîtresse" (an *allegro assai* scherzo in 6-8 time), and "Orgie de brigands: Souvenirs de scènes précédentes," the "souvenirs" being introduced exactly in the manner of the opening of the finale of Beethoven's Ninth, except that the pilgrims' march reappears very effectively *lontano* on solo strings towards the end of the movement. Once again there is a motto-theme (borrowed, as well as the second subject of the first movement, from the *Rob Roy* Overture of 1832), though as Tom Wotton points out in his admirable study[2] it is differently treated: "In the Fantastic Symphony he showed how a theme representing an idea could be modified in accordance with its surroundings; in the *Harold en Italie* Symphony he illustrated the opposite—a theme unaffected by its environment." Wotton goes on to suggest that the burlesque of the *idée fixe* in the finale of the *Fantastique* was the germ of Liszt's idea of "metamorphosis of themes," but it is very much

[1] There are also signs of the influence of the first movement of the Seventh in the first movement of *Harold*.

[2] *Hector Berlioz.* O.U.P., 1935.

more likely that Liszt got the notion from Schubert's *Wanderer* Fantasia.

But it is in *Roméo et Juliette* (1839)—"symphonie dramatique, avec chœurs, solos de chant et prologue en récitatif choral, composée d'après la tragédie de Shakespeare"—that Berlioz's "building up of a world" in a symphony is carried out to the full. It consists of seven movements:

1. (a) Orchestral introduction (Combats; tumult; intervention of the Prince).
   (b) Prologue for chorus and orchestra.
   (c) Strophes ("Premiers transports que nul n'oublie") for contralto solo.
   (d) Recitative and Scherzetto ("Queen Mab") for tenor solo and chorus.
2. Romeo alone; his melancholy (*Andante malinconico e sostenuto*) —Concert and Ball; grand fête at the Capulets' (*Allegro*) (orchestra only).
3. Love-scene (Serene night; Capulet's garden silent and empty— the young Capulets, leaving the ball, pass by singing reminiscences of the dance music). (A short *allegretto* with male chorus, leading to the *Adagio* for orchestra only.)
4. Scherzo: Queen Mab (orchestra only).
5. Juliet's Funeral Procession (chorus and orchestra).
6. Romeo at the tomb of the Capulets (Invocation—Juliet's awakening—delirious joy, despair—final anguish and death of the two lovers) (*Allegro agitato e disperato* for orchestra only).
7. Finale. (The crowd rushes to the cemetery—quarrel between the Capulets and Montagues—recitative and aria of Friar Laurence—oath of reconciliation) (for bass solo, chorus and orchestra).

It is worth pointing out that movements 2, 3 (minus the inessential *allegretto*), 4 and 6, purely orchestral, constitute a more or less normal symphony except that the finale would be in the "wrong" key. As it is, *Romeo and Juliet* is not so much a symphony as a "world" in the Mahlerian sense. Tonality, which plays such an important part in all true symphonies, ancient and modern, is completely disregarded—apart from the fact that the introduction is in B minor and that the finale ends in B major; the vocal element and the additional movements almost obliterate the symphonic outline; Berlioz cares so little about sticking to essentials that he even brings in Queen Mab twice, though Mercutio's speech has nothing whatever to do with the tragedy of Romeo and Juliet. It is not surprising that when

Berlioz revised his symphony for a second edition in 1857 he found it necessary to assert in his preface that the work really was a symphony, not a cantata or *opéra de concert*. And it is very significant that although he lived for another thirty years he never wrote another symphony, except the *Symphonie funèbre et triomphale* of 1840, a mere occasional piece. His next big work inspired by a literary masterpiece—*La Damnation de Faust* (1846)—was styled "dramatic legend."

All this, of course, is not said in disparagement of the magnificent music of a great many pages of *Romeo and Juliet*—for instance the superb love-scene, so classic and restrained, one phrase of which (that sung by the 'cellos on page 140 of the miniature score) was once spoken of by Wagner as "the most beautiful musical phrase of the century." (It is something more than a coincidence that an important love-theme in *Tristan* is practically identical with one motive of it.) The point is that Berlioz took up the symphony where Beethoven had left it, developed it along one particular line as far as it would go—and dropped it. Those contemporaries, such as Félicien David, who imitated him were only his inferiors, while in later times the only important composer who has seen the symphony in anything like the same light is, as I have already pointed out, Gustav Mahler. It is quite wrong to regard Berlioz's programme symphonies as in any way the parents or precursors of Liszt's symphonic poems. The Liszt poems sprang from the overture —the dramatic overtures of Beethoven (*Egmont* and *Leonora* Nos. 2 and 3) and Mendelssohn's concert overtures—not from any kind of symphony; the symphonic poems were actually called "overtures" originally.[1] As for the peculiar inward organism of the Liszt poems, we shall find the origin of that less easily in other orchestral compositions than in the new miniature forms for piano that were being employed in the 'thirties and 'forties by Chopin, Schumann and Liszt himself.

The eighteen-thirties were remarkable for the appearance of a spate of comparatively short piano pieces, the earliest productions of three outstanding piano-composers. Chopin's Op. 2, the "*La ci darem*" *Variations*, was published in 1830. Schumann's Op. 2 (*Papillons*), his first set of *Concert Studies on Paganini's*

[1] The term "Symphonische Dichtung" was first used in 1854, when *Tasso* was performed at a Court Concert at Weimar.

Caprices, and Chopin's first set of mazurkas all came out in 1832, Chopin's first nocturnes and studies in the following year, and Chopin's first valse in 1834. In 1835 Chopin published his first scherzo, Liszt his three *Apparitions*. Hard on the heels of these came Chopin's first ballade and polonaises, Schumann's *Carnaval*, *Davidsbündlertänze*, *Kreisleriana*, *Novelletten* and the rest, and Liszt's *Album d'un voyageur*, which formed the basis of the first set of *Années de Pèlerinage*.

It is characteristic of the romantic musicians in general that they paid more attention to parts than to the whole, as we have just observed in Berlioz's symphonies. The common critical cant puts it that they were remarkable miniaturists but deficient in structural ability. That is partly true, or, rather, a false way of expressing a truth. The critic's duty is not to condemn them for not doing something they had never attempted to do; it is to examine objectively what they actually did achieve and to find if possible why their achievement lay in that particular direction. It is tempting to play with the idea that the emotional intensity which is characteristic of the romantic movement found its expression in spurts of lyrical inspiration rather than in the careful moulding of movements in sonata-form; it is probably this that accounts for the "absolute subordination of the sectional distribution to the ideas contained" to which Parry drew attention[1] in the first movement of Schumann's F sharp minor Piano Sonata (1836). The romantic composers obviously preferred to express a single mood or impression in a small self-contained piece and then to publish it with a group of similar but contrasted pieces, rather than to pour the results of contrasted moods into one large form and work out the resulting conflict. Schumann himself said of *Carnaval*: "The whole has no artistic value whatever; the manifold states of soul alone seem to me of interest."

But there were also purely musical reasons for their preference for miniature forms. As it happens, their musical minds were all constituted in such a way that they could hardly think musically except in terms of small symmetrical forms. This is equally true in different ways of Chopin, Schumann and Liszt. The two main influences on Chopin's musical mind—the environment in which it grew—were Polish folk-songs and dances, and

[1] Article "Sonata" in *Grove*.

Italian opera melody. Some writers have considered musical nationalism itself to be an aspect of romanticism; it is certainly true that some of the most prominent romantics—Weber, Chopin, Liszt, and to a certain extent Schumann—were race-conscious. But the connection between romanticism and nationalism seems to me purely accidental; in the strictly musical sense Weber was less a nationalist than Haydn with his numerous borrowings of Croatian folk-tunes; I shall consider nationalism later as a separate phenomenon. Nevertheless the influence of the mazurka and polonaise, with that of the waltz, largely conditioned Chopin's musical thought as a whole. Dance music is necessarily symmetrical. The nocturnes, especially the earlier ones, show the melodic (which in this case is equivalent to formal) influence of Italian opera melody, again a symmetrical pattern. Chopin's *rubato* and delicate ornamentation take away every suggestion of squareness from his forms but the periods remain well-defined, symmetrical, comparatively short. There is little carrying on of a thought; it is turned over, lovingly dwelt on, exquisitely played with. In the tiny forms in which Chopin excelled one asks for no more. But in the scherzos and still more in the sonatas and concertos, delightful as each section is (generally a perfect miniature taken by itself), one misses the continuity of musical form at its best. Instead of a true whole, we are given, generally, three smaller wholes beautifully welded together. The smaller Chopin's form, as in some of the preludes, the more perfect it is.

Of the larger forms, that in which he succeeded best was his own invention: the ballade. Whether or not the Ballades were inspired by the poems of Mickiewicz, Chopin magically contrived to give them a curious *narrative* tone—perhaps from the use in all four of 6-4 or 6-8 time. With them, although differently titled and in common time, we may class the magnificent *Fantaisie* in F minor. All five are far more truly, inwardly, programmatic than the symphonies of Berlioz, but the programmes are not known for certain—it is better to disregard the gossip of Liszt, Kleczynski, Huneker and the rest—and no one wants to know them. The point is that by making his music suggest an underlying narrative, *not* by telling us that it was inspired by such-and-such a story, Chopin rides away with his rhapsodical forms leaving us with the feeling that they are quite satisfactory.

Moreover, in these works he escapes more successfully than else-where from the comparatively short-breathed inner organism of the dance forms. Especially in the *Fantaisie* and the Fourth Ballade in the same key, his musical thought sweeps along with far more continuity than usual.

Squareness is even more noticeable in Schumann's short pieces and those longer ones, the *Arabeske*, the *Blumenstück* and the *Humoreske* (all three dating from 1839), which like the Chopin scherzi consist in effect of several short pieces tacked together. But it is due to a different cause. Whereas Chopin's symmetry is purely musical in origin, Schumann's is literary. Schumann's approach to music was indeed far more literary than any earlier composer's, far more, even, than Berlioz's, which after all amounted to no more than a desire to pay homage in music to the genius of Shakespeare, Goethe and Byron. Liszt's culture appears fairly imposing, but it was not acquired till he was a young man. Schumann had literature in his blood. His father was publisher, newspaper editor, lexicographer, novelist, miscel-laneous writer and translator of Byron. (August Schumann's last literary work consisted of translations of *Beppo* and three cantos of *Childe Harold* in the original metres.) And this literary approach conditioned the structure of Schumann's music in a curious way.

It is not perhaps of special importance that the end of *Papillons* was inspired by the masked ball at the end of Jean Paul's *Flegeljahre*, that the Intermezzo, Op. 4, No. 2, has a section inspired by Gretchen's "Meine Ruh' ist hin" in *Faust*, that the *Kreisleriana* were suggested by a character of E. T. A. Hoffmann's, part of the *Novellette*, Op. 21, No. 3, by the "When shall we three meet again" lines in *Macbeth*, and so on. Chopin, too, wrote a nocturne (Op. 15, No. 3) "after a performance of *Hamlet*," as he noted on the manuscript. Literature left much deeper marks than this on the structure of Schumann's music. It led him to think of music far too much in terms of verse or rhapsodic prose—admittedly the two forms of literature in which words approach most nearly to the condition of music. His remark that he had "learned more counterpoint from Jean Paul than from my music-master" is a characteristic piece of romantic extravagance but it contains a grain of truth. If he did not learn counterpoint from Jean Paul he learned form from him, the form of the humorous or sentimental aphorism. His Jean Paulism even broke into articulate speech in the first edition of the *Davidsbündlertänze*, in which No. 9 was prefaced with the remark that "Hereupon Florestan finished, and his lips quivered painfully" and No. 18 was headed "Quite superfluously Eusebius remarked as follows, but his eyes beamed blissfully the while."

Even stronger than the influence of the fantastic, aphoristic prose of Jean Paul and Hoffmann (himself strongly influenced by Jean Paul) is the influence of verse, particularly of Heine's four-line stanza. Hadow has put this so clearly, once for all,[1] that it would be presumptuous to try to improve on him: "All tune implies a certain fundamental unity—otherwise it would be chaotic, and a certain variation of detail—otherwise it would be monotonous. This identity in difference can be obtained in two ways, which we may call respectively the Continuous and the Discrete. In the former a series of entirely different elements is fused into a single whole: no two of them are similar, yet all are so fitted together that each supplies what the others need. In the latter a set of parallel clauses are balanced antithetically: the same rhythmic figure is preserved in all, and the differences depend entirely upon qualities of tone and curve. The former is the typical type of Beethoven, the latter that of Schumann.[2] . . . In the last movement of the D minor Trio, in the *cantabile* tune of the first *Novellette*, in the well-known theme of the *Bilder aus Osten*, in a hundred other examples, we find a definite square-cut scheme, exactly analogous to the structure of a stanza of verse. There are very few of Beethoven's instrumental melodies to which it would be possible to adapt metrical words; there is scarcely one of Schumann's which could not be so treated. His

[1] *Studies in Modern Music* (first series). Seeley, Service & Co., eleventh impression, 1926.

[2] Hadow gives as examples of "continuous" melody the opening subject of Beethoven's 'Cello Sonata in A and the chief melody of the slow movement of the *Pathétique* Sonata. Berlioz is full of even longer "continuous" melodies, e.g., the fugue subject of the "Sanctus" of the *Requiem*. He noted in his *Memoirs* that, as his melodies "are often on a very large scale, an immature or unappreciative mind cannot properly distinguish their forms. . . . Such melodies are so unlike the little absurdities to which that term is applied by the lower stratum of the musical world, that it finds it impossible to give the same name to both." In other words they are not "discrete."

relation to poetry extends even to the fact of versification." In addition to Hadow's examples, the reader may care to look at the *Abschied* of the *Waldszenen* for piano, the opening melody of which seems to have been based on a verse inscribed as a motto on the manuscript. Again: the *Intermezzo* of the *Faschingsschwank* and the B flat minor *Romance*, Op. 28, No. 1, cry out for words. Indeed there is some ground for belief that Schumann consciously drew direct inspiration for instrumental melodies from verse. The slow movements of the Piano Sonatas in F sharp minor and G minor, and the *Intermezzo*, Op. 4, No. 4, originated as songs; may he not in later years have dispensed with the intermediate stage of a vocal setting?

If the influence of aphoristic prose and the poetic stanza shaped Schumann's piano music even more squarely and sectionally than the influence of the dance shaped Chopin's, it is easy to understand why Schumann's musical style can be mated so perfectly, so effortlessly with actual verse. The bulk of Schumann's songs—the Heine *Liederkreis*, Op. 24, the *Myrthen* cycle, the first set of *Lieder und Gesänge*, Op. 27, the Eichendorff *Liederkreis*, Op. 39, the *Frauenliebe und-leben* cycle, the first three books of *Romanzen und Balladen*, Opp. 45, 49 and 53, the *Dichterliebe* cycle, greatest of all, and a number of others—all date from 1840, the year of the composer's marriage; they were the last great purely romantic outpouring of Schumann. The next year or two saw the production of a number of works—the Piano Concerto, the First Symphony, the first chamber works, the *Andante and Variations* for two pianos—which are essentially works of transition, and then we see Schumann unconsciously but more or less completely succumbing to the more classical, moré purely musical influence of his adored Mendelssohn, and shaking himself free from that of literature. He passes out of the ranks of the true romantic composers, though square, stanza-like construction and the "rhyming verse" type of melody continue throughout his would-be-classical sonatas and symphonies and are a serious weakness in them, melodic themes complete in themselves being incompatible with development in the Beethovenian sense. But the songs, above all the Heine songs of the *Dichterliebe*, are perhaps the most perfect examples of fusion of music with poetry in existence, surpassed not even by Wolf's *Mörike-Lieder*. There are greater songs in the world;

Schubert, for instance, could take a Heine lyric and make it something far bigger (e.g., *Der Doppelgänger*). Schumann is seldom greater than his poet; but he miraculously enables the poet to become through him a musician.

Not that he merely makes adequate and beautiful settings of words. One has only to compare Schumann's songs with those of the next greatest German song-writer of the period—Robert Franz, whose first set of songs came out in 1843—to see how supreme he is. Franz can set a lyric beautifully, transmuting its spirit into music and all with "just note and accent." Schumann brings to the lyric music that needs nothing but those words, and just those words, to give it articulate expression. Again: an examination of Schumann's songs will help to show how deeply the influence of verse had permeated his piano music. Perfectly vocal as his song-line always is, one has often to do nothing but incorporate it in a slightly recast piano part to get a character-istic Schumann piano piece—as Schumann himself did with the early songs which he turned into slow movements of sonatas.

With Liszt's songs, so unequal in artistic value, we need not concern ourselves here, though we shall have to return to one or two of them later when we consider Liszt from other points of view. But we must note the construction of his early piano pieces, for they are really symphonic poems in miniature. Not so much the studies, fantasias, and bravura pieces, of course, but the miniature tone-poems and impressions, the *Apparitions*, the *Harmonies poétiques et réligieuses* and the first two books of the *Années de Pèlerinage*. One can hardly fail to be struck by the squareness of construction of most of the pieces, both in inner organism and general outline. The three *Sonetti del Petrarco*, the *Canzonetta del Salvator Rosa* and the three pieces of the *Venezia e Napoli* supplement, for instance, are frankly based on song melodies, while *Au Lac de Wallenstadt* and *Les Cloches de Genève* might easily be also. It is doubtful whether Liszt came under the influence of Schumann's piano pieces, but he certainly came under that of Chopin's melody and of Bellini's (directly as well as through Chopin: cf. the Bellinian phrase in sixths in the first *Apparition*); and melodic build is often decisive in conditioning musical organism. The *Eglogue* again consists solely of repetitions of a couple of short, square-cut scraps of— admittedly charming—tune.

Now Liszt's large-scale instrumental pieces, such as the symphonic poems, are simply enlargements and elaborations of these square-cut sectional forms. The symphonic poems, with the exception of *Les Préludes*, are so little known to modern musicians and have had so much ignorant and malicious nonsense written about them that any fair-minded critic is bound to perform a few Donnerlike prefatory exercises in the way of fog-clearing. The most extraordinary misconception about them is that their formal structure is conditioned by their "programmes." Dannreuther[1] says that "with the exception of the little masterpiece *Orpheus*, which is pure self-contained music, all are impromptu illustrations, corresponding to some poem, or picture or group of concepts expressed in words. They are mere sketches arranged in accordance with some poetical plan, extraneous, and more or less alien to music." Again Hermann Kretzschmar, in his ever-popular *Führer durch den Konzertsaal*, informs his readers that "Liszt went considerably further than his predecessor (Berlioz) and completely subordinated even the form of a composition to the programme." The fallacy seems to have been echoed by every sciolist who has ever written about Liszt, even by such an astute critic as Ernest Newman.[2] Apart from the fact that neither *Festklänge*, *Hamlet*, *Heroïde funèbre*, *Orpheus* nor *Hungaria* possesses a programme at all—for a title is not a programme—the true relation of the other symphonic poems to their programmes has been completely misunderstood until a few years ago. In only two cases, *Mazeppa* and *Hunnenschlacht*, can it be said that the musical form is in any way conditioned by the programme, and both these works, whatever their artistic worth, are nevertheless perfectly clear in construction. *Mazeppa*, for instance, consists simply of two independent sections: the ride (in simple ternary form, ABA, with a 34-bar introduction and a 35-bar epilogue) and the triumph (three strophes, the third elaborated, with 29 bars of introductory fanfares and a 33-bar coda looking back to the theme of the ride). As Joachim Bergfeld has convincingly shown,[3] only one of the twelve symphonic poems, *Ce qu'on entend sur la montagne*, is at all confused

[1] *Oxford History of Music*, Vol. VI.
[2] Ernest Newman: *Richard Strauss*. John Lane, 2nd edition, 1921. (See pp. 50–1.)
[3] *Die formale Struktur der Symphonischen Dichtungen Franz Liszts.* Eisenbach, 1931.

in form and even in that case the confusion is in no way due to the programme. In every other case the formal outline of the poem is perfectly comprehensible from a purely musical point of view, no less than seven of the twelve being laid out in that development of simple ternary form that modern German theorists beginning with Alfred Lorenz prefer to call the *Bogen* (i.e., bow or arch).[1]

We may take *Les Préludes* as a typical example, though its musical quality is far below that of Liszt at his best. As Bergfeld shows, it is in ternary form, with a 34-bar introduction. The A section falls into two main parts: the short *andante maestoso* and the more important part beginning with the cantabile melody for 'cellos and second violins, stating the two chief themes at full length. A 22-bar transition passage, *allegro ma non troppo*, leads to the middle section which also falls into two parts, Ba (*allegro tempestuoso*) and Bb (*allegretto pastorale*), connected by an 18-bar bridge (*un poco più moderato*); Ba being a stormy development of the two themes, Bb introducing a new theme and then combining it with the rather slimily chromatic second subject. Then the A section is repeated (*allegro marziale*), though with both themes martially transformed and with the *andante maestoso* following the main part of the section instead of preceding it. Though the point has escaped Bergfeld, if we neglect the introduction and the two brief *andante maestoso* passages at beginning and end, we find *Les Préludes* to be in perfectly orthodox sonata-form: A corresponding to the exposition, B to the development, and the metamorphosis of A to the recapitulation. This hardly looks like "the complete subordination of the form to the programme." As a matter of fact, *Les Préludes* was not composed "in accordance with" the programme at all. It was composed in 1848, perhaps earlier, as the overture to a suite of pieces for male chorus, *Les quatre Elémens*,[2] to words by Joseph Autran, the themes all being taken from the choruses. When Liszt brushed up his overture as a separate

---

[1] Liszt's *Hamlet* is an almost perfect specimen of *Bogenform*: ABCDCBA. The section B begins at the *Allegro appassionato ed agitato assai* marking; C at the *sehr heftig* outburst at the peak of the rushing semiquaver passage; D—the crown of the arch—is the middle section "hinting at Ophelia"; then comes C in a varied form, a passage *not identical with but analogous to B*, and finally A (condensed and fused with the theme of C).

[2] *La Terre, Les Aquilons, Les Flots* and *Les Astres*.

piece three or four years later, he cast about for a suitable poetic motto, failed to find one, and finally concocted the programme as we know it to fit the existing music. It is true he borrowed the title of one of Lamartine's *Méditations poétiques*, but the pretence that the programme itself is "after Lamartine" is a little hoax that was exposed only in 1931 by Peter Raabe.[1]

Even *Die Ideale*, its score sprinkled with quotations from Schiller, has a comprehensible if not completely satisfactory musical form, though a form that can be grasped only when one overlooks the chunks of Schiller and the sections into which they misleadingly appear to divide the piece.

But if literary influences left little or no mark on the outward form (architecture and general lay-out) of Liszt's orchestral works, which are essentially developments of the Beethovenian overture or enlargements of the piano miniature, it seems probable that they are responsible for a curious weakness in the inward form (the actual musical organism): the weakness of "vain repetitions." The least careful listener can hardly fail to notice that Liszt has a mania for singing his songs twice over, but it may be worth while to examine the part that mere mechanical repetition plays in a piece—*Orpheus*—that even the hostile Dannreuther acknowledged to be a "little masterpiece," and to discuss the reason for this weakness.

We may pass over the introduction: two symmetrical harp arpeggios on two chords, each pivoting on the G of the horns. The *poco più di moto* begins with a 6-bar phrase and its rather obvious 6-bar answer; then the whole 12-bar passage is repeated note for note but with different scoring, the first bar of the repetition rhythmically overlapping the last of the original statement. Observe what follows. We get a little 3-bar figure—two bars merely harmonic and rhythmic, the third a motive from the first theme—which is at once exactly repeated; then the whole 6-bar block is repeated note for note a minor third higher, with a 5-bar tag to the second repetition. Liszt has already laid himself open to a charge of inflation, yet he now proceeds to repeat the whole of this 17-bar slab, just as it stands, altering only the little concluding tag so as to modulate into the next section of the piece. In other words, the whole passage of thirty-four bars is constructed on the simple principle of a wallpaper pattern. And examination

[1] *Liszts Schaffen.* Stuttgart, 1931.

of the majority of Liszt's scores will show that, although the first section of *Orpheus* happens to be a particularly bad case, this was Liszt's usual way of going about things. Far from being wild and rhapsodical, he is only too often square and mechanical. He hits on good spontaneous ideas but does nothing with them but modify them and arrange them in well-balanced patterns.

The obvious comment is that this is a rather easy way of composing, as Rimsky-Korsakov and other of Liszt's disciples quickly discovered. And it would be only natural, though possibly unjust, to deduce from Liszt's procedure that he was *incapable* of writing music that developed on Beethovenian lines, one musical shape spontaneously (or with the interplay of technique) begetting another in the composer's mind so that a whole movement is developed from one or two themes as a plant from the seed. But it will be more useful to consider why Liszt dropped into this "wallpaper pattern" type of construction. He himself, in his essay on "Robert Schumann's Piano Works,"[1] wrote that "it is a mistake to regard repetition as poverty. From the point of view of the public, it is indispensable for the understanding of the thought, while from the point of view of art it is almost identical with the demands of clarity, structure and effectiveness." In any case the "impotence" theory seems just a little too easy; for Liszt demonstrably had an exuberant musical imagination. But it is probably here that literary, non-musical influences did affect Liszt's music harmfully. His creative imagination did not function purely and exclusively in terms of music; his themes instead of being purely musical ideas were also partly the symbols of definite emotions, of literary or visual concepts. Consequently the driving power, the forward impulse, within his music was no longer purely musical either. Instead of one musical shape begetting another in a living, growing, rhythmic organism, there were ideas or emotions to be driven home, pictures to be painted, by dwelling on their musical symbols. Arnold Schering has remarked of the romantics that "the dazzling idea as such was sufficient unto itself and called not for elaboration but for enthusiastic repetition." That is true of the romantic composers in general and particularly true of the arch-romantic Liszt. With none of the others is it such a serious weakness. In the *Orpheus* passage the music does not

[1] *Ges. Schriften.* Vol. II, p. 103.

move forward at all, except in the sense that time elapses while it is being played. We are not infectiously swept along by its rhythms or melodic energy, not even levered along by its harmonic progressions. There is a real loss of musical vitality through the substitution of a non-musical for a musical motive power.

The absence of development in the Beethovenian sense in Liszt's music is partly concealed by his ingenious use of the ancient device of theme-transformation,[1] which reminds one of the now-forgotten music-hall science known, if I remember rightly, as "chapeaugraphy" by which a black felt ring ingeniously twisted into the shapes of various characteristic hats enabled the performer to impersonate now Napoleon, now a Nonconformist minister. Liszt brought off some astonishing feats of transformation: for instance, the mockery of the "Faust" themes in the "Mephistopheles" movement of the *Faust* Symphony. Wagner probably learnt a good deal of the art of leitmotive manipulation from his father-in-law-to-be, just as Liszt himself probably got the idea from Schubert's *Wanderer* Fantasia. But theme transformation is but a poor brainspun affair. It comes off when, as in *Les Préludes*, the various shapes are all based on a more or less colourless, inexpressive original (the chapeaugraphist's piece of felt) which can be played either "martially" or *amoroso*, i.e., where the expressive force lies simply in the manner of performance and not in the theme itself. But when the originals themselves are living, expressive melodies, such as those in the slow movement of the E flat Concerto, the transformations are apt to be unintentional caricatures (*vide* the finale of that Concerto) as hideous as the intentional ones in the *Faust* Symphony. Still, Liszt's conception of the single-movement concerto developed from metamorphoses of one or two basic themes and containing the elements of first movement, slow movement, scherzo and finale, was of enormous importance to the evolution of musical form. If it looks back to the *Wanderer* Fantasia on the one hand, it looks forward to Franck and his school, even to Schönberg, on the other. As for the still more remarkable experiment of the Piano Sonata (composed 1852–53), a colossal "first movement" likewise containing the elements of all the other usual movements, it was so bold that, after inspiring a counterpart in the remarkable but

[1] See note on p. 164.

forgotten Sonata in B flat minor by Liszt's pupil, Reubke.[1] it remained uncopied until Arnold Bax took it as his model in his First Piano Sonata in F sharp (composed 1910, though revised in 1917–21 before publication).

II. ROMANTIC MUSIC: ITS TEXTURE AND STYLE

We have already discussed the melody of Chopin and Schumann in so far as melodic form conditions the form of a whole piece, as it necessarily does to a great extent in lyrical music. We must now look a little more closely at the new types of melody that appeared in the eighteen-thirties and 'forties from another point of view: as an element in musical texture and, consequently, as a manifestation of the composers' styles. It would of course be absurd to generalize about the melody of "the romantics"; the highest common factor of Berlioz's long-drawn sensitive lines, of Chopin's delicious curves and fascinating dance tunes, and of Schumann's more homely, square-cut ideas is very low indeed. Yet in the melodic writing of the instrumental composers of that period, one detects certain tendencies, either new or decided developments of what had hitherto been done only sporadically and tentatively. Most striking of all these, and firmly linked with the romantic period by its "literary" nature, was the development of the instrumental recitative.

We have already seen how the influence of verse-forms helped to mould a great deal of Schumann's melodic structure. In the instrumental recitative the influence of verbal declamation on musical line is even more noticeable. It was also, of course, more conscious. In their desire for greater expressiveness or greater precision of expression, the romantic composers tried, as it were, to make their dumb music almost speak. Beethoven had shown them the way[2] in the Piano Sonatas in D minor

[1] Whose one-movement Organ Sonata is, however, still sometimes heard.

[2] There were instrumental recitatives before Beethoven, just as there had been symphonies with choral finales before the Ninth. What matters is not "who did the thing first," a point often difficult to determine, but "who first established it" and "who was the real influence." I doubt whether the instrumental recitatives in either J. S. Bach or his son, Karl Philipp Emanuel, had much influence on the nineteenth-century romanticists, though it is just possible that they did.

(Op. 31, No. 2) and A flat (Op. 110), and above all in the finale
of the Ninth Symphony. The device is effective mainly as a
dramatic contrast to a more normal type of melody, and consequently its effectiveness is in inverse proportion to the frequency
of its employment. Æsthetically it is equivalent to Wilhelmine
Schröder-Devrient's celebrated effect in *Fidelio* of speaking the
line "Tödt' erst sein Weib!" instead of singing it. By all
accounts it was electrifying. But Schröder-Devrient, great artist
though she was, stooped to the exploitation of her stroke of
inspiration and in later years filled all her parts with spoken
interjections. The instrumental recitative is a rhetorical effect
and it has been used by composers in fairly exact proportion to
their rhetorical tendencies. Schumann used it hardly at all;
Chopin very little; Berlioz more frequently; Liszt—always the
ultra-romantic—so much that it became an integral part of his
instrumental style and, especially after its development in
Wagner's hands, of that of all but the most conservative orchestral writers.

Chopin's use of the instrumental recitative is almost as restrained as Beethoven's. The end of the B major Nocturne,
Op. 32, No. 1, is typical. The piece as a whole is a reverie,
purely melodic and very simple; but then come "sombre sounds
as of a kettle drum" as Niecks puts it, a passionate recitative—
and silence. The recitative has no musical interest in itself but
its contrast with what has preceded it is dramatic in the extreme;
the least imaginative listener involuntarily invents for himself
some dramatic happening. One of Beethoven's most romantic
traits is here raised to a higher power of romanticism. (For
one thing, Beethoven would never have *ended* a piece on this
note.)

The left-hand octave passage in the C sharp minor Nocturne,
Op. 27, No. 1—another piece depending very largely on a
totally unexpected coda thought, though this time the coda is
purely lyrical—illustrates very well how nearly allied the interpolated recitative may be to the cadenza (the non-bravura type
of cadenza, of course). The passage is half recitative, half
cadenza. And the same may be said of the passage in Schumann's
Der Dichter spricht (Op. 15, No. 13). Whether considered as
cadenzas or recitatives, these breaks in the regular metrical pattern are highly effective. But they remain mere interpolations;

one cannot recognize them as the beginnings of a new instrumental language.

With Berlioz it is different. Always inclined to the continuous
rather than to the discrete type of melody, Berlioz's normal
melodic line often comes surprisingly near to instrumental
monologue perhaps because some of these melodies were originally allied with words, as we know the opening *largo* melody
of the *Fantastique* to have been. If the cor anglais melody of
the *Roman Carnival* is an example of pure "continuous"
melody, each phrase growing spontaneously out of the preceding
one, but not corresponding to it in pattern, yet undeniably
remaining a melody even in the most conservative sense of the
word, the opening theme of *King Lear* is an instance of "continuous melody" going very near the borderline of declamation.
It does, however, stay just on this side of the line; the unaccompanied violin melody that opens the "Tristesse de Roméo" in
Roméo et Juliette steps right over it. Whether you agree with a
French critic[1] that the passage "gives the impression of notes
taken at random" or whether you feel that it does admirably
conjure up the vision of Romeo alone and melancholy, depends
entirely on your possession or non-possession of that valuable
gift, so capriciously bestowed by Providence, the ability to enjoy
Berlioz.

But Berlioz was easily outstripped by Liszt in the employment
of instrumental declamation. It pervades an immense amount
of his work, not only the orchestral compositions but the piano
pieces. In *Vallée d'Obermann* one section is expressly marked
recitativo but actually the main theme itself, and consequently
practically the whole piece, is recitative. Arnold Schering has
suggested that the sudden interpolations of unaccompanied
declamatory passages in Liszt's works are a "gypsy ornamental
mannerism" (*Zigeunermanier*). It is an interesting idea and the
close relationship between instrumental recitative and cadenza
might be adduced as supporting evidence. But though gypsy
influence may have had something to do with Liszt's penchant
for this bastard type of melody (for such it is), that is not the
whole explanation. At least equally potent was the influence of
literature, of verbal declamation. When Liszt told Agnes
Street-Klindworth in 1860 that throughout his Weimar period

[1] Arthur Coquard: *Berlioz*. Paris, N.D.

(the eighteen-fifties) he had been striving for "the renewal of music through its inner connection with poetry," he was not, of course, referring to this particular feature of his music but rather to his programme music in general. Yet the phrase throws invaluable light on his view of the relationship of the two arts.

The whole difference between Berlioz and Liszt in this respect may be seen at a glance by comparing the introduction to the *Roméo et Juliette* Symphony with the opening of the *Dante* Symphony. *Dante* opens with a tremendous unison passage for strings, trombones and tuba which declaim the famous inscription on the portal of Hell, actually printed under the notes in the score:

> "Per me si va nella città dolente:
> Per me si va nell'eterno dolore:
> Per me si va tra le perduta gente.
>
> .   .   .   .   .
>
> Lasciate ogni speranza voi ch'entrate!"[1]

Another theme in the first movement corresponds similarly to Francesca's words: "Nessùn maggior dolore, che ricordarsi del tempo felice nella miseria."[2] And a distortion of this latter theme, more *arioso* than recitative, provides the subject of the central *fugato* section of the "Purgatorio" movement of the Symphony. Now Berlioz also introduces a declamatory passage for unison brass to depict the intervention of the Prince in *Roméo et Juliette*. But, although Shakespeare had entered his spirit at least as possessively as Dante ever entered Liszt's, he did not allow the poet to control his musical inspiration. His recitative effectively suggests the arrival of a commanding personality, the making of an important pronouncement; the passage is as unmistakable in meaning as anything in the whole range of programme music. But Berlioz's horns and trombones do not declaim Escalus's "Rebellious subjects, enemies to peace" speech

---

[1] In Cary's translation:

> "Through me you pass into the city of woe:
> Through me you pass into eternal pain:
> Through me among the people lost for aye.
>
> .   .   .   .   .
>
> All hope abandon, ye who enter here."

[2] "No greater grief than to remember days
Of joy when misery is at hand" (Cary's translation).

or any part of it. And although the composer has marked the passage "Fièrement, un peu retenu et avec le caractère du récitatif," it is actually as melodious, in the conventional sense, as many other of his "continuous" melodies; more so than the violin passage already referred to in the "Tristesse de Roméo." Moreover it is diatonic, whereas Liszt's impassioned, rather histrionic monologues are usually marked by chromatic intervals.

When one considers to what extent this type of melodic line was developed in Liszt's work—*Hamlet* (1858), for instance, really consists of nothing but recitative-like material—the general trend of melodic evolution (or, if you prefer it, degeneration) from Mozart, through Beethoven and Berlioz to Liszt and Wagner, is immediately comprehensible. Other factors contributed to the evolution of mid-nineteenth-century melody, but it is fairly obvious that the instrumental recitative of Berlioz and Liszt paved the way for the melodic style of *Die Walküre* and *Tristan*.

Still, we must not underestimate the importance of those other factors in the development of melody and of musical texture in general: the increasing freedom, chromaticism and dissonance of harmony and, hardly less important, the increasing sensitiveness of composers in general to *style*, to the closer relationship of their material to their medium.

Melody is, as Wagner put it, the "surface" of harmony. That, at any rate, is one way of looking at it. Directly instrumental music began to break away from its origins in simple song and polyphonic vocal music, composers began to think melodically —and more especially, to feel at the keyboard—in terms of the component parts of chords. By Bach's time the type of melody derived from chords was nearly as common as the type of melody based on scales and deriving from song. Melody is the most spontaneous element in music and so these harmonically derived melodies are usually based only on quite normal unadventurous chords. But as harmony, a more calculated, intellectual element, adds new chords and new uses of old chords to the vocabulary, composers soon find it easy to think melodically in terms of these which have become normal in their turn. The eighteenth-century composers never went far out of sight of ordinary triads and chords of the seventh, in a melodic sense; Liszt, to whose ears the augmented triad was more or less a harmonic commonplace, could easily and spontaneously write the opening melody of the *Faust* Symphony.[1]

Now the great progressive harmonist of the eighteen-thirties and 'forties was Chopin, who in turn came across new chords mainly because he was a stylist exploring new effects peculiar to his special medium, the piano. Like the other romantics, he was exquisitely sensitive to the *expressive* quality of harmony, but the sheer loveliness of a sound effect is at least as often at the bottom of Chopin's new harmonies as desire to intensify the emotional expressiveness of the music. The delicious *leggierissimo* shower of notes sprinkled over the chords of the C sharp minor Scherzo, Op. 39 (composed 1838–39), is an obvious instance of Chopin's delight in a new pianistic effect, of which half the charm lies in the sparkling little points of dissonance.

Chopin was peculiarly alert to one fact that academic musical theorists stubbornly refused to recognize till many years later: that there is no such thing as an abstract chord, that the layout of a chord, its sound-medium, even the way it is played, can alter not merely its colour but its essence. And what is true of single chords is naturally true of harmonic progressions. Hadow, in one of the most penetrating passages of a fine piece of criticism,[2] gives an example from one of Chopin's earliest works: "In the twelfth bar of the well-known Nocturne in E flat (Op. 9, No. 2), there is a connecting passage which, when we see it on paper, seems to consist of a rapid series of remote and recondite modulations. When we hear it played *in the manner which Chopin intended*" (my italics) "we feel that there is only one real modulation, and that the rest of the passage is an iridescent play of colour, an effect of superficies, not an effect of substance."[3] But Chopin's chromatic harmonies are by no

[1] I am quite aware that Hugo Riemann has "proved" in his *Geschichte der Musik seit Beethoven* (Berlin, 1901) that the melody in question is *not* based on a progression of augmented triads. But Riemann was capable of proving anything—even that all music is essentially composed of 8-bar phrases (no matter how extended, curtailed or telescoped), a dogma devoutly accepted by many Germans to this day.

[2] The third part of his "Chopin" in *Studies in Modern Music* (Second Series).

[3] Who would suppose that such an innocent passage contains the germ of present-day atonality? Yet it does. The expansion of tonality by chords and whole passages foreign to the key led gradually but inevitably to the bursting of tonality.

means limited to such impressionistic colour effects as these. They frequently, as in the A flat section of the C minor Polonaise (Op. 40, No. 2), form part of the firm tissue of his most vigorous music. Still there can be little doubt that the composer's pianistic technique smoothed the way for many of these things which seemed painfully ugly to those contemporary critics who could judge them only in the light of past experience. The words of Moscheles, not only a fine pianist but a fine all-round musician, are very enlightening: "Chopin has just been playing to me, and now for the first time I understand his music. . . . The harsh modulations which strike me disagreeably when I am playing his compositions no longer shock me, because he glides over them in a fairy-like way with his delicate fingers."

Chopin's chromaticism and his parentheses in remote keys were partly derived from Spohr, whose chamber music he admired enormously. Spohr's harmony exercised little direct influence on his younger contemporaries;[1] it worked mainly through Chopin. But Chopin's chromatic seed fell not on stony ground but into the fertile minds of Liszt and Wagner. From the harmonic point of view, Liszt—except the Liszt of the last period, to whom we must return in a later chapter—was little more than Chopin-raised-to-a-higher-power, though, even in the early eighteen-thirties, his restless intellect had already been fired to feverish dreams of an *ordre omnitonique* which sounds in theory very much like an anticipation of twentieth-century atonalism. (On the perfectly sound axiom that "When everyone is somebody, then no one's anybody.")

The other two great romantic composers contributed much less to the development of harmony, individual as their harmonic writing certainly was. Schumann could be very bold at times. The finale of the Second Piano Sonata, Op. 14, for instance, was very advanced for 1835. And even in 1857 an English

[1] Though here and there in Spohr, it is true, one finds curious anticipations of Wagner. Edgar Istel (*Die Blütezeit der musikalischen Romantik in Deutschland*: Leipzig, 1909) draws attention to a passage in Spohr's *Alchymist* (1830) strikingly anticipatory of *Tristan*:

critic could find in the first movement of the D minor Symphony (composed 1841) "discords enough to perpendicularize one's hair. In the finale these painful noises are again indulged in." It was not that Schumann invented new and poignant dissonances. He merely used the familiar ones very boldly and with little consonant respite. His consonances are often brief and the resolutions frequently fall on unaccented beats. The first movement of his A major String Quartet, Op. 41, No. 3 (1842) contains a striking example of his sustained use of seventh and ninth chords (see bars 44–52 after the double-bar-and-repeat). We may put it that although Schumann made no great contribution to the harmonic language, his norm of consonance—i.e., the degree of dissonance he could accept as pleasant and normal —was considerably in advance of that of the average musician of his day.

Even that could not be said of Berlioz. It seems somewhat ironical that Chopin, the real modernist of the day, should have held that "Berlioz's music would justify any man in breaking with him." (For his part, Berlioz detested Chopin's *rubato*.) Berlioz's harmony was unorthodox enough but it was peculiar to himself and was largely the result, not, of course, of his alleged "defective education," but of his peculiarly original way of thinking in terms of music, i.e., directly in terms of the orchestra without that conscious or unconscious sense of the keyboard that necessarily haunts and intimidates the creative minds of ninety-nine out of every hundred musicians. If Berlioz "wanted D flat after G," as Schumann remarked of a passage near the beginning of the *Symphonie fantastique*, he just wrote it without any fuss. And he made no bones about using unprepared chords of the ninth. But, broadly speaking, his norm of consonance was remarkably low. With all his adoration of Beethoven he found in the finale of the Eighth Symphony "harsh passing notes which theory may explain, but which are bound to be more or less painful to musical ears"; a Bach air shocked him by "the harmonic asperities and the false relations"; naturally the *Tannhäuser* Overture struck him as "bristling with chromatic successions and with modulations and harmonies of extreme harshness," though, on the other hand, he found "the harmonic sequences" of the *Lohengrin* Prelude "melodious and charming . . . without the least harshness." The "double discords" at bars 21–23 of the Prelude to Act III of *Lohengrin*, a piece for which he had considerable admiration as a whole, seemed to him "intolerable."[1]

Indeed, passing notes and appoggiaturas, the backstairs by which most of our parvenu discords have sneaked into polite society, were Berlioz's special abomination. Edmond Hippeau has pointed out[2] that in his music "there is no passing note without a harmony of its own, so that in fact, in this melodic structure, there is no passing note." "Like all generalities," comments Wotton,[3] "this may not be the whole truth but it is sufficiently near it for our purpose"; and he goes on to quote an article by Berlioz written in 1835 sharply attacking Hérold's abuse of appoggiaturas in *Zampa*. It is easy to understand, therefore, why Wagner's harmony pained him so often even before *Tristan*, and why the prelude to *Tristan*, with its chromatic melody and harmony and its incessant appoggiaturas, was a complete enigma to him.

Berlioz's own breaches of the harmonic canons of the day are of quite a different nature from those of his progressive contemporaries. They do not often take the form of chromatic progressions, though Faust's celebrated "Invocation to Nature"—to take the most obvious example—is sufficient proof that Berlioz could use chromatic harmony in a masterly way when it suited his purpose. His unorthodoxy lies in the "clumsiness," "harshness," "amateurishness" of his part-writing and of his use of quite simple diatonic chords. Or, rather, in his writing of things that look clumsy and amateurish, and sound harsh, to those who judge music by its appearance on paper and by its effect as piano music. But Berlioz himself did not judge his music by its appearance on paper and was physically incapable of discovering what it would sound like on the piano, much less of *thinking* in terms of the piano. Tom Wotton, the soundest Berlioz scholar of our day, put forward an interesting theory that his harmony may have owed something to his practice of the guitar. It may have. But it owed nearly everything to his grasp of the *orchestra* both as a whole and in its component parts.

[1] He was equally conservative in clinging to the old-fashioned "natural" horns and trumpets.
[2] *Berlioz et son temps.* Paris, 1890.
[3] *Hector Berlioz.* O.U.P., 1935.

Ernest Newman has stated the case perfectly in his essay, "Berlioz, Romantic and Classic".[1] "Everyone knows that many effects that seem strange or ugly on the piano are perfectly pleasurable on the orchestra, where they are set, not in the one plane, as it were, but in different planes and different focuses. I fancy that when Berlioz imagined a melodic line or a harmonic combination he saw it not merely as a melody or a harmony but as a piece of colour as well; and the movement of the parts was not only a shifting of lines but a weaving of colours. Many things of his that are ugly or meaningless on the piano have a beauty of their own when heard, as he conceived them, on the orchestra, set in different depths, as it were, with the toning effect of atmosphere between them; not all standing in the same line in the foreground, with the one white light of the piano making confusion of their colour-values." Here then, as in Chopin's piano music, we have a revolt against the "abstract chord." The chord and the chord progression do not exist as things-in-themselves; they are inconceivable to the composer except in one particular lay-out and way of scoring.

This is perhaps the most important of all the aspects of Berlioz's scoring—that scoring which still sounds so fresh, which to-day charms even those who do not care for his music in general, but which Mendelssohn found "so utterly slovenly and haphazard that one ought to wash one's hands after turning over a score of his." It matters very little that he had a certain weakness for "acres of drums and yards of brass"; he was only following the example of Gossec, Méhul and his own master, Lesueur, in writing for enormous forces, and the huge Wagnerian orchestra might just as easily have arrived by way of Meyerbeer as by way of Berlioz. His innumerable effects of instrumental combination are for the most part either such as were bound to be discovered by some clever orchestrator sooner or later (e.g., the strings and flutes in the "Sanctus" of the *Requiem*) or such as are too peculiarly Berliozian for any later composer to borrow without facing a charge of plagiarism (e.g., the flutes and trombone pedal-notes in the "Hostias" of the same work). And some of the effects popularly supposed to have been invented by him were, in fact, only popularized by him; his harp-harmonics, for instance, were borrowed from Boieldieu's

[1] In *Musical Studies.* John Lane, 3rd edition, 1914.

La Dame blanche (1825), his subtle and elaborate dynamic markings were modelled on the practice of Spontini. Even his "muted clarinet" playing in a leather bag, in *Lélio*, had been anticipated by Spontini in *Fernand Cortez*. The essence of Berlioz's great revolution in the handling of the orchestra lies in the fact that he thought in terms of it as Chopin thought in terms of the piano. We must not overlook the importance of Weber, but nevertheless it is Berlioz who has the best claim to be considered the first great orchestral stylist.

His sense of style shows itself equally in the handling of orchestral masses and in the tracing of individual instrumental lines. The marvellous oboe melody in the "Tristesse de Roméo" *ought* to be inconceivable on any instrument but that for which it was written, though unhappily the composer was so misguided as to blare it out later on cornets and trombone; but the melodic line seems almost to have been generated in the composer's mind by the quality of the oboe's tone. The distortion of the *idée fixe* in the "Witches' Sabbath" of the *Fantastique* owes most of its deliberate vulgarity to the tone-quality of the E flat clarinet to which it is given.

The virtuoso is always a stylist and Berlioz was a virtuoso of the orchestra just as Chopin and Liszt were virtuosi of the piano and Paganini of the violin. The eighteen-thirties were remarkable for musical virtuosity and consequently for the development of a general sense of musical style. The influence of Chopin's style on his harmonic development has already been mentioned and something must now be said of the development of piano-style, in (or rather under) his hands and Liszt's, for its own sake.

Here, again, we must be fair to their predecessors. Both Dussek and Clementi had been more conscious than Beethoven of the possibilities of the piano as a sound-producing machine pure and simple. The student of Field will find that the Irish master (who died in 1837) gave Chopin much more than the idea of the nocturne. Field's widespread left-hand parts, his poetic *fiorature*, his delicious washes of treble colour, his singing melodies in middle parts, have influenced—through Chopin or even directly (as one feels is the case with Arnold Bax)—the whole of modern stylized piano-music. Only second in importance to Field was Francesco Pollini (1763–1846), pupil of Mozart, admired by Liszt, who in his *Trentadue esercizi in forma*

di toccata (1820) opened up various new possibilities of the keyboard, including the effect—popular with Liszt and Thalberg—
of bringing out a *cantabile* melody in the middle register while
both hands are also busy simultaneously with florid accompaniment. Even Thalberg, now only remembered contemptuously
for his *Variations on "Home, Sweet Home"* and as a rival virtuoso
to Liszt, contributed elements to the new piano style. Still,
none of these names can compare in importance with those of
Chopin and Liszt; and one has only to compare the first edition
of Liszt's *Études* (1826) with the later ones (1839 and 1852) to
see how his technique as a composer was influenced not only
by his own technique as a pianist but by the music of Chopin.

To enumerate Chopin's new "effects" would be as difficult
as to catalogue those of Berlioz. Almost every page of his mature
work illustrates the nature of the new piano style he established,
though no one work epitomizes it more completely than the
Berceuse. It has as its basis a candid recognition of the fact that
the piano is a percussive, not a singing, instrument, coupled with
an instinct amounting to genius for inventing melodies that
would be actually ineffective if sung or played on an instrument
capable of sustaining tone but which, picked out in percussive
points of sound each beginning to die as soon as born, are en-
chanting and give an illusion of a singing that is often lovelier
than singing itself. Chopin undoubtedly learned that secret
from Field—indeed, the old harpsichord and clavichord writers
understood how to conceal the defects of their instruments in
similar ways—though, curiously, the melody of the popular
Nocturne in E flat, Op. 9, No. 2, often spoken of as the most
Field-like of all Chopin's works, is one of the few instances in
Chopin of melody not peculiarly suited to the piano.

The *Berceuse* is also a miniature encyclopædia of the effects
Chopin produced by the use of the sustaining pedal, by chromatic
filigree-work over a diatonic foundation, by the contrast of
registers. And, finally, no work shows more clearly how completely Chopin's virtuosity is subordinated to his poetic idea.
Liszt forgets too often that virtuosity should be merely the
instrument of the poet; Chopin never does.

At the same time, we may as well admit frankly that virtuosity
for its own sake has its own peculiar thrill. And it is certainly
true that Liszt's piano effects are not all so purely virtuosic as

is commonly supposed. The brilliant passage-work of his Piano Sonata is not "empty" as sciolists would have us believe; indeed, much of it is actually thematic. Liszt himself played (and therefore had conceived) as delicate, silvery washes of background tone-colour passages which latter-day virtuosi have obliged us to accept as mere showy ornamentation, "fireworks." "The gods themselves fight in vain against stupidity"—and treacherous interpreters of their messages. Again: consider such a passage as the opening of *Au bord d'une source*. In the form in which it is generally known, with its left-hand crossings, it looks like a virtuoso-piece; not very difficult, perhaps, but still written for effect. But pause for a moment over the same passage as it was originally conceived for the *Album d'un Voyageur*:

No one would dream of calling that virtuoso-music; the mere look of it on paper shows what it is, a quiet, delicate, pellucid mood-picture. But the later form in *Années de pèlerinage* is nothing but a recasting of this *in such a way that its proper interpretation is actually easier*. Not a note is changed or added, only the accompaniment recast and the whole differently distributed between the hands. And a little careful study will soon show that other of Liszt's piano compositions are similarly reducible to less virtuosic, but also less pianistic, terms.

Not the least interesting feature of Liszt's piano-writing is its influence in turn on his orchestral style. As an orchestrator, Liszt learned his job as he went along. When he wrote his earliest orchestral works he literally did not know how to score. He roughed them out in short score with indications of the instrumentation and handed them over to Raff or, in his earliest Weimar days, to the operetta composer, August Conradi. (*Tasso* was orchestrated first by Conradi and later by Raff.) But experience as conductor of the Weimar orchestra taught Liszt how to handle this new medium; he overhauled and improved the Conradi-Raff versions of the scores; he tried over the different variants of his own versions with his orchestra;[1] and finally he emerged as a genuine master of the orchestra[2] who was later to exercise in certain directions, notably among the Russian nationalists, an influence second only to that of Berlioz.

Liszt was not a Berlioz in the handling of the orchestra, of course; but he excelled in clear, bright, highly effective colouring. And his orchestral music differs fundamentally from the French master's in that it is generally pianistic in origin. I do not mean that it is often, like *Mazeppa*, actually based on piano music; the orchestral versions of the first and second *Mephisto Waltzes* actually preceded the piano versions. But the pianist's mind, even quite often the pianist's hand, is apparent everywhere. The passage near the beginning of *Les Préludes*, where second violins and 'celli have a *cantabile* melody against an arpeggio accompaniment, and the Mephistopheles movement of the *Faust* Symphony are but two of the most obvious instances. It would be difficult to find a bar of Liszt's orchestral music that is not in some way related to piano music.[3]

Indeed, Liszt's supple fingers have left their print even on the harmonic-contrapuntal processes of more modern music. If he derived his love of passages in thirds and sixths from the ensembles of Italian opera, it was his obedient fingers that naturalized them in his own music. One feels those fingers in such passages as the chromatic love-theme in *Les Préludes*— the "second subject" if, as I have suggested, we consider the

[1] He told Christian Lobe in 1856 (*Franz Liszts Briefe*, Vol. VIII) that each of his first six symphonic poems—*Orpheus, Prometheus, Tasso, Mazeppa, Festklänge* and *Les Préludes*—had been written out and tried over in three or four different versions before he was able to decide on the final one.

[2] Liszt's mature scoring shows traces of the influence of *Tannhäuser* and *Lohengrin*.

[3] Compare also an acute criticism of Liszt's orchestration by Sibelius (reported by Bengt de Törne in his *Sibelius: a Close-Up*; Faber & Faber, 1937): "While he was writing his scores he sat at the piano, pressing the pedal, and everything sounded perfect. But in the orchestra there was no substitute for the pedal accommodating enough to avoid the danger of sudden emptiness, and fuse all the different and sometimes incompatible groups of sounds."

piece as being in sonata-form—and the passage in *Die Ideale* headed "Du, die du alle Wunden heilest." And these in turn begot the B major passage near the end of Strauss's *Zarathustra*, the similar ones in the love-scene of *Feuersnot*, and in general many of those passages in modern music where melodic lines are thickened out two-dimensionally.

Chopin and Liszt were stylists because they were great pianists, Berlioz partly because he could not play the piano at all. It was Schumann's misfortune to be neither a virtuoso nor a non-pianist. Of all the great romantic composers he was the least sensitive to relationship between idea and medium. His piano-works—and until 1840, his great "song year," he wrote practically nothing but piano pieces—are genuine piano music in the sense that they are obviously conceived for two hands on a keyboard, but they betray an almost complete insensitiveness to the new pianistic resources that were being opened up by Field, Chopin and Liszt. (His modern use of the sustaining pedal is the only important exception.) However beautiful as music, his pieces are never remarkable as piano music. They lie nearly all in the warm, rich middle register of the instrument, for he entirely neglected the upper register from which every true piano-composer during the last hundred years has drawn delicious colour-effects. When he does experiment with an "effect," such as the dominant seventh struck as an arpeggio and then released note by note, at the end of *Papillons*, it nearly always fails to come off.

Paradoxically, Schumann's orchestral and chamber works are moulded even more than Liszt's orchestral pieces by the hands of the pianist. Not, of course, in this case by the hands of a virtuoso but by the hands of a man accustomed to think of music too often in terms of two handfuls of sound; the *Manfred* Overture (composed in 1848), perhaps his finest orchestral work, is a particularly obvious case. Schumann was notoriously unadventurous as an orchestrator. His scoring, though thick, is not quite as ineffective as is sometimes asserted, but that is only because the orchestra is such a beautiful instrument in itself that, provided one has common sense and observes certain rules of thumb, it requires positive genius to make it sound ugly.

His chamber music is equally pianistic. How completely the piano dominated Schumann's ideas in his first experiments in concerted writing may be seen from the *Phantasiestücke* for piano, violin and 'cello, Op. 88, composed in 1842, the first two of which are completely dominated by the piano. Even the three String Quartets, Op. 41, written the same year, are decidedly pianistic in feeling. Of all Schumann's chamber compositions, perhaps the three finest are works for piano and strings: the Piano Quintet and Piano Quartet (both dating from 1842) and the D minor Trio, Op. 63 (1847); all three suffer from the same defect, much too frequent doubling of the piano by the strings. A surprising proportion of the music would be logically complete, even artistically satisfying, without the string parts. Sometimes the strings say the same thing as the piano in a different way, sometimes in exactly the same way; in either case they are redundant, merely adding to the volume of sound. With all their wealth of beautiful ideas, these works are far from satisfying as examples of a genre in which perfection of workmanship counts for more than in any other type of composition except perhaps the solo song.

But consideration of Schumann's chamber music brings us face to face again with a fact mentioned in the last chapter. This Schumann of the eighteen-forties was no longer quite the same man as the composer of the host of romantic piano pieces and of the majority of the songs. His music remained to the end marked with romantic and predominantly lyrical traits, but it became much less literary, more concerned with purely musical, even technical, considerations. Instead of Hoffmann and Jean Paul and Heine, his inspiration was now Mendelssohn (above all in the first movement of the Piano Concerto, 1841) and Bach (see particularly the fugues and pieces for pedal-piano, Opp. 56, 58, 60 and 72, written in 1845). Mendelssohn himself had been a much earlier renegade from pure romanticism. Now Schumann followed in his wake and the remainder of his output belongs mainly to what we may call the neo-classical reaction against romanticism.

III. THE NEO-CLASSICAL REACTION: CHORAL AND CHAMBER MUSIC OF THE PERIOD

If a great many elements in the so-called romantic movement are obviously derived from Beethoven, the quasi-classical reaction from it towards pure music can also claim descent from him. To put it crudely, the romantics tried to extend and develop music on Beethovenian lines, the neo-classics tried to continue and maintain the Beethovenian tradition. Mendelssohn's *Lobgesang* (1840) is a more legitimate descendant of Beethoven's Ninth Symphony than Berlioz's *Roméo et Juliette* (1839), though unhappily, as is so often the case, the legitimate offspring is much less interesting than the bastard. And this shady half-brotherhood of romanticism and neo-classicism is noticeable in other features: mildly literary leanings, a mild love of the pictorial, a certain affection for motto-themes and theme-transformation, a feeble tendency to experiment—and a very strong tendency for composers to take a very lofty view of themselves and their art, very different from the comparatively humble view of the inspired craftsmen of pre-Beethovenian days. Nor is this close relationship with the romantic movement at all surprising, apart from the common Beethovenian parenthood; all the neo-classic composers of any importance were either men like Mendelssohn and Schumann, who had passed through a definitely romantic period themselves, or their camp-followers, the Sterndale Bennetts, the Gades, and the rest.

Nor was the reaction against romanticism peculiar to the Leipzig school. Berlioz, who was neither a member of a school nor the founder of one, had (as we have already seen) from the first concealed under an ultra-romantic exterior a strong vein of pure, cool, classically objective musicality. As he grew older he too sloughed off his romantic skin and by the fifties emerged as an almost pure classicist. Liszt alone preserved the flame of romanticism and handed it to Wagner, in whose hands it became the great conflagration of the "music of the future," roaring picturesquely through the remainder of the nineteenth century. And even Liszt turned aside in an old age half-austere, half-impotent, to write strangely beautiful things which if they are romantic in any sense of the word are but the ashes of

romanticism. But those last pieces of his, the "third year" of
the *Années de Pèlerinage* and the other late piano pieces, belong
to a period far ahead of that which we are considering now;
they mark the birth of modernism as much as the old age of
romanticism. Only one point is worth noting about them here:
their austerity is not unconnected with impotence. And Liszt
had been the most exuberantly vital of all the great romantic composers. It is noticeable that of the renegades from romanticism,
Mendelssohn—who possessed less musical vitality than any of
the others—was the first to go; then Schumann, then Berlioz,
more or less in ascending order of musical *élan*. And in each
case the products of the later period, whatever their compensating values, lack much of the life of the first romantic crop.

In Mendelssohn's case the compensating elements are piti-
fully few. It is one of the great tragedies of music that the boy
of seventeen who, in 1826, the year before Beethoven's death,
had written such a masterpiece as the *Midsummer Night's Dream*
Overture, to say nothing of the Octet of a year earlier, should
have fizzled out into the anæmic yet prolific craftsman of the
great bulk of the later works. In his few early romantic works,
Mendelssohn showed himself a master of poetic and pictorial
suggestiveness. The scherzo from the Octet is completely worthy
of the stanza from Goethe[1] which it originally bore as a motto.
As Wagner said,[2] "Mendelssohn was a landscape-painter of the
first order, and the *Fingal's Cave* Overture is his masterpiece. . . .
Note the extraordinary beauty of the passage where the oboe
rises above the other instruments with a plaintive wail like sea-
winds over the seas." That is only just. *Fingal's Cave* (composed in 1830) is a magnificent piece of evocative music; the
very opening phrase on bassoons, violas and 'cellos alone conjures
up, to the imagination prepared by the title of the work, a vivid
picture of grey, sullen sea and leaden cloud. The opening bars
of the *Scottish* Symphony (completed 1842) possess a little of the
same evocative power, but the Symphony as a whole symbolizes
only too well the course of its composer's career: the brief touch
of inspired romanticism at the beginning followed by a dreary
waste of mere sound-manipulation, relieved only by the oasis
of the light-handed scherzo, and ending in a blaze of sham

[1] "Wolkenzug und Nebelflor," etc., from *Faust*.
[2] See Dannreuther's article "Wagner" in *Grove's Dictionary*.

triumph. At thirty-three, even the more or less romantic subject
of Early Victorian Scotland failed to fire Mendelssohn's creative
imagination. *Die erste Walpurgisnacht*, of which the earliest
version dates back to 1831, is—if possible—even less alive than
the A minor Symphony, in spite of its highly romantic subject.[1]

The one lovely element that did survive from Mendelssohn's
earlier works into his mature, classical period is the sweet,
Virgilian purity of the idyllic passages,[2] a quality as uniquely
Mendelssohnian as his feeble persistent 6-8 rhythms. (Lack of
rhythmical vitality is one of Mendelssohn's most serious weaknesses.) Even this idyllic element deteriorates in his later works,
becoming squarer and more solid, less magical and more bourgeois, as it were. The slow movement, the so-called "Pilgrims'
March," of the *Italian* Symphony (finished in 1831) is fresher
than "Happy and blest are they" in *St. Paul* (1836), and "Happy
and blest" sounds more spontaneous and poetic than "For He
shall give His angels charge over thee" in *Elijah* (1846). But
even in *Elijah* one of the luminous moments that still light up
that rather dull masterpiece for the most jaded listener comes
from a gleam of the old Virgilian magic: the soprano entry with
the first phrase of "He, watching over Israel."

[1] This was not the view of his contemporaries, however. Berlioz,
who was certainly an authority on witches' sabbaths, was in 1843
"much inclined to look upon this oratorio as the most finished work
Mendelssohn has hitherto produced. . . . His work is perfectly clear in
spite of its complexity; the vocal and instrumental effects are marvellously intermingled in an apparent confusion that is the very acme of
art. Two magnificent features, in absolute contrast, are the mysterious
piece of the placing of the sentinels ('Disperse, disperse!'), and the
final chorus, where the voice of the priest rises calm and reverent at
intervals above the infernal din of the false demons and sorcerers. One
scarcely knows what to praise most in this finale, the instrumentation,
the choruses, or the whirlwind movement of the whole." Is it that
we need a sense of historical perspective to appreciate the *Walpurgisnacht* properly, or was Berlioz deliberately flattering Mendelssohn? The
"letter to Heller" in which this passage occurs was published in
Berlioz's *Voyage Musical* in 1844; it is now Chapter LV of the *Memoirs*.

[2] Even the "fairy" element inherited from Weber which is such an
attractive feature of such early works as the *Midsummer Night's Dream*
Overture and the popular *Rondo capriccioso*, Op. 14, undergoes a
change when it appears in later compositions (e.g., the *Midsummer
Night's Dream* Scherzo of 1843). The outward substance is much the
same but the spirit that had informed it has disappeared.

After the first phrase the light dims slightly. That often happens with Mendelssohn. His music is full of fine first phrases killed by the dead matter that follows them. The Violin Concerto (1844) is an outstanding example; even the *Hymn of Praise* opens quite imposingly. But the case which best repays examination is that of the first movement of the *Italian* Symphony, for its weakness is not peculiar to itself or to Mendelssohn, but is common to the great bulk of the pseudo-classical music written between the death of Beethoven and the advent of Brahms. The opening—the quick repeated wood-wind chords into which the violins cut so gaily—is delightful: a brilliant idea, brilliantly scored. But by the time it has got to bar 10—that is, in no time at all—its spontaneous life is exhausted; the continuation (bars 11–18) is simply cobbled on and keeps the music going only through the sheer momentum of the opening. Then the skilful technician takes a hand. With his opening motive, now given to the wind and horns, and a neat, empty little quaver figure on the strings he builds up a marvellous imitation of living musical tissue; the bass scale brings a heralding touch of genuine life returning; a bustling little climax is built up from the scales in contrary motion—and we break into the opening theme again, *tutti*. Mendelssohn and the other neo-classical composers of the period were far more skilful than Liszt in giving an appearance of life to dead tissue; their music seldom seems to stagnate as his often does. But the single ideas that Liszt gives us so many opportunities of hearing are generally much more interesting, much more vital, than the pleasant platitudes so skilfully eked out by Mendelssohn and his camp-followers. It would be difficult to find in Liszt any idea quite as feeble as the second subject of the first movement of the *Italian* Symphony, the banality of which cannot be disguised even by the rather obvious trick of augmentation at the end of the first phrase.

Perhaps the most interesting feature of Mendelssohn's big orchestral works is his attempt to make the forms of symphony and concerto more concise, to make them organic wholes rather than collections of separate movements. His A minor Symphony, for instance, has a snatch of the slow introduction repeated at the end of the first movement and the whole work is played through without a break. His concertos also have their movements connected, but in this respect Mendelssohn hardly went beyond

Spohr or Beethoven, and even the finest of his transition passages, that to the slow movement of the Violin Concerto, is markedly inferior to Beethoven's unforgettable entry upon the finale of the *Emperor*. The *Hymn of Praise*, of course, stands alone as the most dismal attempt to follow the lead of Beethoven's Ninth Symphony ever conceived by human mediocrity.

Mendelssohn's mild experiments with the symphonic form are far less interesting than Schumann's. For the path trodden by Schumann was followed by the majority of the later symphonists and was to lead ultimately to such a masterpiece of compression as Sibelius's Seventh; it lay in exactly the opposite direction to that chosen by Berlioz, who took the way of expansion and diffusion that led to Mahler and his vast symphonic "worlds." Schumann himself tried an experiment or two in expansion— two trios instead of one, and in the *Rhenish* Symphony an additional slow movement—but, broadly speaking, his influence was strongly in the direction of compression.

Schumann's First Symphony dates from 1841 and is full of romantic traits. It was originally conceived as a "Spring" Symphony, the introduction being entitled "Spring's Awakening," the finale "Spring's Farewell." And, perhaps taking a hint from Beethoven's Ninth, there are thematic links between the movements. The brass theme of the slow introduction generates the main theme of the ensuing *allegro molto vivace* and is also suggested with striking effect by the trombones in the finale. Again, at the end of the slow movement the trombones solemnly intone a theme, related to the chief melody of the movement, which is immediately snatched up as the subject of the scherzo, which follows without a break. Schumann wrote two other symphonic works in the same year as the B flat Symphony: the *Overture, Scherzo and Finale*, Op. 52 (practically a symphony without a slow movement) and the original version of the D minor Symphony—finally published ten years later, with much thicker scoring, with instructions that the movements are to follow each other without a break, and with other changes as "Symphony No. 4."[1]

There are many reasons for regarding this D minor Sym-

---

[1] Schumann at first thought of styling the revised version a "Symphonistische Phantasie." The original version was discovered by Brahms and published on his initiative in 1891.

phony as the most important "pure" symphony produced for forty years after Beethoven's death. Schumann was never a very remarkable symphonic *thinker*—his finest piece of sustained, logical argument is the magnificent first movement of the *Rhenish* Symphony (written in 1850)—but the sequences of the D minor are never as naïve and empty as those of the B flat; he fakes the working of his themes with the skill of a Mendelssohn, even if he does not score nearly as well. But the planning of the D minor and the knitting of the whole together are so new and so suggestive that the work is a real milestone in the history of the symphony. The organic connection of the separate parts of the symphony is contrived as follows:

(1) The "fairly slow" introduction is based on a broad theme in even quavers, A. At bar 22 (of the later version only) the violins introduce the main theme of the whole symphony, B. B at once becomes the first subject of the *allegro* and, either in this main form or in two others closely derived from it, "continues" (as Parry says) "almost ceaselessly throughout the whole movement, either as actual subject or accompaniment."[1] In fact, put into the relative major, it takes the place of a "second subject." After 34 bars of typical neo-classical pseudo-development, entirely based on B, we get a new theme in D flat. But the chief characteristic of this new theme is that it is punctuated at every other bar by references to B; we may call this Ba. After a while we hear yet another new theme, a broad *cantabile* melody on the violins. Judging only from the later version, one would say that it had no connection with anything that had gone before; as a matter of fact, it is a counterpoint to theme B and in the original version was actually accompanied by it; we may therefore consider it as Bb. The rest of the movement is entirely based on Ba and Bb and ends in the tonic major, without a bar of orthodox recapitulation. The whole of the *allegro* is therefore essentially monothematic.

(2) The slow movement opens with a new theme on the oboe, but at bar 12 the violins enter with theme A from the introduction to the first movement and with it completely overshadow the oboe tune. One of the loveliest passages in the whole symphony is that in which a solo violin plays a triplet arabesque

[1] Article "Symphony" in *Grove*.

variation of this theme—Aa, shall we say—while the rest of the orchestra go quietly on with their even quavers.

(3) The scherzo hurls two themes at us simultaneously: a string theme in crotchets which turns out to be an inversion of the first six notes of A, and wind chords derived from Ba, though there is no actual reference to B. The trio melody consists simply of Aa in triple, instead of compound duple, time. This trio is in B flat and recurs after the repeat of the scherzo, dying away quietly and vaguely at the close. The transition from the quiet B flat close of this movement to the triumphant D major of the finale is then effected in a remarkable slow transition passage of sixteen bars entirely based on B on the violins and Ba on the trombones.

(4) The finale opens with Ba which is immediately extended, and the rhythmic figure evolved from it dominates the whole movement. It is so persistent throughout the development, indeed, that Schumann could afford to omit the first subject altogether in the recapitulation. A master-stroke, like a general throwing in his carefully concealed reserves at the crisis of a battle, is the appearance of a broad, swinging *cantabile* theme, entirely new, for the coda; the effect is all the more striking in a work where hitherto nearly all the themes have been so closely connected.

The so-called Second Symphony of Schumann, dating from 1846, is much less interesting than the D minor yet by no means without points that deserve attention. (From the different point of view of purely musical value, its slow movement in particular must be ranked very high indeed.) Here again the slow introduction is thematically important, but the broad theme enunciated by the brass is in this case a mere motto-theme, quoted at the end of the scherzo and in the coda of the finale, not a germ from which the whole symphony is developed. But the unity given by a motto-theme is the equivalent of a uniform consisting of a simple armlet. To change the metaphor, it merely rubber-stamps the movements as belonging to each other. The device was obviously borrowed from Berlioz, whose motto-themes have perfectly definite literary meanings; but when, meeting it in absolute music, we ask for its credentials there it is unable to produce them. The use of a simple generating theme, developing on different lines in each movement, as in the D minor Symphony, is another matter altogether.

As in the First Symphony, the scherzo of the C major has two trios, and this time, following the example of Beethoven's Ninth, it precedes the slow movement. The finale is unorthodox, too. The theme of the *adagio* is introduced, and an important new theme appears half-way through and dominates the whole movement.

The Third (*Rhenish*) Symphony, with the exception of the finale, shows the "classical" Schumann at the height of his powers, but from the point of view of structural innovations it has only one noteworthy feature: the interpolation of an additional slow movement, the profoundly impressive *adagio* inspired by the ceremony of Archbishop von Geissel's elevation to the cardinalate in Cologne Cathedral.[1] At any rate, it proves beyond cavil that in his earlier experiments Schumann had not adopted doctrinaire views on the necessity of unity and compression in the symphony. In some respects, too, the *Rhenish* suggests a return to the composer's earlier romanticism; it is certainly far more romantic than its predecessor. And, like Mendelssohn's two best-known symphonies, it is frankly inspired by, and evocative of, a definite landscape and atmosphere. Apart from the "Cologne Cathedral" movement, the whole symphony —from the very first broad, exuberant, open-airy bars—does vividly call up the very air of the Rhineland to those who know and love it. The second movement was originally entitled "Morning on the Rhine." All this, like Mendelssohn's vision of Holyrood in the *Scottish* Symphony and his pilgrims in the *Italian*, is thoroughly typical of the not unsatisfactory compromise between absolute music and programme music fashionable at that period, the compromise from which were also born the concert overtures of Mendelssohn, Sterndale Bennett and the rest.

Almost equally important with his symphonies are Schumann's chamber works. In the field of chamber music the neo-classical group enjoyed a practically undisputed superiority. The whole-hogging romanticists left chamber music severely alone—we need hardly pause to consider Chopin's 'Cello Sonata *et hoc genus omne*—for, owing to its restrictions, the medium is ill-adapted to express emotional exuberance or to produce picturesque effects.

[1] This movement was the only one in which Mahler found it unnecessary to make alterations when he rescored the Symphony.

Programmatic chamber music is still exceedingly rare. On the other hand, that fineness of workmanship of which Mendelssohn was such a master, and which his followers prized so highly, counts for more in chamber music than in almost any other type of composition. Moreover, the intimacy of the medium made it ideal for a composer like Schumann who was not intended by nature to be a public speaker yet who had tired of the solo piano and was ambitious to do more than go on coining whimsical or poetic aphorisms. Accordingly, not only Mendelssohn and the later Schumann but their numerous imitators composed chamber music prolifically.

Here again Schumann's contribution has proved to have more enduring qualities than that of his idol. Both Schumann and Mendelssohn made the mistake of writing chamber music too pianistically. Attention has been drawn in the previous chapter to this weakness of Schumann's. Mendelssohn is equally afflicted by it, and he has an additional fault from which Schumann is free: he often writes orchestrally, as if each part were to be taken by a body of strings instead of by a solo instrument. He is particularly fond, for instance, of *tremolo* effects that cry aloud for volume of sound, although one would have expected him of all composers to be fertile in devising suitable and effective figuration. The opening of the D major Quartet, Op. 44, No. 1 (1838) is only one of the many passages of Mendelssohn's chamber music that would sound about six times more effective if they were orchestrated. In the preface to his youthful Octet (1824) Mendelssohn actually asked that the piece should be played "in a symphonic style" and, as everyone knows, he afterwards substituted a version of the delightful scherzo of this work for the original minuet of his C minor Symphony.[1] The only possible excuse for "orchestral" chamber music is that listeners more or less unconsciously make allowances and with the inward ear hear the music as it *should* sound. It seems a poor excuse, but piano music has always made similar demands on the listener. And certainly the listener who is un-

[1] Even in this early work, and again in the String Quartet in E flat, Op. 12, written five years later, we find Mendelssohn attempting to bind the whole composition together by harking back in the finale to earlier movements—in the Octet to the scherzo, in the Quartet to the first movement.

willing to meet chamber music half-way must resign himself to getting little pleasure either from Mendelssohn or from César Franck and a good many other more modern chamber-music composers who have disregarded the limitations of the medium instead of deliberately turning them to account.

Like Schumann, too, Mendelssohn allows the keyboard instrument too much predominance in chamber works for piano and strings, a predominance made all the more noticeable when the string-writing itself sounds pianistic; the strings seem all the time to be desperately trying to ape—or even to parody—the piano. On the whole, Mendelssohn's works for 'cello and piano are better in this respect than his trios. The once popular D minor Trio (1839) far too often suggests a brilliant piano solo with not particularly *obbligato* string parts. On the other hand, the scherzo of the C minor Trio, Op. 66, is delightful and well-balanced—as well as being one of the few successful examples in Mendelssohn's later music of the characteristic "fairy" element so prominent in his youthful productions.

The chamber music of Schumann, with all its defects, is more satisfying than that of the man he admired so much and who is generally considered his superior in technical dexterity. In the long run, Schumann's emotional warmth, the patent sincerity lit up by an afterglow of romanticism, has outweighed his weaknesses—the *rosalias,* the miscalculated effects of syncopation, and so on—in the affection of most musicians. Mendelssohn's skilful, facile manipulation of his material—skilful in everything but *style*—has failed to keep most of his chamber music alive, though one must regret that complete oblivion has overtaken the A major Quintet. An orchestral composer with next to nothing to say can manage tolerably by saying it brilliantly. That cannot be done with chamber music, though Mendelssohn came very near to doing it with his D minor Trio.

On the whole, the Piano Quintet, the first of all piano quintets, must be considered the crown of Schumann's chamber music. It would be difficult to find a work more typical of the blend of romantic spirit and more or less classical form characteristic of so much German music written during the eighteen-forties. The introduction in the finale of the chief theme of the first movement, in counterpoint with the chief subject of the finale itself, was evidently suggested by Mendelssohn's E flat String

Quartet; but Schumann improved on his model and there is no other trace of Mendelssohnian influence in the work. If musical epigrams must be expanded and strung together in the manner of a connected argument, it is difficult to see how they could be handled better than in the Schumann Quintet; the individual ideas are so happy that it seems ungracious to quibble about the work as a whole. Or even about the scoring; for it must be admitted that, except for the advantage of having two tone-colours instead of one, there seems to be no reason why the whole work should not have been scored for two pianos. It is incomprehensible why Schumann, having discovered this most satisfactory of all combinations of piano and strings, should have exploited its possibilities so little. Almost as incomprehensible as the neglect with which it has been treated since, for in nearly a century it has had barely half a dozen worthy successors.

Schumann's two Violin Sonatas, both dating from 1851, are of special interest in two respects. They were the first important sonatas for violin and piano since Beethoven's, and with the *Rhenish* Symphony of the year before they refute the popular belief that Schumann's creative power declined seriously in the years immediately before his mental collapse. (The weakness of some of the works written during this period is no evidence to the contrary; it is by no means unusual for the greatest masters to produce poor compositions while at the height of their powers.) The first Sonata, in A minor, is Mendelssohnian— perhaps more so than anything else, except the first movement of the Piano Concerto, that Schumann ever wrote—and suffers particularly from the familiar complaint of piano-doubling. But the second, in D minor, is a masterly work foreshadowing Brahms. Its third movement is one of the most beautiful of all Schumann's compositions and is perhaps the only instance in the whole of his chamber works of music made lovelier by the method of scoring. The opening, where the simple theme is shared by violin chords *pizzicato* and piano chords *una corda*, is unique and unforgettable. Later the theme of the scherzo is worked into the movement; indeed the link between the two middle movements of this Sonata is closer, more organic and more subtle than in any similar case in the previous history of music.

In the field of cantata and oratorio the supremacy of the neo-classics was by no means as undisputed as in that of chamber music. Berlioz's *Requiem* (1837) and *Damnation de Faust* (1846), and Liszt's *Graner Festmesse* (1856) are products of full-blooded romanticism that can well hold their own beside the oratorios and cantatas of Mendelssohn or Schumann's *Das Paradies und die Peri* (1843), *Der Rose Pilgerfahrt* (1851), and *Szenen aus "Faust"* (1844–53). Berlioz's *Te Deum* and *L'Enfance du Christ* (both 1854) really belong to his last, classical period, but it is very difficult to label his compositions and put them into categories. And, broadly speaking, the same may be said of the choral music of the period in general. Romantic and classical tendencies are much less easily distinguishable in it than in contemporary instrumental music. As we have seen, Mendelssohn's *Walpurgisnacht* struck Berlioz as a highly successful essay in romanticism; even *Elijah* is strongly romantic in conception and, occasionally, in the actual music (e.g., the "Baal" choruses). The same may be said of *Das Paradies und die Peri*. And in the Berlioz *Requiem*, where an intensely romantic imagination had fastened on the familiar text for its own artistic purposes, there are many pages of music which in their restraint, their pure beauty, can only be called classical. In fact, at this point the old familiar labels become so well-worn that the writing on them is no longer legible; if we must have labels we must look for fresh ones.

Berlioz himself spoke of his *Te Deum*, his *Requiem*, his cantata *L'Impériale* and the *Symphonie funèbre et triomphale* as his "architectural" works, referring not only to the exceptionally large forces employed—the four additional brass bands of the *Requiem*, the organ, orchestra, and three choirs of the *Te Deum* —but to "the form of the pieces, the breadth of style, and the deliberateness of certain progressions, the goal of which is not at once perceived," which "give these works their strange gigantic physiognomy and colossal aspect."[1] But Liszt more clearly expressed the aims of Berlioz and himself in an article "On the Church Music of the Future" published in the *Gazette musicale* in 1834,[2] three years before the composition of the Berlioz *Requiem* and more than twenty years before he put his ideas into practice in the *Graner Festmesse* (1856) and *Ungarische*

[1] *Memoirs.*
[2] Reprinted in Vol. II of his *Geşammelte Schriften* (1880–83).

Krönungsmesse (1867).[1] At the time when he wrote this article Liszt was much under the influence of Lamennais. Accordingly he demands a "musique humanitaire" appealing to mankind in general, to "the people" who will be the pillars of the Church of the Future. And this "humanitarian music" "should be devotional, strong and effective; it should unite on a colossal scale theatre and church; should be at one and the same time dramatic and sacred, splendid and simple, ceremonial and sincere, fiery and free, stormy and calm, clear and profound."

Whether or not Berlioz had Liszt's words in mind when he wrote his "architectural" settings of the *Te Deum* and the Roman Mass for the Dead, whether or not Liszt himself remembered them all those years afterwards, that does define the nature of their religious music. The third choir of sopranos and contraltos *unisono* in Berlioz's *Te Deum* "represents" (according to the composer himself) "the mass of the people, taking part from time to time in a vast sacred concert." And both *Requiem* and *Te Deum* are written throughout in a vein completely incompatible with a ritual ceremony performed within the enclosed space of a church or cathedral; they suggest the worship of a whole people in the open air, bowed in awe before a god, terrible and omnipotent but hardly identifiable with the Christian God, or praising him for giving them victory over their enemies. The music is a curious mixture of the tender, the austerely monumental, and the dramatic.

Liszt's religious music is equally dramatic and far more subjective. His famous setting of the *Thirteenth Psalm* (1855), for instance, is passionate and intensely personal. He declared that there were passages in it "written with tears of blood" and that in the solo tenor part "which penetrates and dominates both chorus and orchestra," "I let *myself* sing and absorbed King David as it were into my own flesh and blood."[2] Nothing could be further from the ideal of Catholic church music. And in *Psalm CXXXVII*, written four years later, a finer piece of music though less well known, the picturesque element is added to the dramatic. The setting (for soprano solo, small female choir,

[1] *The Hungarian Coronation Mass* with Liszt's oratorio *Die Legende von der heiligen Elisabeth* (1865) will be considered later as products of musical nationalism.
[2] Letter to Brendel, *Franz Liszts Briefe*, Vol. II.

solo violin, harp and organ) was, indeed, probably inspired by
Bendemann's painting of "The Jews mourning by the waters
of Babylon" at Cologne. And the *Hundred and Thirty-seventh
Psalm* in turn is surpassed in drama by the *Graner Festmesse*
(or, to give it its proper title, *Missa solennis for the consecration
of the Basilika at Gran*) and in picturesqueness by the *Hungarian
Coronation Mass*. One particularly interesting feature of the
Gran Mass is the experiment of binding together the various
movements by liberal theme-quotation. For instance, the
"Gloria," "Resurrexit" and "Hosanna" are all founded on one
basic theme, the "Sanctus," "Christe eleison" and "Benedictus" on another. Again, a motive based on the Gregorian
intonation G,A,C is used by Liszt as a "tone-symbol of the
Cross," not only in the *Gran Mass* but in *St. Elisabeth*, the
Dante Symphony and the *Hunnenschlacht*. Only in the oratorio
Christus (completed in 1866) does Liszt adopt a more restrained,
impersonal, genuinely Catholic attitude to his text. But the
austerity of *Christus* is often dangerously near dullness, and even
here there are picturesque passages, such as the miracle of the
storm, and dramatic ones, such as the "Stabat Mater."

Admittedly the musical texture of Mendelssohn's two big
oratorios is very different from Liszt's; they were written a
couple of decades earlier, for one thing. Yet *Elijah*, at any rate,
is thoroughly dramatic in intention. In his letters to Schubring,
who helped him with the concoction of the text, Mendelssohn
asks for "questions and answers, replies and rejoinders, sudden
interruptions." He wants the personages to be living characters,
"not mere musical images, but inhabitants of a definite active
world." In spite of this, the result is *not* dramatic as a whole.
But that is only because Mendelssohn had the smallest possible
spark of dramatic instinct in his musical make-up. When he
aimed at drama, he generally achieved talented amateur
theatricals (e.g., the pseudo-rage of "Cónsume them all").
Whenever the dramatic spark threatens to break into flame, his
formalizing instinct promptly smothers it, as in "Stone him to
death" in *St. Paul*.

Indeed, largely for this reason—that it is frankly formalized,
the story being interspersed as in the Bach *Passions* (on which it
is frankly modelled in some respects) with *Choräle* in which the
congregation break the spell of the drama with their quiet,

thoughtful commentary—*St. Paul* is a more satisfactory artistic whole than the later work. The two best numbers are completely undramatic and make no pretence at being dramatic. "Happy and blest are they" is idyllic, "But our God abideth in heaven" austere and dignified (in the latter the influence of Bach is again perceptible in the use of a *Choral* tune as *canto fermo*). It is characteristic that nearly all the best work in both oratorios is given to the chorus.

Elijah makes hardly the slightest pretence at being a religious work till nearly at the end—the last five or six numbers—and at that point whatever vitality the music has hitherto possessed flickers peacefully out. None but a Bible-worshipping people like the Victorian English, who assumed that everything Biblical, from the list of the dukes of Edom in *Genesis* to the highly erotic *Song of Solomon*, was connected with the religion of Christ, could possibly have accepted the music of *Elijah* as religious. A modern critic can hear it only as a dramatic story told in a rather unsatisfactory way in music that is occasionally genuinely dramatic, e.g., the "Baal" choruses and "Behold, God, the Lord passed by," but much more often merely theatrical, e.g., the "rain" scene, which sounds uncommonly like opera gone wrong. In fact *Elijah* is the counterpart of contemporary German romantic opera in exactly the same way that Handel's oratorios were the counterparts of his operas; but it is much less successful. One of the masterstrokes of the work is the opening, the overture being preceded by a recitative in which Elijah prophesies the drought—a brilliant pretext for the insertion of the particularly arid movement that follows.

Berlioz's *Damnation de Faust* is also open to the criticism that it is bastard opera. It has actually been staged, though in this form it is a dismal failure. (*Elijah* in costume is much too funny to be dismal.) But, having admitted that it is a very unsatisfactory artistic whole, one must recognize the beauty, subtlety and vitality of nearly all its parts. The orchestral brilliance of the Hungarian March, the poetry of the scene by the Elbe (up to the moment of Faust's awakening), the nobility of Faust's invocation to Nature, the haunting simplicity of Gretchen's songs ("simple, sensuous and passionate" if any music in the world is), the combination of malice and power in the part of Mephistopheles—all these are unmatched in any music written before and in very little written since. The direct influence of Berlioz's *Faust* on later music is perceptible at least as late as Richard Strauss; the orchestral part of the last eighteen bars of recitative leading up to "The King of Thule" has left marks on more than one page of Strauss.

But the most enlightening way of considering Berlioz's *Faust* is to compare it with Schumann's *Scenes from Faust*. Schumann's was the later work in point of date: his Part III was written during 1844–47, Parts I and II in 1849–50, and the Overture in 1853; Berlioz's original *Eight Scenes from Faust* were set in 1829, the complete work as we know it in 1846. Nothing could illustrate more graphically the difference between French and German romanticism than a comparison of these two works, both unsatisfactory as wholes, each containing many magnificent parts.[1] The very selection of passages for musical treatment is enlightening. Berlioz's episodes are nearly all pictorial or even mere pretexts for musical tricks (the fragments of the peasants' dance and the march heard in the orchestra after Faust's first monologue; the combination of soldiers' chorus and students' song at the end of Part II); nearly half of Schumann's work in bulk, and by far the finest part of it musically, is a setting of Goethe's last scene, mystical and philosophical. Needless to say, Schumann's approach is far more worthy of Goethe's subject, and his music—square-cut, but noble and thoughtful—is very nearly worthy of the poet's words. Yet in the few cases where we can measure part against part, the opening of Schumann's Part II with Berlioz's chorus of sylphs, Schumann's setting of "Des Lebens Pulse schlagen" with Berlioz's "Nature immense" (not equivalent, but comparable), Berlioz wins. What is the explanation? Perhaps it is that, like Trabb's boy in *Great Expectations*, "he had too much spare vivacity, and it was in his constitution to want variety and excitement at anybody's expense." Berlioz got his excitement at Goethe's expense, but like Trabb's boy (and Trabb's boy's creator) his exuberant imagination carries him lightly through spheres where angels would fear to fly.

Schumann's nobility and thoughtfulness are offset by two faults, the first peculiar to himself, the second common to a

[1] A similar interesting parallel might be drawn between Mendelssohn's *Italian* Symphony and Berlioz's *Harold en Italie*.

great deal of German music at this period: squareness of structure (mature fruit of his early tendency to "verse" melody) and sluggishness of pulse. Mendelssohn's sing-song rhythms do at any rate get him over the ground; much of the music of Schumann, much of Liszt, a tremendous proportion of early Wagner (and a considerable proportion of late Wagner) seems almost to stagnate. The general slowing down of the *tempo* of the music of this period is at least as noticeable as its tendency to increased dissonance. And in this third part of Schumann's *Faust*, noble as it is, the texture so slowly unfolded is hardly interesting enough to hold the attention of a modern audience. The fiery vivacity of Berlioz's imagination has preserved his music, occasional romantic extravagances and all, and kept his slightly ridiculous conception of *Faust* alive to this day, while the far profounder thought of Schumann's *Faust* sounds weary and faded.

As for *Paradise and the Peri*, Schumann's only other choral work of first-rate importance, its once bright colours are now hopelessly dulled. The Chorus of Houris that opens Part III, a sort of feeble anticipation of rather poor Rimsky-Korsakov, is interesting as one of the earlier essays in that pseudo-Orientalism which *L'Africaine*, *Aïda* and the Russians afterwards made fashionable. As in most of Schumann's later works, there is much that can still be recognized as romantic in intention and which seemed quite excitingly romantic to his contemporaries; but the modern musician brooding over the score is more likely to be struck by the absence of the genuinely romantic spontaneity of the early, aphoristic Schumann. This older Schumann, not too skilfully manipulating the imposing forces of chorus and orchestra, is a disappointing sequel to the dashing Florestan and dreamy Eusebius of the piano pieces and songs. Nevertheless, even in the still duller *Pilgrimage of the Rose*, there are gleams of the old poetry, such as the exquisite orchestral motive— strikingly anticipatory of mature Wagner—that opens the penultimate number.

Romanticism, literary romanticism, was Schumann's very life-blood; when it sobered in his musical veins, his inspiration drooped accordingly. With Berlioz, perhaps, it was more in the nature of a cloak or *panache*; he threw it off—and rid his music of extravagances that had disfigured it. His love of the picturesque, his mania for dragging in extraneous episodes by the hair of the head, were ineradicable. So *L'Enfance du Christ* has its "march by night," its "cabalistic dance of the sooth-sayers," its trio for harp and two flutes (supposed to be performed by three young Ishmaelites), *Les Troyens* (1863) its "Royal hunt and storm" and its comic duet for the two sentinels, *Béatrice et Bénédict* (1862) its "épithalame grotesque." But even these artistic excrescences consist for the most part of very restrained music. The "Chasse royale et orage" is more impressionistic than realistic; the trio of the young Ishmaelites is as limpid and simple as a composition of the mid-eighteenth century. As for the overture to the second part of *L'Enfance*, "The Flight into Egypt," it is a flawless little masterpiece of purely classical music, and the movements that follow, the famous chorus of shepherds and "The Repose of the Holy Family," are hardly inferior.

Les Troyens, too, is flooded with the same quiet light. (Consider above all the exquisite duet, "Nuit d'ivresse et d'extase infinie!") It shines even in the witty, light-handed *Béatrice et Bénédict*. (Take, for instance, that other, almost equally lovely duet for Hero and Ursula, "Nuit paisible et sereine!") The history of music records few more striking paradoxes than this: that when the romantic movement had conquered the whole world of music in the nineteenth century, the only important composer who went on composing serenely beautiful music, filled with the classical spirit and fulfilling the classical ideal, was he who a quarter of a century earlier had been considered the most extravagant of the romantics.

The world still thinks of Berlioz as an ultra-romantic—mainly because it does not know his later, classical works. And it does not know *Les Troyens* and *Béatrice et Bénédict* mainly because they lack stage-values. That is true also of Berlioz's earlier opera, *Benvenuto Cellini* (1838). With all their wealth of fine music, Berlioz's three stage-works are so undramatic, and so different in conception from the other operas of their day, that they can hardly be said to belong to the general history of opera at all. Without ancestry (except perhaps Gluck and some of the eighteenth-century Italians) or posterity (except perhaps Cornelius's *Barbier von Bagdad*), they certainly have no place in the history of its development.

II

WAGNER AND THE OPERA

I. OPERA IN THE 'THIRTIES AND 'FORTIES

A CRITIC of the music of the past may choose either of two viewpoints. He may make the most of his sense of historical perspective and try to hear the music of a bygone period as contemporaries heard it; or he may prefer to take his stand on enduring values and judge all music purely and simply as it affects a man of his own time. In the one case he will probably not understand the true significance of a work; in the other he will be liable to ascribe undue importance to works now dead beyond hope of resuscitation. In practice most critics contrive to rub along fairly satisfactorily by compromising between these two ideal viewpoints. Better still, if one has time, patience and imagination, one can take a sight from both and correct the one view by the other; such criticism has a stereoscopic depth and roundness which make it as satisfying as criticism can ever be. But in dealing with the operas of the 'thirties and 'forties of the last century, the two viewpoints are so distant that it is almost impossible to correlate them. To the contemporary opera-lover the period must have seemed a prolific one, teeming with new, live works—works contemporary in every sense, in some cases even alarmingly revolutionary. To-day the masterpieces of the period have almost without exception vanished from the repertoire; at best one can hope to hear nothing more than occasional concert excerpts from Donizetti or Meyerbeer or a sporadic half-dead "revival" for the benefit of some star singer—though such things as Nicolai's *Merry Wives of Windsor* (1849) may still be heard at Continental opera-houses from time to time. The only genuine survivals from the period are those alarmingly advanced works, the first fairly mature operas of Wagner and Verdi, which live on as the most hackneyed of repertory pieces.

It is difficult to think oneself back into a time when Auber's *La Muette de Portici* (*Masaniello*) could "bewilder" German

77

musicians—it came out in 1828, the year after Beethoven's death—and could seem "romantic, extravagant, revolutionary in spirit . . . heady enough to intoxicate."[1]

Yet it *was* all that to contemporary musicians, as even Wagner acknowledged forty years later:[2] "It was completely new . . . the first real drama in five acts, with all the attributes of a tragedy, in particular a tragic end. I remember that this circumstance made a considerable sensation. Hitherto an opera had always had to end happily—no composer would have dared to send people home with a sad impression in their minds. When Spontini conducted his *La Vestale* in Dresden, he was enraged when he found that we intended, as was customary in Germany, to let the opera conclude with the scene in the cemetery."

But Auber wrote no worthy successor to *La Muette* and its only truly French progeny were such productions as Hérold's *Zampa* (1831) and Halévy's *La Juive* (1835). Berlioz's magnificent *Benvenuto Cellini* (1838) stands in a class by itself. (Though in justice to Halévy it must be said that in one respect, the free writing for chromatic brass, *La Juive* is far ahead of most contemporary works, including *Cellini* itself.) All these are, in a sense, romantic operas; romantic in subject but musically only pale reflections of the more robust romanticism of contemporary instrumental music, related to it much as late Puccini is related to Debussy and Stravinsky. The best of the so-called French romantic operas were the work of foreigners: Rossini's great swan-song, *Guillaume Tell* (1829), which should never have been allowed to fall out of the repertoire, and the mature works of Meyerbeer, *Robert le Diable* (1831), *Les Huguenots* (1836), *Le Prophète* (1849) and *L'Africaine* (produced 1865, but begun much earlier). But Meyerbeer was essentially a cosmopolitan, combining French, German and Italian elements.

The most characteristic work of the French operatic school of the period was done in another field, that of light opera and operetta. Auber's mass of light operas (I deliberately avoid the hopelessly ambiguous term *opéra comique*), including such still-

[1] Dannreuther: *Oxford History of Music*, Vol. VI.
[2] *Erinnerungen an Auber* (1871). Owing to a misplaced quotation mark in the *Oxford History* this passage, quoted there, appears as if it were Dannreuther's own.

remembered works as *Fra Diavolo* (1830), *Le Domino noir* (1837) and *Les Diamants de la Couronne* (1841), as well as a host of quite forgotten ones, are as completely unromantic musically as anything one could imagine. At most we can only point to a few isolated phrases such as the opening bars of the overture to *Les Diamants* or Zerlina's "Voyez sur cette roche" in *Fra Diavolo*, which, without being at all romantic in themselves, seem to be ever so faintly coloured by the romanticism of the contemporary atmosphere. As a composer of light opera, Auber considered himself purely as a craftsman supplying the works demanded by the public and that attitude in itself puts him in a different category from the romantics—who, however else they differed, were at one in taking themselves and their art very seriously even in their lighter moments. As a craftsman Auber never rises much higher than the finale of Act II of *Fra Diavolo*; sometimes he seems little better than a more resourceful predecessor of Offenbach. But he is seldom lacking in grace, never in sparkle. In other words, he was a talented manufacturer of good commercial art and, like most such manufacturers, was liable to not infrequent strokes of genuine inspiration.

The same may be said of the great Italians of the period. Operatic conditions in early nineteenth-century Italy have already been briefly described. Composers working in such a milieu could hardly be expected to be very sensitive to general cultural tendencies. Moreover, the romantic movement in general was primarily Franco-German. Nevertheless, the Italian opera subjects of the eighteen-thirties show a tendency towards romanticism and away from the old hackneyed themes drawn from ancient history and classical mythology, and in the next decade Italy produced in Verdi a romantic composer of the first rank—though Verdi, still, differed from Berlioz and the German romantics in regarding himself as a craftsman with a small c rather than an Artist with a capital A. To say that is not to deny that Verdi took his art very seriously; it is well known that he did, and that as his position in the musical world grew stronger he was able to form the taste of his public as well as to cater for it.

The production of Verdi's first important opera, *Nabucodonosor* (or *Nabucco*, as it is generally called) in 1842 actually marked not only the advent of a new composer but the dawn of a new age in Italian opera. Of the older generation, Rossini had finished his operatic life in 1829 with *Tell*, Bellini had died in 1836, and Donizetti was at the very end of his career—his last important work, the brilliant comic masterpiece *Don Pasquale*, dates from 1843. *William Tell* is as thoroughly romantic as any work of Weber's, but the romanticism of Bellini and Donizetti is of a more limited nature. In fact, Donizetti's is limited to his choice of subjects: for instance, *Lucrezia Borgia* (1833) (after Hugo), *Lucia di Lammermoor* (1835) (for Scott was one of the foundation-stones of the literary romantic movement), and *La Favorita* (1840) (based on a French play, *Le Comte de Commingues*). Even in *Lucia* there are few traces of musical romanticism. Donizetti, like Auber, survives only as a composer of sparkling comic opera in the vein of Rossini.

The case of Bellini, a far more gifted composer, is very different. His romanticism is apparent not only in some of his subjects; it saturates his melody, the very heart of his music— for his harmony, his orchestration and his choral writing are generally feeble. Bellini's melody is generally not only beautiful in line, a vehicle for lovely voices;[1] it is often full of peculiarly romantic *morbidezza*, melancholy and passion. Its influence on the melody of Chopin and Liszt has already been mentioned. One has only to examine Pollione's "Vieni in Roma" in *Norma*, for instance, to realize the extent of Chopin's debt to Bellini or (perhaps it would be more correct to say) the indebtedness of both to the Italian operatic composers of the beginning of the century. Cecil Gray has made an even higher claim for the Italian master: "It would probably not be going too far to say that Bellini is to a great extent the father of modern melody. The particular vein of passionate ecstasy and elegiac melancholy which suddenly comes into music in the first half of the nineteenth century, and sharply distinguishes it from that of all

[1] The music of all these century-old Italian composers is far too often judged, and condemned, by its appearance on paper or by inadequate modern performances. When Bellini or Donizetti conceived a melodic line, he conceived it in terms of exquisite vocal tone manipulated through a perfect vocal technique—and he knew that his singers would give it him. It is as absurd to condemn their music because modern singers cannot sing it properly as it would be to condemn Chopin's nocturnes or Brahms's intermezzi because they would sound ineffective on a harpsichord.

preceding centuries, has its source in the operas of Bellini and nowhere else."[1]

The young Verdi was naturally very strongly influenced by Bellini's melody, as he was in other respects by the work of Rossini and Donizetti. (As one would expect, the music of the young and immature Verdi is a rather weak synthesis of the main elements in these three masters of the previous generation.) The famous chorus in *Nabucco*, "Va, pensiero, sull' ali dorate," for instance, is thoroughly Bellinian; and Bellini's influence is still easily perceptible in works written ten years later. Dannreuther has pointed out in the *Oxford History of Music* (Vol. VI) that the great quartet in *Rigoletto* (1851) is modelled on that in Bellini's *I Puritani* (1834). "In so far as the outlines of form are concerned, the two quartets are closely alike in the cast of the melody, the changes of harmonic centres, the culmination of vocal effects towards the close, and in the contrivance of the coda." And he goes on to quote the chief melody of the *Rigoletto* quartet beneath that of "A te, o cara" in *I Puritani*. The demonstration of the Bellinian origin of Verdi's tune is perfectly convincing. But the difference is far more instructive than the similarity. Dannreuther draws attention to Verdi's "advance . . . in the direction of *la musica caratteristica*, the change for the better with regard to the independence of the vocal part-writing, the individualization of the characters, together with a wider range of harmony," but he has nothing to say about the much greater vitality of Verdi's melody. Yet here we can put our finger on the essential difference between Bellini and Verdi. Verdi's tune has a warmth, a passion, a coarse energy that makes Bellini's seem cold and bloodless. By comparison with Verdi, Bellini sounds ultra-refined and almost classical. Verdi is the first full-blooded romantic of Italian opera—and incidentally the link between Bellini and Mascagni.

Just to what extent he was the operatic champion of literary romanticism may be seen from a glance at his subjects: *Ernani* (1844) (Victor Hugo's *Hernani*), *I due Foscari* (1844) (Byron's *The Two Foscari*), *Giovanna d'Arco* (1845) (Schiller's *Jungfrau von Orleans*), *Macbeth* (1847) (for we must remember that Shakespeare had been borrowed by the literary romantics, just

[1] *The History of Music*. Kegan Paul, 2nd edition, 1931.

as the *surréalistes* of our day have laid claim to Blake and Lewis Carroll), *I Masnadieri* (1847) (Schiller's *Die Räuber*), *Il Corsaro* (1848) (Byron's *The Corsair*), *Luisa Miller* (1849) (Schiller's *Kabale und Liebe*), *Rigoletto* (1851) (Hugo's *Le Roi s'amuse*), *Il Trovatore* (1853) (Gutierrez's *El Trovador*), *La Traviata* (1853) (*La Dame aux Camélias* by Dumas *fils*), *Simone Boccanegra* (1857) (on another play by Gutierrez), *La forza del destino* (1862) (*Don Alvaro* by the Duke of Rivas, a leading Spanish romanticist), *Don Carlo* (1867) (Schiller's *Don Carlos*). The exceptions are few, and only two—*I Vespri Siciliani* (1855) and *Un ballo in maschera* (1859), both on conventional Scribe libretti—are important. *Aïda* (1871) and the two Shakespearean masterpieces belong to a new period and must be considered separately.

But one subsidiary motive is noticeable in Verdi's choice of subjects, that of patriotism. In *Nabucco* the captivity of the Jews obviously symbolizes the captivity of the Italians; *I Lombardi alla Prima Crociato* (1843) similarly uses the First Crusade as a mere stalking-horse. "The 'crusade,' in the minds of the listeners," says Bonavia,[1] "had not the Holy Places for its objective, but the cities of Italy. The subject was meant to remind Italians in general, and the Lombard city [Milan] for which it was written in particular, of their ancient military glory; the music expressed in song what poets like Giusti and Fustinato expressed in their verses." *Attila* (1846) again deliberately played on patriotic, anti-Austrian feeling, and probably owed its success to that fact rather than to its not very remarkable musical value; the libretto contains, among other things, the famous line addressed to Attila by the Roman envoy, Ezio, "Avrai tu l'universo, restì l'Italia a me!" ("You shall have the universe, if I may have Italy.") *La Battaglia di Legnano* was frankly inspired by the revolutionary movement of 1848 and produced in Rome in January, 1849, on the eve of the proclamation of the Roman Republic.

In this self-conscious nationalism—for musical nationalism is by no means the affair of mere folk-idiom that it is commonly assumed to be—as well as in his passionate romanticism, Verdi proclaims himself a typical mid-nineteenth-century musician. Both in his general attitude to opera and its problems and in the

[1] *Verdi.* By Ferruccio Bonavia. O.U.P., 1930.

actual texture of his music, he was a progressive second in daring only to Wagner. But whereas Wagner was very conscious of "problems," became disgusted with opera, and evolved from philosophical first principles what he regarded as an entirely new art-form in its place, Verdi modified and developed the conventional opera-form, as he found it, in the light of nothing but his own sound artistic instinct. In place of the old "pretexts for music," he selected genuinely dramatic libretti, often subjects that in this more cynical age provoke ridicule by their characteristically romantic dwelling on the horrible and on violent contrasts. But the libretti of all his best works are full of emotional situations, situations that really can be enhanced by music. And his music itself pulsates with an emotional, dramatic life which, as we have seen, makes the more aristocratic art of Bellini from which it sprang sound pallid and rather lifeless.

Even in an early work like *Nabucco*, there are things such as Abigaille's cabaletta in Act II, "Salgo già del trono auro," which, square-cut as they are, avoid the banal by virtue of naked, vital energy and announce the arrival of a new force in Italian music. Moreover, as Roncaglia and Francis Toye have pointed out,[1] "the overture was the first since *William Tell* to be linked with the development of the theatrical action"; the depth to which the Italian overture had descended may be judged from the prelude to *I Puritani*, which is no feebler than most of Bellini's overtures.

I Lombardi marks a further advance in expressiveness, both melodic (the death of Oronte) and harmonic (Giselda's "Salve Maria" in Act I), and *Ernani* contains in crude forms all the elements of Verdi's robust middle period: the effective, genuinely dramatic ensemble (trio in Act IV), the broad, unforgettable, rather vulgar tune ("Si ridesti il Leon de Castiglia" in Act III), the rudimentary leitmotive, used to drive home a dramatic point but not employed systematically (Ernani's horn-call, the opening theme of the Prelude, used in Acts II and IV), and the rest. Incidentally, Elvira's phrase, "Ohimè, ohimè, si perde" in Act II is not to be taken as a deliberate reminiscence of her "Ernani, involami"; this little cliché was one of Verdi's favourite melodic gambits (cf. "Libiamo ne' lieti calici" in the first act

[1] *Giuseppe Verdi: his Life and Works.* By Francis Toye. Heinemann, 1951.

of *La Traviata*). But in Verdi's next opera, *I due Foscari*, indubitable leitmotives are multiplied.[1] As Francis Toye points out, "a certain orchestral figure is associated throughout with the Council of Ten; the same holds good for the private meditations of the Doge; Lucrezia's agitation and Jacopo's despair both have themes of their own recurrent throughout the opera."

We must blame the conditions in which Verdi worked, the commercial demand that he was constantly supplying, for the poorness of much of his work. Between *I due Foscari* (produced in November, 1844) and *Luisa Miller* (December, 1849), Verdi provided his public with seven operas of which only one, *Macbeth*, is of any real value.

Macbeth (1847) was not only the finest thing Verdi had done so far but, as Bonavia says, "the first Italian opera of the nineteenth century to admit the need for lyrical restraint and to make a wider use of an essentially dramatic style." That exactly defines the nature of Verdi's contribution to the æsthetics of Italian opera. In *Macbeth* "he did not forgo completely the use of lyricism; but he denied its supremacy, he denied that arias *were* infallible and inevitable; he sought a juster balance between the lyrical and the dramatic."[2] A good deal of light is thrown on Verdi's own views by a letter of his to Cammarano: "There are two very important moments in the opera: the duet between Lady Macbeth and her husband, and the sleep-walking scene. If these fail, the whole opera falls to the ground. These two pieces must not on any account be sung. They must be acted and declaimed in a very sombre, veiled tone. Unless this can be done, the whole effect will be lost." He objected to Mme Tadolini as Lady Macbeth on the ground that she "sings to perfection, and I should prefer Lady Macbeth not to sing. Mme Tadolini has a splendid voice, clear, pure and powerful; and I should like in Lady Macbeth a hard, hoarse, gloomy voice." But it would be wrong to conclude that Verdi had taken to theorizing about the nature of opera and the need for reforming

[1] The point at which the old, well-tried operatic device of "thematic reminiscence" merges into leitmotive proper is not easily determined. The word "leitmotive" should really be reserved for the quasi-symphonic theme used systematically throughout a work, but I employ it here in the wider sense.

[2] Bonavia: *Verdi*.

it; it was simply that he had got hold of a subject which, as with his lifelong admiration of Shakespeare he immediately recognized, would have been preposterous if handled in terms of the old predominantly lyrical opera. And it must be confessed that enough of the old incongruous lyricism remains, even in the revised version of 1865, to "date" the work hopelessly. The sleep-walking scene could have been written by no one but the mature Verdi; but Lady Macbeth's "Vieni! t'affreta!" in Act I, with its concluding splash of coloratura, shows the Verdi who was only the more dramatic heir of Bellini.

Luisa Miller marks another advance, particularly in Verdi's orchestral writing (already very far ahead of Bellini's or Donizetti's), and then with *Rigoletto, Il Trovatore* and *La Traviata* we reached the mature second-period Verdi—the Verdi who incidentally compelled J. W. Davison in 1855 to admit that although "he is neither a Rossini, nor an Auber, nor a Meyerbeer; far from it . . . he is not, as some would insist, a nonentity." In *Il Trovatore* one detects for the first time in Verdi the influence of Meyerbeer—an influence deepened in *I Vespri Siciliani, Don Carlo* and *Aïda.* And in many respects it is certainly a throwback to vulgarized Bellini. But *Rigoletto* and *La Traviata* are both masterpieces of their kind.

Because these operas are now commonplaces to us, it is difficult to realize how extraordinarily fresh, colourful and dramatic they must have sounded in the eighteen-fifties. There is in both a certain amount of poor music, music poor alike in quality and in treatment. There are still plenty of conventional set-numbers, still coloratura arias. But in at least two celebrated cases, "Caro nome" and "Ah fors' è lui," the coloratura—if properly sung, instead of being treated as vocal fireworks—is dramatically justified. These are not show-pieces, though it is disgustingly easy for a bad artist to turn them into show-pieces. The musical characterization in both *Rigoletto* and *La Traviata* is very fine; the principals, if not always the minor characters, really exist in terms of music. Knowing their music, one knows them—and never forgets them. And everything "comes off" so marvellously in the theatre. Theme-quotation—or use of the leitmotive, if you will—has often been used far more subtly but nowhere with more overwhelming dramatic effect than when Rigoletto hears the snatch of "La donna è mobile" at the end of the opera. Verdi could be subtle, too; witness the modulation at "Se una pudica vergine" in the last scene of *La Traviata*. But he never makes the fatal mistake of being too subtle for the theatre with its strong lights and broad effects.

Alike in *Rigoletto* and *La Traviata* and in the series of strangely unequal works that followed (*I Vespri Siciliani*, *Simone Boccanegra*, and the rest), with all Verdi's emphasis on dramatic feeling, this feeling is expressed through the music itself rather than through any attempt to fuse music and play into a satisfactory artistic whole. As a play the average Verdi opera is an unsatisfactory, often ridiculous, piece of stage-carpentry which we accept because the music, if properly performed, compels us to forget it. Verdi was never further from Wagner than during the 'fifties and 'sixties.

As regards the actual texture of his music, of course, Verdi had not yet even at this period sloughed off the traces of the school from which he sprang. His dynamic melody had very nearly done so, but beside the many happy touches of orchestration there are far too many pages of conventional, rule-of-thumb scoring. Harmonically, Verdi's style is still more uneven; sometimes strikingly expressive (as at the crisis of Violetta's pleading with Germont in Act II of *La Traviata*), but frequently very conventional and sometimes even absolutely banal in the worst Italian tradition.

Far more enterprising in this respect was Glinka, the so-called "father of Russian music," who also began his creative career under the influence of Bellini. Glinka, indeed, although he soon struck out on original lines of his own, must be considered as, next to Verdi himself, the most important offshoot of the older Italian school. Its other Italian disciples are so negligible that their very names are almost forgotten.

Glinka's first opera, *A Life for the Tsar* (1836), enjoys a popular reputation as "the first Russian opera," which it most certainly was not. It is in many respects a typical product of the Russian "gentlemanly dilettantism" of the period, a style that combined imitation of Italian opera with a rather unintelligent appreciation of the flavour of native folk-music and considerable technical incompetence. *A Life for the Tsar* differs from its predecessors in quality rather than in kind. Much of the texture is amateurish and colourless; often the tang of folk-song is very mild indeed—if not completely absent. Still feebler are the imitations of Polish national music used throughout to characterize the enemies of the Russians. However, one or two actual folk-tunes are used in the score, and in one or two numbers, such as the unison chorus in Act I, with its pizzicato accompaniment suggesting balalaikas, and the bridal chorus in 5-4 time in Act III, Glinka did succeed brilliantly in writing music with unmistakably Russian melodic inflections. And these melodies sound spontaneous, not like mere laboured imitations of folk-music.

The most serious weakness of *A Life for the Tsar* is its harmony, usually perfectly obvious and insipid in the contemporary Italian manner. Glinka not infrequently writes a modal melody and kills it with diatonic harmony. But in one respect the opera does stand far in advance not only of all previous Russian operas but of all contemporary operas. As Russian critics delight to point out, Glinka was a pioneer in the use of the leitmotive—or, at any rate, of wholesale theme-quotation as a means of dramatic expression. Leitmotives are employed far more extensively in *A Life for the Tsar* than in any opera by Weber or any other composer before Wagner. Wagner's *Das Liebesverbot*, in which leitmotives are employed tentatively, appeared in the same year as *A Life for the Tsar*, *Ernani* and *I due Foscari* eight years later. To take only one instance out of many: practically the whole dramatic pathos of the hero's last monologue as he awaits the dawn that will bring him death depends on the recollection of theme after theme—six in all—associated earlier in the action with his daughter, her betrothed, and his adopted son.

With all its defects, *A Life for the Tsar* has several features premonitory of things in later Russian opera: the perfunctory nature of the love interest, the crisp, slightly Weberian overture (though it has none of Weber's magical romanticism), Antonida's cavatina (in which the unaccompanied, or barely accompanied, voice echoes the arabesque phrases of flute or clarinet), the bright, transparent texture (choral and orchestral) of the peasants' chorus in Act III. But in this respect *A Life for the Tsar* is completely thrown into the shade by Glinka's second opera, *Ruslan and Lyudmila* (1842).

Ruslan is far weaker than its predecessor from the dramatic point of view; indeed, it hardly exists at all as a drama, being merely a sequence of fantastic happenings, dreamlike in their incoherence. But musically it is one of the most remarkable operas of the first half of the last century. There are still traces of the influence of Weber (the overture, the "magic dances" in Act III, the fight music in Act IV, etc.) and the Italians (Farlaf's *buffo* aria in Act II), but by far the greater part of the music is absolutely original, and served as the stylistic model for the entire "nationalist" Russian school.

The bard's song in the first act, for instance, contains the germs of both the so-called Russian "heroic" style (broad and modal) and the lyrical style of Borodin and Rimsky-Korsakov (slightly facile diatonic melody, simple but delicately coloured harmony, transparent part-writing). The "heroic" style of Borodin's B minor Symphony and other works in the same vein is also foreshadowed in the 5-4 chorus in honour of Lel, the Love God, also in Act I.

Then again, the attractive Oriental conventions of later Russian music are almost entirely modelled on those in *Ruslan*. The importance of the Oriental element in Russian music has been greatly exaggerated; Russian composers were attracted by Orientalism not because it was in their blood, but because it was an exotic form of art brought to their notice through Russia's military penetration of the Caucasus and Central Asia. The melody of the Persian chorus that opens Act III, the first theme of Ratmir's aria in the same act, and two of the themes of the *lezginka* are genuine Oriental tunes, but the treatment—the triplet arabesques and luscious orchestration—is merely a convention devised by Glinka. Ratmir's romance in Act V, apparently wholly faked, actually exercised as much influence on later Russian "Oriental music" as any of the genuine specimens in *Ruslan*. The Persian chorus, like Finn's ballad in Act II, is interesting too as one of the earliest examples of a type of variation-writing much practised by Russian musicians, the melody being repeated unchanged against ever new harmonic and orchestral backgrounds.

But the most interesting of all the new features of *Ruslan* are the boldness of the harmonic texture and the use of technical ingenuities to produce "fantastic" effects. Whereas *A Life for the Tsar* is very tame from the harmonic point of view, *Ruslan* may almost be said to mark the beginning of a new epoch in

harmony. The descending whole-tone scale used as the leitmotive of the villain Chernomor is probably the first appearance
of that artificial scale in music. The music of Lyudmila's abduc-
tion—the bass descending in whole tones, the treble in major
thirds, with inner parts producing clashes of naked seconds and
sevenths—is characteristic of Glinka's harmonic experiments.
The scene between Farlaf and Naina in Act II (making play with
augmented and diminished triads), Chernomor's march, the
fight in Act IV (with more clashing seconds), and above all the
astonishingly modern *lezginka*, with its ruthless carrying through
of melodic and harmonic patterns, are all far in advance, harmonically, of anything that was being written for the Western
opera stage at that time or for years afterward. But Glinka's
advance was along quite different lines from Chopin's—the
chromatic highroad followed by Liszt and Wagner—and it was
only after another quarter of a century that Russian music began
to be affected, through Liszt, by Western harmonic developments. On the other hand, Liszt knew and admired *Ruslan*,
and it is possible that some elements in his later style were
suggested by Glinka.

In the history of opera as such, Glinka cuts a much less impressive figure. Although his operatic methods were to influence
Borodin and Rimsky-Korsakov to some extent, and despite the
great musical interest of *Ruslan*, neither of his operas is good
enough as a stage-work to win a place in the repertoire outside
Russia. Historically he is a most interesting figure, a disciple
of Bellini and (as regards the magical romanticism of *Ruslan*)
Weber, who adapted the methods of both his models to his own
ends and created a style as distinctive as Verdi's. But it is
curious that, while admitting the influence of the Italians,
Glinka himself always depreciated Weber, drawing from Liszt
the caustic comment "You and Weber are like two rivals for
the affection of the same lady." Which was not unfair, for,
allowing for the difference of the Russian temperament, *Ruslan
and Lyudmila* belongs to the family of *Oberon* and *Euryanthe*
and is perhaps, after them, its most distinguished member.

In Germany itself Weber's immediate progeny were few and
comparatively unimportant. With the exception of Schumann's
single opera, the unfortunate, wholly unsuccessful *Genoveva*
(1850), Lortzing's *Undine* (1845) and Nicolai's *Lustigen Weiber*

von Windsor (1849), the only purely German romantic operas
of importance between Weber and Wagner are those of Heinrich
Marschner. (Spohr survived Weber by many years, but most of
his operas belong to his younger days; *Die Kreuzfahrer* (1844)
is a not very important exception.) The only interesting features
of *Genoveva*, the break with the long accepted convention of the
"set number" and the employment of leitmotives, are obviously
copied from *Euryanthe*; and some of the best things in *The
Merry Wives*—above all, the opening of the scene in the moon-
lit forest (identical with the opening of the overture)—are
decidedly Weberian.

The subjects of Marschner's three best-known operas show
the thorough-going romanticism of his taste. *Der Templer und
die Jüdin* (1829) is based on *Ivanhoe, Der Vampyr* (1828) on a
novel by Byron (or rather by Polidori, his secretary-physician),
while *Hans Heiling* (1833) deals with the wooing of a girl by a
goblin prince who takes human form. The two latter are
particularly significant; Marschner delighted in vampires and
goblins, the *macabre* and terrible, and his sombre music surpasses
even Weber's in depicting the incidents beloved of German
Schauerromantik. But on the whole Marschner was distinctly
Weber's inferior. In fire and imagination, in melodic invention, harmonic sense and orchestration, he can hardly be compared with his master. Wagner undoubtedly took hints from
him and Brahms, perhaps deliberately, quoted an 8-bar melody
from the *larghetto* of the *Hans Heiling* Overture in his early
Scherzo in E flat minor for piano (composed 1851). But
Marschner added little to the vocabulary of music in general.

That cannot be said of Meyerbeer. Whatever one thinks of
the intrinsic merits of Meyerbeer's music—whether one agrees
with such distinguished and diverse critics as Rossini, Schumann
and Wagner in condemning it, or with one or two modern
English critics in finding it full of merits—it is impossible to
deny that it exercised an enormous influence not only on contemporary opera but on opera for several decades, as late as the
eighteen-seventies. Meyerbeer's art was almost entirely synthetic, a compound of the most effective elements of German
romantic opera, Italian opera and French heroic opera mixed to
suit the taste of the Paris public, and not even his very great
talent could save his operas from frequently degenerating into

comic nightmares of romantic extravagance. (He had a special weakness for highly romanticized history.) Yet these brilliant pastiches, disparate and apparently "style"-less as they are, did after all receive the stamp of the composer's musical personality. The adjective "Meyerbeerian," usually a term of abuse, does not mean merely "noisy and spectacular grand opera, full of calculated effects of stage and music"; it does also indicate a certain musical style. And this style, much of which really derives from Spontini, as well as "Meyerbeerism" in the vulgar sense, left marks on *Rienzi* and *Tannhäuser*, on *Don Carlo*, *I Vespri Siciliani* and *Aïda*, and on most of the operas of Halévy, Gounod, Saint-Saëns and the young Bizet. Even on Mussorgsky; the opening bars of Act I, Scene 4, of *Les Huguenots*[1] contain striking anticipations of *Boris Godunov*, and other instances might be quoted.

Of Meyerbeer's half-dozen early Italian operas, only one, *Il Crociato in Egitto* (1824) is of the least interest, and *Il Crociato* itself is in some respects a work of transition. It was with his first French opera, *Robert le Diable* (1831), that Meyerbeer established himself in the first rank of opera composers—and incidentally sent Rossini into retirement. *Robert*, its libretto owing more than a little to that of *Der Freischütz*, is perhaps the wildest of all Meyerbeer's romantic nightmares, full of the most extravagant musical and dramatic contrasts but not without genuinely beautiful passages (e.g., the famous "Robert! toi que je t'aime"). And the orchestration was then new and striking. Meyerbeer's scoring is often justly condemned as noisy, and to the end of his life he was so unsure of himself that, like Liszt, he scored passages in alternative versions and made his final decision only after testing both at rehearsal; yet he possessed a fine sense of orchestral colour, understood the peculiarities of the various instruments far better than most of his contemporaries, and was in many respects a pioneer. For instance, he originated the French fashion of using a pair of cornets as normal constituents of the orchestra, and in *Robert* showed Berlioz what could be done with natural horns by writing for them in three or four crooks simultaneously. The scene of

[1] Cf. a similar melodic pattern in the Overture to *L'Africaine*, also sung by Inès in the finale of Act II. But the *Huguenots* example also anticipates the "police" theme in *Boris*.

the resurrection of the nuns in Act III of *Robert* is a superb piece of orchestration; the bassoon triplets, the low brass chords, the touches on the gong—every detail is peculiarly effective.

But by general consent Meyerbeer's best work is *Les Huguenots* (1836). Like everything else of his, it is patchy; but the good patches cover a much bigger area than usual and the fourth act is indisputably a masterpiece. The celebrated "consecration of the daggers" is not by any means great music but it is dramatically effective, and the duet that occurs a little later in the act is as nearly "great" as anything in opera between *Oberon* and *The Flying Dutchman*. It is based on one of the most beautiful melodies Meyerbeer ever wrote; not long-breathed—Meyerbeer was incapable of sustained lyrical flight—but genuinely warm-blooded and alive. The aptness of the key (G flat major), the subtlety of the orchestration, the effective echoing of the vocal phrases by the 'cellos (not the less effective because the device is obvious), all combine to produce an unforgettable impression— and an impression that was not forgotten by a good many later composers. Equally beautiful is the luscious scoring of the celebrated bathing chorus in Act II, while the tocsin in Act IV, overtones to the actual bell used being simultaneously suggested by clarinets and bassoons, probably suggested the numerous similar effects in Russian music (*Boris*, *Khovanshchina*, *Pskovityanka*, Rimsky-Korsakov's *Overture on Three Russian Themes*, etc.). Very interesting, too, is the use of unusual solo instruments, the viola d'amore in Raoul's romance in Act I, the bass clarinet in the trio in the last act (where it has an effective piece of instrumental recitative).

Le Prophète (finished 1843, produced 1849), even more than *Les Huguenots*, shows Meyerbeer's dissatisfaction with the old, conventional set-numbers of grand opera. The first two acts in particular are perhaps the most successful of all his rather half-hearted attempts at greater continuity of texture. The breaks are fewer and the music is partially bound together by the recurrence of certain themes, notably the striking chorus of Anabaptists, "Ad nos, ad salutarem undam," known to most people only through the fine organ piece based on it by Liszt. One number, "O mon fils," is peculiar in betraying the influence, unusual in Meyerbeer's work, of Chopin. But nothing in *Le Prophète* reaches the height of the *Struensee* overture of

1846, part of the incidental music to his brother's play of that name, and after *Le Prophète* Meyerbeer's powers show a distinct falling off. Neither *L'Étoile du Nord* (1854), partly based on the *Feldlager in Schlesien* of ten years earlier, nor *Dinorah* (1859) added anything to his reputation—though the pretty Shadow Song in the latter opera still survives—and *L'Africaine* (begun in 1838, completed 1863, performed 1865) is more remarkable for the influence it undoubtedly exercised on *Aïda* than for its own sake. Despite interesting passages, such as the short prelude to Act II, the sham Orientalism of *L'Africaine* has faded sadly, much worse than that of Glinka's *Ruslan*.

Indeed, "faded" is the inevitable epithet for Meyerbeer's music as a whole, as it strikes the modern listener. The orchestral colouring, once so novel, now impresses only those who possess that sense of historical perspective referred to at the beginning of this chapter, and the other elements of his musical style have worn even worse—mainly because their novelty tickled the fancy of so many less ingenious, but more naturally gifted, composers who appropriated them and wore them out. Meyerbeer has suffered as much as Liszt, much more than Berlioz, from the fact that his imitators are better known than himself. And, unlike Liszt's, his music has not enough inner vitality to reward the efforts of those conscientious students of musical history who, from a sense of justice, would like to revive it. Paradoxical as the statement may appear, Meyerbeer's operas have died because they are too intellectual and not tuneful enough. They are brilliant compendiums of nearly all that was interesting and modern in the music of their day; but that has not preserved them. Half the vulgar spontaneous melodic vitality of, say, *Il Trovatore*, would have kept them in the repertoire to this day. In fact *Il Trovatore* itself, as nearly a mere mixture of Bellini and Meyerbeer as Verdi was capable of writing at forty, rather cruelly demonstrates the superiority of the Italian composer. If, as Dannreuther says, "the rôle of Azucena is but that of Fidès in *Le Prophète*, translated into Romany," the greater musical vitality of Azucena is only too obvious. Meyerbeer's favourite substitutes for a genuine life-pulse in his music, his incessant, well-marked rhythms, now seem curiously wooden.

Meyerbeer also fares badly if one compares even the best of his scores with Wagner's *Rienzi* (completed 1840, performed

1842), a work deliberately written in his vein and aimed at his public, that of the Paris Opéra. Wagner had already written two operas, one in the true German romantic opera tradition, *Die Feen* (completed 1834, performed 1888), a charming and by no means unindividual essay in the genre of Weber and Marschner, the other, *Das Liebesverbot* (completed and performed in 1836), betraying strong French and Italian influences. But *Rienzi* is the earliest work of his still in the repertoire (in those countries that possess a genuine opera repertoire) and *Rienzi* challenges Meyerbeer on his own ground and beats him.

Although *Rienzi* suffers from the rhythmic monotony that pervades áll Wagner's music right up to *Lohengrin*—and a good deal of it after—it possesses a certain broad ponderous movement that bears it forward as Meyerbeer's music is very seldom borne. In the whole of Meyerbeer it would be difficult to find any long orchestral movement as good as the *Rienzi* overture, any melody as broad and sweeping as Rienzi's prayer, any stretch of fairly sustained dramatic music as fine as the latter part of Act II: the attempted assassination, the condemnation of the nobles, and their subsequent pardon. *Rienzi* contains an enormous amount of poor music, music that is commonplace, meretricious and pretentious, yet it was one of the finest operas of its day. And it contains enough signs premonitory of the later Wagner's style to make it of enduring interest to the Wagnerian student. Not only accidental things, like the sounding of the *Parsifal* bells at the beginning of the overture and the characteristic turn in Rienzi's prayer, the opening of the finale of Act IV, and so on, but the tendency to chromaticism (mild enough in the duet of Act I, more pronounced in the introduction to Act II), the type of phrase used to accompany the entrance of the Goddess of Peace in the pantomime, the texture of several passages in the latter part of Act II (e.g., after Rienzi's words, "Zu End', ihr Römer, sind die Feste," and after Cecco's "Du wirst's bereu'n!"), all these point already to the Wagner of the eighteen-fifties.

Der fliegende Höllander (completed 1841, performed 1843) no longer belongs to the cosmopolitan world of Meyerbeer. It is pure, honest German romantic opera in the Marschner tradi- tion, but far more powerful than anything of Marschner's, indeed the finest of all German romantic operas up to that time. The directness, the drama, and the vivid pictorial power of the

overture, at once announce that a new and potent spirit is working in the old operatic form. In the *Dutchman* Wagner for the
first time got hold of the type of subject that he afterwards
considered the only one suitable for musical-dramatic treatment:
the legend, with its simple outline and its handful of profoundly
significant characters. The action is all concentrated closely
around Senta and the Dutchman, characters with real dramatic
life very different from the conventional operatic lay-figures of
Rienzi (and Meyerbeer and early Verdi in general). That alone
gives the opera a certain unity, and the musical treatment makes
that unity far more complete. The outlines of the old set forms
are still perceptible but the texture is more continuous than in
Rienzi or *Le Prophète* (Wagner even intended originally to have
the work performed in one act; this may be done by omitting
the last twenty-six bars of Act I, the first eighteen of Act II,
and the last twelve of Act II). The numbers are bound together
both by the general feeling—the atmosphere of storm, physical
and emotional, and the all-pervading harmonic tension—and by
the numerous thematic links. Leitmotives are used in *The
Flying Dutchman* more freely than in any previous opera, more
than in *Das Liebesverbot*, far more than in *Rienzi*. Comparatively crudely, it is true; the motives are seldom modified, much
less transformed in Wagner's later manner; but they are already
used fairly systematically—and hence necessarily with less
immediate dramatic effect than in, say, *A Life for the Tsar* or
Ernani.

Tannhäuser (completed and performed 1845) is no great
advance on *The Flying Dutchman*. Some passages, such as the
celebrated march in Act II, are closer in feeling to *Rienzi* than
anything in the intervening work. The tromboning of the
pilgrims' chorus tune, against a persistent accompaniment figure,
at the end of the overture, is distinctly Meyerbeerian—though
glorified Meyerbeer. (The magnificent "Venusberg music" was,
of course, written for the Paris production of 1861.) Neither
action nor music has the striking unity of its predecessor. But
the musical language employed in *Tannhäuser* is more chromatic
than that of any previous work. *The Flying Dutchman*, despite
its harsh harmonic tang, has only passing touches of chromaticism.
Even *Tannhäuser* naturally remains predominantly diatonic.
But many of its pages show Wagner speaking naturally and

confidently in chromatic melody and a chromatic, Chopinesque harmony bristling with suspensions and appoggiaturas and passing-notes. It is true the "chromatic melody" generally slides cautiously in semitones (the 'cello melody at bar 17 of the overture, "O du mein holder Abendstern," etc.) instead of moving easily hither and thither over the surface of the chromatic chords (as in the melody of "O sink' hernieder Nacht der Liebe" in *Tristan*), but it was only natural that a composer who had so accustomed himself to chromatic idioms in 1845 should have arrived at the musical language of *Tristan* a dozen years later.[1]

However, chromaticism plays a much less important part in *Lohengrin* (completed 1848, produced 1850). Nothing in Wagner's music is more remarkable than his effortless adoption of what almost seems like an entirely fresh musical language, even a new style of scoring, in each new work—the outstanding examples, of course, are *Tristan* and *Die Meistersinger*. The pink and gold romantic chivalry of *Lohengrin* is perfectly matched by the diatonic music with its sweet, pellucid orchestral colouring; excessive chromaticism would have been out of place. On the other hand, diatonic as they are, things like the chorus in Act I, "Wie fasst uns selig süsses Grauen," with its numerous expressive suspensions and appoggiaturas, are thoroughly typical of Wagner's mature part-writing.

But if its harmony seems retrograde, *Lohengrin* is far in advance of its predecessors in every other respect. Dramatically it is much more "tight" than *Tannhäuser*; the action contains fewer incidents appealing to the mind rather than to the feelings, and therefore, according to Wagner's own theories, unsuitable for music. And the dramatic unity is deepened by the musical unity much more even than in *The Flying Dutchman*. The texture is now almost continuous; the traces of the old set-numbers are still perceptible enough but they amount to no more than, say, the coccyx which is all that is left of the human tail. There is still plenty of what appears to be, and essentially is, old-fashioned recitative, but Wagner was very anxious that it should not be treated as such. As he told Liszt (letter of

---

[1] Even in *Tristan* semitonal movement of parts is the rule rather than the exception. It remained for Schönberg to treat Wagnerian harmony and the melodic possibilities latent in it with anything like the ease and boldness of Brahms's handling of diatonic harmony and melody.

September 8th, 1850), he indicated the spoken stress of the words so clearly in his music that the singers have only to sing the notes with the right values in the tempo indicated. This applies also to the recitative in *Tannhäuser* (see also letters to Schindelmeisser, May 30th, 1852, and Hermann Levi, May 18th, 1876).

The homogeneity of the musical material has already been mentioned. Leitmotives are used far more lavishly and systematically than ever before, though they still remain dramatic labels; they have not yet become the generating themes of a symphonic web, for the "symphonic web" has not yet come into existence—the orchestra still "accompanies." Yet texture and orchestration are already hardly separable. And the scoring, with its triple wind and its separation of orchestral groups, not only reinforces the homogeneity of the whole opera but opens out wide new perspectives in the handling of the modern orchestra.

In short, *Lohengrin*, despite its undeniable squareness of rhythmic structure and its stodgy tempo (that characteristic sluggish German-romantic tempo) is a masterpiece. It is the apogee of German romantic opera and it is difficult to see how German romantic opera could have developed far beyond it. Actually it never did develop further.

II. WAGNER AND THE MUSIC-DRAMA

When Wagner put the finishing touches to the score of *Lohengrin* in March, 1848, he could hardly have realized that he had finished with "romantic opera," indeed with opera altogether, and that his future works for the stage would belong to an entirely new genre, sprung from romantic opera, it is true, just as that in turn had sprung from the earlier *Singspiel*, but differing far more fundamentally from the opera of the day than Weber's works had differed from the *Singspiel*. He even proceeded to plan more "romantic operas," wrote the libretto of *Siegfrieds Tod* (the basis of the later *Götterdämmerung*), and planned a *Friedrich Barbarossa* and a *Jesus of Nazareth*. Ernest Newman has asserted that "*Siegfried's Death* was impossible in the musical idiom of *Lohengrin*; and Wagner must have known this intuitively. This is no doubt the real reason for his writing no music for six years."[1] It may have been. But, as everyone knows, much happened to Wagner during those six years. From dissatisfaction with the Dresden Royal Opera his restless mind led him to dissatisfaction with the political condition of Saxony, of Germany and of the world. Political theorizing led to revolutionary practice, and that to exile and the impossibility of getting his operas produced in Germany. Wagner had always been an exceptionally self-conscious, introspective artist, and he had always had a weakness for theorizing in print. Now, largely with the purpose of clearing his own mind, he poured out a flood of prose works in which he exposed the nakedness of the existing forms of opera and stated the *rationale* of his proposed "art-work of the future": *Art and Revolution* (1849), *The Art-work of the Future* (1850), *Opera and Drama* (1850–51), *A Communication to my Friends* (1851), and various others of less importance.

The "art-work of the future" is now the art of seventy years ago. But although Wagner's theories did not bring into existence a new art-form, except in his own works, they have left a very considerable impression on the development of opera. Modern opera is, after all, generally closer to music-drama than to the old opera. Nowadays people who have obviously never read a word of his prose works talk glibly of his "reforms" and his "theories," and then airily dismiss them and proceed to judge his works by the æsthetic standards of common grand opera. Wagner may not be the great all-round "artist" he was commonly held to be thirty or forty years ago; his great "composite art-works" may have turned out to be almost as predominantly musical works as any ordinary opera; but no one is in a position to pass judgment on a Wagnerian music-drama who does not know what Wagner was really aiming at—and he is not likely to learn that from a few paragraphs of facile generalization in a text-book of "musical appreciation." The only way, a horrible one, is to plod wearily through the turgid pages of *Oper und Drama*, the Sinai tablets of Wagnerian music-drama.

Opera and Drama consists of three sections, the first two (which may be summarized briefly) critical and analytical, the third constructive and therefore demanding more careful consideration. Part One deals with "Opera and the Essence of

[1] *Wagner as Man and Artist.* John Lane, 2nd edition, 1925.

Music." The extremely unsatisfactory nature of opera as an art-form has long been generally acknowledged by serious artists (says Wagner) but, instead of seeking for the fundamental error responsible for this unsatisfactoriness, they have been content to blame the taste of the public and the weakness of the composers who have pandered to it. He, however, has discovered this fundamental error: "The fact that a means of expression (music) has been made the object; and that the object of expression (drama) has been made the means."[1] The supreme merit of a librettist is that he gives the composer good material to set to music, "provides a dramatic background for certain musical forms" in which the musician wishes to compose.

The musical foundation of opera is the aria, evolved from the folk-song type of melody through the desire of singers to show off, and Gluck's so-called operatic revolution "really consisted of nothing more than the revolt of the composer against the singer." After Gluck the composer's supremacy was more or less assured and the music itself was more expressive of drama, but the poet-dramatist's position was no better than before. Nor was it with Mozart. Mozart "embarked with the utmost indifference upon the composition of any text he was offered. All he did was to pour the fiery stream of his music into the operatic forms, developing their musical possibilities to the utmost." As for Méhul, Cherubini and Spontini, they—following in Gluck's footsteps—had certainly done their best to express dramatic feeling in their music, but their art had failed to hold its own against the purely melodic operas of Rossini and Weber. For, although Weber did bring the aria back to the sincerity and simplicity of folk-song, the Weberian opera remained melody-opera just as much as the Rossinian; the drama was still a mere pretext for the music.

"Up to now this melody has been merely song-melody." But in the meantime a new, more subtly expressive type of instrumental melody had been developed by Beethoven, yet a type not completely satisfactory in itself. "In the works of the second half of his artistic life," those in which the old, conventional formal moulds are broken by his profound emotion, "Beethoven is mostly unintelligible, or at any rate liable to be misunder-

---

[1] My quotations from *Opera and Drama* are taken, or adapted, from the translation by Edwin Evans, Senior. (William Reeves, N.D.)

stood, where he tries to convey some particular meaning with special clearness. He abandons the absolute-musical . . . in order to speak in a language which, not being attached to a purely musical context, is only held together by a poetical idea that cannot be clearly expressed in the music itself." And these "exterior traits and peculiarities of Beethoven's later manner" were imitated by composers who were not moved by anything like Beethoven's inner spirit, by Berlioz in his programme music and by Meyerbeer in his operas. Whereas in the opera of earlier times "the orchestra had never been anything but the harmonic and rhythmic support of the melody," it had now produced a peculiar kind of melody of its own and "was now itself to be trained to behave 'dramatically'." "By arbitrary combinations of this peculiar kind of mosaic melody, the composer was able whenever he so desired to appear strange and peculiar; and this he did with the aid of the orchestra." The new resources of the orchestral palette were used to produce more striking and "characteristic" effects. What Meyerbeer demanded of his poet-dramatist was "a huge, parti-coloured, historico-romantic, satanico-pious, dogmatico-lewd, sancto-nonsensical, mystico-daring, sentimentally roguish, stagy conglomeration of all sorts, in order to provide him with opportunities for inventing fearfully curious music." Everywhere in opera, then, in Gluck, in Mozart, in Rossini, in Weber, in Meyerbeer—and in Verdi, though Wagner does not mention him (presumably because he was as yet unacquainted with him)—music, which should be merely the means of expression, "has tried to dictate the object of the drama." The result has necessarily been profoundly unsatisfactory.

At the same time the new instrumental language is not completely intelligible by itself and "in his grandest work," the Choral Symphony, Beethoven "at last felt the necessity of throwing himself into the arms of the poet" in order to make the meaning of his melody absolutely clear and unmistakable. Not that he was "moved to spontaneous creation by any poet's thought"; "even his 'Joy' melody does not appear to have been invented in consequence of the poet's lines, but to have been composed only through the emotion caused by remembering the general content of Schiller's poem. Only where Beethoven tries to correspond to the poetic content by rising to dramatic directness of expression (as in the 'Seid umschlungen Millionen' and the combination of this theme with 'Freude, schöner Götterfunken''), do his melodic combinations show continual evidence of their evolution from the text; then the unparalleled variety of expression reached by his music becomes allied with the poem in its highest sense; and this to such a degree that henceforth the music is inconceivable apart from the poem. The organism of music is capable of bearing living melody only when fructified by the poet's thought. Music is the female, destined to bring forth—the poet being the real generator; and music reached the very peak of madness when it aspired not only to bear but also to beget.''

Accordingly Part Two is devoted to the art of the poet-dramatist, ''The Drama and the Essence of Dramatic Poetry.'' Before coming to his main theme, however, Wagner pauses to condemn the individual arts on the curious ground that they ''merely indicate. A real presentation would become possible to them only if they became possessed of the power of simultaneously addressing the whole range of man's artistic sensations, of communicating to his entire perceptive organism and not merely to his powers of imagination.''[1] So instead of individual arts he wants a ''unified art-work,'' one single Art, which shall *not*, however, consist, as his enemies seem to think, of lumping all the individual arts together, ''reading a romance by Goethe in a picture-gallery adorned with statues, during the performance of a Beethoven symphony.''

Now our modern drama, springing from two main sources, the romance and the Greek drama, is ''an appeal to understanding, not to feeling'' and ''the course to be taken by the drama of the future will be a return from understanding to feeling.'' The poet of the future will make sure that the intellectual element in his work is transformed into feeling. And, if he is to do that successfully, he must choose the right type of dramatic subject, ''which must be such that the action is com-

---

[1] Wagner was notoriously incapable of leaving anything to the imagination. The afterthought of introducing both Venus and Elisabeth's bier in the last scene of *Tannhäuser*, instead of symbolizing them by a glow on the Venusberg and by tolling bells, was characteristic. Wagner told Uhlig that he was afraid ''the former ending gave only a *hint* of what had actually to be communicated to the senses.''

pletely justified both in character and scope by the feeling that prompts it." Judged from this point of view, the ideal dramatic subject is the legend: concentrated, inexhaustible, eternally true, but more intense and elevated than anything in everyday life. As a matter of fact, Wagner had come to this conclusion at least six or seven years earlier, in his *Dutchman–Tannhäuser* days. He wrote to Karl Gaillard (January 30th, 1844) that "subject matter ought to be selected which is capable of musical treatment only. I would never take a subject which might be used just as well by an able playwright for spoken drama. . . . It is the province of the present-day dramatist to give expression and spiritual meaning to the material interests of our own time, but to the operatic poet and composer falls the task of conjuring up the holy spirit of poetry as it comes down to us in the sagas and legends of past ages. . . . Here is the way to raise opera to a higher level from the debasement into which it has fallen as the result of our expecting composers to take as their subjects commonplaces, intrigues, etc., things which modern comedy and drama without music are far more successful in presenting."[1]

But the poet can appeal only partially to the feeling through "an articulate language capable only of description and indication, unless he intensifies this language . . . and that can be accomplished only by the effusion of ordinary speech into the tone-language," which is "the inner man's most primitive medium of utterance." Indeed a quasi-melodic tone-language of vowels alone must have been "the first emotional language of mankind," and this "melody" "became rhythmical through being accompanied by suitable gestures" and appeared to be an inner expression of that which was outwardly indicated by gesture. This primitive tone-language was converted into the roots of word-language by the addition of consonants. By grouping together roots with a common consonant (*Stabreim*, alliteration) the primitive poet not only "presented to the ear a succession of similar sounds but bound together similar objects into a complete mental picture." But "the poetic impulse, originally an activity of the inner feelings, gradually became an affair of the understanding" and this link between tone-language and word-language was broken. Our modern word-language

---

[1] M. M. Bozman's translation (from *Letters of Richard Wagner, selected and edited by Wilhelm Altmann*. Two vols., Dent, 1927).

"enables us to communicate our feelings, but only to the understanding," so "feeling sought refuge from an absolute speech of this intellectual kind and sought it in that absolute tone-language which constitutes our music of the present day."

The problem, therefore, is to bring word-language and tone-language together again. "Poetic creation" addressed direct to the feeling "is impossible in modern speech." But if the poet "waits for the situation where he wants melody (as the most complete expression of exalted feeling) to step in and transform the nakedness of articulate speech into the fullness of the tone-language, he will involve both understanding and feeling in complete confusion"; in fact, he will have produced something like *"modern opera."* The artist must from the beginning create in a medium compounded equally of word-language and tone-language.

The nature of this compound is the subject of Part Three, "Poetry and Music in the Drama of the Future." "Hitherto the poet has endeavoured in two different ways to give emotional expression to articulate speech: by metre (rhythm) and by terminal rhyme (melody)." Neither of these is really satisfactory. Iambic verse puts words into fetters, and in the theatre is spoken either as prose or as a nonsensical sing-song; terminal rhyme certainly holds the attention of the ear but is essentially an intellectual device depending on the alternate raising and fulfilment of expectation.

A reunion of verse as we know it and melody as we know it (that is, as people conceived them in 1851) is impossible. One of two things must happen. Either "the rhythmic line of verse, after being broken up by melody into its separate portions, is controlled by it in a new way, according to melody's own absolute measurements," in which case the terminal rhyme tends to be "sunk without a trace." Or "if melody subordinates itself to verse, or contents itself with merely contributing fullness of musical tone to its rhythms and rhymes, it not only shows up the untruth and unloveliness of the verse-shapes, but deprives itself of its own sensuous beauty." "The bond of union between melody and verse has still continued to be the accent of ordinary speech" and Gluck's "concern was to give a melodically strengthened, but true, rendering of the natural expression of speech." But to do that, he was obliged to break up the verse into prose. And his melody with it; "for nothing but musical prose can remain of any melody, the purpose of which is to strengthen the rhetorical accent of verse already rendered in the same way."

What is needed for the art-work of the future is a new kind of verse. Just as it is necessary to suppress "everything accidental or unimportant in the action" (both in the situations and in the motives behind them), so everything "that distorts what is necessary to feeling" must be cut out of speech, leaving "nothing but the kernel, the purely emotional element." The poet will have to go back to "the sensuous substance of the roots of speech," to that primitive quasi-melodic tone-language of vowels and to those primitive groupings of emotionally related roots produced by a common consonant, by alliteration. The rhythm will be determined by the symmetrical return of accents, the natural spoken accents. And the musician will take this highly compressed emotional language and "broaden out this compression to its highest degree of fullness," intensifying the emotion to the uttermost.

And not by melody alone. The emotional relationship partly expressed by alliteration can be intensified or subtilized by key and modulation. "If we take for example a line containing initial rhymes of similar emotional character, such as 'Liebe giebt Lust zum Leben' ('Life's delight is love'), the musician will feel no incentive to modulate. . . . If however we take a line containing mixed feelings—such as 'Die Liebe bringt Lust und Leid' ('Love's passion of pleasure and pain')—the musician will feel obliged to modulate from the original key, suitable to the first feeling, to another key suited to the second. The word 'Lust' will have to receive an accentuation quite different from that given to it in the line, 'Liebe giebt Lust zum Leben,' for the note here sung to the word 'Lust' will involuntarily become a sort of 'leading note' pressing forward into the key in which 'Leid' is to be expressed. Thus 'Lust und Leid' will be the statement of a special sensation; special, that is, in its representation of two contradictory sensations conditioning and belonging to each other—a statement possible only in music, thanks to its faculty of modulation. We will now see how modulation, together with the content of the verse, is able to lead back to the first feeling. We will take the line 'Die Liebe bringt Lust und

Leid' and follow it by a second: 'Doch in ihr Weh auch webt sie Wonnen.'[1] In this case the note for 'webt' would beoome one leading back into the first key; for at this point the second feeling returns to the first, now enriched.''

The musician's power lies in his ability, through key-relationship, to convey in a single emotional impression a variety of "feelings originally one in character." "The easiest way to realize how great this power is, is to imagine the sense of both the above lines more definitely stated, so that, between the leaving of the first feeling and the return in the second line, a whole succession of intervening lines express a mixture of intermediate feelings—some strengthening, some reconciling; and all this continuing until the final return of the principal feeling. In order to realize the poetic intention, modulation would here have to pass through the most varied keys and back again. All these keys, however, will be closely related to the original key. Being the basis of the principal feeling, the main key will show its fundamental relationship to all the others. . . . If we consider all this as a musical-poetic *period* we may, taking the 'period' as determined musically by a principal key, put it that that artwork is the most perfect in which many such periods are presented so as to follow one another naturally in the realization of one grand poetic purpose. This purpose is the finished drama.''

So far we have considered the musical element in the artwork principally as melody. But melody is only the surface of harmony and it is only "the compound sound, simultaneous harmony and melody, that completely brings home to one the emotional content of the melody." The harmony should not exist for its own sake, should not need to be "understood." "The attention of the feeling must not be drawn to the effectiveness of harmony merely *as* harmony." Nor must the harmony be that of the conventional operatic ensemble. There must be no "participators in the action who serve merely to supply a harmonic background to another character's melody, except in a few rare cases where they are necessary to complete comprehension. Even the chorus as hitherto employed in opera will have to disappear, for the chorus is vitally effective in the drama

---

[1] Edwin Evans, Senior, suggests:

> "True love doth lighten loss;
> For 'tis from woe she weaves her wonders."

only when the mass-like character of its utterance has been got rid of. A mass can never interest; it merely startles us." But the musician does possess an "immeasurably capable medium through which the harmony can be made evident." This is the modern orchestra, which must be allowed "a more integral participation in the drama than thitherto."

Even from a musical point of view the orchestra's part must be completely self-sufficient; owing to the difference between vocal timbre and instrumental timbre, orchestral harmonies that need the voice-part to complete them are unsatisfactory. One of the fundamental errors of opera was the treatment of the voice merely as another kind of instrument; not, of course, in the sense of being written for "instrumentally," but as a vehicle of "absolute" (i.e., essentially instrumental) melody. Indeed, many people do not really appreciate opera melodies till they hear them played by instruments alone—for instance, by military bands— "free from the vowels and consonants which to this kind of melody are only an obstruction calculated to hinder them from grasping it." (Nowhere does Wagner show less understanding than here of the exquisite technique of the Italian composers and librettists, who knew quite as well as he how to make vowels and consonants a part of the music.) In the art-work of the future, however, the voice-part will be quite different. It will as far as possible state the emotional content of the verse by resolving the vowel-sounds into musical tone, and it will also appeal to the intellect as articulate speech. In short, it will be "the connecting link between articulate speech and tone-speech." This voice-part or verse-melody will be borne on the surface of the orchestral harmony as a boat is borne on the surface of water. But it will be a *sung* part, not a declaimed part. (The singers who "bark" Wagner merely caricature him.)

As we have already seen, modern instrumental music "undeniably possesses a capacity for speech." Not precise speech; but we shall not now want it to be precise in itself; the voice-part will give precision to the message. The special virtue of instrumental music is just that it can express all that is inexpressible in articulate speech. In this respect it is akin to gesture, and in the art-work of the future, gesture, hitherto limited to ballet-pantomime, must be immensely subtilized and developed —always in harmony with the orchestra through the common link of rhythm.[1] Instrumental music can also, through the power of association, recall past emotions and hence (as these vague emotions have been defined by the voice-part earlier in the drama) more precise thought-impressions. This, in fact, was the original function of the leitmotive. Similarly, by its power of expressing indeterminate emotion, it can awaken in us emotional premonitions and prepare us for what is to come.

So much for the separate elements of the art-work. It only remains to see how they are to be united in a single form corresponding to the single content of the drama. "The central point of dramatic expression is the actor's articulate verse-melody, towards which absolute orchestral melody is drawn as a *premonitory* preparation and away from which the 'thought' of the orchestral motive leads as a *remembrance*. . . . That which we see in the movements of the exponent of the verse-melody is—dramatic gesture; that which makes this clear to the ear being the orchestra, the original function of which is to be the harmonic support of the verse-melody. In the complete expression of all that the actor communicates to eye and ear, the orchestra plays a sustained part, supporting and explanatory; the unifying bond of expression therefore proceeds from the orchestra."

The orchestra must begin by "exciting our feeling from a general state of tension to a special sensation of premonition." And this will have to be done by something very different from the contemporary operatic overtures "which, assuming that they contained anything to understand at all, would have to be played after the drama, instead of before, to become intelligible"; the "premonitory" sensation cannot be spread over the whole course of the opera (as Wagner himself had tried to do in the *Dutchman* and *Tannhäuser* overtures). And when the curtain goes up, we must not be let down again to the emotional level of everyday life; language, action, gesture must all be emotionally "larger than life." "Wherever the word-tone-speech of the characters happens to sink, for the purpose of defining a dramatic situation, more or less to the level of an intellectual medium of expression as in everyday life," the orchestra must keep up the emotional temperature "by means of its powers of musical statement in remembrance and premonition."

[1] Here, in one sentence, Wagner expresses the essence of *modern* ballet.

The drama will consist of a chain of emotional situations or musical-poetic periods, "organized members mutually completing and supporting each other like the organic members of the human body." And these members will be natural forms arising from the emotional content, very different from the detached, artificial forms of the old opera into which the content has to be arbitrarily forced. Similarly, the situations in which the orchestra will be called upon to sustain the emotional temperature "must never be determined by the arbitrary will of the musician, as a sort of ingenious sound-concoction, but only by the poetic intention. The decoration by mere absolute music of situations of abatement and preparation, as in conventional opera *ritornelli* and the like, destroys all pretence at unity of expression." But now, "by means of the orchestra these melodic situations will become so many signposts for our feeling throughout the whole of the drama's complex construction," though "they will fall into the background again the moment the actor advances to complete expression in the verse-melody."

"These melodic situations (in which premonition is remembered while remembrance is converted into premonition) necessarily spring only from the main dramatic motives." As the drama itself is to be highly compressed and reduced to essentials, the musician in faithfully carrying out the poet's design will find that his music, too, is bound together in a unified form. Hitherto there has been no attempt to give a unified form to the music of a whole opera; only the separate arias and so on have had form, and purely musical form at that. Again in the field of absolute symphonic music, form has been an affair of more or less arbitrary pattern; for the return of themes has not always been fully justified by feeling; but in the art-work this return will be justified by the poetic intention. In fact, the return of the principal motives of the dramatic action, "so naturally conditioned by relationships as to give it the character of rhyme," will bind the whole drama together into a unified artistic form. "The unifying cohesion of themes hitherto attempted by the musician only in the overture must be applied to the drama itself."

Wagner concludes with a number of general observations: that poet and musician are not to restrict one another but to inspire each other; that there is no *a priori* reason why poet and musician should be one and the same person; that as the German language "still displays an immediate and recognizable connection with its own roots," it is more suitable for the art-work of the future than French or Italian; that translated opera is idiotic and disastrous; that the actor-singers in the new art-work will have to sing in accordance with the sense of the words and not merely in accordance with the sense of the melodic line; that they will also have to use gesture intelligently; and that, after all, this art-work will be wasted on the contemporary opera public which merely wants to be amused: there will have to be an entirely new public. And that last condition was the one point in *Oper und Drama* that Wagner never succeeded in realizing. As the result of the most extraordinary exertions in the entire history of art, he brought into existence his great unified art-work, found the artists to perform it, and built the theatre for it to be performed in. But he never created that new public. The *Wagnervereine* of the last century did very nearly bring it into existence, but their efforts are now expended, little is left, and Wagner's vast synthetic art-pearls are now usually cast before very much the same public as that which hissed *Tannhäuser* in Paris in 1861.

Opera and Drama is first and foremost an *apologia* for the *Ring* and it is only in the *Ring*[1] that he keeps faithfully to the principles enunciated here. It will have been noticed that he attached enormous importance to alliteration, which he was then using in the poem of the *Ring*. But alliteration plays a much less important part in the poem of *Tristan* (comp. and orch. 1857–59; perf. 1865) and considerable use is made of the despised terminal rhyme; Wagner was no rigid *doctrinaire*. And *Die Meistersinger* (comp. and orch. 1862–67; perf. 1868) is written wholly in rhymed verse. *Parsifal* (comp. and orch. 1877–82; perf. 1882) also has rhymed stanzas alternating with free verse.

One has only to glance at the score of *Das Rheingold*, the first work in which Wagner put the theories of *Oper und Drama* into practice, to see how radically the new art-work, music-

---

[1] The chronology of *Der Ring des Nibelungen* is as follows:
Poem: begun 1848, completed 1852.
Das Rheingold: comp. and orch. 1853–54; performed separately 1869.
Die Walküre: comp. and orch. 1854–56; performed separately 1870.
Siegfried: comp. and orch. 1856–57 and 1865–71.
Götterdämmerung: comp. and orch. 1869–74.
Complete *Ring*: performed 1876.

drama, differed from the most advanced form of contemporary opera, represented by *Lohengrin*. The last traces of discrete melody and set-number have disappeared; only vestiges of recitative remain. The whole musical texture is fluid and continuous. Even the leitmotives, as Newman has pointed out, are no longer vocal in origin, and consequently no longer extended melodies as in his earlier works but concentrated instrumental themes of the nature of symphonic germ-ideas, and so capable of being developed more or less symphonically. Actually *Das Rheingold* is the most orthodox of all Wagner's attempts to keep to his own rules; ultimately, indeed before very long, the musician in him began to disturb the balance insisted on in *Oper und Drama* and find a surprising number of cases where the rules were better overridden. "It would be impossible to make the tissue of the *Rhinegold* intelligible without the voices," says Newman,[1] "but the orchestral part of the *Götterdämmerung* would flow on with hardly a break if the vocal part were omitted; so also would large sections of *Tristan* and the *Meistersinger*. It was inevitable that under these circumstances the vocal writing should occasionally become a little perfunctory." He goes on to point out that even in *Tristan*, where the balance between voices and orchestra is generally considered to be most perfect, there are many passages where the vocal line seems to have been added almost as an irrelevant afterthought to the symphonic tissue or where it simply doubles the orchestral melody. And in *Parsifal* the vocal writing is generally quite perfunctory.

On the other hand, even before *Tristan*, the old type of "absolute" melody suppressed throughout *Das Rheingold* had begun to reappear in the voice-parts: notably in Siegmund's "Winterstürme" in *Die Walküre*. As for *Die Meistersinger*, of course, it is full not only of "absolute melody" but of the ensembles and choruses forbidden in *Oper und Drama*. "Am stillen Herd" and the Prize Song may be passed over as justified by the dramatic situation but, from the point of view of 1851, the exquisite quintet is inexcusable. Nevertheless, *Die Meistersinger* is based on the fundamental principles of *Oper und Drama*; it was only that as Wagner ripened artistically, he detected and weeded out the inessential from his theories.

His supreme justification is that he did achieve genuine drama

[1] *Wagner as Man and Artist.*

played out by genuine living characters, characters as real to our minds as those of Shakespeare. He did get rid of the libretto that was *merely* a pretext for music, of the characters who were first and foremost musical instruments. In earlier opera, including Wagner's own works, it was not uncommon to find one genuinely alive character, perhaps two: Beethoven's Leonora, Rossini's Figaro, Verdi's Lady Macbeth and Luisa Miller and Violetta, Glinka's Ivan Susanin, Wagner's own Rienzi, Senta and the Dutchman, Tannhäuser. (But hardly one in the whole of Meyerbeer, not even Valentine in *Les Huguenots* or Vasco da Gama in *L'Africaine*.) The rest were all lay-figures. A whole group of living, even if rather theatrical characters, such as Verdi gives us in the protagonists of *Rigoletto*, is altogether exceptional. But with the later Wagner, practically all the characters, even the minor ones, are living, thinking beings conceived in the round, beings whom we can *know*. They may be bores, like Wotan and King Mark, or fools, like Parsifal, but they *exist*. And each group exists in its own musical world, the chromatic world of *Tristan*, the diatonic world of *Die Meistersinger*, the great all-containing world of the *Ring*, and can no more be imagined outside it than Hamlet can be thought of as strolling into *The Merry Wives of Windsor*.

I say "musical world" advisedly, for ultimately Wagner's characters, solidly conceived as they are, are kept alive mainly by their music. Without music they are solid, but dull and dead; their music is the breath of their life. The concentrated power of characterization in their leitmotives stamps them for ever on our minds, as Dickens's characters are stamped by some mannerism or trick of speech; their whole musical utterance widens and deepens our knowledge of their characters till we know them as we know a character in Henry James. (The part of Hagen in *Götterdämmerung* will particularly repay study from this point of view.) Sometimes the leitmotives themselves change and grow with the character, as Siegfried's gay horn-theme in *Siegfried* becomes the more staid and manly motive of *Götterdämmerung*. In one instance, particularly memorable, a character is fully developed before she is summarized once and for all in a single leitmotive. But perhaps that is because the earlier Brünnhilde has been a goddess, or a woman not yet accustomed to mere womanhood. The wonderful clarinet-theme in *Götter-*

dämmerung, which seems to concentrate into two bars the whole
of feminine grace and tenderness and strength, announces a new
Brünnhilde; new, yet obviously the same Brünnhilde who had
announced to Siegmund the coming of death in *Die Walküre.*

Even from the purely dramatic point of view, then, the mature
Wagner's leitmotives are something more than mere labels.
And musically they may be regarded as the "subjects" of some
of the most remarkable symphonic music ever written.

III. WAGNER THE MUSICIAN

It has long been realized by the world in general that, whatever Wagner himself may have thought, however sincerely he
may have theorized, the music in the Wagnerian music-drama
is the one element that matters supremely. Those who still
consider that he possessed the greatest creative musical mind
since Beethoven and those who consider him merely the *cleverest*
composer of the nineteenth century (and no one not a fool can
deny that he was that) agree on this point. Ernest Newman has
put it clearly in *Wagner as Man and Artist*: "So far from the
poet in him shaping and controlling the musician, it was the
musician who led the poet where he would have him go; so
far from drama being with him the end and the music the
means, it was music that was more than ever the end, to which
the drama served only as means;[1] and so far from Wagner being
first and last a dramatist, the whole significance of his work lay
precisely in the fact that he was a great symphonist. . . . It was
not for nothing that Wagner always claimed descent from
Beethoven rather than from even the greatest of opera writers,
such as Gluck and Mozart and Weber. . . . He himself always
proudly pointed to *Tristan* as the supremely successful realization of all his theories as to the expressive capacity and the
formal possibilities of music. Very well; *Tristan* is of all his
works the most symphonic, the one that least needs the apparatus
of the stage, the one in which the actors could most easily be dispensed with for long stretches of time with the minimum of loss."

[1] But there is still a vast difference between the hegemony of music
in Wagner and the hegemony of music in his predecessors. The drama
may still be secondary in importance to the music but it is a complete
justification of it, not a mere occasion for it.

When we come to examine in some detail the thematic construction and formal architecture of the scores of *The Ring* and *Tristan* and *Die Meistersinger* and *Parsifal*, we shall see that Newman is perfectly right, that when we speak of Wagner as a symphonist we are not merely expressing an æsthetic preference but stating, probably without realizing it, a matter of fact. But first of all we must examine the material of which these "symphonies" are woven, the actual texture of the mature Wagner's music: melodic, harmonic and orchestral. We involuntarily divide it into those three elements, but as Wagner himself pointed out, he thought so completely in terms of orchestral texture that it is almost unjust to speak of his harmony and his scoring as separate elements; and his melody stands in the same unusually close relation to his harmony. His texture is really one-and-indivisible. But it is analysable.

The most cursory comparison of the scores of *Lohengrin* and *Das Rheingold* shows that Wagner's style underwent a considerable, if not a radical, change during those five or six years. In his earlier operas a style originally derived from Beethoven and Weber (above all from *Fidelio* and *Euryanthe*), Marschner, Spontini and Bellini, with harmonic hints probably from Chopin and Spohr, and orchestral ones (with a few melodic ones as well) from Berlioz, had been gradually forged by the force of his genius into the perfectly original medium of expression employed in *Lohengrin*. But *Das Rheingold* takes us into a new musical world and the difference is not to be accounted for merely by a theory of unconscious inward ripening. For one thing the texture was naturally conditioned by the ideas outlined in *Oper und Drama*. And it is fairly obvious that Wagner had come under some new musical influences, of which the most important was probably that of Beethoven's C sharp minor Quartet, which he had just heard in Paris (in 1853) and which had made a profound impression on him and must have opened to him new vistas in instrumental music. After that there was bound to be much less *Lohengrin*-ish squareness of rhythm and structure.

At about the same time Wagner also began to come under the influence, especially the harmonic influence, of Liszt; though Liszt's influence is more perceptible in *Die Walküre* than in *Rheingold*. Wagner was always a little coy about admitting this indebtedness to his future father-in-law. "There are

many matters which we are quite frank about among ourselves,"
he wrote to von Bülow (October 7th, 1859), "(for instance, that
since my acquaintance with Liszt's compositions my treatment
of harmony has become very different from what it was formerly), but it is indiscreet, to say the least, of friend Pohl to
babble this secret to the whole world in the prominent first lines
of his short article on the prelude to *Tristan*."[1]

Still, we must guard against exaggerating this influence,
considerable as it undoubtedly was. Chantavoine, for instance,
suggests[2] that "the agitation that troubles Sieglinde's sleep in
the second act of *Die Walküre* (the four bars preceding Sieglinde's
'Kehrte der Vater nun heim') is an echo of that which tor-
ments Doctor Faust" in the opening bars of Liszt's Symphony.
As a matter of fact these two works were actually being sketched
at precisely the same time, *Faust* at Weimar (August-October,
1854) and the second and third acts of *Die Walküre* at Zürich
(September-December, 1854). Wagner therefore could hardly
have borrowed from Liszt. All that happened in this case was
that two composers writing in the advanced idiom of their day
happened to hit on similar melodic progressions. Seeing that
Liszt produced *Tannhäuser* at Weimar in February, 1849, and
received the score of *Lohengrin* later in the same year, it is
possible that the influence was reciprocal; both men possessed
an unusual aptitude for assimilation.

Even in *Die Walküre* and the earlier part of *Siegfried* Wagner's
harmony had reached a remarkable degree of complication and,
relatively to most of the music of that day, of dissonance. All
the traits we have already noticed—free use of chromatic chords,
with suspensions, appoggiaturas and accented passing notes
employed more and more frequently in several parts simultaneously[3]—combined to present the composer now thoroughly
accustomed to thinking in terms of them with a musical speech

[1] M. M. Bozman's translation. The nature of Wagner's indebtedness
to Liszt in *Tristan* may be seen from Liszt's song, "Ich möchte hingehn,"
written in the eighteen-forties (the bar for piano alone after the words
"stille wie der Stern versinken"); the "yearning" appoggiatura effect
is absolutely Tristanesque.

[2] *Liszt.* By Jean Chantavoine. 4th edition. Paris, 1920.

[3] Though even Mozart had used chromatic appoggiaturas simultaneously in all parts in the G minor Symphony (1788). See the first
movement, bars 50 and 52 of the development, for the extraordinary
transitory "chords" so produced.

of unprecedented richness, subtlety and expressiveness. Tonality
is often temporarily obliterated, as in the famous chromatic
progression at Wotan's "In festen Schlaf" in the third act of
Die Walküre. And Wagner's ear could now accept a degree of
dissonance considerably more advanced than could most other
musicians of his day. The dominant seventh is commonly used
in *Die Walküre* as a chord consonant enough not to need resolution at all. Eliminating the inessential in a way that has been
taken again and again throughout the history of harmonic
progress, mainly because he does not want to interrupt the continuous texture of his music by commonplace full closes, Wagner
brings us to the dominant seventh, takes it that either we can
imagine the resolution or do not need the resolution, and plunges
into the next sentence.

The same thing is noticeable in bars 3, 7, 11 and 13 of the
Tristan prelude. Like much else in *Tristan*, these unresolved
dominant sevenths are at once firmly rooted in the present and
pointers to that future which is *our* present. From a purely
technical point of view, they are treated as consonances, self-
sufficient; indeed chords of the seventh and ninth are used as
"normal" chords throughout *Tristan*; but emotionally they were
still dissonant enough, and in this context are still so to-day,
for the absence of resolution to fill us with that sense of yearning
for fulfilment which is the emotional keynote of the whole of
Tristan. Wagner had by this time progressed so far in this
chromatic tone-language of his and Liszt's that to express very
great and sustained emotional tension, he was obliged to intensify
(or did instinctively intensify) the relative dissonance of that
language to a degree seldom reached again in music during the
next half-century. Simultaneous appoggiaturas and suspensions
are so multiplied, so overlap, and are so complicated by the
flattening or sharpening ("chromatic alteration") of notes in
normal chords—not only in triads, as earlier composers had done,
but in higher-powered chords[1]—that the ears of the musicians

[1] Essentially the complete substitution of a semitone appoggiatura
for the real note—another instance of the omission of resolution. The
true note often, though not invariably, appears in the *next* chord. In
other cases the alteration is equivalent to the introduction of a chromatic
passing-note unpreceded by the true note. Heinrich Rietsch (*Die
Tonkunst in der zweiten Hälfte des* 19ten *Jahrhunderts*: Leipzig, 2nd
edition, 1906) suggests that chromatic alteration is analogous with the
mediæval *musica ficta.*

of seventy years ago were exquisitely tortured by the lack, during seemingly interminable stretches, of anything they could recognize as consonant. *Tristan's* role in the development of modern music has consisted partly in accustoming musicians' ears to this degree of dissonance as normal, beautiful and consonant, and thus preparing them for still higher degrees of dissonance.[1]

It has also prepared them for the twentieth-century's partial break with tonality. It is perfectly true that the chromaticism of *Tristan* is from first to last underlaid by a more or less solid tonal basis; there is nothing in it as nearly atonal as the Prelude to Act III of *Parsifal*. But it is equally true that *Tristan* did much to weaken the key-sense, the hitherto instinctive need for clear tonality felt by musicians in general. (Not only by the innumerable "altered" chords but by the absence over long stretches of a single tonic triad.) Wagner's apologists and slightly "superior" modern theorists have, between them, managed to convey an exaggerated impression of the comparative orthodoxy of Wagner's harmony and tonality. It has even been said that to analyse any chord in *Tristan* is "as easy as peeling a banana." But it is worth noting that two of our finest modern English theorists have held different views as to the right way of peeling the very first banana in the work:

According to Sir Donald Tovey[2] the remarkable wood-wind

chord at bar 2 of the Prelude is really $\begin{matrix} A \\ D \\ B \\ F \end{matrix}$ sharp; that is, a so-

called "French sixth"; the G sharp is an "appoggiatura prolonged till it seems to make a strange foreign chord before it

---

[1] Ironically enough, Wagner professed dislike for "harmonic harshness." He wrote to Bülow during the *Walküre* period (October 26th, 1854): "I know there are subjects that cannot be expressed except by harmonies that are bound to grate on the ear of the musical Philistine. When, however, I have noticed such in my own works I have always been led by a definite impulse to disguise the harmonic harshness as much as possible and finally to manage so that (to my mind) they were no longer perceptible." Which of course shows how far his idea of "harshness" differed from that of his contemporaries.

[2] Article "Harmony" in the *Encyclopædia Britannica*.

resolves on the short note," the A. But according to Sir George

Dyson,[1] this "strange foreign chord" $\begin{matrix} \text{G sharp} \\ \text{D sharp} \\ \text{B} \\ \text{F} \end{matrix}$ is the true chord,

"in its implication a variation of the diminished seventh, the D
sharp being a chromatic appoggiatura on D natural . . . and
Wagner so resolves it on to the dominant (E) of the key of A
minor," the A of the oboe being merely a passing-note. Common
sense and Wagner's scoring support this view, but Tovey's is
that generally accepted by German theorists, e.g., by Louis and
Thuille (*Harmonielehre*: Stuttgart, N.D.), Schreyer (*Harmonielehre*, Dresden, 1905), and Arnold Schering (*Jahrbuch Peters*,
1936); the "G sharp appoggiatura" theory was started as long
ago as 1881 by Karl Mayrberger (article in the *Bayreuther
Blätter* for that year). Schönberg (*Harmonielehre*, third edition,
Vienna, 1922) declares that each view is equally feasible. Incidentally, Ernst Kurth in his standard work on Tristanesque
harmony[2] takes yet another view, holding that here the F
natural is the "altered" note, not the D sharp; that is, that the

essential harmony is $\begin{matrix} \text{A} \\ \text{D sharp.} \\ \text{B} \\ \text{F sharp} \end{matrix}$ Yet he undermines his own

argument by pointing out that the F, B, D sharp, G sharp chord,
Tovey's "strange foreign chord," is a sort of *Leitharmonie*
throughout *Tristan* (in various enharmonic forms), that this is
the chord which marks the climax of the *Tristan* prelude—and
that Wagner had always shown a marked liking for it (it occurs
even in *Tannhäuser*).[3] As for the chords at bars 11 and 12 of
the *Tristan* Prelude there are nearly as many different conceptions of them as there are theorists who have written about
them. So much for easy "banana peeling." This sort of contro-
versy is hardly more profitable than attempts to solve the
celebrated "hen and egg" problem.

[1] Article "Harmony" in *Grove's Dictionary*.
[2] *Romantische Harmonik und ihre Krise in Richard Wagners
"Tristan"* (Bern, 1920).
[3] Both original and later versions of the Venusberg music: "Wo in
den Armen Glühender Liebe."

It is more sensible to look at the full score and consider this extraordinarily pregnant phrase in its horizontal aspect and its instrumental colouring; to note how on the dying fall of the 'cello melody Wagner drops this "strange foreign chord," the most poignant discord he could devise, and how he resolves it: each part, except the first bassoon, creeping semitonally to its place in the dominant seventh which, as we have seen, is all the resolution Wagner gives it; to observe how beautifully the second oboe and the two clarinets are used to stress the "strange foreign chord" and how they fade out before the alleged resolution of the G sharp. It is in this indivisibility of horizontal line-drawing, harmonic feeling, and instrumental thinking—all equally important and combined in a single thought—that lies much of the wonder of Wagner's mature mastery, as marvellous in the diatonic idiom of *Die Meistersinger*, most remarkable of all examples of Wagner's chameleonlike ability to adapt his manner to his matter, as in the chromaticism of *Tristan*.

Wagner's melody as a thing in itself is generally "continuous." He himself used the expression *"unendliche Melodie"* to indicate that there were no more recitatives in his works, that the apparently declamatory parts were essentially melodic (cf. his letters to Liszt, Schindelmeisser and Levi referred to on page 97). But I use it here in Hadow's sense, as opposed to discrete melody. Wagner's melody at its best is a superb development of the continuous melody of Beethoven, generally held together by a hint of sequence; the lapses into discrete tune on the one hand (as in the opening of Siegmund's "Winterstürme") or into quasi-recitative, vocal or instrumental, on the other, mark temporary fallings off in inspiration. The sense of melodic continuity is heightened, the concealment of any traces of underlying strophic construction achieved by that baulking of cadences already referred to. The last note of one phrase becomes the first of the next; the voice ends the phrase but the orchestra immediately starts another; or, more often, as mentioned above, the expected "last" note and chord are omitted altogether. As one would expect, the melody becomes more *purely* melodious (i.e., melodious in what Wagner considered the "instrumental" sense) in the highly emotional passages and nearest to recitative when the emotional temperature falls in mere narrative passages.

Too frequent concert performance of the celebrated purple patches in Wagner's works has drawn far too much attention to the virtuosity of his scoring. To understand his real attitude to the orchestra it is far more profitable to open one of his scores at random and study the subtlety of his handling of perhaps a single instrumental group, the extraordinary expressiveness he often obtains by the layout of the chord alone, his unerring rightness of instinct in adding a touch of "doubling" to a phrase, than to concentrate on such glamorous high-lights as the ride of the Valkyries, the fire-music, the forest murmurs and the *Götterdämmerung* funeral march. The triple wind, the often elaborately divided strings, the tubas introduced to strengthen the orchestral bass, the free use of chromatic brass, often employed melodically, all these features which collectively made the Wagnerian orchestra "gigantic" were introduced to increase not the volume of noise but the colour-palette, and hence the expressiveness of the orchestral mass. If his scoring once sounded unduly noisy—our modern ears are accustomed to much more deafening outbursts—it was because music calculated for a sunken orchestral pit was being played in ordinary opera houses and concert halls. The loudest *fortissimo* at Bayreuth did not drown the voice.

Wagner's mature orchestration *per se* can be studied most easily in *Die Meistersinger*, thanks to the comparative—but only comparative—simplicity of the harmonic-contrapuntal texture. One of the most curious of the facts that emerge from study of the score is the almost incessant employment of the horns. In the whole of the overture, for instance, the horns are silent for only nineteen bars; indeed not only in *Die Meistersinger* but in all Wagner's mature works, the foundation-colour is not string-tone but strings-plus-horns. (Even Brahms seems to have been slightly influenced by his practice in this respect.) Consider bars 59–63 of the overture, a little passage that illustrates this use of string-and-horn foundation-tone and also Wagner's general treatment of orchestral polyphony at an average moment.[1] Here we have a piece of four-part writing in which

---

[1] In his edition of Berlioz's *Traité de l'instrumentation* (Leipzig, 1905) Strauss points out that Wagner's position as "the perfecter of the modern orchestra, in distinction from Berlioz its creator" rests on three main points: "First, the employment of the richest polyphony. Second,

two of the parts are of equal melodic importance and must be well differentiated, yet at the same time bound well together in a homogeneous harmonic mass. The first and second violins unison are amply sufficient to bring out the highest part, while violas and 'cellos playing in a very sonorous register and backed up by two horns sing the tenor melody with great power. Bassoons, bass trombone and string basses supply a firm foundation, while the remaining part, though of secondary importance, is by no means "undernourished" in the hands of four wood-wind and two horns and is in such danger of standing-out unduly when the brighter trumpets take it over at bar 62 that the latter are marked down to *forte*, though all the other instruments are playing *fortissimo*. Note, too, how the tenor trombones, also marked down to *forte*, are discreetly used to emphasize the purely harmonic points of the passage. A more perfect balance of orchestral harmony and counterpoint could hardly be devised.

But by far the most interesting field of modern Wagnerian criticism is not texture, which has now been fully explored by critics, but structure, which has until recently been badly neglected. When Wagner's music was spoken of as "symphonic" by those who thought more highly of it than of the "collective art-work," the word was generally used to imply no more than that the orchestral web was beautiful, self-contained music equal in value and dignity to the music of the great symphonists. It was recognized that the leitmotives were endlessly modified and developed in much the same way that symphonic themes are worked out, but it was generally supposed, even by those who had got beyond the infantile pastime of detecting and labelling new leitmotives, that their recurrence was dictated by the poetic-dramatic action. But thematic recurrence is one of the most important elements in musical form[1] and it thus seemed true to say that in a precise as well as in a general sense the formal structure of the music was controlled by the drama, and the general principles of *Oper und Drama*

---

the introduction of the valve-horn which did more than anything else to make this polyphony possible. Third, the demanding from all instruments of the orchestra a technical virtuosity such as had hitherto been required only of solo-players."

[1] The others being key-recurrence and, a long way after, recurrence of striking rhythms, orchestral colour-schemes, and dynamics.

seemed to confirm that view. But as long ago as 1883 Edmund von Hagen[1] drew attention to the formal symmetry of the first act of *Die Meistersinger* and Guido Adler, lecturing at Vienna University in 1904,[2] pointed out that "Wagner was not opposed to formal architecture, either in the building up of a whole scene or in the parts of one and the same scene. . . . Many of these parts are more or less close to real, definite forms. . . . In *Tristan* one finds a series of passages, musically symmetrical and which contribute more than a little to the holding together of the entire structure of the music-drama." But it was left to Alfred Lorenz to demonstrate in his masterly *Das Geheimnis der Form bei Richard Wagner*[3] how completely the basic principles of musical form underlie the vast musical-dramatic structures of Wagner's mature works.

Yet Wagner himself had stated plainly enough in his letters and theoretical writings that with him the primary act of creation was just as much musical as poetic. For instance, in the letter of January, 1844, to Karl Gaillard, already quoted from in the previous chapter,[4] he says, "It is not my way to choose some story or other, get it versified, and then to begin to consider how to make suitable music for it. For this mode of procedure I should need to be twice inspired, which is impossible. The way I set to work is quite different. In the first place I am attracted only to matter the poetic and musical significance of which strike me simultaneously. Before I go on to write a verse or plot or scene I am already intoxicated by the musical aroma of my subject. I have every note, every characteristic motive in my head, so that when the versification is complete and the scenes are arranged the opera is practically finished for me; the detailed musical treatment is just a peaceful meditative after-labour, the real moment of creation having long preceded it." The poetic-dramatic substance, being mentally associated with music from its inception, was thus naturally controlled to some extent by those broad conceptions of form common to

[1] *Gesammelte Aufsätze.* Berlin, 1883.

[2] *Richard Wagner: Vorlesungen gehalten an der Universität zu Wien.* Leipzig, 1904.

[3] Published in four parts: I. *Der Ring des Nibelungen* (Berlin, 1924). II. *Tristan und Isolde* (1926). III. *Die Meistersinger von Nürnberg* (1931). IV. *Parsifal* (1933).

[4] See page 102.

music and poetry—a very different matter from the concoction of verse as a suitable verbal framework for the conventional musical forms of pre-Wagnerian opera. As for details, it is well known that Wagner never hesitated to alter his words to fit a melodic or rhythmic idea. And not only was the overture to *Die Meistersinger*, i.e., much of the most important material, composed before a word of the poem was written, but the music of Walther's songs[1] and the Eva–Sachs scene, and the melody of the *Choral* in Act III, were all written before the words of these passages.

Lorenz's investigations take as their starting-point the passages in *Oper und Drama*, quoted on pages 105 and 108, in which Wagner speaks of musical-poetic "periods" and "emotional situations" equivalent to organic members of the body, held together by unity of poetic content and unity of musical content, especially unity of key. In the light of these passages Lorenz was able to determine the "periods" of the *Ring* and the three other great music-dramas. An examination of the separate periods soon revealed that each was organized in a more or less clearly defined musical form: for instance, strophic form, that elaboration of ternary form (*Bogenform*) which we have already noticed in Liszt's symphonic poems, or a form borrowed from mediæval German poetry, the *Bar*, explained to Walther by Hans Sachs in the third act of *Die Meistersinger*.[2] Lorenz's method and results will be understood best by analysing fairly fully a complete act, chosen at random: Act I of *Die Walküre*.[3]

From a formal point of view, the Prelude to Act I, that highly effective piece of storm music, is chiefly remarkable for its quite

---

[1] "I've made the verses according to the melody in my head," Wagner wrote to Frau Wesendonck (March 12th, 1862). (*Richard Wagner an Mathilde Wesendonck*. 2nd edition: Berlin, 1904).

[2] Walther sings eleven bars of "Morgentlich leuchtend." "That," says Sachs, "was a stanza [*Stollen*]; now make another like it." Walther does. "Now make me an after-song [*Abgesang*]," commands the old man, "like the *Stollen*, as a child is like its parents, yet rich in new rhymes and tones; something that will round off your two *Stollen*." When that is done, he comments, "There's your complete *Bar*" ("*Seht wie der ganze Bar gelang!*"), and calls for a second *Bar*, "*Abendlich glühend*."

[3] It is interesting to note that those passages in the Fricka–Wotan scene of Act II, generally considered the most boring in the *Ring*, are less clear in musical form than any others in the whole tetralogy.

Lisztian squareness of structure, the first sixteen bars being almost exactly repeated a tone higher, the rest of the piece being similarly organized in 4- or 8-bar sections. In Lorenz's view the prelude ends twelve bars after the rise of the curtain, its last eight bars also constituting the first eight of the first "period."

Period I is short, consisting of only forty-four bars, and depicts Siegmund's exhaustion. Its musical content consists almost entirely of the "Siegmund" motive. After eight bars of storm music, balanced by another eight bars of storm at the end, comes the first main part (A) of the period (4 + 4 bars of the "Siegmund" theme). Then we have twelve bars of miniature development (B) and, after an orchestral pause of nearly three bars at Siegmund's first words, a 4-bar reprise of A—the shortening being compensated for by Siegmund's snatch of melody. The period is therefore in *Bogen* form, the key, D minor as in the prelude. A 13-bar transition passage in which Sieglinde contemplates the stranger leads to Period II.

Here Sieglinde gives him drink, the musical content consisting of statement of the themes of "compassion," "flight" and "love." Formally, the period consists of a *Bar* of two 15-bar *Stollen* (the second a fifth higher) and a 43-bar *Abgesang* (beginning at Sieglinde's "Labung biet ich" and ending on the dominant chord at "harre bis heim er kehrt"). Period III, in which *both* drink from the horn and Siegmund begins to realize that he loves Sieglinde, is not only based on the same musical material, now intensified, and in the same form (two *Stollen* of nineteen and eighteen bars, with a 36-bar *Abgesang*), but altogether so corresponds to the previous period that it might almost be considered a varied repeat of it. Both periods preserve the main key of D minor and Period IV begins in it (where the tempo changes to *Lebhaft*), turning to the tonic major only at the end and then modulating to the key of the next period (Scene Two, with Hunding).

Period IV, in which Sieglinde presses Siegmund to stay, is a sort of coda to the first scene and rather scrappy in form. It consists of five short sections: a tiny *Bogen* of 2 + 4 + 3 bars, based on a variant of the "compassion" motive; a perfect *Bar* with two 4-bar *Stollen* introducing the "Misswende" chord and a 10-bar *Abgesang*; six bars of cantilena—Sieglinde's "So bleibe hier!"; another perfect *Bar* of 4 + 4 + 8 bars; and a beautiful, varied repeat of this *Bar* in the tonic, though finally modulating as already mentioned. Lorenz points out that these four periods that together make up the first scene constitute a sort of gigantic *Bar* with introduction in D minor, Period I being introductory, II and III the two *Stollen*, each seventy-three bars long, and IV the *Abgesang*.

The first two periods of the second scene are both *Bogen*. The appearance of Hunding is marked by a decisive change of key; Period V is in C minor, ending on a dominant chord as Sieglinde puts the food on the table. The form is almost perfectly symmetrical:

(A) 8 introductory bars adumbrating the "Hunding" theme.
(B) 4 bars of the "Hunding" motive in complete form.
(C) 3 bars of "questioning look" chords.
(D) 2 bars (Sieglinde's "Müd am Herd," etc.).
(E) 3 bars for 'cellos based on the "storm" and "Siegmund" themes.
(D) 4 bars of dialogue.
(C) 3 bars of "questioning look" chords.
(F) 4 bars (Hunding's "Heilig ist mein Herd," etc.), the only real break in the symmetry of the period.
(B) 4 bars of "Hunding" motive.
(A) 8 concluding bars in which the "Hunding" motive blazes up and then dies away.

If we neglect the vocal bars, the symmetry is perfect.

Period VI (B flat: Hunding as host) is likewise a *Bogen* broken only by the repetition of one of its members:

(A) 5 bars. "Compassion" and "flight" themes.
(B) 6 bars. Hunding's thoughtfulness ("treaty" motive).
(C) 5 bars. "Hunding" theme and detached chords.
(D) 6 bars of "storm" motive.
(C) 6 bars of detached chords and "Hunding" theme.
(C) 7 bars. The same repeated a tone higher.
(B) 6 bars. Siegmund's thoughtfulness ("woe of the Wälsungs").
(A) 6 bars. "Compassion" and "love" themes. (The "love" and "flight" themes are so closely related as to be practically variants of the same idea.)

Five transitional bars (Hunding's "Trägst du Sorge," etc.) lead to Period VII (G minor), which, like most of the merely narrative or argumentative periods, is less symphonic in nature and consequently less clear in build. Lorenz considers it to be strophic: a

14-bar introduction, two strophes of seventeen and nineteen bars ("Wolfe, der war mein Vater" and "Zu Schutt gebrannt"), and a 5-bar "refrain" hinging on the "Wehwalt" chord. The strophes are just recognizable, thanks to the hunting-horns at the end of each; but it would surely be more sensible to recognize that a nasty piece of narrative grit has got into the musical machinery and interrupted its working. This first part of Siegmund's narration is separated from the second (Period VIII: A minor) by a 10-bar interruption: Hunding's "Wunder und wilde Märe" (two 4-bar strophes) and two bars for Sieglinde. It again requires a great deal of faith to agree with Lorenz that Period VIII is a *Bar* of 8- and 10-bar *Stollen* with twenty-nine bars of *Abgesang*; in contending that "the second *Stollen* may be a complete contrast to the first" he seems to be straining a point to fit his theory. A 7-bar coda, of which the end overlaps the beginning of the next period, leads to the third and last part of Siegmund's narration (Period IX: C minor).

Here the symphonic texture grows more continuous and the form correspondingly clearer. It is an extended *Bogen* with introduction and coda:

Introduction (13 bars).
Bridge-passage on the "woe of the Wälsungs" and "compassion" motives (3 bars).
A: "Misswende" chords; run suggesting the "storm" motive and the second part of the "Siegmund" theme; "die Leichen umschlang da die Maid" (14 bars).
B: "Mit wilder Tränen Flut" (7 bars); "Hunding" rhythm (7 bars); the "Tränen Flut" theme combined with the "Hunding" rhythm (3 bars)—(16 bars in all).
A: "Misswende" chord; first part of the "Siegmund" theme and "storm" theme; "auf den Leichen lag sie tot" (13 bars).
Bridge-passage on the "woe of the Wälsungs" theme (3 bars).
Coda (17 bars), itself a tiny *Bogen* (8 + 4 + 5). (The period ends not at the double bar but with the dominant chord following it.)

Period X, Hunding's challenge, is also a *Bogen*, though an irregular one (41 + 58 + 16 bars), the reprise being much curtailed. The middle section, in turn, consists of two *Bare* of 8 + 8 + 12 and 10 + 10 + 10 bars respectively. The key is C minor, though the period begins in G minor, and so the second scene, while Hunding is on the stage, ends in the key in which it began. Lorenz also points out that it is, roughly, a large-scale *Bogen*, Period X being a sort of shortened reprise of Periods V and VI (the thematic material consisting mainly of the "Hunding" and "compassion" motives), while Periods VII, VIII and IX (Siegmund's narration) are held together by the bars grouped around the "Wehwalt" chord, the germ of the theme of "recognition," "which open the first part of the narration and conclude each section of it."

Period XI (C major, though a minor touch makes the mode indeterminate at the end), Siegmund alone, is a species of prelude to the great love-scene. The first sixty bars, essentially introductory, consist of a long-drawn crescendo of emotional tension based almost entirely on the "Hunding" rhythm, but with several hints at the "sword" theme. The period proper begins with the C major statement of the "sword" motive and consists of eight strophes, each introduced by the "sword" motive as a sort of refrain, and consisting of 8, 6, 7, 8 + 2, 9, 11, 10 and 12 bars respectively. The last four bars sound only the note C in the bass-octaves. With the *pianissimo* C major chord, as Sieglinde softly opens the door, begins the last period of the act, the love-scene.

For the purposes of his analysis, Lorenz divides this colossal period into seven subdivisions. The first, Sieglinde's narrative, is in ternary form with a 29-bar introduction:

A: "Der Männer Sippe" and "Valhalla" theme (22 bars).
B: "Mir allein": "sword" theme: "dem sollte der Stahl" (a rudimentary *Bogen*) (27 bars).
A: "Der Männer alle" and "Valhalla" theme (18 bars).

The second, the rejoicing of the Wälsungs, consists of two strophes (33 and 32 bars respectively) which correspond much more closely than a cursory glance at the score would suggest; the 2-bar "cry of victory" that punctuates the whole section divides each strophe into four members closely corresponding in length and content.

With the opening of the great door begins the profoundly stirring 20-bar introduction to Siegmund's spring song, which Lorenz considers as two strophes (of 29 and 31 bars) corresponding closely in structure though not in thematic content. Each strophe opens with a miniature *Bogen* and closes with a miniature *Bar*. Three transitional bars lead to the next subdivision,

Sieglinde's reply, one of the most interesting of all from the point of view of structure. It is most remarkable that Wagner's imagination working at its highest pressure should have cast his music not only into exact *Bar* form, and a *Bar* of which each section consists of two perfectly balancing members, but into a form in which each member is itself a perfect *Bar*:

First *Stollen*	(a)	"Flight" motive (2 + 2 + 4 bars).
	(b)	"Love" motive (2 + 2 + 4 bars).
Second *Stollen*	(a)	"Flight" motive in diminution (2 + 2 + 4
(merely a		bars).
variation of	(b)	"Love" motive (2 + 2 + 4 bars).
the first a		
semitone		
higher).		
Abgesang	(a)	"Im Busen ich barg" (2 + 2 + 4 bars).
	(b)	"Love" motive (2 + 2 + 5 bars).

So tightly knit is this glorious stream of apparently rhapsodic song! Indeed, as after all we might expect, the more "essentially musical" the poetic content and the greater the intensity of the musical emotion, the clearer is the musical architecture. The eight ecstatic bars that follow are a miniature *Bogen* ("Freia" motive—"foreboding" motive—"Freia" motive) and Sieglinde's 14-bar strophe, "O lass in Nähe," is almost exactly repeated a minor third lower in Siegmund's 14-bar strophe (plus 4-bar coda), "Im Lenzesmond."

Just as Sieglinde's "Du bist der Lenz" consists of *Bar* within *Bar*, so the next section, the mutual recognition, consists of *Bogen* within *Bogen*:

A: The two motives associated with "foreboding"; "Valhalla" theme; "foreboding" themes combined with the "Freia" theme and others (10 + 10 + 20 bars).

B: "Flight" motive; "mich dünkt, ihren Klang," etc.; "flight" and (related) "love" motives (7 + 6 + 10 bars).

A: "Valhalla" theme, preceded by the "Wälsung" and "sword" themes; a recollection of Siegmund's narration, followed by the second "foreboding" motive; dialogue followed by "Valhalla" theme (21 + 16 + 9 bars).

Coda: Ten bars based on the "flight" motive.

It will be noticed that in the reprise of A, the order of the "Valhalla" and "foreboding" themes is transposed: "trio-minuet-trio," as it were.

Lorenz regards the rest of the act as two colossals trophes, of 59 and 61 bars, with a 26-bar coda. The first culminates in the winning of the sword, the second in the passionate embrace; the only thematic correspondence is in the opening members of the two strophes, both based on the "sword" and "Wälsung hero" themes, but they balance each other structurally.

Nor is this colossal Period XII formless as a whole. It is, in fact, a great *Bogen* with its middle section in *Bar* form:

> Introduction: 29 bars.
> A: Sieglinde's narrative ("Valhalla" and "sword" themes). Two strophes (first rejoicing of the Wälsungs).
> B: "Winterstürme" (plus "love" and "flight" themes) (first *Stollen*).
> "Du bist der Lenz" ("love" and "flight" themes) (second *Stollen*).
> "O süsseste Wonne!" (*Abgesang*).
> A: Mutual recognition ("Valhalla" and other themes). Two strophes (second rejoicing of the Wälsungs).
> Coda: 26 bars.

Lorenz also draws attention to the fact that Siegmund's part of the action concludes (end of Act II) in the key, D minor, in which it has begun. Indeed, as one would expect from Wagner's own words in *Oper und Drama*, tonality plays as important a part in the great *Ring* "symphony" and its successors as in the symphonies of Mozart, Beethoven and Brahms.

The result of Lorenz's great analytical work is to demonstrate conclusively that as long as Wagner was true to his own axiom that the poetic-dramatic stuff of opera must be essentially "musical" (i.e., emotional) and not intellectual (argument or narrative), his work was cast in coherent and more or less clear musical forms; and that when argument and narrative do intrude, as in Act II of *Die Walküre* and so much of *Parsifal*, though they injure the form, they do not destroy all vestiges of it. And these forms are not only apparent in the separate periods and their divisions and subdivisions, often down to the smallest units, but, taking into account similarities in the action as well as in the music itself, discernible in whole acts or even larger stretches of the drama. The "Siegmund" portion of the *Ring*, for instance (Acts I and II of *Die Walküre*), is not only unified by key but forms a gigantic *Bar*, of which the second *Stollen* begins and ends in the dominant minor:

First Stollen (*Act I*).	*Second Stollen* (*Scenes* 1 *and* 2 *of Act II*).
Brother and sister as protagonists.	Father and daughter as protagonists.
Their love becomes apparent.	Their profound inner sympathy becomes apparent.
Law, in the person of Hunding, intervenes.	Law, in the person of Fricka, intervenes.
Left to themselves, their dialogue ends in intense rapture of love (consonance).	Left to themselves, their dialogue ends in intense disagreement (dissonance).

Abgesang (*remainder of Act II*)

The two *Stollen* are brought together by the meeting of Siegmund and Brünnhilde.

Finally all the characters are brought together.

Similarly Lorenz declares the whole of *Das Rheingold*, with the exception of the introductory "Rhinedaughters" scene in E flat (dominant of the dominant), to be a gigantic *Bogen* in D flat. (The D flat of the end of *Götterdämmerung* completes the key-circle of the whole *Ring*.) The action of Act I of *Siegfried* is also a perfect *Bogen*. Most interesting of all, *Die Meistersinger* can be shown to be a single *Bar*, of which the first two acts form the *Stollen* and the third the *Abgesang*.

Indeed, *Die Meistersinger* is specially remarkable for the prevalence of *Bar*-form throughout, a prevalence no doubt intentional, for the form was a favourite one of the real Mastersingers who had acquired it from the still older Minnesingers. Seeing that Wagner makes Sachs lecture Walther on the form, he can hardly have been unconscious that he himself was using it throughout the work.

INTERLUDE: MUSIC IN THE EIGHTEEN-SIXTIES

"I had my *Tristan* Prelude played for the first time," wrote Wagner to Mathilde Wesendonck from Paris in January, 1860, "and, as though scales had fallen from my eyes, I saw how immeasurably far I have travelled from the world during the last eight years. This little prelude was so incomprehensibly *new* to the musicians that I had to lead them from note to note as if searching for precious stones in a mine." It was at the concert following this rehearsal that Berlioz failed so dismally to make head or tail of the piece. And if Berlioz could make nothing of *Tristan* in 1860, it is hardly surprising that the unintelligentsia of the Jockey Club, apart altogether from the society politics that also played a part, took a strong dislike to *Tannhäuser* in 1861.

We can judge how Wagner's music sounded to a musical society woman of the period from the memoirs of the Comtesse de Mercy-Argenteau,[1] one of Napoleon III's innumerable reputed mistresses. The Comtesse may not have been very intelligent, but by all accounts she was genuinely musical, an excellent pianist and an admirer of Chopin and Liszt. In the 'seventies she became the patroness and friend of Borodin and other Russian composers, then considered advanced modernists, and did a very great deal to make Russian music known in Belgium. She was interested enough in *Tannhäuser* to attend several of the rehearsals "and got somewhat accustomed to Wagner's music." She even "liked some parts very much, especially the third act," but "wondered how the public would bear the endless contest of the minstrels and the strange and barbarous accents of Venus." We must endorse her verdict that it was "sheer madness to impose *Tannhäuser* on France," on the Paris of Meyerbeer and Offenbach, of Gounod and Ambroise Thomas.

At the same time it is only fair to the musicians who disliked Wagner to point out that a good deal of their distaste was aroused by the undeniable element of vulgarity and sensationalism—the tromboning of melodies and the general attempt to stun and dazzle—in so much of his music up to and including *Lohengrin* and by no means eradicated even from the later and greater works. Sterndale Bennett's condemnation of the *Tannhäuser* Overture as "Brummagem Berlioz"[2] may have been lacking in perspicacity but was by no means the mere exhibition of academic wrong-headedness it appears to be. Henry Davison summarizes the views of the group to which his father belonged in these words: "Where was the wonderful originality of the author of the books? Where was the much-vaunted 'music of the future'?

[1] *The Last Love of an Emperor.* Heinemann, 1926.
[2] See Henry Davison's *From Mendelssohn to Wagner: Memoirs of J. W. Davison, Forty Years Music Critic of "The Times."*

This music" (i.e., the *Tannhäuser* Overture and the introduction, bridal chorus, wedding march and epithalamium from *Lohengrin*) "was clearly of the present. Melody commonplace, harmony sometimes brilliant in effect, but fuller of faults than originality, orchestration borrowed from Berlioz."

In spite of the *Tannhäuser* furore in the German opera-houses of the eighteen-fifties, it is probably true to say that genuine understanding of Wagner was really only hammered out on the domestic pianos of Germany during the 'sixties and 'seventies. The case of the sixteen-year-old Nietzsche and two young friends of the same age is probably typical of what went on in a good many German homes in 1860 and thereabouts. A couple of years earlier, already a keen young musician, he had felt "an inextinguishable hatred for all modern music . . . the so-called 'music of the future' of Liszt and Berlioz," in fact for all the post-Beethovenian composers except Mendelssohn; he considered them vague and obscure, and felt that they aimed at effect for effect's sake. But now he and his friends began to subscribe to Brendel's *Zeitschrift für Musik*, a paper that supported Wagner. They began to take an interest in Schumann and Liszt, and in the autumn of 1862 they clubbed together to buy Bülow's piano score of *Tristan* and played it from morning to night. The musical father of one of the boys would not allow these "Wagner orgies" in his house. "And I must confess," says Nietzsche's sister,[1] "that at first the music did sound frightful as played by them; they apparently did not understand how to make the melody stand out from the rich harmonic background, and our good mother frankly admitted that she took no pleasure in this 'frightful noise,' as she called it."

For some time, particularly outside Germany, the names of Schumann, Liszt and Wagner were associated as pioneers of the new, incomprehensible "music of the future." Even in Germany it was some time before it was realized that Schumann and his immediate circle had more in common with the Mendelssohnian traditionalists than with the "new German school." It was only with the celebrated manifesto of March, 1860, that Brahms and Joachim openly and definitely broke with the progressive party and divided musical Germany into two camps.

[1] E. Foerster-Nietzsche: *The Nietzsche-Wagner Correspondence.* Duckworth, 1922.

This unfortunate declaration stated that "the undersigned have long observed with regret the activities of a certain party whose organ is Brendel's *Zeitschrift für Musik*" (which had admittedly been idiotic enough to hail Liszt as "the Mozart of his time"). . . . "The undersigned declare that they do not recognize the principles expressed by Brendel's paper and can only deplore or condemn the productions of the leaders and disciples of the so-called 'New German' school . . . as contrary to the inmost essence of music." Actually the manifesto was not aimed at Wagner, whose music Brahms admired, but at Liszt. But the progressivists worshipped both and would not have recognized this distinction even if it had been frankly made in the declaration. As for Clara Schumann, she was bitterly anti-Wagnerian and found the music of even *Lohengrin* "horrible," though on the whole she liked "*Lohengrin* better than *Tannhäuser*, in which Wagner goes through the whole gamut of abominations."[1]

Yet at this very time the principal English critic, a friend and on the whole an admirer of Berlioz, saw in her own late husband "the representative of a movement which threatened to upset the old order of things, a musician before whom his heart's idol" (Mendelssohn) "was required to make way, the head of a pretentious regiment of German doctors and metaphysicians, affecting profundity, laying down the law æsthetic, sneering at England and English opinion, yet invading England and ousting English musicians"—this of the Schumann who had hailed Davison's own friend, Sterndale Bennett, in enthusiastic terms —"one who, first from lack of a thorough musical education and then from organic disease was, as a musical composer, a noble failure."

General appreciation of Schumann in England was very slow in coming. When it did come, it was due partly to Clara Schumann herself, who began to visit London annually during the 'sixties and played frequently at the chamber concerts of the Musical Union until it died with its founder, John Ella, in 1880, and at the Monday Popular Concerts. Still more, perhaps, to the persistent propaganda of August Manns at his Crystal Palace Saturday Concerts.

[1] See her letter to Brahms of March 31st, 1859, given in *The Letters of Clara Schumann and Johannes Brahms: 1853–1896*. Two vols. Edward Arnold, 1927.

Both the Monday "Pops," started in 1859, and the Crystal Palace orchestral concerts, started in 1856, made a notable difference to the musical life of London. Both series began as thoroughly popular affairs—Manns in October, 1855, with only a wind band, the St. James's Hall "Pops" as mere ballad concerts—and therefore with popular prices. Whereas Ella's Musical Union had aristocratic audiences with prices to correspond, anyone with a spare shilling could get a seat at the "Pops." The equally aristocratic and expensive Philharmonic had now to compete not only with the progressive and less exclusive New Philharmonic Society (from 1852 to 1879) but with the even cheaper concerts at Sydenham.[1] Both the "Pops" and the Crystal Palace concerts did much to educate the musical public also by using analytical programmes, already introduced to London by Ella, the "Pop" notes being written by Davison (who acted more or less as artistic adviser), those for Manns' concerts by George Grove, most celebrated of English amateurs, who was fortunately the secretary of the Crystal Palace Company.

Manns had been only an unusually talented Prussian army bandmaster, but he must have been a sound musician—Davison wrote of him in 1857 that he "made the orchestra express all the modifications of feeling that an imaginative soloist would give voice to on a single instrument"—and English music, including the English composer, has reason to be grateful to him. He was a progressive, too. As Grove proudly pointed out,[2] "the audience were familiar with Schumann's symphonies and overtures, and with Schubert's symphonies and *Rosamunde* music, at a time when these works were all but unknown in the concert-rooms of the metropolis." (The *Rosamunde* music and *Unfinished* Symphony came to light only in 1866–67, forty-odd years after their composition.) "Brahms's symphonies, piano concertos, *Variations on a Theme of Haydn* and *Song of Destiny*;

[1] Pasdeloup's popular orchestral concerts at the Cirque d'Hiver, started in 1861, did for Paris very much what the Crystal Palace concerts did for London. Chamber music was badly neglected in Paris during the 'sixties, though the Maurin Quartet gave half a dozen concerts a season in the Salle Pleyel. French interest in the genre really dates from the foundation of the chamber-music society, La Trompette, in 1869.

[2] Article "Symphony Concerts" in the *Dictionary of Music and Musicians*.

Raff's various symphonies; Liszt's *Ideale*; Rubinstein's symphonies; Goetz's symphony, concerto, and overtures; Smetana's *Vltava*; Wagner's *Faust* Overture; Sullivan's *Tempest* music and Symphony in E; Benedict's Symphony in G minor, and many other works were obtained (often in MS.) and performed before they were heard in any other place in the metropolis. . . . A very great influence was exercised in the renaissance of English music by the frequent performance of new works of importance by Mackenzie, Parry, Stanford, Cowen and others." (These last, of course, at a somewhat later period.)

But the general state of London's musical culture during the 'sixties may be judged more accurately by a glance at the programmes of the "Old" Philharmonic (directed up to 1866 by Sterndale Bennett, from 1867 by W. G. Cusins). The new works performed in England for the first time by our premier concert-giving society included Spohr's *Seasons* Symphony (1860), Sterndale Bennett's *Paradise and the Peri* Overture and the 'Cello Concertos of Piatti and Davydov (naturally played by the composers) (1862), Beethoven's *Egmont* music (1863), Bennett's G minor Symphony and Joachim's Second Concerto (1864), the *Rienzi* Overture and Molique's Flute Concerto (1865), Sullivan's *Marmion* Overture (1867), Lucas's *Rosenwald* Overture, J. F. Barnett's Overture *Symphonique*, Benedict's *La selva incantata* Overture and Schumann's *Concertstück*, Op. 92 (1868), and a Symphony in G minor by Joseph Woelfl (1869). Programmes more completely out of touch with live contemporary music could not possibly have been drawn up. Besides the *Rienzi* Overture, the only Wagner items in the whole decade were the *Tannhäuser* march (1863) and Overture (1867), and the Prelude to *Lohengrin* (1869). Neither Liszt nor Brahms was represented at all.

London heard its first complete Wagner opera in July, 1870, when the *Dutchman* was given *in Italian* at Drury Lane as *L'Ollandese dannato*. *Tannhäuser* did not arrive till 1876, also in Italian, just thirty-one years after the original production. The parallel with the modern British interest in contemporary opera is too obvious and too painful to need emphasis.

Of the younger British composers of the day only one, Sullivan, has proved to be anything but a complete nonentity. His *Tempest* music, written at twenty, first drew general attention to him in 1862. Then came a cantata, *Kenilworth* (1864), a Symphony, the *In Memoriam* Overture and a 'Cello Concerto (all in 1866), and an oratorio, *The Prodigal Son* (1869). But *Box and Cox*, the first of the operettas by which alone he is remembered, did not appear till 1867; the first work in which he collaborated with Gilbert, *Thespis*, came only in 1871. The 'eighties were the "great" Gilbert-and-Sullivan years. English opera in the eighteen-sixties was represented by such doubtful masterpieces as Balfe's *Bianca* and *Puritan's Daughter* (1860), *Armourer of Nantes* (1863) and *Rose, or Love's Ransom* (1864), Vincent Wallace's *Lurline* (1860) and *Amber Witch* (1861), Macfarren's *Robin Hood* (1860) and *Helvellyn* (1864), and Benedict's *Lily of Killarney* (1862). All these were produced with singers of the rank of Santley and Sims Reeves, so that the legend that British opera has failed because it has never been given a chance is merely—a legend.

Specially typical of the Victorian mania for oratorio and of the Victorian public's complete misunderstanding of its idols were the monster Handel Festivals at the Crystal Palace, the first of which was held in June, 1857. Another was organized in 1859 and from then onward the Festival was held triennially.

Yet England and France were certainly not more backward than Italy. "The condition of Milan—by far the most musical town in Italy—in the 'sixties" is thus described by Mazzucato:[1] "*Music* and *opera* were synonymous words, and no one cared for anything that had not been or could not be performed with success at the Scala. Bach, Beethoven, Mozart, Mendelssohn, Schumann, were as much unknown as if they had never been born. Even as late as 1876, the only copy of Beethoven's symphonies to be had at the Library of the Conservatorio, was a cheap edition printed at Mendrisio, and so full of mistakes as to be in some parts unintelligible."

But in the eighteen-sixties the musically most backward of all the great European countries suddenly awoke and before the end of the decade began to produce works that are still as alive and nearly as fresh as when they were written. The Russian Music Society was founded in 1859, with Anton Rubinstein as its musical director in St. Petersburg, while his brother Nicholas directed the Moscow branch of the Society. Each branch gave

[1] Article "Boito" in the second edition of *Grove*.

ten orchestral concerts a season. Unfortunately the Rubinsteins, of German-Jewish origin, were (like Sterndale Bennett in England) Mendelssohnian in outlook—Anton even more than Nicholas—and had little sympathy either with genuinely contemporary music or with native talent. Nevertheless, the rules of the Society obliged them to perform at least one native work at each concert. Through the Society, too, Russia at last acquired official schools of music, the Petersburg Conservatoire being opened in September, 1862, the Moscow Conservatoire in September, 1866, both of course under the control of the Rubinstein brothers.

The Russian equivalent of the progressive Crystal Palace concerts sprang from the Free School of Music founded in St. Petersburg, also in 1862, by a choral conductor, Gabriel Lomakin. Under Balakirev, who was at first Lomakin's assistant and who succeeded him as director in 1867, the School gave choral and orchestral concerts, the programmes of which included numerous works by Berlioz, Schumann and Liszt, to say nothing of Balakirev himself and the brilliant group of young amateur composers he had gathered about him.

III

AFTER WAGNER

I. EARLY NATIONALIST SCHOOLS

NEXT to the influence of Wagner, the most potent force in the music of the mid-nineteenth century was nationalism, a more or less conscious nationalism springing in practically every case from political causes, generally from political repression. The deliberate Germanness of Weber was a product of the intense national emotion of the War of Liberation against Napoleon[1] and German national consciousness was kept at a high temperature throughout the century, first by Liberal aspirations and the desire for a unified Germany, then by the victory over France and the establishment of the Empire. (Though success was noticeably a less powerful artistic stimulus than striving.) Chopin, Liszt and Smetana were obviously made patriot-musicians by the repression of their respective countries by Russia and Austria. And it should not be overlooked that Grieg's Norway, uneasily yoked to Sweden, was much more aggressively conscious of its Norwegianness than the Norway of to-day. Russia was not suffering from foreign domination but she *was* suffering very badly from a combination of inferiority complex with quasi-mystical imperialism. It is true that Glinka was first filled with the desire to "write music in Russian" by his homesickness in Italy, but the Russian nationalist movement of the eighteen-sixties was a by-product of that strange half-religious, half-political faith in the world-mission of the Slavonic peoples which played such an important part in Russian thought at this period and for some time after.[2]

The musical patriot can display his feelings by the choice of patriotic subjects for his operas and oratorios and symphonic

---

[1] It should be remembered also that Weber's teacher, Vogler, was interested in folk-song and collected melodies from as far afield as North Africa and Russia.

[2] See, for instance, Dostoevsky's *The Idiot* and *The Possessed*, and, above all, his political writings.

works as Glinka, Liszt and Smetana did. But these affect his music only outwardly, leaving its actual substance untouched. The true nationalist goes deeper. He exploits the characteristic rhythms of national dances, like Chopin and Dvořák; generally he goes further and incorporates folk-tunes in his music or deliberately imitates the folk-idiom. Incidentally, one curious result of this is that the folk-tune fancier frequently acquires a certain liking for the folk-music of other countries, and the nationalist who is also an exoticist is following a rule rather than providing an exception. Weber introduced gypsy, Spanish, Chinese and Arabian tunes in *Preciosa*, *Die drei Pintos*, *Turandot* and *Oberon*, Liszt wrote a Spanish Rhapsody and pieces on Polish, Italian, and Russian airs, the Russians delighted in Oriental and Spanish idioms, Brahms showed a marked predilection for Hungarian gypsy music, Dvořák was interested in the songs of the American negroes—and the list could easily be extended.

More interesting than this deliberate but still rather superficial type of nationalism is the unconscious variety: the kind of nationalism that betrays itself in idiosyncrasies of musical thought, such as we shall discover when we examine the music of the Russians, and in a melodic utterance naturally related to folk-music, such as we find on so many pages of the German classics.

The profound influence of German folk-song, both traditional songs and the comparatively modern so-called *Volkslieder*, on the great German masters has never been sufficiently recognized. At the most, it is admitted that Schubert and Weber have stylistic affinities with folk-music. But the influence of those rather square-cut melodies, generally in the modern major scale and frequently centring on the notes of the tonic triad, has gone much deeper than this. A composer living in a country where music is always in the air acquires as an impressionable child a natural musical vocabulary based on what he hears; in terms of that vocabulary he first thinks and creates, and it forms the basic texture of his music. In the case of the great German masters of the past, that musical vocabulary consisted largely of *Choral* melodies and folk-songs.

A comparative study of German folk-music and German art-music reveals the most astonishing affinities. One would hardly suppose the fugue-subject of Bach's C major Concerto for two claviers to have any relationship with folk-music but a comparison with the song "Was wölln wir auf den Abend tun?" in the *Fabricius Lautenbuch* (1603) definitely shows that it has:

A relationship, nothing more. It would be absurd to suggest that Bach elaborated his theme from the folk-tune—though the latter may well have been buried in his subconsciousness; the point is that the fugue-subject obviously springs from the same German stock as "Was wölln wir." Beethoven, Schubert, Weber, Schumann, Mendelssohn—even Mozart to some extent —all contain a certain folk-song element in the alloy that constitutes their musical speech; Haydn, as is well known, was strongly influenced by Croatian folk-music.

With Brahms, however, the folk-song element assumes much more importance than in the music of his great predecessors. German popular music played an even more strongly determinative part in the formation of his melodic style than did the music of Schumann and Mendelssohn, and even survived in it long after their influences had been obliterated by the rapid development of those qualities that are uniquely and unmistakably Brahms's and Brahms's alone. One has only to glance at such *Volkslied* melodies as "Es wohnet ein Fiedler" and "Es stunden drei Rosen" (Nos. 36 and 43 of Brahms's own collection of *49 Deutsche Volkslieder*) to see that many of the themes of his symphonic and chamber music spring directly from this stock. According to Kalbeck,[1] "he said more than once that the beginnings of his composing could be traced back to folk-song."

It is instructive to compare Brahms's own settings of folk-song words with the original melodies to the same words. "Tren-

[1] Max Kalbeck: *Johannes Brahms*. 2nd edition. Berlin, 1908–15 (in eight "half-volumes").

nung" (Op. 97, No. 6), for instance, is very similar to the original tune of "Da unten im Tale" (No. 6 of the 49 *Volkslieder*); "Spannung" (Op. 84, No. 5) is less close to the original (No. 4 of the 49); but in both cases it would puzzle anyone not in the secret to say which was the traditional, which Brahms's setting. Here, of course, Brahms was dealing with simple folk-song words and deliberately trying to catch their spirit. His setting of "Dort in den Weiden" (Op. 97, No. 4) is further from the original (No. 31 of the 49) and altogether too subtle to be mistaken for folk-song. Yet its ancestry is quite unmistakable. It is only that we have got one generation, as it were, beyond true folk-song. And, as Kalbeck has shown, the melody of Op. 97, No. 4, is one of a whole family of Brahms themes: the basic theme of the B major Trio, Op. 8 (pub. 1859, revised 1890), the setting of "Edward," Op. 75, No. 1, the finale of the Horn Trio, the first choral entry in the funeral march of *Ein Deutsches Requiem* (1868), the coda of the slow movement of the F minor Piano Sonata (comp. 1853), and the second subject of the intermezzo of the G minor Piano Quartet (pub. 1863).

Brahms's use of actual folk-melodies in his compositions, on the other hand, is comparatively rare. The slow movements of the first two Piano Sonatas, Opp. 1 and 2 (1852–53), are both based on old *Minnelieder*, the first on the still popular "Verstohlen geht der Mond auf," the second on "Mir ist leide." The "Hungarian song" of Op. 21, No. 2 (1853), is merely a pretext for variations, the student songs of the *Academic Festival Overture* (1880) are introduced for a special purpose, and the Hungarian Dances (1869–80) are mere arrangements (with three exceptions) and arrangements not of genuine folk-melodies but of popular tunes by such composers as Kéler-Béla (No. 5), Rizner, and Adolph Nittinger.[1] The *Tzigane* element that matters in Brahms's music is absorbed like the *Volkslied* element, as in the finale of the Violin Concerto (1878) and the slow movement of the Clarinet Quintet (1891).

Chopin's nationalism appears to be of the same variety as Brahms's. Niecks says[2] that "everyone acquainted with the national music of Poland as well as with the composer's works

---

[1] Kalbeck challenges this, but produces no evidence that the tunes are true folk-melodies.

[2] *The Life of Chopin.* Two vols. Novello, N.D.

knows that he is indebted to it for some of the most piquant
rhythmic, melodic, and even harmonic peculiarities of his style.
. . . Generally speaking, however, Chopin has more of the spirit
than of the form of Polish folk-music. The only two classes of
his compositions where we find also something of the form are
his mazurkas and polonaises; and, what is noteworthy, more in
the former, the dance of the people, than in the latter, the dance
of the aristocracy. In Chopin's mazurkas we meet not only with
many of the most characteristic rhythms, but also with many
equally characteristic melodic and harmonic traits of the chief of
all the Polish dances." The twelve examples of Polish music,
"melodies and snatches of melodies," given by Niecks on
pp. 217–18 of his second volume, confirm this, though he admits
that they were "chosen with a view rather to illustrate Chopin's
indebtedness to Polish folk-music than Polish folk-music itself."

Liszt's virtuosic exploitation of actual folk-material in the
famous Rhapsodies (1847–85) and his deliberate imitation of it
in *St. Elisabeth* (1865) (the music associated with the Hungarian
magnate, etc.), and the *Hungarian Coronation Mass* (1869) are
of a very different nature. To use folk-tunes as mere excuses
for orchestral or pianistic fireworks, decorating them outwardly
instead of drawing out their inner essence, to treat them as
"Far and high the cranes give cry" (see No. 3 of Korbay's
collection of *Hungarian Melodies*)[1] is treated in Liszt's *Hungarian
Fantasia* (1853) and the Fourteenth Rhapsody, is to abuse them
vilely. Liszt draws nothing out of the tunes, adds nothing to them
—except tawdry ornamentation. At the most one can only plead
as Liszt's excuse that an element of virtuosity and showmanship
is common in the make-up of Hungarian gypsy musicians, and
that they are much addicted to elaborate ornamentation.

We have already seen that Liszt's instrumental recitatives
have been considered a "gypsy mannerism." But it would be
difficult to trace any other real penetration of his natural musical
style by the idioms of Hungarian gypsy music; I doubt whether
even the rapid repeated notes in his piano pieces were suggested
by cymbalom music. (Of the true Magyar folk-music, since
brought to light by Bartók and Kodály, he seems to have been

---

[1] This particular tune seems to be a fairly modern popular melody,
not a true folk-tune, though the composer is not definitely known.
But that does not affect the point at issue.

extraordinarily ignorant.) When he does "go Hungarian" as in
the *Coronation Mass* and the passages referring to Hungary in
St. Elisabeth, he obviously does so deliberately, quoting traditional tunes or fragments of them, or else concocting synthetic
"Hungarian music" from the melodic and rhythmic clichés
characteristic of the genuine article.

The same distinction between natural absorption of the folk-
idiom and artificial imitation of it may be studied even more
profitably in the work of the different members of the Russian
school. Their compositions also throw a great deal of light on
the problem of the introduction of actual folk-melodies into art-
music, on its fertilizing power and on its limitations.

Borodin, Mussorgsky and Balakirev, like Brahms and Chopin,
seem to have absorbed folk-music into their very blood so that
its rhythms and melodic shapes naturally crept into nearly
everything they wrote. Yet Borodin only twice uses actual
Russian folk-tunes: in *In Central Asia* and for the chorus of
peasants in the last act of *Prince Igor* (comp. 1869–87; prod.
1890); the music of the Polovtsy in the same opera is practically
all evolved from a single Oriental tune. Mussorgsky frequently
quotes folk-melodies. Balakirev never "quotes" them but often
uses them as the thematic nuclei of his works, evolving from
them a wealth of sound partially derived from them yet essentially the stuff of his own exuberant imagination. Tchaïkovsky
frequently introduces folk-song themes but his own melodic style
has so little affinity with the folk-idiom, especially in his later
works such as the finale of the Fourth Symphony (1877) and the
finale of the String Serenade (1880), that they seldom or never
coalesce. Rimsky-Korsakov was much more conscious in his
approach to folk-music. He not only borrowed liberally from
its treasures but, on his own confession, deliberately concocted
synthetic pseudo-folk-melodies. Defending himself in his
memoirs[1] against the charge of too frequent use of actual folk-
tunes in his earlier operas (said by hostile critics to be a sign of
the poverty of his melodic invention), he says: "As regards the
invention of folk-songish melodies, they must naturally be based
on the curves and motives of genuine folk-songs. How can two
things resemble each other as wholes if they do not resemble each
other in any single detail? Hence, how can any melody be

[1] *Letopis moey muzïkalnoy Zhizni.* 4th edition. Leningrad, 1932.

'folk-songish' if its separate curves are not copied from those of genuine folk-songs?'' It never occurred to him that there is a vast difference between the natural inspiration of one piece of art by another and the clever imitation of one by an expert. Unlike Mussorgsky and Borodin, Rimsky-Korsakov never really assimilated the folk-idiom; from first to last it remained little more than an external decoration of his musical thought, though a decoration to which his music owes a very great deal of its charm; he always found it easy to drop it, as in *Servilia* (1900), *Pan Voevoda* (1902), and innumerable passages even in much more characteristic works.

It is probably true to say that the Russians used actual folk-material far more freely than had ever been done before. Russian opera is full of folk-tunes, often introduced very effectively: as aria—Olga's "Stay with me, my love" in Korsakov's *Maid of Pskov* (*Ivan the Terrible*) (1873) and Marfa's song in Act III of Mussorgsky's *Khovanshchina* (comp. 1873–81; prod. in Korsakov's version 1886); as chorus—the revolution and coronation scenes of *Boris* (1874); leitmotive—Ivan the Terrible's theme in Rimsky-Korsakov's *Tsar's Bride* (1898); or orchestral interlude—prelude to Act III of his *Snowmaiden* (1882). But the problem of weaving folk-tunes into purely instrumental music is much more difficult. Not easy even when the composer tries merely to give a folk-tune a suitable instrumental setting, increasingly difficult—to the point of impossibility—the further he gets from mere arrangement and the nearer to genuine composition on a folk-song basis.

A folk-song is a complete musical entity (or rather, when deprived of its words, a maimed artistic entity), a fully developed whole containing no growing power. To break it up into its constituent motives is not only vandalism but useless vandalism, for the beauty of a folk-tune generally lies in its phrases as wholes, and smaller melodic fragments from it are usually quite commonplace. To vary it melodically destroys its folkishness at once (the theme is almost the least important part of genuine variations) and it has no harmony to vary.[1] To dress it up with *gorgeous*

---

[1] A good deal of Russian folk-music is polyphonic, but no one knew that in the eighteen-sixties. When Melgunov published his collections of polyphonic folk-music in 1879 and 1885, Rimsky-Korsakov condemned them as "barbarous."

ornamentation or instrumentation, as Liszt did with his *Tzigane* tunes in his Rhapsodies, is like putting a peasant into a brilliant uniform. In fact, as some wit has said, almost the only thing you can do with a folk-tune, once you have played it, is to play it louder. But there is one way of spinning a longish piece from a folk-tune without destroying either its form or its spirit, the way discovered by Glinka in *Ruslan* (Finn's ballad and the Persian chorus): repetition of the tune, with little or no modification, against ever new but always sympathetic backgrounds of harmony and instrumental colour. Glinka's orchestral piece, *Kamarinskaya* (1848)—"from which," as Tchaïkovsky said, "all the Russian composers who followed Glinka (including myself) continue to this day to borrow contrapuntal and harmonic combinations directly they have to develop a Russian dance-tune"[1] —is another brilliant essay in this method, though in this case the method inevitably exposes the poverty of the basic theme. The Prelude to Act IV of Balakirev's incidental music to *King Lear* (1861) is a particularly beautiful example of this type of variation, the theme being an English folk-tune.

Balakirev also evolved a type of overture based on three folk-tunes, a slow melody generally being used to open and conclude the piece, while the main section consists partly of "changing background" variations, partly of contrapuntal combinations of the themes. His own *Overture on Three Russian Themes* (1859), *A Thousand Years* (1864, revised in 1887 as a symphonic poem, *Russia*), and *Overture on Czech Themes* (1867, revised in 1906 as a symphonic poem, *In Bohemia*), and Rimsky-Korsakov's *Overture on Russian Themes* (1866, revised 1880) are planned on these lines. All these are attractive, racy compositions and *Russia* is a good deal more; in this magnificent work Balakirev's imagination really took fire from the folk-material, as it did again from the rubbing together of two or three dry sticks of Armenian and Caucasian themes in the piano fantasia *Islamey* (1869), and by some mysterious process these permutations and combinations of three borrowed tunes are filled with the breath of life and coalesce into an artistic whole. But *Russia* and *Islamey* are almost the only instances in Russian music of

[1] The influence on later Russian composers of Glinka's brilliant, clear, transparent scoring, based on equally clear, transparent part-writing, has also been inestimable.

genuinely inspired treatment of folk-material. Rimsky-Korsakov's Piano Concerto (1883), Sinfonietta (1884), Violin Fantasia
(1886), and the rest, merely demonstrate in one way or another
the almost impossibility of breaking in folk-music to the ends of
any but the simplest forms of instrumental art-music.

Far more interesting than this obvious, self-conscious "folk-
song nationalism" is that more profound kind of nationalism
which manifests itself in special ways of thinking and feeling,
some peculiar to music, others common to the whole art and
literature of a country. The preference of Balakirev and other
composers for borrowed folk-material rather than invented
material as the basis of works absolutely original and individual
in essence, for instance, has literary parallels in the borrowing
by Pushkin and Gogol of folk-tales as the bases of so many of
their most characteristic stories. That which gives the music or
the story enduring value as a work of art is in each case the
treatment, the elaboration; and that is completely individual.
But the *given* basis seems to be almost indispensable; without
some form of it, Russian art is usually painfully insipid.

Indeed, the whole relationship between Russian art and such
données is peculiar and has in several respects conditioned its very
nature. Naturally all the arts in all countries are frequently
inspired by all sorts of external *données*: music by poetry,
characters in fiction by characters in real life, and so on. But
Russian art is peculiar in that practically *all* its best products in
music, painting and literature depend on such bases, and that
cause and effect stand in unusually close relation. And as the
donnée is usually something in real life, we recognize this
quality as "realism" or "artistic truth." There is no need to
insist on the almost photographic realism of the Russian novelists;
the lyric note in Turgenev, the sublimating breadth of Tolstoy's
vision of humanity, Dostoevsky's fantastic imagination cannot
conceal, indeed barely modify, their intense realism. Pushkin
and Gogol, Gorky and Chekhov, with all their differences, have
this in common. The most important school of Russian painters,
the so-called *Ambulants*, Kramskoy, Gay, Repin and the rest,
aimed at "brutal realism" and "despised formal beauty";
they "systematically sacrificed the form to the subject."[1]

This trait, natural to the Russian character, was recognized

[1] L. Réau: *L'art russe de Pierre le Grand à nos jours.* Paris, 1922.

by the leading Russian critics and writers on æsthetics and directly encouraged by them, particularly about the middle of the last century when progressive ideas in art and politics were fermenting with special intensity. Chernyshevsky (1828–89) and Dobrolyubov (1836–61) both preached the doctrine that life is more important than art and that the function of art is to show us life as it is actually lived (and thus to widen and deepen our understanding of other men's lives), to explain it and to comment on it. Dobrolyubov, in particular, desired tendentious, propagandist art. When Tolstoy came out in 1898 with his denunciations of beauty as the end of art, of empty technical dexterity, and so on in *What is Art?* he was merely redigesting a great many ideas that by that time had grown rather stale.

The first Russian musician to fall a victim to this passion for artistic "truth" was Dargomïzhsky. His realistic leanings are apparent in some of his songs and in his feebly Glinka-ish opera *The Rusalka* (1856). But it is in his very daring setting of Pushkin's "miniature tragedy," *The Stone Guest* (comp. 1868; perf. 1872), that his "truthfulness" has fullest play. Dargomïzhsky's avowed aim was "the note as the direct expression of the word" and he set Pushkin's play, just as it stood, to what he called "melodic recitative," the vocal line being always controlled by the sense and natural inflection of the words but at the same time retaining—at any rate, in intention—the rhythms and curves of genuine melody. Actually Dargomïzhsky was too poorly gifted to avoid a great deal of very dry declamation, "true" enough but seldom characteristic of the individual and not often as graphic as in the passage where Leporello gasps out his invitation to the statue. All this sounds like Wagnerism very imperfectly understood and Dargomïzhsky was certainly acquainted with the score of *Tannhäuser* as early as 1856.[1] Moreover, the score of *The Stone Guest* contains a few rudimentary and inexpressive leitmotives—though these were by that time part of the stock-in-trade of all opera composers. But with Dargomïzhsky the voice-part is all-important, the orchestra generally supplying a mere unobtrusive background.

The score of *The Stone Guest* is full of interesting points: the

---

[1] He was present with Mussorgsky and Rimsky-Korsakov at the first Russian performance of *Lohengrin* in October, 1868, and poured mockery over it. But *The Stone Guest* was then practically finished.

complete absence of key-signature throughout, the chromatic side-slipping of diminished sevenths when Juan is gradually admitting his identity in the last act, the use not merely of the whole-tone scale *qua* scale but of themes in the whole-tone mode and, in one or two instances, whole-tone harmonies as well. But, despite its interest and historical importance, the work is artistically dead, not only because Dargomïzhsky was rather sterile in genuine inspiration but because no musician, however gifted, could have made anything of such a rigidly doctrinaire art-form. Mussorgsky tried to follow Dargomïzhsky's example by setting Gogol's comedy, *The Marriage* (1868), but broke down after completing the first act. And Rimsky-Korsakov amused himself in 1897 by setting Pushkin's *Mozart and Salieri* on similar lines and dedicating it to Dargomïzhsky's memory. But the real value of Dargomïzhsky's realism lies in its influence on Mussorgsky's *Boris Godunov* and *Khovanshchina* and Rimsky-Korsakov's *Maid of Pskov*, to say nothing of many of Mussorgsky's songs (e.g., "The Orphan, "The Street Arab," "Darling Savishna" and the "Nursery" cycle). In the three operas mentioned, Dargomïzhsky's theories are not only practised by two composers far more gifted than himself, but very considerably adulterated with a lyrical element derived from Glinka. The resulting genre is essentially hybrid but such is the force of Mussorgsky's original genius that, at any rate in *Boris*, the two disparate elements are forced into a surprisingly satisfactory whole.

Yet another form of "truth to life," of closeness to the *donnée*, is the pantomimic element that plays such an important part in Mussorgsky's operas (e.g., the "writing" themes in *Boris* and *Khovanshchina*), songs (e.g., "Master Pride" and "The Magpie") and instrumental music, e.g., the Intermezzo in B minor (1862), suggested by the sight of peasants plunging through deep snow-drifts, and almost every number of the *Pictures from an Exhibition* for piano (1874). Nor is this peculiar to Mussorgsky. Rimsky-Korsakov's most characteristic operas abound in pantomimic themes, music far removed from tone-painting yet obviously visually inspired (e.g., the fussy, pompous theme of the Tsar and the themes associated with the wicked sisters in *Tsar Saltan* (1900) and the motives of Dodon, Polkan and Amelfa in *The Golden Cockerel* (comp. 1907)).

Another peculiarity of the Russian creative mind in general is its inability to conceive organic wholes. The Russian thinks most naturally in episodes and produces his general effects by the accumulation of episodes. This trait, which is not necessarily the weakness it appears to be, was pointed out a century ago by the critic Chaadaev and has been again in our own day by Prince Mirsky and Maurice Baring. It is obvious in the plays and novels of Tolstoy, in Dostoevsky's novels, in Chekhov's plays; Pushkin's *Boris* is actually more episodic than the opera Mussorgsky based on it. Naturally the same disjointedness (and the same lack of dynamic "drama" in the ordinary sense of the word) is very apparent in Russian opera. From Glinka's *Ruslan* to Borodin's *Prince Igor* and Korsakov's *Sadko* (completed 1896; perf. 1898), it is difficult to think of one really characteristic Russian opera that is not essentially episodic in structure and lacking in conventional "dramatic interest."

The same peculiarity can be detected in Russian music in general. With the exception of Borodin's symphonies and one or two other works, Russian symphonic music in general is patchy and sectional—with the sections badly joined. That is particularly true of Tchaïkovsky's instrumental works; as he himself confessed, "my *seams* always showed and there was no organic union between the separate episodes." Even in the first movement of the *Pathétique* Symphony (1893), where the intensely felt episodes are more or less fused together by the emotional heat, the impression left by the parts obliterates in retrospect that made by the whole. Mussorgsky was almost completely lacking in a sense of independent musical form and Rimsky-Korsakov's so-called "symphonic" music has only an artificial form produced by sedulous aping of Liszt's "wall-paper pattern" methods of construction described in a previous chapter.[1]

Russian music is full of marvellous *passages* but it seldom achieves perfection of form except on the smallest scale, in miniatures and epigrams such as Borodin's songs (e.g., "The False Note") and Skryabin's Preludes for piano (e.g., Op. 33, Nos. 1 and 3). On the other hand, Russian music contains some highly interesting examples of free organic forms, arising more or less naturally out of the musical content, from the themes and their treatment, with only the lightest constraint from any

[1] See pages 40–41.

preconceived structural outline. The first movements of Borodin's First Symphony, Balakirev's First Symphony and Piano Sonata, and Tchaïkovsky's *Pathétique* Symphony all repay study from this point of view.

The success of Russian musicians in the miniature forms is not unconnected, too, with the Russian gift for conciseness, economy of texture and directness of expression. From Pushkin to the present day, these have been the distinguishing marks of practically every Russian writer of distinction. Gogol's highly ornamented early tales are exceptional; generally speaking, luxuriance and elaboration are quite foreign to Russian prose and Russian poetry. The same national trait is noticeable in Russian music; indeed it is just this simplicity of statement and economy of texture, together with its intense rhythmic vitality, that have made the influence of Russian music so valuable as a corrective to that of German romantic music, with its tendency to turgidity and prolixity.[1] Balakirev admittedly lacks this tightness of texture and Russian composers tend more than Russian writers to an irritating repetitiveness due to various causes: in Tchaïkovsky's case to imitation of classical forms not necessitated by his material, in Rimsky-Korsakov's to his Lisztian processes of thought. But the music of Mussorgsky's operas is nearly as superior to Wagner's from a dramatic point of view in its power of producing extraordinary emotional effects with the simplest means (cf. Boris's hallucination at the end of the "nursery scene," his death, or the murder of Khovansky in *Khovanshchina*) as it is immensely inferior to it as pure ("symphonic") music. Similarly the clear transparent, but brilliant and piquant, orchestration of such rather brittle scores as Rimsky-Korsakov's *Scheherazade* (1888) served as a healthy antidote to the sumptuous, excessively complicated scoring of Wagner and his most important disciple, Richard Strauss.

It would be possible to continue almost indefinitely this examination of general Russian traits as manifested in Russian music. Russian orchestration, with its clarity and its emphasis on bright, unmixed orchestral timbres (a style of scoring

---

[1] Hans von Bülow once wrote of Schumann as having "contributed to that deplorable anti-rhythmic tendency from which we are suffering in Germany and which too often obliges us to take the anti-toxins of Russian music."

originated by Glinka, developed by Balakirev, Borodin and Tchaï-kovsky, and carried to its highest development by Rimsky-Korsakov and Stravinsky) is the obvious counterpart of the Russian love of bright colours. The objectivity of the great Russian novelists is matched by the objectivity of most of the great Russian composers—the later Tchaïkovsky, Rakhmaninov, and perhaps Skryabin are the only important exceptions—just as the pure lyrical vein in Glinka, Borodin, Rimsky-Korsakov and Tchaïkovsky is the exact counterpart of the lyrical poetry of Pushkin, Fet and Alexey Tolstoy. Common, too, to all Russian art (and folk-lore) is a curious matter-of-factness of imagination, a fantasy without fancy.

No composers in the world have written more avowedly fantastic music than the Russians. But this fantastic music of theirs always turns out on examination to be essentially mathematical: a logical working out of a certain rigid symmetrical pattern or device, seducing and tickling the ear by its strangeness and harmonic ruthlessness. Harmonic tricks (particularly use of the piquant "ambiguous" chords, the augmented and diminished triads with all their possibilities of enharmonic change) and artificial scales (the whole-tone scale, and the scale of alternate tones and semitones invented by Rimsky-Korsakov) are also an important part of the stock-in-trade of these dealers in mathematical sound-fantasy. Technical device, in fact, is itself used as the indispensable *donnée*. We have already noticed all this—the logical working out of a curious progression, the use of the whole-tone scale, and so on—in Glinka's *Ruslan*. Dargomïzhsky's three orchestral pieces, the *Kazachok*, the *Fantasia on Finnish Themes* and the fantasy scherzo *Baba-Yaga* (1865–69) are full of harmonic curiosities of this kind, some astonishingly bold and harsh, inserted in a harmonic texture which in other respects might almost have been written by a very amateurish contemporary of Haydn. The chromatic world of Chopin and Liszt was quite foreign to Dargomïzhsky, and the harmony of *The Stone Guest*, where it is not astoundingly advanced, as in the celebrated whole-tone passages and a few others, is astoundingly commonplace.

It seems to have been the impact of Liszt, and more especially of his *Episodes from Lenau's Faust* (1860) and *Totentanz* (1865) about 1866, that first opened the ears of Russian musicians to the resources of modern harmony. Even then Mussorgsky continued, like a Dargomïzhsky of genius, to pick out bold, new, crude but curiously "right" harmonies at the piano (e.g., the chords in the duma-scene of *Boris* where Shuisky says, "I sought a chink and peered through"), and Borodin, following Glinka's hint, went on exploiting whole-tone basses (e.g., the B minor Symphony (1877) and his song, "The False Note") and the fascination of unresolved seconds (as in "The Sleeping Princess," a song written in 1867). But it was Rimsky-Korsakov, with his penchant for the intellectual, mathematical element in music, who by his synthesis of mildly Lisztian chromaticism and Lisztian methods of symmetrical construction with the harmonic ingenuities of Glinka and Dargomïzhsky produced the most remarkable specimens of coldly fantastic music—and, incidentally, cleared the way for Stravinsky. *Scheherazade*, Tsar Berendey's march in *Snowmaiden*, the witches' sabbath in *Mlada* (1892), the submarine ballet in *Sadko*, most of the Tartar music in *Kitezh* (perf. 1907), almost the whole score of *The Golden Cockerel*, show at its best this interesting method of tickling the ear. The prelude to the *Cockerel* epitomizes the whole system in its most highly developed form: the first part, associated with the Tsaritsa, based almost entirely on the chromatic scale and the minor third; the second, associated with the Astrologer, essentially diatonic (despite the semitonal wrench at each bar) and consisting of alternate 6-4 and 6-3 chords on a bass descending by whole-tones.

Although Russian composers in general have been boldly experimental harmonists—even spinning whole passages, as we have just seen, from mere harmonic curiosities—harmony seldom seems to be an essential part of a Russian composer's original conception. The interaction of melody and harmony so often apparent in the music of the great German masters is comparatively rare in Russian music. The conservatoire-trained Tchaïkovsky is an exception, and occasionally in Glinka and Borodin one finds melody and harmony that seem to have come into being simultaneously, but the bulk of Russian music seems to have been conceived primarily in terms of line and timbre; the harmony is support, spice, sound-padding—but not living tissue.

That is true also of the contrapuntal element in Russian music. Genuine, spontaneous contrapuntal thought seems to be quite foreign to the Russian nature. Russian composers frequently show considerable skill in writing clean, simple, effective secondary parts and in combining and dovetailing themes (e.g., in Borodin's orchestral piece *In Central Asia* (1880) and the finale of the fourth scene of *Sadko*); Rimsky-Korsakov and S. I. Taneev were masters of academic counterpoint but their more deliberately contrapuntal compositions—Korsakov's String Quartet (1875), Sextet (1876), and Third Symphony (1874), and Taneev's chamber music in general—are exceedingly dry. So is most of Tchaïkovsky's contrapuntal writing. Of genuine polyphonic thought there is extraordinarily little.

On the other hand, one finds certain thought-processes quite foreign to Western European music. If the Russian composer is weak at theme-development on Beethovenian lines and generally produces only forced, unnatural imitations of it, he has other resources. Borodin was incapable of harmonically developing a theme as Wagner develops, say, the "Rheingold" cry throughout the *Ring*, but by inserting grace-notes and then broadening them into essential notes—a peculiarly Russian process —he evolved from bars 5–6 (reckoning from the choral entry after the solo) of the chorus of Polovtsian girls in Act II of *Igor* the theme of Konchakovna's cavatina; from that, the melody of Konchak's big aria; and from this in turn the music of Yaroslavna's lament in Act IV. Stravinsky has employed the same method of development in *Les Noces* (1917) and other works.

And Balakirev and Borodin worked out in the eighteen-sixties an entirely new type of monothematic symphonic first movement. In two cases all the essential material is stated in the slow introduction, as in Brahms's rather later First Symphony, while the *allegro* is a sort of constructive analysis of this nucleus: the opening movement of Borodin's First Symphony (completed 1867) preserves the outline of classical sonata-form but ignores its spirit (thematic dualism) and concludes this "constructive analysis" with a final most satisfying coda-synthesis;[1] that of Balakirev's First (begun 1866, though not finished till 1898) ignores even the outline of sonata-form. The first movement of Borodin's Second Symphony, the popular

[1] See the present writer's *Studies in Russian Music* (William Reeves, 1935) for a detailed discussion of this movement with music-type examples.

B minor, has no such pregnant introduction but is completely dominated by the powerful opening subject; the lyrical second subject is merely an unimportant contrasting idea and in the development is promptly hammered into the shape of the principal theme.

The key-schemes of Borodin's symphonies also throw considerable light on the peculiarity of the Russian sense of key-relationship. The First Symphony is in the following keys: (1) E flat, (2) E flat, (3) D–D flat–D, (4) E flat; the scherzo (omitting the introductory chords inserted by Balakirev) and slow movement of the Second each begin a semitone higher than the end of the preceding movement. Rimsky-Korsakov's early "symphonic picture" *Sadko* (1867) is planned thus: D flat— D natural—D flat. And there are numerous similar instances in Balakirev. Such semitonal modulations are not, of course, peculiar to Russian music. They occur in Schubert and Grieg, and Bruckner was very fond of them. But with German composers they are exceptional, definitely romantic devices. With the Russians, modulation to a key a semitone or tone away is as natural as modulation by a fifth or a fourth. As Calvocoressi has pointed out,[1] "in certain scales of Russian folk-music, the second degree plays a part similar to that of the dominant in the major and minor scales."

The Czech school founded by Smetana, though it produced a great deal of delightful music and one really great master, is less remarkable than the Russian. The Czech mind differs much less than the Russian from the German and Italian musical mentalities that we are accustomed to accept as "normal"; even the superficial manifestations of nationalism are less distinctive in Czech music. The reason is obvious. The Czechs were subjected for centuries to Teutonic cultural penetration, as the Russians, Poles and Hungarians never were. Until the eighteen-sixties Russia had been a musical backwater; neither of its capitals possessed even a conservatoire of music. (And the increasing influence of the Petersburg and Moscow Conservatoires in the 'seventies and 'eighties, with their Teutonic methods of teaching composition, coincided with the decline of intense national feeling and the decay of specifically Russian trends of musical thought.) Bohemia has, ever since Mozart's day, and

[1] Article on Balakirev in *The Musical Quarterly* (January, 1937).

before, been in the main stream of European music, and Berlioz considered the Prague Conservatoire second only to that of Paris. The very musicality of the people who had already adopted the airs of *Figaro* as popular songs when Mozart came to Prague to produce *Don Giovanni*, was a menace to the purity and homogeneity of their national music.

But although Czech folk-music is less intensely national than that of Russia and some other countries, and bears many traces of German and even Hungarian gypsy influences, its individuality is still quite clearly marked; that of Slovak music still more so. And the Hussite melodies preserved from the fifteenth century are an entirely peculiar type of chant or *Choral*. But it is characteristic of Czech popular music that its most distinctive dance-measure, the polka, is a comparatively modern invention, little more than a hundred years old. Smetana and Dvořák, in so far as they built on a basis of national music at all, derive from a comparatively modern "popular music," more akin to the German *Volkslieder* of Silcher and Zuccalmaglio and the Hungarian melodies of Kéler-Béla than to the ancient and comparatively unspoiled folk-melodies of Russia, many of which date back (on the evidence of the words) to the old pagan times. And the nationality of their music in general manifests itself not in strange, un-Western modes of thought, but in the naïve spontaneity of melody, the simplicity and naturalness of harmony, the slightly facile technique, one would expect of gifted members of a nation of *Musikanten*.[1]

Smetana's nationalism, moreover, was from the first modified by foreign influences, notably that of Liszt; there are even traces of Auber and Donizetti. In his early Piano Trio (1855) there are rhythms and turns of phrase (see, for instance, bars 5–9 of the first *alternativo* of the second movement) closely akin to those which in Dvořák have been supposed to be of negro origin, and which we may therefore conclude to be genuine Czech traits. But the three symphonic poems, *Richard III*, *Wallenstein's Camp* and *Hakon Jarl* (1858–61), are Czech neither in subject nor in

[1] The German word *Musikant* is untranslatable. Generally used contemptuously, it indicates the village fiddler, the leader of the café band and their kind—men who usually have the essential stuff of music in their very blood but possess little or no musical culture. Schubert and Mahler both sprang from this fertile soil.

musical substance, and though Smetana might easily have introduced Czech folk-tunes in *Wallenstein*, he did not do so. Indeed the deliberate use or imitation of folk-music seems to have been distasteful to him. The use of actual folk-tunes for the opening chorus and furiant in *The Bartered Bride* (1866) and the second of the three lullabies in *The Kiss* (1876) is quite exceptional, though a celebrated Hussite chant, "Ktož jsú Boží bojovníci," is introduced for historical purposes in the opera *Libuše* (1872) and the symphonic poems *Tábor* (1875) and *Blaník* (1878)—and in Dvořák's *Husitská* overture (1883). The ten *Czech Dances* for piano (1878) are Smetana's only "arrangements" of folk-music. According to his biographer, Zdeněk Nejedlý, "local colour was not enough for Smetana, either from the national point of view—for nationality was to him something more than a mere ethnographical curiosity—or from the artistic, for this pastime of reproducing local colour was irreconcilable with the sincerity of his æsthetic feeling. He never, as he said, 'counterfeited' the art of the people. He held that national character was manifested not in outward show but in the thought and substance of a work."

Yet much of the charm of his mature work, from *The Bartered Bride* onward, lies in its faint flavour of popular song. Presumably Smetana, like Mussorgsky and Borodin, caught something of the accent of folk-song naturally and without any conscious effort, though he certainly never caught it as thoroughly as they did. Nevertheless, it is significant that he was frequently accused in his lifetime of being insufficiently Czech.

His disciple, Dvořák, a far more imaginative musician and far more resourceful technician, was probably just as much and just as little a nationalist as Smetana. (Even the popular *Slavonic Dances* (1878 and 1886) are not based on actual folk-themes.) Curiously enough he is nearest to Smetana in his latest and better known works, the Fourth and Fifth Symphonies (1889 and 1893), the *Carnival* Overture (1891), the F major String Quartet (1893) and still more in the five symphonic poems, *The Water Sprite*, *The Golden Spinning Wheel*, *The Noonday Witch*, *The Little Dove* and *Heroic Song*, than in the so-called First, Second and Third Symphonies (1880, 1885 and 1875),[1] which

[1] The numbering of Dvořák's symphonies is very misleading chronologically.

are marked by far more genuinely symphonic thought than anything of Smetana's.[1] The loose structure, the transparent texture, the general naïveté and delightful tunefulness of the later Dvořák are strikingly akin to Smetana. But the only striking melodic traits common to both and also occasionally found in Czech folk-music are the little "knight's move" motives, pentatonic in flavour, noticeable in the opening bars of the *Bartered Bride* overture: cf. the chief theme of Smetana's *Vyšehrad* (1874), Martinka's song in Act I, Scene 7, of *The Kiss*, the opening of the slow movement of Dvořák's Second Symphony, the alleged "Swing low, sweet chariot" flute tune in the *New World*,[2] the opening theme of the finale of the same symphony, and many other examples. But they are also common enough in the music of other countries and composers! The Czech equivalent of the fundamental Russian-ness of Mussorgsky appeared only with the advent of Leoš Janáček in the early twentieth century, though even Janáček's most popular opera, *Jenůfa*, does not contain a single actual folk-tune.

The highest common factor in Scandinavian music is even more difficult to determine than the same quantity in Czech music. Debussy's famous impression of Grieg's pieces for strings—"the delightful taste of a pink sweet filled with snow" —defines not unfairly the nature of a great deal of Scandinavian music. And this quality, the musical equivalent of sweetness, of delicate pastel shades, and of romantic nostalgia, is the only musical quality one can isolate as peculiarly Scandinavian. (It

---

[1] The only trace of intellectuality in Smetana is his skill in Lisztian transmogrification of themes. The most remarkable example of this is the opera *Dalibor* (1868), the music of which is so exclusively developed from the leitmotive of the hero himself that there is some ground for the claim that the opera is "monothematic." Lisztian, too, are the numerous orchestral passages in thirds.

[2] No doubt Dvořák's undeniable interest in negro music was due to such superficial affinities with Czech music. Compare also the second bar of the Czech folk-song, "Pod tím naším okenečkem":

with a familiar theme in the *New World* Symphony and with the third bar of "Swing low, sweet chariot."

is apparent also in the work of certain Scandinavian writers: for instance, the Danish poet-novelist Jens Peter Jacobsen.) The "hardy Nordic" strain is curiously unobtrusive. The harsh intellectual virility of Ibsen is matched by Sibelius and by Sibelius almost alone, though Grieg's G minor Ballade for piano (1875) does show that the Norwegian master was not solely a manufacturer of sweetmeats.

Nor is it possible to speak of a Scandinavian, or even a Norwegian, "school" as one speaks of "the Russian nationalists" or "the Smetana-Dvořák-Suk tradition" in Czechoslovakia. When in the eighteen-sixties Grieg and Nordraak revolted against the Mendelssohnism of Gade "and enthusiastically struck out in the new direction now followed by the Nordic school" (as Grieg put it), it appeared as if a "movement" had begun. But Nordraak, the potential leader through whom Grieg had "learned to know both Nordic folk-music and my own nature," died in 1866 at twenty-four, and Grieg, left alone, was not the man to lead an artistic movement or form the centre of a school.

His slightly older contemporary, Svendsen, was completely cosmopolitan. Except his four Norwegian Rhapsodies (c. 1880) and a number of orchestral arrangements of Norwegian, Swedish and Icelandic folk-songs, Svendsen's music is as completely lacking in national colour as Anton Rubinstein's ponderous imitations of Mendelssohn are in Russian-ness. One recognizes in it the characteristic Scandinavian sweetness; some of it is coloured in pastel shades akin to Grieg's. But other elements took the place of native folk-music in forming Svendsen's musical style; Wagnerism and French influences are even more apparent in it than the influence of Liszt and Schumann in Grieg's.

As a nationalist in the more superficial sense, Grieg stands midway between the Czechs and the Russians. His numerous transcriptions of Norwegian melodies, from the early set for piano, Op. 17 (1870), to the Symphonic Dances of 1898 and the seventeen Slåtter for piano, Op. 72, of 1902, are generally models of what folk-song arrangements ought to be. And his own personal melodic style seems to be rather more saturated with the folk-idiom than Smetana's, for instance, is. But the structural and other peculiarities of his music seem to be quite personal; there is nothing in it but the already mentioned "pink sweetness" that one can fasten on as a specifically Scandinavian quality.

Technically Grieg was far from being the equal of Smetana, much less of Dvořák or Borodin or Tchaïkovsky. The youthful *Autumn* overture (1866; re-orchestrated 1887) is spoiled by the dullness of the academic, thoroughly Teutonic working-out; the Piano Concerto (1868; drastically revised 1906–7) and the sonatas are essentially salon music put under a microscope—and the last of the sonatas, the C minor for violin and piano (1887), "just one damned tune after another," is structurally the most feeble of all; even the *Symphonic Dances*, fine as they are, are a long way from being genuinely symphonic. (The G minor Ballade evades architectural problems through the loophole of variations.) Recognizing his weakness, Grieg preferred to work in the smaller forms, the song and the short piano-piece.

Yet he is far from being a perfect miniaturist. The great miniaturist must be a magnificent craftsman, making every bar tell, never using a note too many, making the most of the medium in which he works. And Grieg is not. His workmanship is usually neat, but he drops so easily into conventional figures, particularly in his song-accompaniments. His little piano-pieces have nothing of the epigrammatic quality of Skryabin's. The perfecting finality of Chopin's "last lines" bears comparison with the best of Heine or any of the great sonnet-writers; Grieg seldom achieves anything better than the mildly happy after-thoughts of the songs "Sunset," Op. 9, No. 3, and "First Meeting," Op. 21, No. 1. In most of the later songs he is content simply to finish when he has said what he has to say, a somewhat negative virtue. Nor are these little piano-pieces particularly pianistic; those that are are trivial and school-girlish, while the best of them, things like the *Peasant's Song*, Op. 65, No. 2, *Evening in the Mountains*, Op. 68, No. 4, and the *Cradle Song* that follows it, seem to be piano music only by accident.

The most serious of all Grieg's weaknesses is his inability to conceive more than two bars of music at a time. Even when he gushes—consider the 'cello melody of the first movement of the Piano Concerto—he cannot sustain the melodic flow. A melody as long-breathed as that of the setting of Hans Andersen's "Hytten," Op. 18, No. 7, is quite exceptional with him. Harmonically, of course, he is more interesting. Broadly speaking, his chromatic harmony is an individual twig of the Wagnerian tree, a demonstration that Wagner's harmony could be employed in the charming salon-piece as well as in heroic and passionate drama. Frankly impressionistic experiments as bold as the *Klokkeklang* for piano, Op. 54, No. 6, with its clashing of opposed fifths (dating from 1891) are rare with him, and most of his once novel chords (e.g., the chords of the ninth and eleventh and the tonic sevenths and ninths which he exploited *ad nauseum*) sound over-sweet to modern ears. Broadly speaking, Grieg's poetic harmony, despite its influence on Delius and one or two other composers, is as peculiar to himself as his melodic style and has added little to the common stock of musical resource.

II. BRAHMS AND THE GREAT INSTRUMENTAL TRADITION

Just as the literary-romantic movement in the music of the 'thirties and 'forties came to its full flower in Wagner, the half-romantic neo-classicism of Mendelssohn and the later Schumann reached its full maturity only with Brahms. Contemporary partisanship and the dramatic sense of musical historians have combined to set these two great figures in strong contrast, and certainly their music has little in common. (The coda of the slow movement of Brahms's F minor Piano Sonata (comp. 1853) and Sachs's "Dem Vogel, der heut sang" in Act II, Scene 3, of *Die Meistersinger* are almost the only points where they touch.) Admittedly Wagner thought little of Brahms's compositions, but Brahms was always deeply interested in Wagner and repeatedly expressed admiration of his music. Brahms did not admire Liszt. (And Liszt in turn thought Brahms inferior in imagination to Raff!) But even his dislike of Liszt's music seems to have been based not on Liszt's abandonment of "absolute" music, his modernity, or any of the outward symbols of musical thought that were disputed about in those days, but on the very essence of his music, the fact that it seemed to pay so much attention to outward effect and so little to inner feeling. Brahms demanded "soul" and depth of feeling in music and had comparatively little use for fire, brilliance and surface emotionalism; he had little love of sound, even lovely sound, for sound's sake. In these respects his influence was perhaps actually harmful, especially to his English admirers. (It is not altogether a coincidence that the true English Brahmins were eclipsed by a composer—Elgar—who combined a deep admiration for Brahms with a pronounced strain of Lisztian emotionalism.)

Above all, Brahms demanded solidity, particularly solidity of workmanship. And however unjust may be the still widely held view that Liszt's music is empty and superficial, it is undeniable that as a technician and as a thinker-in-sound he was a child by comparison with Brahms. His wall-paper pattern method of construction is often irritating even to those who delight in the richness, pregnancy and vital fire of the separate particles of his music; to Brahms it probably seemed merely pitiable. Whereas Liszt and Berlioz, and even to some extent Schumann and Wagner in their different ways, brought extremely active minds to bear *on* music—as it were *from outside*—Brahms, like Bach and Haydn and Mozart and Beethoven, did practically all his thinking *in* music, in terms of sound only. Hence the complexity, the satisfying richness of his texture. Hence, too, his comparative conservatism; he was content, broadly speaking (though not nearly so content as hostile critics used to assert), to think in the accepted forms and idiom of the day, though he thought in them with powerful individuality; but his mind was not of that restless, speculative cast which sets a composer consciously worrying about new possibilities and new forms.

Brahms, then, was essentially a throwback to the Beethovenian or pre-Beethovenian type of non-literary composer. But if his music is non-literary it is by no means "absolute," any more than a good deal of Bach or Haydn or Beethoven is "absolute" music. It is well known that the first two movements of the D minor Piano Concerto (1859) are remnants of a Sonata for Two Pianos (1854) which nearly became not a concerto but a symphony. And Kalbeck learned from Dietrich and Joachim that the opening theme of the first movement was suggested by Schumann's attempt to commit suicide by throwing himself into the Rhine and that the melody of the second movement, "a slow scherzo in sarabande tempo," was that which we now know as the theme of the funeral march in *Ein Deutsches Requiem* (1868). We know, too, from a letter from Brahms to Clara Schumann (December 30th, 1856), that the *adagio*, which bore the inscription "Benedictus qui venit in nomine Domini," is a "portrait" of Clara. The composer of a projected symphony with that content and of the C minor Piano Quartet (1875, though sketched out twenty years earlier), of which he said himself that it was "a sort of illustration to the last chapter of the man in the blue dress-coat and the yellow waistcoat" (i.e., Goethe's Werther),[1] could have had no deep-rooted objection to programme music as such or to subjective expression in music.

Historically Brahms's position as the heir of Mendelssohn and Schumann is too obvious to be disputed; much more obvious than his heirship to Beethoven. The influence of Mendelssohn is the less important of the two, but it is obvious enough, from the finale of the C major Sonata, written in 1853 (the A minor subject in 6-8 time), to the slow movement of the First Symphony (1876), essentially a glorification of the nocturne in Mendelssohn's *Midsummer Night's Dream* music and the slow movement of the G minor Piano Concerto. But if Brahms is only mildly Mendelssohnian, he is profoundly Schumannesque.[2] (Granted that he gives us super-Schumann and super-Mendelssohn.) Schumannesque in both feeling and actual musical material; Schumannesque in his love of syncopation, Schumannesque alike in his piano-writing—the writing of a virtuoso Schumann—and in the pianistic feeling of his orchestral music and even sometimes of his chamber music, though in Brahms's case this is true of the general texture rather than of the ideas themselves. It is no mere accident that the D minor Piano Concerto and the great Piano Quintet in F minor (1864) were for a time conceived, and the latter actually published, as sonatas for two pianos; even the *Variations on a Theme by Haydn* (1873) were issued simultaneously in versions for piano

[1] Letter to Billroth (October 23rd, 1874). He had already indicated the "suicidal" nature of the first movement to Deiters in 1868. Compare also the letter to the publisher Simrock of August 12th, 1875: "You might put a portrait on the title-page! A head with a pistol in front of it. Now you'll have some idea of the music. I will send you my photograph for that purpose! Can you also have a blue dress-coat, yellow pantaloons and topboots, as you seem to like colour-printing?" Brahms's relation to Clara Schumann had been tragically like that of Werther to Lotte.

[2] All the more remarkable in that until the autumn of 1853, when he had already written the C major and F sharp minor Piano Sonatas, the Scherzo, Op. 4, and a number of songs (including the well-known "Liebestreu"), Brahms knew practically nothing of Schumann's music—and, incidentally, nothing at all of Chopin's.

duet and for orchestra—and, according to Orel,[1] the piano version was the original despite the fact that Brahms had had an orchestral version in mind from the first. But for that matter, it is well known that Brahms cast even the symphonies in the form of duets for two pianos, though naturally bearing orchestral possibilities in mind, before scoring them.

Brahms's thick, careful, unenterprising orchestration also apparently perpetuates a bad Schumannesque tradition. But there is this difference between Brahms's scoring and Schumann's: that Mahler was able to touch up, almost to rescore, Schumann's *Rhenish* Symphony and make it sound much better without injuring its nature, while it is obvious that to "improve" Brahms's scoring would be to destroy the very essence of his music. Schumann's thickness is the result of incomplete grasp of orchestral balance and so on, lack of self-confidence leading to a continual playing for safety; Brahms's thickness is deliberate, part and parcel of his polyphonic musical thinking and the perfect counterpart of his emotional gravity. Brahms deliberately disregarded all that had been done by Weber, Berlioz, Liszt, and Wagner to develop what we may call the romantic orchestra, went back to the old Viennese masters, and slowly and painfully through the two Serenades, Opp. 11 and 16 (written in 1859), the D minor Concerto, the *Ave Maria* (published in 1861), the unpublished symphonies that preceded "No. 1 in C minor," the *Deutsches Requiem* and the *Haydn Variations* evolved an orchestral style entirely his own and perfectly adapted to his needs. This style, which Riemann has happily styled "Gothic instrumentation," is in some respects an elaboration of a chamber style, a super-chamber medium called into existence for the expression of ideas too broad and powerful for actual chamber music. Technically it is, as Geiringer puts it,[2] "fundamentally an intensification of the 'openwork' (*durchbrochene Arbeit*) of the Viennese classical school. The motives and themes wander continually from one instrument to another; long-drawn-out melodies are divided among the various instruments, so that the lead is continually changing from one section of the orchestra to

---

[1] Article, "Skizzen zu Brahms' Haydn Variationen," in the *Zeitschrift für Musikwissenschaft*, 1923.

[2] Karl Geiringer: *Brahms, his Life and Work* (translated by H. B. Weiner and Bernard Miall). Allen and Unwin, 1936.

another." Brahms's orchestra rarely sounds "beautiful" in the ordinary sense of the word, except as almost everything not deliberately ugly must sound more or less beautiful on such a lovely instrument as the full orchestra, but like Hardy's "haggard Egdon," it appeals "to a subtler and scarcer instinct, to a more recently learnt emotion, than that which responds to the sort of beauty called charming and fair." And, *mutatis mutandis*, the same is true of the sonorous layout even of Brahms's chamber-music. His two String Quartets, Op. 51 (1873) are far less beautiful in sound than Borodin's exquisitely euphonious Quartets in A and D (1879 and 1885); yet in the long run one's ear tires of the sheer loveliness of Borodin's perfect quartet-writing, particularly in the Second Quartet, quicker than of Brahms's harsh asceticism.

The one orchestral instrument that does seem to have fired Brahms's imagination for its own sake and colour was the horn. The wonderful horn solo leading to the coda of the first movement of the Second Symphony (1877), the opening theme of the Second Piano Concerto (1881) and the horn-writing in the seventh of the *Haydn Variations* were obviously inspired by the timbre of the instrument, while the material of the Horn Trio of 1868 is almost entirely controlled by it (notwithstanding which, Brahms cheerfully acquiesced in the replacement of the horn by a viola). It was only towards the end of his life, when he came under the spell of the marvellous clarinet playing of Mühlfeld, of the Meiningen Orchestra, that Brahms was inspired to the same degree by another instrument and produced the superb Clarinet Quintet (1891) and the two Clarinet Sonatas (1894). Despite the intimacy of the two men, even the magic of Joachim's fiddle and his freely given technical advice failed to draw from Brahms, even in the Violin Concerto (1878), anything as thoroughly violinistic as these works are clarinetish. Nevertheless, a great deal of the effect of Brahms's orchestra comes from the "bite" of his string-writing.

One other peculiarity of Brahms's orchestration is worth noticing: his ability to make his wind sound, not like an organ, but as that least musical of instruments would sound if it had any genuine power of expression (cf. in particular the slow movement of the Third Symphony (1883) and the eighth of the *Haydn Variations*). The effect is produced not by the unpleasant "organ

registration" scoring of actual organists such as Bruckner and
Franck, which is merely bad orchestration and does not even
sound like an organ, but by skilful disposition of his instruments.
Schumann does the same thing by different technical means in
the *adagio* of the *Rhenish* Symphony.

Brahms was also the successor of Schumann in the modern
use of the very old device of theme-transformation to bind
together the separate movements of large-scale works.[1] He
makes no experiments on the lines of Schumann's D minor
Symphony, but rests content with the conventional four movements. He seldom makes obvious quotations from one movement
to another—the finales of the Clarinet Quintet and of the String
Quartet in B flat (1875), which both weave first-movement
themes into their concluding variations, are exceptional—and it
is only in his earliest piano sonatas (and, exceptionally, in the
allegretto of the Second Symphony) that we find him indulging
in obvious theme-transformation *à la* Liszt: basing the finale of
Op. 1 on a rhythmical transformation of the opening theme of the
first movement and the scherzo of Op. 2 on the theme of
the preceding *andante*. Already in the third Sonata, Op. 5, the
thematic allusions are subtler and more organic; so subtle, in
fact, that they are generally missed altogether. The "Rückblick" intermezzo is always spoken of as "looking back to the
theme of the *andante*," but, as Edwin Evans, Senior, has pointed
out,[2] it actually looks back not only to this particular theme but
in bars 5–7 to the trio of the scherzo, in bars 12–13 to the final
cadence of the first movement, and in bars 20–21 to bar 56 of the
andante. Again, the finale alludes at bars 3–4 to the scherzo, at
bars 6–7 to the trio, at bars 151–52 to the *andante* (bars 5–8 of the
poco più lento), and in the following four bars to bars 92–93 of
the *andante*, while the theme at bars 40–43 of the finale is a sort
of counterpart of the theme at bars 146–49 of the first movement.

[1] See, for instance, many "pavanes and galliards," Schein's *Banchetto
Musicale* (1617), innumerable keyboard suites by Kuhnau, Handel and
their less familiar contemporaries, Pergolesi's Fourth Clavier Sonata, to
say nothing of Schubert's *Wanderer* Fantasia.

[2] *Handbook to the Pianoforte Works of Johannes Brahms*: William
Reeves, N.D. This book and its three predecessors—handbooks to
the *Vocal Works* and *Chamber and Orchestral Works* (first and second
series)—contain the most detailed technical analyses of Brahms's
music available in English.

The movements of the B major Trio, Op. 8, are linked in the same subtle way by reference to a single basic theme never stated in its simplest form.

In the mature Brahms this subtle allusiveness is carried very far, so far indeed that it becomes difficult to assert that it was deliberate at all and not the spontaneous, unconscious result of a single creative mood. That the chromatically descending thirds in the wind at the opening of the *sostenuto* introduction to the First Symphony, which contains the germs of the whole of the thematic material of the ensuing *allegro*, are a deliberate motto-theme can hardly be doubted; they are clearly quoted at bar 5 of the *andante sostenuto* and in the opening of the finale. (Though we may not agree with Kalbeck in calling them a "fate" motive.) But what are we to say to the theories that the clarinet melody of the *poco allegretto* springs from the second subject, the oboe melody, of the *andante*; that the majority of the themes of the Second Symphony are deliberately linked by the semitonal drop and rise of the very first bar, a feature common to so many of them—but also to themes in other of Brahms's works (for instance, the finale of the Third Symphony and the third movement of the F major 'Cello Sonata)? Dr. Colles[1] wisely "questions whether its recurrence in the finale" (of the Second Symphony) "is devised at all." But, deliberate or spontaneous, its subtle binding effect is undeniable.[2]

Even now we have not come to an end of Brahms's indebtedness to Schumann and his then far surpassing him in skill and subtlety. To discuss adequately his innumerable modifications of conventional sonata-form, most of them elaborations of hints from Schumann and Mendelssohn, if not from Beethoven,

[1] *Oxford History of Music*, Vol. VII ("Symphony and Drama," 1850–1900).

[2] Edwin Evans, Senior, has also pointed out that the *grazioso* violin theme of the third movement of the Fourth Symphony (1885) (p. 84 of the Eulenburg miniature score) is a variant of the striking *marcato* subject first stated by wind and horns in the first movement, and that the continuation of the *grazioso* subject also quotes, in the second violin and viola parts, the opening theme of the first movement. Even more important is his observation that not only is the finale of the Symphony a passacaglia but the passacaglia spirit pervades the whole work, particularly the first movement. He also shows that the principal subjects of the first movement, the *andante* and the passacaglia can all three be combined in perfectly satisfactory counterpoint.

would require a monograph dealing with the whole range of his chamber music. But one other point may be dealt with briefly here: the element of stanza-like construction in Brahms's themes. We have already noticed this in very obvious forms in Schumann's instrumental music; it is also generally present, though much less obvious, in Brahms's—though it was probably due here to another reason than admiration for Schumann or even the direct influence of folk-melody, which is inevitably stanza-like in structure.

Kalbeck is probably right when he suggests that it is often due to the direct influence of verse, as seems to have been the case with Schumann himself. In one of Brahms's note-books the poem by C. O. Sternau, "Junge Liebe," of which the first five lines are prefixed to the *andante* of the F minor Piano Sonata, is immediately followed by some more verses, "Bitte," by the same poet. The first stanza is as follows:

"O wüsstest du, wie bald, wie bald
Die Bäume welk und kahl der Wald,
Du wärst so kalt und lieblos nicht
Und sähst mir freundlich ins Gesicht!"

Can it be a mere coincidence that these words, as well as their mood and content, exactly fit the melody of the "Rückblick" in the same sonata? And Kalbeck also surmises that "possibly, indeed most probably, the anapæstic swing" of the great tune of the finale of the First Symphony "is based on some equally stirring poem." That is certainly more probable than that the opening theme of the finale of the G major Violin Sonata (1879) should have been directly inspired by Klaus Groth's "Walle, Regen, walle nieder," as we know from the song "Regenlied," Op. 59, No. 3, it actually was. Brahms himself told Dietrich that the 6-8 theme in the finale of Op. 1 was suggested by Herder's version of "My heart's in the Highlands" ("Mein Herz ist in Hochland'"—for Schumann's setting as a song, see his Op. 25, No. 13); the melody fits the complete stanza. And in two other well-known cases Brahms frankly admitted his indebtedness to Herder's translations[1] in the published music: the Ballade, Op. 10, No. 1 (on the Scottish ballad,

[1] The great collection of *Stimmen der Völker in Liedern* which he discovered in 1854. "Next to the Bible," says Kalbeck, "it was one of his favourite books and again and again excited him to composition."

"Edward"), and the Intermezzo, Op. 117, No. 1 (on "Lady Anne Bothwell's Lament"); and as the second of these dates from Brahms's last years—it appears to have been composed about 1890—we may take it that Brahms was indebted to the direct verbal inspiration of poetry in his instrumental works throughout his life. In both these cases the imprint of the words is very obvious. The first three bars of Op. 10, No. 1, exactly fit "Dein Schwert, wie ist's von Blut so roth? Edward, Edward!", the five bars of *poco più mosso*, Edward's reply, "O ich hab' geschlagen meinem Geier todt" (one-bar interlude) "Mutter, Mutter!"; the first four bars of Op. 117, No. 1, are obviously a setting of the two lines prefixed to the piece,[1] and although the *piu adagio* appears to be very far removed from verse-melody it is actually, as Edwin Evans, Senior, shows, a simple variation of a melody that both fits and expresses the stanza beginning "Dein Vater als er zu mir trat."

In that last point we have the clue to one of the main differences between Brahms's use of stanzaic melody and Schumann's. Even in the D minor Ballade the second of Edward's replies is an inversion of the first. Brahms's extraordinary skill in variation-writing, in which he equals Beethoven himself (if he does not actually surpass him), often completely disguises quite simple melodic outlines. And the square strophic origin of his phrases is constantly concealed by rhythmic extensions and overlappings of phrases. The beginning of the D minor Ballade itself gives an early example of Brahms's ingenuity in avoiding those "rhyming" cadences which make Schumann's music so often sound annoyingly square-cut. The first subject of the slow movement of the First Symphony contains several masterly examples of avoidance of the obvious, melodically and metrically: without the interpolation of bars 5, 10–11, etc., the passage would still make sense but it would sound very square and pedestrian. A still finer interpolation occurs at bars 24–25. Both the principal subjects of the *Tragic* Overture (1880) are purely melodic; both cease to be purely melodic just at the points where they might have lapsed into the commonplace. Brahms may be seen at work as a craftsman by comparing the early A minor Sarabande for piano (1855) with the second movement of the String Quintet,

[1] Kalbeck again points out that Op. 117, No. 3, fits the very next song in Herder in exactly the same way: "O weh! O weh, hinab ins Tal."

Op. 88 (1882), where the same music is used, but now with the cadence carefully "darned over."

Brahms shows the same metrical skill in a good many of his songs—the "Sapphische Ode" and "Feldeinsamkeit," to take a couple of very familiar and obvious examples—though naturally the very many songs in which he approximates to, or actually drops into, the *Volkslied* vein are metrically simple and square-cut. And it is noteworthy that, while so many of his instrumental themes are of song-origin, the melodies of his songs are almost invariably "instrumental," in Wagner's sense of the word. They are conceived in terms of the voice; the "Sapphische Ode" is, as Dr. Colles says,[1] "a melody as inseparable from contralto tone as that of the slow movement of the Violin Concerto is from the oboe"; and the melodies would often lose something, occasionally a great deal, if divorced from the words. Nevertheless, the voice is treated first and foremost as an instrument, the words—and Brahms's literary taste was not irreproachable—merely as an occasion for music. Words would give Brahms a melody but, as we have just seen, the melody was quite often self-sufficient; the words could then be thrown away. And in quite a large number of the songs one feels that it would not have mattered seriously if Brahms had thrown away their words, too, treated the melodies a little differently, and used them for instrumental compositions as he actually did with the "Regen-lied" in the G major Violin Sonata and with "Wie Melodien zieht es" in the first movement of the A major. In one cele-brated case, "Wie bist du, meine Königin," it would have been much better if Brahms had actually done so; for, although the melody is one of the loveliest that even he ever wrote, it makes nonsense of both the accentuation and the punctuation of Daumer's verses. There are notable exceptions, of course; the *Vier ernste Gesänge* of 1896 are unthinkable apart from their Scriptural texts. But broadly speaking, although Brahms's songs *qua* music reach greater heights and sound profounder depths than Schumann's, they contain nothing like the exquisite unity of verse and music that we find in, say, the *Dichterliebe*.

But although essentially a lyrical composer, even in his sym-phonic works, Brahms is much less obviously so than either Schumann or Mendelssohn or any of his contemporaries. Neither

[1] *Oxford History of Music*, Vol. VII.

Bruckner, Borodin, Tchaïkovsky, Dvořák nor Franck possessed anything like Beethoven's or Wagner's seemingly endless power of conceiving pregnant germ-themes and developing them symphonically. Bruckner's long-drawn ideas generally lack both the fertility of good themes and the beauty of genuine melodies: take, for instance, the opening subjects of the Second, Seventh and Eighth Symphonies (1873, 1884 and 1892). Borodin certainly got hold of a striking main theme for his E flat Symphony and treated it in an entirely original way,[1] but he does very little with the still more striking subject of his Second Symphony but hammer it home relentlessly. Tchaïkovsky, so fertile in attractive tunes, was completely incapable of writing a true "theme" and apparently never tried to write one till he reached the *Pathétique*, for the first movement of which he hatched the not very striking four-note motive which by no means dominates it. Dvořák created a magnificent theme for the first subject of the *allegro maestoso* of his D minor Symphony (1885) and borrowed another magnificent one from Brahms for the second, and handled them really symphonically, but for the most part he was content to deal in delightful tunes. Franck borrowed from Liszt's *Les Préludes* the striking opening theme of *his* D minor Symphony (1889), but did nothing with it but transform it a little on Lisztian lines, though other ideas do seem to spring naturally out of it (e.g., bar 3, and again the third bar of the *allegro*).

Brahms himself is not remarkable for striking thematic invention, as distinct from melodic invention, and the first movement of the Second Symphony resembles the Franck work in that the "theme"—the three-note motive of the 'cellos and basses—is in itself comparatively unimportant or, at any rate, plays the part of mortar rather than of brick, although practically every *tune* in the movement springs out of it and seems to continue it. The first movement of the First Symphony is certainly evolved from the opening theme—so completely that the movement is almost monothematic—but the theme itself is remarkable for nothing but its possibilities, which no one could suspect. The Fourth has a striking theme but it is treated by variation methods instead of being "developed" in the usual sense of the word. Only in the Third Symphony of Brahms, and here in the magnificent

[1] See page 152.

finale even more than in the first movement, do we meet with genuine "symphonic thinking" at all comparable with that in the Third, Fifth, Seventh and Ninth Symphonies of Beethoven. And what is true of the symphonies in particular is true of the concertos, chamber works and other instrumental compositions in general. Often the opening theme is quite frankly a lyrical melody, as in the *Tragic* Overture, the Violin Concerto, the B flat Piano Concerto and the String Quintet, Op. 88 (1882); sometimes, as in the opening movements of the Piano Quintet (1864), the Piano Trio, Op. 87 (1882), and the D minor Violin Sonata (1888), the essentially melodic nature of the theme is slightly disguised.

The great difference between the symphonic lyricism of Brahms and that of his more naïve contemporaries—Tchaïkovsky and the Dvořák of the Fourth and Fifth Symphonies—is that Brahms was so much more skilful in covering up his tracks. Tchaïkovsky presents his tunes, usually very attractive tunes, comparatively naked, or at any rate, dressed only in brilliant orchestration, counter-melodies and savoury accompanying harmonies, trimmed with rushing scales and the like. Bruckner gravely entangles his Schubert-and-Wagner-and-water melodies in webs of obvious and very organist-like counterpoint and blobs of rather Wagnerian harmony, decked out with baroque, rather crude, orchestration that is not so Wagnerian as we used to think. (But that, it seems, was the fault of the pious disciples who insisted on improving it.) Borodin contrives all sorts of symphonic subtleties, but the very clarity of his texture, the straightforwardness of his racy themes, distracts attention from these subtleties. Franck's tunes are obvious, too, and his post-Lisztian harmonies and organist-like orchestral methods only emphasize their obviousness. But with Brahms the statement of a subject in its simplest form is, in his instrumental music, quite exceptional; even the simplest of the forms in which it actually appears is generally reducible to still lower terms, in other words, is itself a variation. The purely melodic, perhaps even strophic, origin of much of his texture is completely concealed. It is this constant avoidance of the obvious that makes so much of his music profoundly and enduringly satisfying; it never seems to have revealed the last of its secrets.

It is no doubt true also that Brahms's personality was stronger than that of any of his contemporaries except Wagner, that his fine, bracing pessimism is stronger and healthier than Tchaïkovsky's neurotic melancholy or Franck's sentimental mysticism —which is, after all, largely sublimated Gounod: the *molto cantabile* string tune in F major in the first movement of the Symphony (1889) is practically identical with the theme that "expresses the happiness of the blessed" in *Mors et Vita* (1885). But personality alone is of little value in art, or Haydn and Mozart would cut poor figures beside Berlioz and Balakirev. And after all "bracing pessimism" and "sentimental mysticism" really mean "astringent, but essentially diatonic, melody and harmony" and "luscious chromatic melody and harmony," and "musical neurosis" the attempt to squeeze tremendous quantities of emotional expression out of melodies that are really only very attractive, ear-haunting quasi-ballet-tunes. However, we do owe it to some stupendous convulsion of the soul that Tchaïkovsky once, and once only, in the *Pathétique* Symphony, achieved a natural, more or less satisfactory form for his ideas.

In his Fourth and Fifth Symphonies (1878 and 1888), for instance, Tchaïkovsky seems to have cast his first movements in sonata-form only because that was the traditional first movement form, not because the ideas themselves, their treatment, or the emotional sequence demanded that form; they do not demand it and it does not really suit them. And, as Tchaïkovsky himself ruefully admitted, in all his big instrumental works "the seams show" and there is "no organic union between the separate episodes." Brahms, whom Tchaïkovsky despised as an uninspired, academic composer, is almost unrivalled in his ability to conceal his seams, to unite his episodes organically—or, at any rate, even in his off-moments, to give one the impression that he has so united them. (The transition from the development to the recapitulation in the first movement of the Third Symphony is a good example.)

Brahms's command of the technique of composition would alone suffice to make his instrumental architecture more satisfactory than that of his contemporaries. Admittedly his form never springs immediately and spontaneously from the content, the musical ideas as it were generating the form as they unfold; but of that there are few examples in the whole range of music.

Music generally needs some sort of frame—poem, programme, abstract form—as roses need a trellis. Brahms accepted the convention of classical sonata-form, modifying it to suit his personal needs, as he accepted the convention of the classical orchestra and the classical chamber-music combinations, or as a stage-composer, unless he happens to be a Wagner or a Mussorgsky, accepts a certain operatic convention. He was no more hampered by sonata-form than he was hampered by the fact that his orchestra did not allow him to write chords for flutes only or chromatic melodies for the trumpet; his ideas, unlike Tchaïkovsky's, were admirably suited to it. He is never tempted to break through it by an overflowing, spontaneous, lyrical outburst as Dvořák so often is, or by experiments like Borodin's and Franck's.

Even the manner of his theme-quotations from movement to movement distinguishes him sharply from the other symphonists of his period. As we have seen, his quotations are so subtle that, despite their effectiveness as binding agents, we can hardly be sure that they are intentional quotations at all. The motto-theme, programmatic as in Tchaïkovsky's E minor Symphony, or purely musical as in Lalo's G minor (1887), the naïve little fantasia on the themes of the preceding movements which Dvořák inserted near the end of the finale of the *New World*, Franck's and Saint-Saëns's more skilful adaptation of crude Lisztian theme-transformation in each movement (the so-called "cyclic form" of which Franck's Quartet (1889) is perhaps the finest example), and Bruckner's trick of tying up all the threads in the finale and sealing them with a grandiose *Choral* were all equally foreign to Brahms. He attempted neither to expand the symphony by substituting whole groups of themes for single subjects, as Bruckner did, nor to make it more concise by telescoping slow movement and scherzo as in the Franck D minor. It never occurred to him to invent substitutes for the sonata as Franck did in his *Prélude, choral et fugue* (1884) and *Prélude, aria et final* (1887).

So, great figure as he is, Brahms contributed little to the historical development of music, almost as little as Bach or Handel. He did not enlarge the harmonic language—though he did show musicians, at a time when chromaticism was gaining ground rapidly, that there were still new things to be done with the old diatonic idiom. Tchaïkovsky left his mark on Rakhmaninov and Arensky, Dvořák on Suk and Novák—and Coleridge-Taylor; Franck's methods and ideas were taken up and developed by d'Indy, Chausson, Lekeu and Roussel; and Saint-Saëns, through his best pupil, Fauré, may be considered the grandparent of a school that includes such distinguished musicians as Ravel, Roger-Ducasse, Koechlin and Florent Schmitt. Even Bruckner's influence is traceable in Mahler. But Brahms stands practically alone. The Herzogenbergs, Grädeners and the rest who came under his influence all seem to have been nonentities. Only the young Reger and the Hungarian Dohnányi really owe much to him. It is true that Brahmsian influences are perceptible here and there in Dvořák, in the early works of Richard Strauss, e.g., the F minor Symphony and C minor Piano Quartet (comp. 1883–84), in some of Mahler's songs, e.g., the third of the *Lieder eines fahrenden Gesellen* (comp. 1884), and even for a short period in Schönberg (the *Kammersinfonie*, Second String Quartet, and the *Klavierstücke*, Op. 11), yet neither the mature Strauss nor the mature Mahler owes anything whatever to Brahms, and Dvořák and Schönberg are essentially poles apart from him. But something of his spirit and technique was caught by Parry and anglicized in much the same way that Sterndale Bennett had anglicized the idyllic vein in Mendelssohn. *Blest Pair of Sirens* (1887) and Job's "Man that is born of woman" in Parry's *Job* (1892) are outstanding among the few pieces of pseudo-Brahmsian music of which Brahms himself need not have been ashamed.

III. THE PROGRESS OF NON-WAGNERIAN OPERA

Notwithstanding that various other composers—Weber, Meyerbeer, Verdi, Glinka—had challenged the tyranny of the operatic set-number and experimented with the leitmotive, at any rate for dramatic purposes, the appearance of leitmotives or mild attempts at continuity of texture in any new opera in the eighteen-sixties and 'seventies inevitably resulted in its being condemned as "Wagnerian." Actually Wagner's influence, both that of his music itself and that of his theories, was extremely slow in making any real impression on the opera of the time;[1] his theories, in particular, were misunderstood by his friends almost as completely as by his enemies. (They are probably very imperfectly understood by the majority of people to this day.) Even so it seems incredible that such operas as Bizet's *Pêcheurs de perles* (1863), *Djamileh* (1872), to say nothing of *Carmen* (1875), and Saint-Saëns's *La Princesse jaune* (1872) could ever have been considered Wagnerian. Or that Bizet himself could have written of Verdi's *Don Carlo*, "Verdi is no longer Italian; he wants to play the Wagner."[2] The word "Wagnerian" seems to have been generally employed simply as a term of abuse for anything new, unorthodox or unpleasant in the music of the day.

Actually by far the most popular operatic model in the eighteen-sixties was not Wagner but Meyerbeer. His direct musical influence is obvious in Verdi's operas of this period, in Gounod and Bizet, in Saint-Saëns's operas of the following decade, and in the *Judith* (1863) and *Rogneda* (1865) of Serov, the avowed champion of Wagner in Russia and the most popular Russian opera-composer of the 'sixties. Apart from specifically musical influence, moreover, the average opera of the period kept in essentials—relative importance of voice and orchestra, compromise between set-numbers and continuous texture and so on—very close to the model of *Le Prophète* and a long way from the model of *Lohengrin*.

The operas of Tchaïkovsky, for instance, from *The Oprichnik* (1874) to *The Queen of Spades* (1890), conform to operatic conventions hardly distinguishable from those of Meyerbeer and his French disciples (above all, Bizet) or of middle-period Verdi, and are as absolutely uninfluenced by Wagner's theories as by those of Dargomïzhsky and Mussorgsky. Tchaïkovsky concisely expressed his view of the æsthetics of opera in a diary-entry dated July 13th, 1888: "I have never come in contact with anything more antipathetic and false than this unsuccessful attempt to drag truth into this sphere of art, in which every-

---

[1] In the last century musical influences penetrated much more slowly than they do to-day. As we have seen, Brahms knew nothing of Schumann and Chopin, till 1853, and it is probable, says Toye, that Verdi had *heard* nothing of Wagner's—though no doubt he had seen his scores—till 1865.

[2] Letter to Paul Lacombe (March 11th, 1867).

thing is based upon falsehood, and 'truth,' in the everyday sense of the word, is not required at all." As for Wagner, he considered him a symphonist by nature; as an operatic composer, "paralysed by theories."[1] "In his efforts to attain *reality, truth* and *rationalism*, he lets *music* slip out of sight. . . . Not a single broad, rounded melody . . . The singer has always to pursue the orchestra; his note is of no more importance in the score than some note for the fourth horn." He admired Wagner's mastery of the orchestra but thought it "too symphonic, too overloaded and heavy for vocal music."[2]

Tchaïkovsky's best opera, *Eugene Onegin* (1879), is a fine example of dramatic lyricism. Always subjective in tendency, Tchaïkovsky seems to identify himself with each of the protagonists in turn, with Onegin, with Tatyana and with Lensky, and writes for them melodies full of subjective feeling and therefore emotionally "true," though this truth is very different from that aimed at by Dargomïzhsky. Leitmotives are used sparingly; the set-numbers, though retained, are joined; and the orchestra, though subordinated to the voices as long as the latter really have to sing, is handled interestingly—almost symphonically—in the patches of recitative. In one passage, after Tatyana's entrance after the *écossaise* in the first scene of Act III (hailed by the chorus with conventional, dramatically "false" cries), Tchaïkovsky uses a device particularly beloved of Puccini: recitative dialogue against a lightly scored melodic background in the orchestra—a sort of pretty bastard of Wagnerism.

In Tchaïkovsky's second most successful opera, *The Queen of Spades*, similar methods are applied, though subjective feeling is carried so far in the musical interpretation of Hermann's character that he is no longer recognizable as the hero of Pushkin's story. And although the orchestral writing is more symphonic than in *Onegin*, the opera is dramatically more conventional than that work. Tchaïkovsky's archaizing tendency, which had shown itself in Triquet's couplets in Act II of *Onegin*, is carried much further in the pastoral interlude "The Faithful Shepherdess" and the old Countess's song from Grétry's *Richard Cœur de Lion* interpolated in Act II of *The Queen of Spades*.

Of more historical interest than Tchaïkovsky's operas are his

[1] Letter to Mme. von Meck (November 26th, 1877).
[2] Letter to Mme. von Meck (May 5th, 1879).

ballets: *Swan Lake* (1877), *The Sleeping Beauty* (1890) and *Nutcracker* (1892). These, and more especially the two latter, really mark the beginning of a new genre: the symphonic ballet. Just as Tchaïkovsky's symphonic themes are often open to the accusation of being glorified ballet music, much of his ballet music is as rich in texture as his symphonic music (see, for instance, the passage in Act I of *The Sleeping Beauty*, just before the famous waltz, in which the four princes entreat the king).

Mussorgsky's blend of Dargomïzhskian "truth" with more lyrical, mainly folk-songish, elements produced one undeniable masterpiece in *Boris*—mainly because the composer happened to be a strikingly individual musical genius.[1] But the very original operatic convention he evolved is, after all, a hybrid and possibly owes more than is generally thought to hearsay about Wagner. And his two later, uncompleted operas, *Khovanshchina* and *The Fair of Sorochintsy*, show a much stronger lyrical tendency than *Boris*. Mussorgsky always used leitmotives sparingly, and purely for dramatic ends. But the main differences between the Mussorgskian and the Wagnerian music-drama are in the treatment of the orchestra (Mussorgsky never uses it symphonically, however interesting or important its share in the texture) and in the declamation (with Mussorgsky the equivalent of natural speech, whereas Wagner's is the equivalent of elevated, poetic speech).

As for the other Russian opera-composers, Borodin contented himself in *Igor* with the outworn conventions of the set-number, while Rimsky-Korsakov steered a singularly erratic course, beginning with a half-lyrical, half-Dargomïzhskian hybrid on the same lines as *Boris* (*The Maid of Pskov*) and following it with a lyrical work in Glinka's vein, *May Night* (1880). In *Snowmaiden* (1882), still a thoroughly lyrical work, he uses leitmotives systematically àlmost on Wagnerian lines, though, as he claims in his memoirs, his leitmotives are more subtle than Wagner's "which often remind one of coarse military trumpet calls." His own leitmotives are sometimes fragments of extended melodies, sometimes mere chord-progressions or even single unusual chords (such as that of the Wood Spirit)

---

[1] The fact that Mussorgsky transferred to *Boris* music originally written for an opera on the subject of *Salammbô* throws an amusing light on his liberal view of "dramatic truth."

only to be distinguished by "a good trained ear." But nothing
else in *Snowmaiden* is at all Wagnerian. In *Mlada* (1892),
written just after Korsakov's first hearing of the *Ring*, the
orchestration and, to a slight extent, the harmonic idiom are
somewhat Wagnerian. Again in *Kashchey* (perf. 1902) and *The
Golden Cockerel* (comp. 1907), even to some extent in *Tsar
Saltan* (perf. 1901), the influence both of Wagner's music and
of Wagner's theories is apparent, and in all Korsakov's later
works the leitmotive system is extremely elaborate.[1] And his
view of opera was not so very different from Wagner's. As he
put it in the preface to *Sadko* (1898): "An opera libretto should
be considered and judged only as an integral part of the music.
Apart from the music it serves only as a filling-out of the bare
action; it is certainly not an independent literary work. I have
not hesitated to take liberties with the poetic metre wherever
the music demanded them. In opera the poetic rhythm must
be subordinated to the musical, not vice versa." On the face of
it, that seems directly opposed to what are commonly supposed
to have been Wagner's theories; but, as we have seen, it is not
so very far from Wagner's real view and his actual practice.
(In spite of this, Korsakov soon flirted with Dargomïzhskian
"truth" once more in *Mozart and Salieri* (1898).)

Most of Korsakov's operas, then, are song-operas with a more
or less elaborately developed orchestral texture and "continuous texture" operas with many vestiges of set-numbers
and, most interesting of all, with numerous scenes organized
on broad symphonic lines not dissimilar to those of a Lisztian
symphonic poem or those that Lorenz has traced in subtler,
more veiled forms in Wagner. In *Sadko*, for instance, the
harbour scene possesses, as Korsakov himself pointed out, "a
clear and broadly laid out symphonic form (somewhat in the
manner of a rondo)" and the recurrence of the choral lullaby in
the first scene of Act I of *Tsar Saltan* gives that, too, a rondo-like
form. There are several scenes in *Tsar Saltan*, and other of
Korsakov's operas, where this musical formalization arises
naturally out of the symmetries and repetitions characteristic of
the folk-tales of all countries and which Southey caught so

[1] Detailed thematic analyses of Rimsky-Korsakov's operas are given
by N. van Gilse van der Pals in his *N. A. Rimsky-Korssakow: Opernschaffen*. Leipzig, 1929.

happily in "The Three Bears." These features in themselves
must have made the stories peculiarly attractive to Rimsky-
Korsakov.

Even German opera remained remarkably free from Wagnerian influence till the appearance of Humperdinck's *Hänsel
und Gretel* (1893), Richard Strauss's *Guntram* (1894) and
Wolf's *Der Corregidor* (1896). Except Wagner's own works at
one end of the scale and Johann Strauss's brilliant operettas at
the other, the German operas of the 'fifties, 'sixties, 'seventies
and 'eighties were nearly all still-born. Only two are of any
importance—Cornelius's *Der Barbier von Bagdad* (1858) and
Goetz's *The Taming of the Shrew* (1874)—and neither shows
more than the slightest traces of Wagner's influence. The Goetz
opera is frankly Schumannesque and is interesting mainly for
its lighthanded, beautifully polished workmanship. *Der Barbier*
has the same qualities and something more—a dash of real
genius. Here the parentage is not so much Schumannesque as
Berliozian and Lisztian; when the shade of Wagner appears it
is only to be mocked at (cf. the "Wagnerian turn" when Abul
bows to Nureddin, Scene 5, bar 12). The score employs all the
resources of what was then ultra-modern harmony and orchestration with an almost Rossinian wit and lightness of touch;
Abul's patter song "Bin Akademiker, Doctor und Chemiker"
is in the direct line of descent from "Largo al factotum" and
musically far superior to anything of Sullivan's.[1] In fact, *Der
Barbier*, so badly received by the Weimar audience in 1858, is a
work that might easily have become the model for modern
German comic opera, a genre that was really set on quite the
wrong path by *Die Meistersinger*, musically much finer than
Der Barbier, but altogether too symphonic for comic opera.
Unfortunately Cornelius himself succumbed to Wagnerian influence in his later *Cid* (1865) and extinguished his own bright
talent. *Der Barbier* had no true successor, though Wolf's
Corregidor has something of its spirit. It is curious to note,
however, that Smetana sometimes employs a very similar
operatic technique and a very similar harmonic and orchestral
technique; not so much in *The Bartered Bride* and his other

---

[1] Generally speaking, it is Sullivan's music that has kept "Gilbert
and Sullivan" alive. But in the patter songs, exceptionally, the success
is mainly Gilbert's.

comic operas as in the heroic-romantic ones. *Dalibor*, for instance, obviously belongs to the same "school" as *Der Barbier* —though the school is that of Liszt, who, barring his boyish *Don Sanche* of 1825, never wrote an opera in his life.

Dvořák in his comic operas *Tvrdé palice* (*The Pigheaded Peasants*)(comp. 1874, prod. 1881) and *Selma sedlák* (*The Peasant a Rogue*) (1878) naturally worked more or less on Smetana's lines, though his orchestral writing is generally more elaborate than that of *The Bartered Bride*. In the grand opera *Dmitrij* (1882) he tackled a bigger subject, the historic sequel to the events depicted in *Boris Godunov*, and poured over it some magnificent music, but, as contemporary critics pointed out, the work is cast in the mould of Meyerbeerian grand opera, or, rather, in a modernized form of it. In his later comic-fantastic *Čert a Kata* (1899) and romantic-fantastic *Rusalka* (1901), the latter his operatic masterpiece, he draws near to the later operas of Rimsky-Korsakov. · In short, Dvořák, like most of the opera-composers of the last half of the century, muddled along with hybrid forms of opera that recognized the inadequacy of the old-fashioned set-forms yet were unable to let go of them and launch out boldly on Wagnerian lines, that admitted the use of leitmotives and some elaboration of the orchestral part of the score but in real essentials declined to recognize Wagner's existence. In other words, the tendencies already noticeable in the opera of the eighteen-thirties and 'forties continued to develop independently and more or less uninfluenced by Wagnerian theory.

This may be seen more clearly still in French and Italian opera, more firmly rooted in the past than that of either the Czechs or the Russians. Such operas as Ambroise Thomas's *Mignon* (1866) and *Hamlet* (1868), Gounod's *Faust* (1859), *Mireille* (1864) and *Roméo et Juliette* (1867), Delibes's *Le Roi l'a dit* (1873) and *Lakmé* (1883), Bizet's *Pêcheurs de perles* (1863), *Jolie fille de Perth* (1867) and *Carmen* (1875), Saint-Saëns's *Samson et Dalila* (1877) and its successors, even the still more modern operas of Massenet, *Hérodiade* (1881), *Manon* (1884) and the rest, merely continued the tradition of Boieldieu, Halévy and Meyerbeer, while the Auber tradition degenerated into the operettas of Offenbach. The family likeness of all these works, despite their obvious differences, is really remarkable.

Granted that Gounod was slightly more enterprising in his harmony than the rest (though his explorations took him only into the more luscious spheres of dissonance) and that both his melody and his orchestration owe enough to Berlioz to give them a certain modest distinction; that Delibes had a remarkable gift for ballet music—*La Source* (1866), *Coppélia* (1870) and *Sylvia* (1876) really matter more than *Le Roi l'a dit* and *Lakmé*; that Bizet wound up a career of workmanlike mediocrity with a burst of real genius; that Saint-Saëns was a brilliant craftsman with a flair for assimilating everything assimilable in Berlioz, Liszt and Gounod; that Massenet also worthily carried on the Gounod tradition without merely imitating Gounod—and, incidentally, threw off a number of charming songs. Granted, in short, that all these composers had artistic personalities of their own. They all accepted without question the operatic conventions of Meyerbeer and Auber, though their operas show a stronger tendency than Meyerbeer's to lyrical melody: melody sometimes over-sweet, often merely insipid, yet generally spontaneous. But the invention of good tunes was not Meyerbeer's strongest point, while melody of the feminine Gounod-Massenet type—however different in quality—has long been the backbone of French music, as apparent in Berlioz, particularly the later Berlioz, as in much of Debussy and Ravel—for instance, the string melody in D flat, *expressif et très soutenu*, in *L'Après-midi d'un faune* (1894) or Ravel's *Pavane pour une Infante défunte* (1899)—or in Honegger for that matter (cf. his *Pastorale d'été* (1920)). The little duet for Carmen and Escamillo, "Si tu m'aimes, Carmen," near the end of Bizet's masterpiece, is a fine example of this type of melody not at its best—for it is at its best when it is used to express light, delicate, and subtle things—but at its most passionate and most nearly virile.

The fact that *Carmen* stands head and shoulders above the other French operas of its time has originated a fairly widespread impression that Bizet was a musical innovator a good deal in advance of his time or, at any rate, an artist with higher ideals than most of his rivals. Nothing could be less true. No nineteenth-century composer ever took a more level-headed, businesslike view of the craft of opera composition than Bizet, and neither musically nor operatically did he make any attempt to break with convention. Like the great craftsmen-composers of the eighteenth century, he regarded himself purely and simply as a manufacturer of good commercial articles—the exact antithesis of the romantic view· of art—and he was fortunate enough to find in Carvalho, the director of the Théâtre Lyrique, a retailer so eager for his wares that he went on commissioning them regularly despite their very modest success.

As for his musical tastes, Marmontel tells us[1] that his favourite masters were "Auber, Halévy, Gounod and Thomas." And he followed faithfully in their footsteps. He toyed cautiously with the leitmotive and occasionally fancied he was something of a modernist and once went so far as to declare that "the tra-la-la and roulade school, the school of falsehood, is completely dead; let us bury it with tears, regrets, or emotion, and . . . forward!" But at the very time that he wrote this he was, as Gauthier-Villars points out,[2] "writing Catherine's '*copieuses roucoulades*' and the frightful ensemble at Glover's entry [in *La Jolie fille de Perth*] which would have made Auber himself flinch." His cautious views on technique in general and orchestration in particular are expressed in a letter to Paul Lacombe: "Let each part have about it sufficient atmosphere for it to move in. . . . Owing to the special timbre of each of the wood-wind, it is inadvisable to use them *en corps*. . . . The greater my experience the more I am convinced that wind and brass must be employed very circumspectly. . . . You use the horn as an ordinary instrument—which is very wrong; the great difficulty of producing certain stopped notes on it rules it out as a harmony instrument. . . ." His most daring harmonies are generally the result of nothing more startling than free use of appoggiaturas, often sounded simultaneously with the true harmony note. *Carmen*, then, and the delightful incidental music to Daudet's *L'Arlésienne* (1872),[3] are the masterpieces of a craftsman who aimed at nothing higher than the pleasing of his patrons, the public. Except that he drew the attention of musicians in general to the delightful possibilities of a pseudo-Spanish idiom, and mildly anticipated Italian *verismo* in *Carmen*, it cannot be claimed for

---

[1] *Symphonistes et virtuoses.* Paris, 1881.
[2] Henry Gauthier-Villars: *Bizet.* Paris, N.D.
[3] The local colour is more authentic in *L'Arlésienne* than in *Carmen*. The prelude, lullaby and farandole are all three based on genuine Provençal themes.

Bizet that he contributed much to the progress of his art. But that might also be said of much greater composers. Bizet, like Handel and Brahms, did remarkable things within the convention he accepted.

The one French opera-composer of this generation who was not only individual but struck a really new note was Edouard Lalo.[1] Lalo, like Dargomïzhsky and Boito and Busoni, was one of those composers gifted with more intellect than creative power who enliven the history of music from time to time. As may be seen from his best score, *Le Roi d'Ys*,[2] he was more enterprising than most of his compatriots (other than the Wagnerians, who will be considered in a later chapter) alike in his conception of musical drama and in his harmony: see, for instance, the progression at Karnac's song, "Et, pour suprême affront, j'ai survécu," in Act II, Scene 2. Yet the musical material he works with—the melody and general texture—is unmistakably mid-nineteenth-century French and he owes nothing, except perhaps his leitmotives, to Wagner; Lalo was neither a Wagnerian nor a revolutionary of any other brand. Nor was he a nationalist, despite his use of genuine Breton folk-songs (e.g., in the opening chorus and in the nuptial scene). Too often he is almost commonplace; even at its best his music is seldom as vital as it is interesting and individual.

Much the same may be said of Boito, whose *Mefistofele* (1868) is, if nothing else, a landmark in the history of Italian opera.[3] *Mefistofele* is so different from the average Italian opera of the eighteen-sixties that the accusation of Wagnerism almost universally levelled at it was not unnatural; nevertheless, Boito's admiration for Wagner dates from long after the composition of *Mefistofele*. His openly expressed contempt for the vulgarity and "imbecility" of the Italian music of his day and the more

[1] Whose *Symphonie espagnole*, incidentally, was performed just a month before *Carmen*. Lalo's *Spanish Symphony*, *Russian Concerto* and *Norwegian Rhapsody* are typical of the geographical mania that possessed French composers at this period.

[2] Belatedly produced in 1888, though the brilliant overture and another excerpt from it were publicly performed as early as 1876, while the nuptial duet was written as early as 1867 for another opera, *Fièsque*.

[3] His second opera, *Nerone*, occupied him for the rest of his life. He completed it only in 1916 and it was produced posthumously in 1924.

substantial elements in his own style were the result of his admiration of the older German classics, particularly of Beethoven. In spite of the remnants of 'aria, duet and so on, *Mefistofele* blows a good many of the old conventions of Italian opera to smithereens. It is true that Margaret sings a coloratura aria in prison and that the broad tune that clinches the duet for Helen and Faust in Act IV has an unmistakably Verdian ring, but Boito's free (but hardly fuller) handling of the orchestra, his treatment of recitative, his rhythmic freedom (cf. the constantly changing time-signatures at the opening of Act I) were all well in advance of their time. Harmonically, he was less progressive; a certain fondness for augmented triads hardly redeems his harmony from commonplaceness. But, all in all, it is not surprising that the Milan audience of 1868 found *Mefistofele* disturbingly revolutionary and that there was a scene comparable with that at the Paris *première* of *Tannhäuser* seven years earlier.

Unfortunately the novelties of 1868 have long been commonplaces and Boito's music as a whole lacks the beauty or vitality of many more conventional works. The "Prologue in Heaven" has a serene, epic breadth but little else in the opera is on the same level. Boito's real importance is that he was the first Italian composer to treat the composing of opera as anything but a job for a musical craftsman. He brought to the task a fine brain and a first-rate literary talent; unhappily as a musician he was markedly inferior to most of the mere craftsmen. It was only when his brain and his literary skill were harnessed with the music of one of the finest craftsmen of the nineteenth century that they were able to produce real masterpieces.

Whether Verdi owed anything to Boito, apart from his obvious debt to him as a librettist of genius, is as problematic as whether he owed anything to Wagner. *Aïda* (1871) and the Requiem Mass (1874), if not *Don Carlo* (1867), show that his musical mind was developing more vigorously at sixty than ever before. Even *Don Carlo*, unequal as it is, contains things as fine as any he had ever written; harmonically and in the handling of the orchestra, too, *Don Carlo* looks forward to *Aïda*. Toye draws attention to an orchestral passage in Don Carlo's "Io la vidi," possessing "an indubitable flavour of Wagner," and to the "decidedly Wagnerian" nature of the short orchestral passage, *andante sostenuto*, when Radames is led in, in the first scene of

Act IV of *Aïda,* of the accompaniment to Amneris's "Nei disperati aneliti" a little later, and of Radames's phrase soon after this, "È la morte un ben supremo." Yet the only really important "outside" influence in either work is Meyerbeer's. *Aïda* may be regarded as a final sublimation of Meyerbeerian grand opera. Even the G flat end of the great final duet was obviously suggested by the duet in the same key in *Les Hugue-nots,* but its lyrical superiority is the measure of the difference between the two composers.

But, despite these slight Wagnerian traces and rather less slight Meyerbeerian ones, *Aïda* is Verdian through and through —and as a whole on a much higher level than any of his previous works. One has only to study such passages as Aïda's "O cieli azzuri" near the beginning of Act III and Amneris's "Ah pieta! ah! lo salvate, Numi, pietà!" in the judgment scene of the last act, which both look back to familiar phrases in *Il Trovatore,* and Radames's "Gli Dei l'adducano" in Act IV, Scene 1 (which looks forward to the love-duet, "Labbra di foco," of *Falstaff,* Act I, Part two), to realize how *Aïda* links the old Verdi with the new. The most noticeable tendency is the increasing classicism of the melody, the approach to Bellinian purity; not through any cooling or slowing down of the lyrical flow, but in the refining of it. In Aïda's "O cieli azzuri" and still more in her exquisite "Vedi? di morte l'angelo" in the last scene, the old lyricism of the *Rigoletto* period is exquisitely subtilized, the passion expressed far more spiritually; and all this without any loss of spontaneity.

Verdi's orchestration is subtilized equally with his melody. It is incredible that the man who had so often treated the orchestra so perfunctorily—despite such passages as the music of the apparitions in *Macbeth*—should have written such marvellous pages of scoring as the famous opening of the third act of *Aïda,* with its combination of first violin arpeggios, second violin *tremoli* and viola pizzicati—all muted—with the harmonics of the divided 'cellos, and the still lovelier accompaniment to "Vedi? di morte l'angelo," with its extraordinarily subtle sub-division of the first violins. Indeed from this point to the end of the opera almost every bar of the string-writing is as interest-ing as it is lovely.

Nor is the scoring of *Aïda* remarkable only in such purple

patches. One can hardly speak of "Verdi's orchestra" as we can
of "Wagner's" or "Rimsky-Korsakov's," yet the score of *Aïda*
has an unmistakable quality of its own, due perhaps to the subtle
predominance at crucial moments of the flutes, most beautifully
written for: consider, for instance, the flute-writing in the low
register in "Celeste Aïda" (the duet with the voice and then the
long trill), the use of three flutes in the priestesses' dance in
Act I, the solo in the introduction to Act III, and, particularly
fine, the flute chords at "Là, tra foreste vergini" in the finale
of Act III. The "side-slipping" of 6-3 chords here, an effect
of which Verdi was rather fond and which Puccini afterwards
worked to death, anticipates the "side-slipping" of diminished
triads in the opening scene of *Otello* and of second inversions of
dominant sevenths about thirty bars before the end of the first
part of Act III of *Falstaff*.[1]

Nevertheless, *Aïda* is after all Meyerbeerian grand opera,
spectacular, emotionally crude and violent; it is even disfigured
by musical vulgarity of the worst Meyerbeerian kind (e.g.,
"Su! nel Nilo"). It is a "setting" of a conventional "libretto,"
though a very fine setting of an exceptionally good libretto. It
is not yet pure musical drama. Verdi achieved that only after a
long interval of silence, in *Otello* (1887) and *Falstaff* (1893),
when Boito provided him with libretti that are dramatic poems
valuable in themselves, and faithfully handed on to him the
living characters of Shakespeare himself. Here at last, at the
height of his musical powers and working on such magnificent
material, Verdi takes his place beside Wagner as a musical
dramatist. (Not, of course, as an "absolute" musician.) Here,
like Wagner, he gives us characters musically alive in every
note, true and uncaricatured; not only the great dominating
characters—Othello, Iago, Falstaff—but practically every minor
one as well. *Falstaff*—if not *Otello*—actually achieves a more
perfect balance between music and drama, and between voice
and orchestra, than any of Wagner's works; and achieves this
balance with a technical ease that makes Mussorgsky appear,
from this point of view, little better than a bungler.

The orchestra seldom distracts one's attention from the voice,

[1] Verdi had anticipated this delicious passage in a similar chain of
sevenths in *Otello*, where the strings enter *dolcissimo* after Iago's
account of Cassio's dream.

even when, as in Othello's monologue "Dio! mi potevi scagliar" (Act III, Scene 3), it happens to have more melodic interest than the voice-part (e.g., at the words, "Tu alfin, Clemenza"). The delicious tune that accompanies both Falstaff's reappearance in his new doublet, with hat and stick, near the end of the first part of Act II, and the ensuing snatches of conversation, is even more unobtrusive than the melody that enters with Tatyana in the last act of *Eugene Onegin*. Yet the handling of the orchestra in *Falstaff* is, in its way, as remarkable as anything in Wagner. The orchestral humour ranges from the simplicity of the absurd underlining of Falstaff's "No's" in the monologue on honour to the celebrated orchestral trill when he describes the effect of wine. Again, the pantomimic curtsey before Mrs. Quickly's "Reverenza!" and her "dalle due alle tre" motive, later used orchestrally, are perfect examples of the purely dramatic leit-motive.

Yet the method and the music are not in the least Wagnerian. Beyond these few comic motives and the love-music of the young people, there are no leitmotives in *Falstaff*. In *Otello* there are none at all, though the reappearance in the last scene of the "kiss" music from the love-duet of Act I is perhaps the most overwhelmingly effective, certainly the most poignant, piece of theme-quotation in the whole range of opera.

Whereas in *Otello* the outlines are broader and the dramatic effect naturally deeper, *Falstaff* is the finer piece of workman-ship. The wedding of words and music is even closer; musically, the fragmentary style results in almost impressionistic effects—though the spirit is unmistakably that of true Italian *opera buffa*, the spirit of Rossini. The harmony has lost the last traces of banality and over-lusciousness. In *Otello* music still has slightly the upper hand; Verdi could not write tragedy without lyricism. There are still a few set-numbers in *Otello*—Iago's drinking-song, the serenade to Desdemona, the bonfire chorus, the willow song, and so on—though they are always cunningly justified dramatically; the love-duet at the end of Act I is as fine a com-pound of lyrical beauty and dramatic truth as one could conceive. In *Falstaff* there are none, except Fenton's and Nannetta's songs in the last act and the final fugue. In *Otello* there are still traces of the old Verdi: for instance, Desdemona's "E un dì sul mio sorriso" (finale of Act III) and her last farewell to Emilia;

in *Falstaff* there are none. But beside the individualization of characters in the final ensemble of Act III of *Otello*, the (quite justly) celebrated "truth" of the *Rigoletto* quartet and the finale of Act II of *Aïda* seem almost childish, and the vocal scherzi of *Falstaff* (those in Act I, "Pizzica, pizzica," and the final fugue) are unsurpassed in the whole range of comic opera.

In dramatic truth, that will-o'-the-wisp of opera-composers, there is little to choose between the tragedy and the comedy, between Othello's "Dio! mi potevi scagliar" or the opening of the last scene of Act III of *Otello* and Ford's jealousy monologue or Falstaff's reflections on the "Mondo ladro, mondo rubaldo" (Act III, Part One). Verdi's dramatic power is evident in his expression of falseness alone; a whole monograph might be written on his treatment of Iago's falseness (above all, in the "Cassio's dream" passage) and Amneris's "Fu la sorte dell' armi a' tuoi funesta, povera Aïda!", of Falstaff's humbug and Ford in disguise.

One point can hardly fail to strike the student of Verdi's last two operas: the chastity—there is no other word for it—of the love-music in both. In *Otello* there is only the slightest trace, in *Falstaff* not even that, of the powerful animal passion of the earlier Verdi.[1] Like all the other great romantic composers, he ended his career as a pure classicist. But the "vulgar melody" of his early days, having died in himself, was just being reborn in his young compatriots.

Mascagni's *Cavalleria rusticana* (1890) certainly inaugurated an outburst of "verism" in Italian opera, with subjects drawn from contemporary life, but mostly characterized by "truth" to a "life" as sordid as Zola's naturalism. Leoncavallo's *I Pagliacci* (1892), Giordano's *Andrea Chénier* (1896), and the other "verist" works are more indebted to *Carmen* than to Mussorgsky—to whom, indeed, they owe nothing. But although these so-called "verists" aped some of the external methods of Wagner and the Verdi of *Otello*, using crude leitmotives in the crudest way, making a shallow pretence at continuity of texture and so on, their spirit was that of the earlier Verdi; their "dramatic truth"

---

[1] "Labbra di foco" is a sort of idealized, purified echo, no doubt accidental, of a phrase from the by no means chaste music of the *Parsifal* flower-maidens "Dir zur Wonn' und Labe gilt mein minniges Mühen!"

consisted of violent, stagily effective melodrama expressed in terms of vulgar, but forceful and sometimes striking melody, banal harmony and noisy, commonplace orchestration. Their tradition was carried on in more recent years by Zandonai, whose *Francesca da Rimini* (1914), though based on a text by d'Annunzio, is superior to Mascagni's operas only in technical workmanship.

From the dramatic point of view, Puccini's earliest operas, *Le Villi* (1884) and *Edgar* (1889), have little in common with *verismo* though the music of *Edgar* bears the same stamp as *Cavalleria rusticana* and is very nearly as vulgar. Yet even *Edgar* contains evidence of Puccini's remarkable gift for warm, luscious, living melody (e.g., Edgar's song near the beginning of Act II). The characteristic Puccinian repetition of a final note, a musical trait obviously derived from the numerous feminine endings of the Italian language, gives an unmistakable stamp to Edgar's "Bella signora" in the last act. And Puccini's remarkable aptitude for picking up harmonic novelties appears in the 8-bar passage near the end of Act I (at Edgar's cry, "Egli lo vuole!"), entirely based on the side-slipping of diminished seventh chords, and the similar progression of 6-5 chords accompanying the recitative before Edgar's already mentioned "Non più dal tuoi sguardi" in Act II. The trick is, of course, borrowed from *Otello*; we hear a modification of it near the end of *Manon Lescaut* (1893); by 1898, when Mascagni wrote his *Iris*—musically far superior to *Cavalleria*—it was a commonplace of Italian opera (cf. the series of thirteen diminished sevenths in Iris's "Ho fatto un triste sogno" in the first scene); yet when Richard Strauss wrote a few consecutive sevenths in *Ein Heldenleben*, first performed in the same year as *Iris*, he was considered extremely daring.[1] Whether or not Debussy acquired the device from Satie's *Sarabandes* (1887), the Italians certainly anticipated him.

Manon Lescaut shows an immense advance on *Edgar*; musically it is one of Puccini's richest works and as far superior to Massenet's *Manon* of nine years earlier as it is inferior to it dramatically. It is curious that, although Puccini's melody in general has more than a dash of Massenet in its blood, this is not at all apparent in *Manon Lescaut*; indeed the strongest

---

[1] Admittedly the *interval* of the diminished seventh is not a "real" seventh, being enharmonically identical with a major sixth.

external influence perceptible in *Lescaut* is Wagner's. Specht[1] says truly of the duet for Manon and Des Grieux that "never did Puccini reveal such indebtedness to *Tristan* as in this fevered duet, with its rising sequences, its yearning chromatic figures and imploring sevenths"; though the beginning and end of the intermezzo between Acts II and III are even more Tristanesque. Nevertheless, both melody and harmony of *Manon Lescaut* as a whole are thoroughly Puccinian in their spontaneity, ardour and *morbidezza*. Only he still tends to write long-sustained melodies depending for their effect on the balance of phrases, while in his later works the melodic interest is more compressed so that the line—still long-breathed and still spontaneous-sounding (cf. "Un bel dì" in *Madam Butterfly*)—actually consists of a chain of linked melodic motives.

Of Puccini's next three operas, *La Bohème* (1896), *Tosca* (1900) and *Madam Butterfly* (1904), that is to say, the three on which his popular reputation mainly rests, *Butterfly* is by far the finest musically and *Tosca* the most crude both in its music and as a dramatic conception. (Though even *Tosca* has some interesting harmonic effects: e.g., at Angelotti's entrance and the effect of fourths, reminding one of the most primitive form of mediæval *organum*, when Cavaradossi begins to paint.) All three are extremely effective as stage-works, and in all three the general musico-dramatic convention of *Otello* is cleverly adapted to very different ends. *La Bohème* is musically a curious mixture of banality and brilliant invention, held together by intense emotional sincerity and by Puccini's very individual musical personality. The orchestration alone is sufficient to illustrate both Puccini's skill and his weaknesses. The combination of glockenspiel, solo trumpet, high wind and pizzicato strings near the beginning of the second act is brilliant, but the *tuttis* sound curiously "tuney." Take the *fff* climax of the Mimi-Rudolph duet in Act I: the melody is not only sung by both soloists in octaves but spread over three octaves in the orchestra—piccolo, flutes, first oboe, first clarinet, all four horns, first and second violins and 'cellos—the harmony being left to trombones, harp, violas and a few odd wind. The effect is hysterical in the worst Tchaïkovskian manner.

[1] Richard Specht: *Giacomo Puccini* (translated by Catherine Alison Phillips). Dent, 1933.

Madam Butterfly has a good many of the same weaknesses—
they are inherent in Puccini's musical nature—but they are
much less apparent than in *Bohème*. *Butterfly* is seldom banal
and, moreover, possesses a curious exotic charm derived largely
from the genuine Japanese motives which Puccini borrowed and
made completely his own. Specht says that although "hundreds
of gramophone records [of Japanese music] were sent him from
Tokio, only infinitesimal doses of the music found a way into
his work." But Mosco Carner has shown[1] that a considerable
number of actual Japanese and Chinese melodies and melodic
fragments are introduced in *Butterfly* and *Turandot*, to say
nothing of numerous pentatonic patterns and rhythmic elements
derived from Japanese and Chinese music. In *Butterfly* alone
Carner has been able to identify several unaltered Japanese
melodies: for instance, three bars of the Japanese national
anthem in the orchestra when Goro speaks of "L'Imperial
Commisario" and a "Cherry-blossom Song" when Butterfly
empties her sleeves of her little possessions ("Una cintura. Un
piccolo fermaglio. Uno specchio"), both in Act I, as well as a
number of passages derived from identifiable Japanese motives.
The chorus of children in Act I of *Turandot*, "Là, sui monti
dell'est," is a brilliant example of Puccini's skill in patching
together tiny Oriental motives to form a new and apparently
spontaneous melody; the tune is in one sense completely
Puccini's, yet it is built up entirely of motives from the "Song
in Honour of the Emperor" (the old Chinese imperial hymn)
and from an old Confucian hymn.

But *Butterfly* has many good qualities other than its delightful
flavour of exoticism. The dramatic action and dramatic emotion
conceal or excuse the structural and other weaknesses of the
music, or rather those qualities that would be weaknesses if the
score were symphonic instead of operatic. Granted that Puccini
was incapable of reaching the height of *Otello*, *Butterfly* and
Turandot are the only post-Verdian Italian operas worthy to be
mentioned in the same breath with it. When Butterfly awakes
at dawn and sings "Dormi amor mio," it is difficult not to think
of Desdemona's willow song, though the music is as different from
it as a little Japanese geisha is different from a noble Venetian lady.

[1] Article, "The Exotic Element in Puccini," in *The Musical Quarterly*,
January, 1936.

Puccini's next two works, *La fanciulla del West* (1910) and *La Rondine* (1917) were failures, but he closed his career with two, or rather four, masterpieces, *Il Trittico* (the three one-act operas, *Il tabarro*, *Suor Angelica* and *Gianni Schicchi*) (1919) and *Turandot* (1926). *La fanciulla* aims at realism, *verismo*, and falls into *Tosca*-like melodrama; *Il tabarro* aims at the same thing and achieves it perfectly. Even the final murder is "in the picture"; it does not give anything like the brutal shock of Butterfly's suicide. And the music as a whole is as near to naked "dramatic truth" as any Italian is likely to get; Puccini achieves "truth" without sacrificing his essential lyricism. And *Il tabarro* possesses something more than truth and lyricism; it has atmosphere, atmosphere more skilfully achieved, because so much more subtle, than that of *Madam Butterfly*.

It is customary to say that Puccini learned these "atmospheric" secrets from Debussy; and it is true that he was keenly interested in Debussy, as in his other progressive contemporaries, and that the wonderful opening of *Il tabarro* has a sort of *Cathédrale engloutie* flavour. But, as I have already shown, Puccini took over these *organum-* or *faux bourdon*-like effects, these side-slippings not only of triads but of dissonant chords, from Verdi. This counterpoint of two lines of bare perfect fifths that opens *Il tabarro* is, from a purely harmonic point of view, a natural development of, say, the bustling consecutive triads at the beginning of Act II of *La Bohème*. The *Trittico* is full of such *faux bourdon* effects, melodic lines thickened out into lines of "added note" chords or seventh chords of the same effect (e.g., at Giorgetta's "Lo pensavo. Ho quel che ci vuole" and Michele's "Ero tanto felice, ah tanto felice!" in *Il tabarro*; at Suor Angelica's "Addio, buone sorelle, addio" in the second opera; the passage when Schicchi is being hustled into bed and the greeting to the doctor in the third) or chords of the ninth (after Angelica's cry when she learns of her child's death). Indeed, progressions of ninths are freely used: e.g., after Luigi's death-cry in *Il tabarro* and at the opening of *Suor Angelica*; they are only a step beyond the sevenths of earlier days. That being so, there seems little ground for suggesting that Puccini was merely taking a hint from *Petrushka* in the diminished octaves of the out-of-tune barrel-organ in *Il tabarro*.

Apart altogether from its "advanced" harmonies—which by

1919 were not "advanced" at all, of course—*Gianni Schicchi* in particular is a masterpiece from whatever point of view one looks at it. Here again, as *Butterfly* recalls *Otello*, *Schicchi* reminds one—at a distance—of *Falstaff*. But deliciously witty and light-handed as it is, it just lacks the *extra sec* quality of Verdi's masterpiece. Comparison of the music of the young lovers in each opera is instructive: the love of Fenton and Nannetta, as we have seen, is kept on a plane that harmonizes miraculously with the whole of the comic action, that of Lauretta and Rinuccio is expressed in luscious music indistinguishable from that of Puccini's other pairs of lovers. And Lauretta's "O mio babbino caro" is the one artistic blemish in the whole opera.

In *Turandot* Puccini's most striking characteristics are all developed still more fully. The very opening (bars 5–12, with their simultaneous D minor and C sharp major triads) shows that he had accepted polytonality. Again, Act II opens with common chords of E flat, D flat and A over the bass, E natural, D natural, B flat. Puccini's lyricism never reached greater heights than in his last work (though the popular "Nessun dorma" is not one of those heights); Liu's songs are perhaps the peak of his art. The humour of the trio that opens Act II is as delightful as anything in *Gianni Schicchi*. Exoticism in melody, harmony and orchestration is developed almost as far as any Western composer can develop it successfully. And the scoring throughout is superbly effective, though even here Puccini falls into his old trick of over-emphasizing the melody, as in the big *tutti, largo sostenuto*, near the beginning when the guards push back the crowd: the melody is spread over four octaves in all the wood-wind, four horns, a trumpet and all the strings except the double-basses, the harmony being left to the trombones and a couple of trumpets. It is easy to point to a number of recent operas stronger than *Turandot* from a purely *musical* point of view but, considered as it should be—as a musico-dramatic whole —it is by far the most satisfactory operatic work produced during the last quarter of a century.

INTERLUDE: MUSIC IN THE EIGHTEEN-NINETIES

The predominating influence that Wagner began to exercise on European music in the eighteen-nineties is hardly reflected in the programmes of the (not yet Royal) Philharmonic Society for that decade. Admittedly the *Meistersinger* overture had now been stamped with the Society's hall-mark of respectability, like that to *Tannhäuser*, and soloists sang Wotan's farewell and Walther's prize-song. But the Philharmonic appears almost to have exhausted its interest in Wagner with the Memorial Concert of 1883, a programme that would now seem particularly unenterprising if given on a Wagner night at the "Proms." Actually the predominant foreign influences in the programmes were those of Dvořák and the Russians; the novelties of the decade included Dvořák's Fourth Symphony (in 1890), Tchaïkovsky's Fourth (1893) and Sixth (*Pathétique*) (1894), Borodin's B minor Symphony and Dvořák's 'Cello Concerto (both 1896), Glazunov's Fourth Symphony and Tchaïkovsky's Variations for 'Cello and Orchestra (both 1897) and Rakhmaninov's Orchestral Fantasia, Op. 7 (1899). And the programmes also contain the names of numerous "interesting" new foreigners who have failed to stay the course: Peter Benoit, Martucci, Moszkowski, Mancinelli, Sgambati[1] and others.

English music was, as usual, generously treated. Macfarren's more than fifty-year-old *Chevy Chase* overture was still being played in 1891. And there were plenty of English novelties, though the list has a certain pathos to-day: Frederic Cliffe's *Cloud and Sunshine* and vocal duets by Goring Thomas (1890), C. E. Stephens's C minor Symphony (1891), Somervell's *Helen of Kirkconnel* and Cliffe's Second Symphony (1893), Stanford's *L'Allegro ed il Pensieroso* Symphony, Mackenzie's *From the North* and George F. Bennett's *Leonatus and Imogen* overture (1895), Cowen's *In Fairyland* suite, Edward German's Suite in D minor, and Herbert Bunning's overture *Spring and Youth* (1897), MacCunn's *Diarmid* ballet music and Frederick Corder's *Pippa Passes* (1898), Stanford's *Concert Variations on an English Theme* (1899). The new rising stars of English music—Coleridge-Taylor, Elgar, Bantock—began to twinkle in the Philharmonic programmes only at the turn of the century. No critic in the 'nineties could have predicted which of the three would finally

---

[1] Sgambati, a pupil of Liszt, is at least historically important as a pioneer in the renaissance of Italian instrumental music—a movement continued in our own day by such composers as Pizzetti, Respighi, Malipiero and Casella.

turn out to be the star of the first magnitude, or even that he was of any greater importance than any of the ordinary comets that crowded across the heaven of Victorian English music.

Mackenzie was in charge of the Philharmonic during the greater part of the period—a seven-year interlude in the long régime of Cowen. And in 1894 the Society moved from the St. James's Hall, which had been its home since 1869, to the then new Queen's Hall. The new hall also became the home of a new venture. On August 10th, 1895, the first of Robert Newman's Promenade Concerts was conducted by Henry J. Wood. The programme included the *Rienzi* overture, a Liszt rhapsody, the gavotte from *Mignon*, arias by Gounod and Saint-Saëns, a Swiss "echo song" and *Chromatic Waltzes* by one Kistler. But the programmes soon became a little more serious; in less than a month Wood was giving a Sullivan night, a Wagner night, a Gounod night, and a classical night; and before long the promenaders were hearing the first English performances of works by Rimsky-Korsakov and Tchaïkovsky. In a sense, the "Proms" eventually took the place in London's musical life of the quite differently organized Crystal Palace Saturday Concerts, but these also continued until 1901. The St. James's Hall chamber music "Pops" expired earlier, after the season 1897–98.

English opera was in its usual state. That is to say, the masterpiece that was to herald a revival of it—in this case, Sullivan's *Ivanhoe* (1891)—had appeared and had turned out not to be a masterpiece after all. As for opera in England, that too was in its usual state. Covent Garden was putting on the operas of half a century earlier to the almost complete neglect of contemporary art. As Bernard Shaw complained:[1] "I have to sit in our vulgar diamond show at Covent Garden, listening to scratch performances of *Faust* and *Les Huguenots*, whilst Mottl is producing *Les Troyens* in Carlsruhe, Levi conducting *Siegfried* at Munich, and Richter using his left hand at Vienna to conduct *Carmen*, because his right is fatigued with perpetual Wagner." One suspects that in 1988 the International Season will consist

[1] *Music in London* (1890–94) and *London Music in 1888–89*. Four vols., Constable, 1932 and 1937. These reprinted articles of Shaw's, probably the most readable criticism of music ever written, give a delicious picture of musical London in the last decade of the century.

mainly of scratch performances of the works of Berg, Milhaud and Janáček.

Even in the fortunate lands that enjoyed or suffered perpetual Wagner in the eighteen-nineties, conditions were not as happy as they must have seemed to an enthusiast "heartily sick of the London no-rehearsal system, under which, with the best players in the world, equipped with the best instruments in the world, we have orchestras that read everything and know nothing; so that the moment we are confronted by works which can only be played properly by a band thoroughly obsessed with every melody and every accent in the score, we are beaten and disgraced not only by our provincial rivals from Manchester, but by a second-rate German band from Hamburg" (that of the Hamburg municipal opera, under Mahler) "which supersedes us in our own leading opera-house."[1] When in 1891 the twenty-eight-year-old Weingartner made his début at the Berlin Royal Opera with *Lohengrin*, he had "to explain to the musicians that the only way to escape from an indeterminate *mezzoforte*, to which they seemed to have become addicted, was by conscientiously following all the dynamic instructions and by rhythmical phrasing."[2] Again in *Carmen*: "The chorus of the cigarette-makers in the first act never kept together at rehearsal. Finally I asked whether they had been accustomed to a different method of conducting. 'No.' 'Well, why don't you keep time then?' 'We *never* have,' answered one of the ladies of the chorus calmly."

In the Germany and Austria of the 'nineties the feud between the Brahmsians on the one hand and the partisans of Wagner, Bruckner and Wolf on the other was by no means over. (And Brahms was still very little known outside the Teutonic countries, except in England and America.) But as far as one can judge, the German musical world in general, like the English, was essentially little different from what it had been in the 'sixties. And the same may be said of Italy.

In Russia the new developments of the 'sixties—conservatoires and concert-giving bodies—were now well-established. And in 1886 a new figure had made his début in the Russian

[1] Bernard Shaw, op. cit.

[2] Felix Weingartner: *Buffets and Rewards: A Musician's Reminiscences*. English translation by Marguerite Wolff. Hutchinson, 1937.

concert world: the extremely wealthy timber-merchant and music-publisher, M. P. Belaiev, whose "Russian Symphony Concerts," conducted by Rimsky-Korsakov, Glazunov and other first-rate musicians, long played an extremely important part in the musical life of St. Petersburg. Belaiev also founded a publishing house, and his personal tastes, above all his love of chamber music, exercised a perceptible influence on Russian music at this period. The quantity of pleasant but rather light and ephemeral Russian chamber-compositions written and published at this time—incidentally, an entirely new type of "recreation" chamber music—owed its inspiration entirely to Belaiev.

The one country in Europe that had changed astoundingly between the eighteen-sixties and the eighteen-nineties was France. Victory and unification in 1870 made little difference to German art; defeat and the disappearance of the gay and frivolous Second Empire entirely regenerated French art. Even before the war was over—in February, 1871—the Société nationale de musique was founded by Saint-Saëns, Guiraud, Massenet, Fauré, Duparc, Dubois and others "to aid the production and the popularization of all serious musical works, whether published or unpublished, of French composers; to encourage and bring to light all musical endeavour, whatever form it may take, on condition that there is evidence of high artistic aspiration on the part of the author." The Society gave its first concert on November 25th, 1871, and from that time onward its services to French chamber and orchestral music have been incalculable. First performances of most of the major instrumental works of Franck, Saint-Saëns, d'Indy, Lalo, Bruneau, Chausson, Debussy, Dukas, Lekeu and Magnard were given under its auspices.[1] Saint-Saëns was the first director. "But," says Romain Rolland, "from 1881 the influence of Franck and his disciples became more and more felt, and Saint-Saëns began to lose interest in the efforts of the new school." In 1886 he resigned in consequence of the adoption of d'Indy's proposal to include the work of classical and even contemporary foreign composers in the Society's programmes.

[1] A detailed, but by no means exhaustive, list will be found in the last chapter of Romain Rolland's *Musicians of To-day*. (Translated by Mary Blaiklock.) Kegan Paul, 4th edition, 1919.

In addition to the concerts of the Société nationale, two new and very important series of symphony concerts came into existence: Colonne's Concerts de l'Association artistique at the Châtelet, begun in 1873, which gave the classics and French music in general, and Berlioz in particular, and Lamoureux's Société des Nouveaux Concerts (afterwards renamed Association des Concerts-Lamoureux), founded in 1881 and continued after 1897 by Lamoureux's son-in-law, Chevillard. These Lamoureux concerts were of the highest importance for they laid the foundations of the extraordinary craze for Wagner's music and Wagnerian æsthetics that possessed the whole of intellectual France from about 1885 to 1895. Lamoureux championed not only Wagner but the French Wagnerians, d'Indy, Chabrier and the rest. But the immediate influence of Wagnerism was felt less by music than by the other arts and by criticism in general. "Wagner's influence," says Rolland, "considerably helped forward the progress of French art, and aroused a love for music in people other than musicians; and, by his all-embracing personality and the vast domain of his work in art, engaged the interest not only of the musical world but of the theatrical world, and the world of poetry and the plastic arts." And he cites the *Revue wagnérienne*, published monthly from 1885 to 1888, with its extraordinary band of contributors: Verlaine, Mallarmé, Swinburne, Villiers de l'Isle Adam, Huysmans, Richepin, Fantin-Latour, Wilder, Schuré, Soubies, Malherbe and the rest. "These writers not only discussed musical subjects, but judged painting, literature and philosophy from a Wagnerian point of view." And as Edward Lockspeiser has pointed out,[1] there was a close connection between this Wagnerian cult and the Symbolist movement; Dujardin, the editor of the *Revue wagnérienne*, also edited the Symbolist *Revue indépendante* and Mallarmé was completely under the spell of Wagner.

Lockspeiser also points out how the way for this Wagnermania was, remarkably enough, made easy by "post-war" feeling. It was a reaction against literary naturalism and philosophical positivism. "The Franco-Prussian war had annihilated, for the time being, all desire on the part of artists and thinkers to approach the world in any calculating, scientific manner. . . .

[1] *Debussy*. J. M. Dent, 1936.

Flaubert, Taine and Renan were dethroned in favour of Edgar Allan Poe (first translated by Baudelaire), the English Pre-Raphaelites and certain of the Russian novelists." The musicians followed the painters and literary men and before long, as Rolland wittily puts it, some of them "were translating Gounod's or Massenet's ideas into Wagner's style."

But in 1889 the Parisian art world, comparable with that of the Athenians in its love of "new things," was exposed to fresh influences. In that year a world exhibition brought to Paris native musicians not only from every corner of Europe but from Africa and the Far East. Rimsky-Korsakov conducted two concerts of Russian music at the exhibition, his programmes including works by Glinka, Borodin, Tchaïkovsky, Balakirev, Cui, Lyadov, Dargomïzhsky, Glazunov, Mussorgsky and himself, and from this period Russian music began little by little to exert a considerable influence on that of France. Only slightly less important was the fascination exercised on the twenty-seven-year-old Debussy and other young French musicians by the *gamelang*[1] that played in the Javanese "village." In short, folk-music—particularly the more exotic varieties—was the vogue. Grieg, too, reached the peak of his Parisian popularity in the early eighteen-nineties.

In this whirl of enthusiasms and passing fancies a stabilizing factor was introduced in 1894 by the foundation of the Schola Cantorum. The Schola was established by two of Franck's old pupils, Charles Bordes and Vincent d'Indy, that is, by musicians who had come strongly under the influence of Wagner. But, as its name hints, its main object was originally the reform of religious music by reference to the standards of plainsong and the polyphonic masters of the sixteenth century. But gradually seventeenth-century music began to be cultivated, then Bach, Rameau and Gluck, and finally old music of every kind, secular as well as sacred. When in 1900 d'Indy succeeded Bordes as head of the Schola, it admitted by a change of title that it had become an Ecole supérieure de musique. Not only did the Schola train such composers as Roussel and de Séverac, it gave innumerable concerts in Paris and the provinces, revived old

---

[1] A Javanese native orchestra, consisting of percussion instruments of definite pitch plus a two-stringed instrument of the viol type. The music is pentatonic and very subtle in rhythm.

operas, and published a great deal of music, both old and new.

By the end of the century, then, the French musical renaissance was complete. A strong new native art was flourishing, just as Russian music had begun to flourish in the eighteen-sixties, and the various foreign influences that fertilized it, but might easily have smothered it, were almost—not quite—completely absorbed. The last decade of the century saw France finally emerge from her position as a land of second-rate opera and take her place in the front rank of European music.

IV. THE HERITAGE OF LISZT AND WAGNER

Whereas in Germany Liszt's most distinguished, though not most faithful, disciple in the field of instrumental music was the mediocre eclectic Raff[1] whose symphonies vainly attempt to reconcile programmes with more or less conventional symmetrical forms, the Lisztian symphonic poem was cultivated brilliantly, if superficially, by Saint-Saëns in his *Le Rouet d'Omphale* (1872), *Phaéton* (1875), *Danse macabre* (1875) and *La Jeunesse d'Hercule* (1877), and with more originality by Franck in *Les Eolides* (comp. 1876), *Le Chasseur maudit* (1883) and *Les Djinns* (1885), the last of which is the precursor of the fairly numerous modern works in which a solo piano is treated as part of the orchestra. It was in France, too, that theme-transformation in compositions of the sonata type was most logically and elaborately developed in such works as Saint-Saëns's now almost forgotten Third Symphony in C minor (1886) and still more in the orchestral and chamber works of Franck and his school: d'Indy, Chausson, Lekeu and the rest.[2] And Franck must certainly be credited

[1] Raff's two best-known symphonies are No. 3, *Im Walde* (1. Daytime, impressions and emotions; 2, Twilight, dreams, dance of dryads; 3, Night, silence and darkness, passing of the " Wild Hunt " with Odin and Venus; daybreak) (1869), and No. 5, *Lenore* (after Bürger's ballad) (1872). He also wrote *Alpine, Sounds of Spring, Summertime* and *Autumn* Symphonies and one with the motto, "Gelebt, gestrebt; gelitten, gestritten; gestorben, umworben" ("Lived, striven; suffered, fought; died, acclaimed").

[2] In justice to Franck, it should be said that he did not borrow this idea from Liszt, as Saint-Saëns clearly did. The device is employed in Franck's F sharp Trio, Op. 1, No. 1, composed as early as 1841—that is, before any of the Liszt works in which it is used.

with being the first composer, other than Grieg, to take over the chromatic harmony of Liszt and Wagner, multiplied appoggiaturas and all, and employ it in a new and unmistakably personal way. Whether one likes Franck's harmonic methods or not, it is as obvious that they are absolutely Franckish as that they are based on Wagner's—or at any rate on Liszt's. And Franck's disciples were harmonically at least as Wagnerian as their master; indeed, rather more so.

More curious still, it was in France that the first notable Wagnerian, or seemingly Wagnerian, operas began to appear. Whereas *Hänsel und Gretel, Der Corregidor* and *Guntram* came out only in the mid-eighteen-nineties (1893–96), Reyer's *Sigurd* and Chabrier's *Gwendoline* were produced as early as 1883 and 1886 respectively. Even one of Massenet's most gifted pupils, Bruneau, displayed strong Wagnerian tendencies in his *Le Rêve* (1891) and *L'Attaque du Moulin* (1893). But the peaks of French Wagnerism were d'Indy's *Fervaal* (1897) and Charpentier's *Louise* (1900), though the latter—an opera of contemporary life—shows the dramatic, though not the musical, influence of the Italian verists. (Charpentier, like d'Indy, was his own librettist.) In Dukas's *Ariane et Barbe-Bleue* (1907) the still very obvious Wagnerism is modified by the influence of Debussy; the tide had begun to ebb.

On the whole the French Wagnerians are more interesting than historically important. Except Charpentier, they were all just a little too intellectual in their approach to opera, a little too conscious that there is such a thing as an opera "problem," and none of them possessed anything like the creative power that enabled Gluck and Wagner and Mussorgsky to soar above that consciousness. Yet they never allowed themselves to be swallowed up by Wagner, to degenerate into manufacturers of imitation Wagner even to the slight extent that Humperdinck did or the early Strauss. As Colles has put it:[1] "In the work of these composers we see the gradual absorption of the major lessons of Wagner's art while on the whole they successfully maintained the French tradition of vocal clarity and directness of expression." Or, as Romain Rolland more picturesquely expresses it,[2] "You may find in *Fervaal* a few trees like those in the forest of *Sieg-*

[1] *Oxford History of Music.* Vol. VII.
[2] *Musicians of To-day.*

fried; but the forest itself is not the same; broad avenues have been cut in it, and daylight fills the caverns of the Nibelungs."

Even as it is, the influence of Wagner was probably harmful except in giving the death-blow to outgrown musical and dramatic conventions, and in enormously enriching the harmonic vocabulary. All that Wagner stood for was really too foreign to the French temperament for these composers to absorb it as a nourishing food; their Wagnerism was merely a sort of antitoxin. To change the metaphor: it stunted their growth quite as much as it fertilized them. Chabrier's *Gwendoline* is a particularly striking illustration of this. Chabrier's real talent was for robust, sometimes almost vulgar, humour and gaiety; witness his brilliant, sparkling *Le Roi malgré lui* (1887). But he went to Bayreuth, heard *Tristan* and wept, and came home to write a tragic-heroic music-drama, with Danes who cry "Ehèyo! Ehèyo!", and all the usual Wagnerian trimmings. Naturally, as in all these would-be Wagnerian works, French and German alike, the real essence of Wagner is completely misunderstood.

Chabrier handles the chorus more conventionally than Wagner ever did after *Lohengrin*. As for Gwendoline's legend, "Ne riez pas! . . . Ils sont rudes et plus forts que les ourses," it is simply an old-fashioned recitative (actually so marked) and aria, of a kind that could have been written by no one but a Frenchman. Harald's sword song contrives to be Wagnerian and an aria at one and the same time. There is some really fine music in *Gwendoline*, but it is very far from being the essential Chabrier. (Though Gwendoline's spinning-song, "Blonde aux yeux de pervenche" (Act I, Scene 4), certainly has the ring of an Auvergne folk-song, like much of the authentic Chabrier.) The Prelude to Act II is peculiarly interesting in that its latinized Wagnerism is curiously akin to a good deal of early Debussy; it is, in fact, one of the links between Wagner and the composer who quite wrongly regarded himself, and is still generally regarded, as Wagner's complete antithesis.

In d'Indy's *Fervaal* (1897) and *L'Étranger* (1903) one is much less conscious of this inner conflict between the composer's true personality and his idol. D'Indy was always a much more intellectual, much less spontaneous and lyrical artist than Chabrier. His Franckish musical ancestry had endowed him with a chromatic style, closer it is true to Liszt than to Wagner, yet which harmonized well with Wagnerian methods. His own strong personality, the austerity of his taste (so much more refined than his adored master's), and the quite Teutonic soundness of his technique as a composer combined to give his music a stamp of its own. *Fervaal*, for instance, needs only a little more pure inspiration to be a real masterpiece; the prelude to Act III is very fine indeed. On the whole the music is extraordinarily unlike almost everything else in the whole range of French opera, though the true Frenchman peeps out here and there— for instance, in Fervaal's "Jadis, enfiévré par les chantes des bardes" (Act I, Scene 2), indeed, through the greater part of this scene with Guilhen, and again in Grympuig's address in Act II, Scene 3—just as the pupil of Franck is still evident in much of the harmony. And there is just one touch that suggests Russian influence: the throbbing syncopated seconds that accompany Guilhen's "Au nom du soleil" in the Prologue come straight out of Borodin's song, "The Sleeping Princess," though Debussy had borrowed them earlier in the accompaniment to "Le Jet d'eau," a song published in 1890.

Charpentier's *Louise* has little in common with d'Indy's operas but the Wagnerism and the symbolism. But whereas d'Indy's mystical symbolism is part of the very essence of his art, Charpentier's is superficial, pretentious and completely out of place in a would-be naturalistic opera about modern Paris. Indeed, Charpentier's Wagnerism is altogether more superficial than d'Indy's; that he was a lyricist and a pupil of Massenet betrays itself on nearly every page of the score; the notorious "Depuis le jour" is only the most glaring of dozens of instances. Like Puccini, Charpentier borrows every useful weapon in the Wagnerian armoury; he even goes beyond Puccini in trying his hand at pseudo-Wagnerian combination of leitmotives, as in the celebrated passage, also in the first scene of Act III, where Louise sings, " 'Comment veux-tu la choisir?' disait mon père," to the "experience" motive while the orchestra accompanies her with a combination of the themes associated with Louise's love for Julien, Julien's love for Louise (which is a sort of motto-theme for the whole opera),[1] and the paternal hearth. Charpentier even took hints from Puccini himself; the street-cries of Act II of *Louise* were obviously the result of the hints given by

[1] It is an echo from Massenet's *Werther* (1892).

Puccini in *La Bohème*. But Charpentier is a very inferior, shoddy Puccini. His lyricism is more banal and lacks Puccini's ardent, passionate sincerity. As for the once novel realism—the family at supper, Louise reading the newspaper as the curtain falls on the first act, the scene of the night wanderer and the vagrants that opens Act II, the sewing-machine included in the score of the work-room scene, and so on—it is almost as feeble in comparison with Mussorgsky's as the music is in comparison with Wagner's. What could be less realistic than the handling of the chorus in the work-room scene?

But, as d'Indy himself has made clear,[1] the most valuable results of Wagner's influence on French music were not the creation of a quasi-Wagnerian school of French opera, but the revivification of French orchestral music and the actual *creation* of French chamber music which, until 1871, had been practically non-existent. As we have seen in the previous chapter, the downfall of the Second Empire gave French music both a fresh lease in life and a not unwholesome sense of gravity, and this renaissance was curiously stimulated and largely controlled by an extraordinary wave of enthusiasm for Wagner. And, all in all, the French operas written under this influence are less interesting than the chamber works of Franck, Fauré and their disciples, "in which," as d'Indy puts it, "our French sense of proportion and balance was able to temper the extravagances of the Wagnerian spirit, while discerningly employing and profiting by the methods and discoveries of the Bayreuth giant." In other words, Wagnerian harmony and technique were used as the medium for the expression of essentially French ideas.[2]

The same remarks apply equally to the orchestral works of this group: Franck's Symphony in D minor (1889), d'Indy's *Wallenstein* (1880), *Symphonie sur un chant montagnard français* (1886), and *Jour d'été à la montagne* (1905), Chausson's Symphony in B flat (1891), Dukas's Symphony in C (1896) and *L'Apprenti sorcier* (1897), the symphonies of Guy Ropartz and

[1] *Richard Wagner et son influence sur l'art musical français.* Paris, 1930.

[2] D'Indy also attributes to Wagnerian influence (transformation of leitmotives) that employment of "cyclic themes" which is such an important feature of the instrumental music of Franck and his school. But as we have seen, Franck anticipated even Liszt in the revival of this common seventeenth-century device.

Magnard, and so on. "None of these works," as d'Indy says, "can reasonably be accused of being Wagnerian pastiches, yet every one of them betrays in some point or other the influence of the composer of *Tristan*."

But the first important composers really to follow Wagner's lead were not Frenchmen nor did they do their best work—with the exception of one masterpiece—in the field of opera. As early as 1880 Hugo Wolf had completed a String Quartet in D minor which, despite its mainly Beethovenian ancestry, showed a good many traces of Wagner's harmonic influence. Two or three years later the slightly younger Richard Strauss, though still strongly under the influence of Schumann and Brahms, wrote a group of songs, his Op. 10, in which the harmony already shows an awareness of Wagner still greater than Wolf's (see, for instance, the popular "Allerseelen"). And after flirting with the Berliozian "programme symphony" in *Aus Italien* (1887), Strauss produced in the period 1888–90 a trio of orchestral works —*Macbeth, Don Juan* and *Tod und Verklärung*—that injected new life into the Lisztian symphonic poem and at the same time announced that the orchestral wizard Wagner had found an apprentice more wily than the one in Goethe's ballad.

At the same time Wolf, too, began to show his true mettle. In 1888 he published a first modest set of twelve songs and the same year composed the fifty-three *Mörike-Lieder*, a dozen settings of Eichendorff, and nearly half the fifty-one *Goethe-Lieder*. During 1889–91 he completed the *Goethe-Lieder*, wrote the forty-four songs of the *Spanisches Liederbuch*, the six *Alte Weisen* (settings of Gottfried Keller), and the twenty-two songs that make up the first part of the *Italienisches Liederbuch* —the most remarkable outpouring of German song since Schumann's great flood of *Lieder* in 1840. Wolf's opera *Der Corregidor* was composed in 1895 and produced the following year. The remaining twenty-four songs of the *Italienisches Liederbuch* were written in 1896, the three great *Michel-Angelo-Lieder* in 1897.

Not only is the stamp of Wagnerian harmony perceptible in the great majority of these songs, but they mark a revolution in song-writing in general, and the German *Lied* in particular, comparable with that produced in opera by the earlier works of Wagner. Compared with the much more daring songs written by Mussorgsky twenty years or so earlier, Wolf's certainly do not sound very revolutionary. Mussorgsky, particularly in the songs written when he was strongly under the influence of Dargomïzhsky, broke completely with song as it had been understood hitherto; he was willing to subdue music wholly to the words. All he sought, alike in vocal line and piano part, was music that should reproduce and intensify the natural intonation, rhythm and expression of the poem with absolute fidelity and without regard to any other consideration. (Naturally he was not invariably faithful to that ideal, especially in his later songs.) But Mussorgsky's songs were practically unknown in Germany till after Wolf's death; his influence is apparent in Debussy's songs but nowhere in German music. And if Wolf also insisted on the hegemony of poetry, he did so much less drastically than Mussorgsky. Nor did he choose realistic, grotesque or broadly comic subjects like those in which Mussorgsky delighted.

It is not true in any but a limited sense to say that Wolf applied Wagnerian methods to the song. Wagner added music to words of his own—words, artistically incomplete in themselves, that had been deliberately devised for the addition of music; Wolf sets poems that were already artistic entities, with clear metrical patterns of their own. Wagner, at any rate in theory, separated the word-bearing music from the stream of musical emotion in the orchestra; Wolf does quite often make his piano-parts very important (e.g., in "Prometheus," "Ganymed," "Der Feuerreiter" and "Kennst du das Land"), but their alleged "symphonic" nature has been a great deal exaggerated. Wolf's vocal line at its most characteristic is essentially a compromise between what I have called "word-bearing music" and "stream of musical emotion"; it is not purely word-bearing like Mussorgsky's nor absolute "instrumental" melody inspired by the words like Brahms's; it is a stream of emotion exquisitely, painfully sensitive to every shade of intonation and expression in the words. And since Wolf had come very strongly under the spell of Wagner as early as 1875, as a boy of fifteen, this vocal line quite often resembles Wagner's, while the piano-part harmonically underlines every point in the poem with a subtlety that reminds one of Wagner's orchestra. Yet Wolf's methods vary astonishingly according to the tone of the poem, or even poet, he is setting; the Mörike songs, the Goethe songs, the

Spanish and Italian songs—each set unlocks a fresh side to his nature. In some of his youthful songs (e.g., "Bescheidene Liebe," written in 1877, and even "Fussreise," "Der Gärtner" and "Der Musikant," eleven years later) he remains quite close to the *Volkslied* type of melody that has always been so dear to German song-writers; "Bescheidene Liebe" and "Der Gärtner" are even strophic. On the other hand, in such songs as "An die Geliebte" and "Peregrina II," the vocal line is merely sensitive, subtle declamation. But such absolutely naturalistic, almost Mussorgskian declamation as in the two last-named songs is not Wolf's normal method; his declamation is generally emotionally exalted and hence exaggerated. Important syllables, for instance, are abnormally sustained; even a purely lyrical composer would hardly have ventured to hold the high G sharp ("lass uns siegen") at the end of "Morgenstimmung" for more than three bars in moderate time. And this "plasticity of declamation" is, as Georg Bieri points out,[1] a thoroughly Wagnerian trait (cf. Isolde's "Fluch dir, Verruchter" in Act I, Scene 3, of *Tristan*).

Just as in his chromatic harmonies Wolf continues Wagner's work of breaking down the firm lines of tonality—he begins the tiny sixteen-bar-long "Wenn zu der Regenwand" in A and ends it in E, having touched on almost every other key on the way—his sensitive and (from a purely musical point of view) strange melodic lines and his complete breaking up of the regular metrical and rhythmic patterns of a genre that might have been expected to preserve conventional balanced structure long after it had been obliterated in instrumental music, did much to prepare the way for the still more advanced modernity of Schönberg. The ninths that stalk through the accompaniment of "Agnes" are distinctly Schönbergian. Even harmonically Wolf sometimes gives an impression of greater harshness than Wagner, though this is partly due to the forthrightness of his not very pianistic keyboard-writing. But his free use of "altered chords" shows how completely he had mastered Tristanesque harmony, and the intense discords of "Seufzer" shocked even the Wagnerians of the eighteen-nineties.

Richard Strauss, too, has been a prolific song-composer but, although he has enriched the *Lieder* repertoire with such fine

[1] *Die Lieder von Hugo Wolf.* Bern, 1935.

things as the popular "Ständchen," "Cäcilie," "Morgen" and "Traum durch die Dämmerung," he is hardly a "great" song-composer nor have his songs anything like the historical importance of Wolf's. Strauss's real importance is as the rejuvenator of the symphonic poem, which he developed into an entirely new genre, and as the composer who carried the Wagnerian orchestra to its *ne plus ultra*, exhausted the emotional possibilities of Lisztian-Wagnerian harmony as applied to essentially diatonic melody, and demonstrated that it was impossible for anyone but Wagner to write genuine Wagnerian music-drama. And in each case he has initiated a reaction against the tendencies he has worn to death.

To understand how radically new were the symphonic poems of Strauss we must glance back for a moment at the post-Lisztian symphonic poem in general. In every case the symphonic poems of Saint-Saëns, Franck, Tchaïkovsky, Balakirev and the rest were, like those of Liszt himself, still closely related to the Mendelssohnian concert-overture and the dramatic overture of the *Coriolan-Leonora No. 3* type. Each section has a poetic or pictorial or dramatic basis, but the sections are so put together, sometimes skilfully, more often rather naïvely, as to form a more or less balanced musical whole. The only real difference between Tchaïkovsky's *Romeo and Juliet* overture (1870) and his "symphonic fantasias," *The Tempest* (1873) and *Francesca da Rimini* (1877)—except that *Romeo* happens to be much better music—is that the ideas associated with "family enmity" and "the love of Romeo and Juliet" are laid out according to sonata-form while in the other two works the form is that of the "arch." *Francesca* is an example of the most elementary type of ternary form, with a 66-bar introduction: whirlwind of Hell—Francesca—whirlwind of Hell. The structural plan of *The Tempest* is less simple; it is still an "arch," though an imperfect one. It may be represented graphically thus: AxByCDCBA, D (the music contrasting Ariel with Caliban) being the crown of an arch with two members missing from one side. But these two members, x and y, are musical equivalents of two episodes that could not be repeated without reducing the whole piece to absurdity: Ariel receiving Prospero's command to raise the storm, and the storm itself. (A represents the calm sea music, B the solemn chord-passage associated with Prospero, and C the love-themes.) But it is rare indeed to find the form of a pre-Straussian symphonic poem conditioned by programmatic considerations even to this small extent. Almost invariably we find that the making of any specific "literary" points is confined to short sections stuck on to, or dovetailed into, a perfectly clear, self-sufficient musical outline.

The popular *Danse macabre* of Saint-Saëns is an excellent example. The clock strikes twelve and Death tunes up his fiddle in the introduction; the cock crows and the skeletons disperse in the coda; but the piece itself consists merely of incessant variations on two themes which towards the end are combined. The subject may have suggested the themes and their orchestral colouring, but it has certainly not conditioned their treatment or the outline of the music. As for *Phaéton* and *Le Rouet d'Omphale*, they are both in very slightly modified ternary form. The modification in *Le Rouet* consists of the insertion after the middle section (supposed to represent "Hercules groaning in the bonds he is unable to break") of a few bars based on a variant of this second theme and intended, though we should hardly have guessed it if the composer had not told us, to suggest Omphale mocking her victim. In *Phaéton* the reprise of the first section is somewhat condensed and a new chromatic theme in the bass is woven into it; and after the launching of Jove's thunderbolt, as the peak of a more or less natural musical climax, there is a coda in slow tempo brooding over the themes of the *allegro*; but the simple ternary form is not even faintly disguised.

Strauss's earliest symphonic poems, though written little more than a decade later, take us at once into a world in which not only harmony and orchestration are profoundly different from Saint-Saëns's but where the relationship between music and programme is completely altered. Not so much in *Macbeth* which, although it bears a later opus number than *Don Juan*, was actually the first of Strauss's symphonic poems to be written. (Its earliest form dates from 1887.) This fine, hard score—sounding so strangely unlike most of the later, mature Strauss—is cast in a modification of sonata-form, the recapitulation being telescoped into the latter part of the development. But it is not so much a symphonic poem as a symphonic character-study on the lines of, but vastly superior to, Anton Rubinstein's *Faust*, *Ivan the Terrible* and *Don Quixote*; a musical portrait in sonata-form of Macbeth himself, with Lady Macbeth as the "second subject."

Don Juan (1888) is a different matter altogether; this, too, is a musical character-study but with the character shown in action. Here is a piece which, like Liszt's *Der nächtliche Zug* but unlike his symphonic poems proper, does actually attempt to tell a story and which breaks through all the conventions of formal symmetry in telling it. Yet, considered even as a piece of absolute music, *Don Juan* has a fine organic shape of its own, a shape that seems to arise naturally out of its themes; and the constant recurrence of the opening themes associated with Juan himself, binding the whole together, have led many critics to declare that *Don Juan* is a sort of free rondo. It is. But its freedom is such as to make the symphonic poems of Liszt and his immediate followers seem as square and formal as an ordinary mid-eighteenth-century sonata movement by comparison with mature Beethoven. It might be represented graphically by some such formula as this: A,B,A,Ca,Cb,D,A(+D), E(+A and D), B(+C), A,D,A.[1] But some of the sections, for instance B (based on the first important "feminine" theme) and Cb (on the lovely oboe tune), are disproportionately long; themes are freely interwoven, sections skilfully fused into one another. All this blurs the formal outline still further. And the texture already shows signs of that polyphony which Strauss afterwards carried to such lengths in *Ein Heldenleben* and other works, whereas Liszt's remained predominantly homophonic.

Nevertheless, despite all this and despite obvious Wagnerian influences in the harmony and orchestration, *Don Juan*—and Strauss's music in general—owes much to Liszt and is, in fact, a good deal more Lisztian than Wagnerian. Strauss has never, even in *Elektra* (1909), the high-water mark of his chromaticism, approached the essence of *Tristan*; his chromaticism is surface-colouring, not an integral part of his thought; through all the bold dissonances, abrupt key-changes and chromatic harmonies of the most powerful works of his middle period runs a curiously Italian vein, probably derived from Italy *via* Liszt, a stream of

[1] R. C. Muschler (*Richard Strauss*. Hildesheim, N.D.) considers it to be "in sonata-form with thematically free development. The reprise is shortened. The structure resembles that of Wagner's *Siegfried Idyll*, of which Strauss is so fond."

diatonic lyricism pouring itself out in sweetly sensuous melodies and in those cloying progressions of thirds and sixths that originated in the duets of early nineteenth-century Italian opera and were transplanted into symphonic music by the hands of the pianist Liszt. Those thirds and sixths have penetrated Strauss's style more and more completely in later years—the introduction to *Der Rosenkavalier* (1911) is only one of a hundred examples that might be quoted—and his affection for sweet diatonic commonplaces has been the cause of his later remarkable decline, as it was the fundamental weakness of his contemporary Mahler. All these elements are already present in germ-form in *Don Juan*, but, thanks to the tremendous creative vitality that informs the whole piece, they are not yet weaknesses.

The further course of Strauss's development of the symphonic poem is extremely interesting. His next work in this form after *Don Juan*, *Tod und Verklärung* (1890), is an essay in musical story-telling even more detailed than its predecessor. *Till Eulenspiegels lustige Streiche* (1895), *Don Quixote* (1897) and the *Symphonia Domestica* (1904) carry this tendency perhaps as far as it can be carried. Quixote going crazy, Sancho with his short-winded aphorisms, Quixote charging the windmill and overthrown, the bleating of the flock of sheep, the attack on the pilgrims, the imaginary ride through the air, the last drubbing and Quixote's dying sigh; and the squealing baby of the *Domestica* and its squabbling parents—these are all painted in music that comes as near to precise statement of the concrete as instrumental music is ever likely to attain. Not even Honegger's *Pacific 231* (1924) is a cleverer imitation of a steam-engine than the second variation of Don Quixote is of the noise made by a flock of sheep.

But Strauss's true importance, of course, is as a musician not as a musical juggler who has too often amused himself and the groundlings with clever silliness. He has not only stuffed his symphonic poems full of narrative and pictorial points; he has poured into them a lot of fine music. And in effect, he has made the symphonic poem a sort of condensed Wagnerian music-drama without voice-parts. The combination of Strauss's thematic kaleidoscope with his orchestral polyphony produces a general effect so like that of Wagner's orchestra that it is easy to close one's eyes during the performance of a Strauss tone-poem and imagine that it is subtly accompanying, bar by bar, thoughts and emotions that are being simultaneously expressed by actors on a stage. And it is fairly obvious that in the composition of his works Strauss has followed some such definite sequence of thoughts, some such drama played in the theatre of his mind.

It is most interesting to observe how, like Wagner, he has striven—though not always successfully—to give his symphonic dramas satisfactory musical forms. It is difficult at first to discover any musical ground-plan in *Tod und Verklärung*; the sequence of musical ideas—the throbbing chords of ebbing time, the themes recalling "childhood's golden age," the dying man's desperate struggles, and the final death and transfiguration—is satisfactory enough but it appears to be conditioned solely by the psychological drama as the composer conceived it. (Not by Ritter's poem prefixed to the printed score, which was written *after* the music—though possibly by the quite different poem by Ritter which appears on the autograph score.) Nevertheless, closer analysis of the score, an analysis that disregards transitional passages and mere brief appearances of themes, reveals the following plan:

Introduction (ABA):	Throbbing chords, with references to the first "childhood" theme
	Both "childhood" themes
	Throbbing chords and first "childhood" theme
Main Section (CDBCD):	Themes of "struggle" and "despair"
	Theme of "transfiguration"
	"Childhood" themes
	Struggle and despair
	Transfiguration
Conclusion (ACBD):	Throbbing chords
	Struggle
	Second "childhood" theme
	Transfiguration

In other words a short, simple arch; a long and more developed arch, with a considerable affinity with sonata-form; and a brief review of three of the main elements in the score leading to a more extended treatment of the fourth, the theme of transfiguration.

In *Till Eulenspiegel* and *Don Quixote* Strauss solved this problem of form by casting his music in the forms of rondeau (not rondo)[1] and variations respectively;[2] in *Also sprach Zarathustra* (1895), in many respects the least satisfactory of his early works, he just fails to solve it. *Zarathustra* is very nearly what Liszt's antagonists have supposed his symphonic poems to be: loose fantasias, each section based on some poetic idea and the whole bound together only by the use of metamorphoses of basically identical themes. Each section of *Zarathustra* bears a chapter-heading from Nietzsche's book but the music seldom has even a remote connection with the contents of the corresponding chapter, and the Viennese waltz theme that dominates the dance of the Superman is one of the earliest instances of Strauss's curious affection for the simpler elements of the musical past. Yet if *Zarathustra* is merely a rhapsody, it must be admitted that it is a very brilliant rhapsody, that Strauss has woven his score so skilfully from the permutations and combinations of some five or six main themes, and so bound them all together in the "Tanzlied" section which, with its climax the "Nacht-wandlerlied," constitutes about three-fifths of the whole piece (a sort of unified recapitulation of thematic elements stated separately), that one is almost tricked into accepting it as an organic whole. Indeed even Strauss's pseudo-organism is a good deal more satisfactory than the naïve symmetrical structures of Saint-Saëns and Tchaïkovsky.

Zarathustra is interesting, too, as a forerunner of three works —*Ein Heldenleben* (1898), the *Symphonia Domestica* (1904), and the much later *Alpensymphonie* (1915)—in which the symphonic poem was so extended that the composer was almost justified in calling the two later works symphonies. Actually they are hybrids, results of a cross between the programme symphony of Berlioz and the one-movement symphonic poem of Liszt. *Ein Heldenleben*, like *Zarathustra*, is frankly sectional, very nearly a mere fantasia; one must be a thoroughgoing Strauss-worshipper like Specht[3] or Muschler to see in it, as they

[1] i.e. ABACADAE, not ABACABA.

[2] In 1897, the very year of Strauss's *Don Quixote*, d'Indy also produced a set of programmatic variations, *Istar*. Each variation is less complicated than its predecessor till at last the theme is revealed in all its simplicity, symbolizing Istar's naked arrival in the Dwelling of the Dead after parting with a garment or a jewel at each portal.

[3] Richard Specht: *Richard Strauss und sein Werk*. Two vols. Leipzig, 1921.

do, a single great symphonic "first movement" with scherzo
and adagio elements woven into it. Here, even more completely
than in *Zarathustra*, the form is dictated by the programme.
The Straussians try to explain the six sections—"The Hero,"
"The Hero's Adversaries," "The Hero's Helpmate," "The
Hero's Battlefield," "The Hero's Works of Peace," "The
Hero's Flight from the World: Conclusion"—in this way:

   I   Exposition
   II   Scherzo and first part of development
   III   Scherzo capriccioso and slow movement
   IV   Second part of development; beginning of a free reprise
   V   *Andante* and third part of development
   VI   Coda in two sections

which seems to be merely ingenious sophistry. The piece is
held together not by the stresses of musical architecture but by
the power of the composer's imagination—which triumphs even
over formlessness. Of the two later works the *Domestica* is
architecturally more satisfactory than *Ein Heldenleben*, the
Alpensymphonie less so. The *Domestica* is at least concise, and
it needs to be; the composer's imagination is so much less vital
here. The thematic economy, too, is unusual for Strauss; the
first section states the whole of the material—the three themes
of the husband, the wife's two, and the theme of the child. (In
addition the oboe d'amore is associated with the child, as the
solo 'cello is with Don Quixote and the solo viola with Sancho
Panza; and the husband is associated largely with the key of
F major, the wife with B, and the child with D minor and major.)
Then come a scherzo section depicting the child's games, a
lullaby, a slow movement (love-scene and night), and a fugal
finale (awakening, dispute and reconciliation)—all following
without a break and all based on the themes of the first
section.

As for the *Alpensymphonie* it is neither concise nor vital. It
ends as it begins with night and stillness; when the "descent"
begins we hear some of the themes of the "ascent" more or
less in reverse order. But that is the only shape the "symphony"
possesses; the latent arch is completely shattered. All we have
is a series of musical magic-lantern slides—*Zarathustra* and
Heldenleben have at least the continuity of a film—held together
only by a certain amount of theme-recurrence and by the fact

that in them all appears some form or other of the incredibly banal theme of "ascent," the motto-theme of the whole piece.

But the *Alpensymphonie* is a fairly late, isolated work of Strauss's, a feeble reversion to a form of which he had tired. Up to the *Symphonia Domestica* Strauss had been mainly a composer of orchestral programme music who had, more or less incidentally, thrown off a couple of thoroughly Wagnerian operas, *Guntram* (1895) and *Feuersnot* (1901). After the *Domestica* he devoted himself almost entirely to the stage until the Second World War and his consequent years of retirement and exile in Switzerland when he turned to the production of non-programmatic chamber works and compositions for small orchestra, such as the two Sonatinas for Wind (1942 and 1945), the *Metamorphosen* for 23 solo strings (1945), and the Concerto for oboe and small orchestra (1946). He must have been conscious that nothing more could be done with what I have called the "condensed Wagnerian music-drama without voice-parts," that he had carried programme music to the *ne plus ultra*. The expressiveness of music could be extended further only by linking it with words and action. Wagner had been right, after all.

In *Salome* (1905) Strauss created perhaps the greatest of all the Wagnerian music-dramas not actually written by Wagner himself. And even *Salome* is untrue to one vital Wagnerian principle—though admittedly a principle that Wagner himself violated—that the action must be pure "stuff for music" and the words artistically incomplete in themselves, devised so that music should complete them. But Wilde's play, even after being translated into German and slightly cut, is a perfect, self-sufficient work of art. Instead of plastic material for the composer's mind to mould to its will, material devised with that moulding already in view, Strauss was confronted with a mass of hard, beautifully cut verbal gems. He solved the problem by underlaying the text with a colossal symphonic poem, playing for about two hours without a break, and patching on to it voice-parts that sometimes double the orchestral melody, more often lapse into not very distinguished declamation. The effect is extraordinarily like Wagner and it is true that Wagner himself often lapses into this sort of thing, but one never finds in Strauss that subtle inner fusion of word and music achieved by Wagner at his best. On the other hand, Strauss makes brilliant play with

verbal leitmotives (e.g., "Wenn er kommt") musically insignificant, in both senses of the word, yet filled with meaning through
direct association with a verbal phrase.

Elektra (1909) also employs the methods of *Salome*, though
the tragedy is grimmer and even more tense, and the music has
correspondingly less lyrical beauty.   And with *Elektra* began
Strauss's collaboration with Hugo von Hofmannsthal, a collaboration so close that it might almost be said that Hofmannsthal
was to Strauss what Wagner the dramatist was to Wagner the
musician.   Their second work together, *Der Rosenkavalier*
(1911), was a masterpiece—though a masterpiece on very
different lines from *Salome* and *Elektra*.   It is not that the
method is different; the score is still completely symphonic,
though the voices have to do a good deal more singing and less
declaiming.   But that arises from the whole style and texture of
the music.   In *Der Rosenkavalier* Strauss purged his music of
the more advanced chromaticism that had crept into the two
previous operas, returned frankly to the diatonic style natural
to him, and gave free rein to his already mentioned love of
lyrical sweetness and of music's past.   He had already done this
to a considerable extent in the almost Humperdinckian *Feuersnot*
—Diemut's "Süsse Amarellen" song might have been written
by Schubert, and many of the other themes are equally *volks-
liedartig*—and, of course, Zarathustra's waltz is only one of a
number of such passages in the symphonic poems (e.g., the oboe
melody of *Don Juan*, the third variation of *Don Quixote*, the
love-scene and "Weltflucht" of *Ein Heldenleben*).   But *Der
Rosenkavalier* abandons itself almost wholly to these sweet
delights and, pastiche though it is, is one of Strauss's best works.
The final trio, to take a single example, is one of the loveliest
things he has ever written.

Unhappily *Der Rosenkavalier* seems to have been the last
effort of his true genius.   Often dangerously near the banal and
sometimes lapsing into it, the score triumphs because of the
melodic charm and the all-pervading vitality.   Its successors—
Ariadne auf Naxos (first produced in 1912 as part of the music
to Molière's *Le Bourgeois Gentilhomme*; produced in a new
frame as an independent work in 1917), *Josephslegende* (ballet)
(1924), *Die Frau ohne Schatten* (1919), *Schlagobers* (ballet)
(1924), *Intermezzo* (1924), *Die ägyptische Helena* (1928),

Arabella (1933), *Die schweigsame Frau* (1935), *Friedenstag* (1938), *Daphne* (1938) and *Capriccio* (1941)—have generally lacked this vitality and dropped all too often into the completely commonplace. Strauss's excursions into the field of symphonic ballet, which might easily have been highly important, turned out to be quite uninteresting and the operas are noteworthy chiefly as curiosities and for their technical experiments. *Ariadne*, for instance, is not only more of a *singing* opera than its predecessors, but employs only a small orchestra of thirty-seven players[1] and contains some curious attempts to recapture the musical spirit of the rococo age: the song of the nature-spirits, "Ach, wir sind es eingewöhnet," Zerbinetta's coloratura rondo "Als ein Gott kam jeder gegangen," and others, to say nothing of the transcribed Lully and pseudo-Lully in the music associated with *Le Bourgeois Gentilhomme* in the first version. The other trio of the nature-spirits, "Töne, töne, süsse Stimme," is certainly Schubertian, as Specht says, though not for his reason (that it is "a melody which seems to have fallen from Heaven") but because it contains a ridiculous and obviously unintentional quotation from the most popular of Schubert's military marches. Yet in other passages, e.g., Ariadne's "Es gibt ein Reich, wo alles rein ist," Strauss demonstrates that he is as capable as any of the old masters of conjuring fine music out of four common chords.

One of the most interesting of all Strauss's later operas is *Intermezzo*, "a bourgeois comedy with symphonic interludes" as Strauss himself calls it. The composer's foreword, in which he states his view of the whole history of German comic opera and its forms, is even more interesting than the work itself, which is little more than a brilliant experiment. The libretto, written by Strauss himself, is merely an autobiographical incident, an incident of everyday life, and the language is that of everyday life too. To set it in the style of modern German comic opera (that is, in the symphonic style of *Die Meistersinger*, *Feuersnot* and *Der Rosenkavalier*) would obviously have been impossible. Instead Strauss has given the singers a light, swiftly moving musical speech, transparently accompanied and gathering itself

[1] Originally because, as part of the incidental music to a play, it had to be played by an ordinary theatre orchestra instead of by a full opera orchestra. But the transparency of this accompaniment so pleased the composer that he repeated the experiment in *Intermezzo*.

into prolonged cantilena only in the closing scenes of each of the two acts; the lyrical element in the score is developed independently in the orchestral interludes.[1] The composer asks of his singers a sort of conversational *mezza voce*—and clear enunciation. In *Intermezzo* he has in fact created a new model for German comic opera.

Still, on the whole, it is likely that history will decide that the Strauss who matters is the Strauss of the symphonic poems, of *Salome* and *Der Rosenkavalier*, the Strauss who developed the Wagnerian orchestra and the diatonic orchestral polyphony of *Die Meistersinger* to a degree that flabbergasted even the Wagnerians. Strauss was never a revolutionary. The majority of the "cacophonies" of which he was accused thirty or forty years ago are merely the result of a free polyphony still more disregardful of transitory clashes than Wagner's was. Writing of the *Meistersinger* overture, Bernard Shaw says[2] that "only those . . . who judge its reckless counterpoint by the standard of Bach and of Mozart's *Magic Flute* overture, can realize how atrocious it used to sound to musicians of the old school. When I first heard it, with the clear march of the polyphony in Bach's B minor Mass fresh in my memory, I confess I thought that the parts had got dislocated, and that some of the band were half a bar behind the others." And those who judged *Ein Heldenleben* by the standard of *Die Meistersinger* felt just the same about it in turn. But such counterpoint is not "reckless"; it is based on the perfectly safe assumption that the human ear will ultimately accept anything that it can follow and that the musical brain can understand. In the same way Strauss was careful to smooth out the celebrated instance of bi-tonality at the end of *Zarathustra* —B major chords contradicted by the obstinate C major of the basses—with a cunning trombone chord E F sharp C natural to which the

---

[1] The orchestra of *Intermezzo* is small, though not as small as that of *Ariadne*. It consists only of thirty-three strings, double wind, three horns, two trumpets, two trombones, percussion, piano, harp and harmonium—an orchestra larger than that for which Beethoven scored the *Eroica* but a mere chamber orchestra in comparison with the colossal forces employed in many of Strauss's works. He has since become more and more fascinated by the chamber orchestra.

[2] *The Perfect Wagnerite*. Constable, 4th edition, 1923.

two opposed harmonies at first seem to offer alternate resolutions before being heard in stark contrast at the very end. Similarly his abrupt key changes are usually only extensions of the principle that admitted to the key such chords as the Neapolitan sixth, the minor form of the subdominant triad, the major triad on the supertonic, and so on.

Strauss's other "new" harmonies are usually introduced as expressive devices and he is particularly fond of an effect we have already noticed in Verdi, Puccini and Mascagni: the prolonged chromatic or diatonic side-slipping of a discord (for instance, of a chord of the seventh in *Salome* when Herod cries "Diese Rosen sind wie Feuer" and tears off the wreath).[1] Strauss out-Mascagnis Mascagni only by using a more intense dissonance (e.g., the "blood" motive in *Elektra*—D,A,C flat, E flat, G flat; see its first appearance on page 17 of the vocal score, where one of the maids speaks of "das ewige Blut des Mordes"). In *Ariadne* a triad built up of two fourths, instead of the customary thirds, is treated in the same way at the climax where Bacchus appears. And in *Josephslegende* an impressionistic colour-effect is produced, when Joseph is left alone in the evening, by a similar treatment of "added-note chords," i.e., chords in which an appoggiatura is sounded simultaneously with the true note. The passionate consecutive sevenths near the end of the love-scene of *Ein Heldenleben* which seemed so unpleasant to Ernest Newman in 1908[2] are now hardly noticed, and the consecutive seconds with which *Elektra* is sprinkled are only inversions of sevenths.

Needless to say, these discords, introduced (like all the other discords music has ever known) by the movement of parts or as special expressive and colouristic devices, quickly passed into the ordinary harmonic vocabulary in their own right simply as sounds, just as some of Strauss's deliberately ugly themes, such as those of "the hero's adversaries" in *Ein Heldenleben*, and the melodies devised to express the tortured emotions of *Elektra*,

---

[1] Indeed occasional *brief* side-slippings of diminished sevenths may be found in the Viennese classics, of more prolonged ones in Chopin, and of other chords of the seventh in Wagner: for instance, near the end of Act I, Scene 1, of *Siegfried*, where Mime cries "Halte! Halte! Wohin? He! Siegfried!" as the hero disappears into the wood.

[2] *Richard Strauss.* John Lane, 1908 (see pp. 131–32).

helped to prepare the way for the melodic eccentricities of the mature Schönberg and his disciples.

Similarly, as an orchestrator, Strauss has done little but extend and develop the Wagner tradition. Even in his later symphonic poems he had employed the full *Ring* orchestra, with eight horns, and in *Elektra* he enlarges it, demanding an E flat clarinet, two basset horns and a fourth ordinary clarinet (in addition to Wagner's three, plus bass clarinet) and six trumpets instead of Wagner's three, while the strings throughout are written for as follows: first, second and third violins, first, second and third violas, first and second 'cellos, and basses. But colossal orchestras were then in fashion; even the *Elektra* orchestra is not as huge as that required in Schönberg's *Gurrelieder* (1901). As we have seen, the reaction to a small orchestra in *Ariadne* was imposed by the fact that the work was originally intended to be given in a theatre, not an opera-house, but *Intermezzo* showed that the earlier work had taught Strauss a real lesson in vocal accompaniment. The post-1918 reaction against the giant orchestras of the earlier part of the century was general, however, and was possibly due partly to economic as well as to purely artistic reasons.

Granted that Strauss's understanding of the individual instruments and their capabilities is unsurpassable, that his handling of the orchestral masses is often superb, and that his scoring is strikingly individual, it must also be said that his orchestral methods have resulted in the *reductio ad absurdum* of polyphony on the giant orchestra. Rich scoring, subtly mixed colours, carefully kept balance between the parts, numerous holding-notes and free crossing of parts have frequently combined, as in the fugue of the *Domestica* and the "works of peace" section of *Ein Heldenleben*, to produce a mere sonorous muddle. It is highly instructive to compare such passages in Strauss with the *tutti* scoring of Rimsky-Korsakov, who has exercised a far greater influence on modern orchestration in the non-Teutonic countries. Admittedly Korsakov's orchestration is based on an entirely different, mainly homophonic style, but there are a few examples of polyphonic *tutti* in his work (e.g., in the harbour scene of *Sadko*)—all sounding remarkably clear and brilliant, thanks to the sharp individualization of each part by a special timbre or register and to the almost complete disregard, if necessary, of "vertical" sonority.

Strauss's scoring also contrasts strongly with that of his Austrian contemporary, Mahler, who although strongly influenced by Wagner, directly and through Bruckner, really belongs to quite another tradition. Despite his Jewish blood, Mahler's music is essentially Austrian—in the line of Schubert and Bruckner—and, as products of latter-day nationalism, will be discussed in a later chapter. But it is worth pointing out here that, although he was unable to escape the glamour of Wagner's orchestra, Mahler's own scoring was based largely on the methods of Schubert and Bruckner, which in turn, as Egon Wellesz has pointed out,[1] are firmly rooted in the old baroque church and theatre music of Austria. Paradoxically, although Mahler never aimed at Wagnerian-Straussian orchestral polyphony, he often achieved clearer line-drawing in timbre than Strauss has ever done. He used great orchestral masses but was much more anxious than Strauss that everything should be clear and audible; it is well known that his revisions of his scores were always in the direction of economy and clarification. His use of the individual instruments is characterized by brilliant perversity, apparent *mis*-use—against their own nature and against the nature of the music given to them: fanfares for wood-wind, melodic employment of the trumpet, etc. Instead of reserving trumpet-melodies for climaxes, Mahler used the trumpet as freely as any wood-wind instrument—purely for the sake of clear line-drawing through the orchestral mass. And this practice of his influenced the later Strauss in turn, particularly in the *Alpensymphonie* and the more recent operas; Wellesz draws attention to a passage in the *Alpensymphonie* (page 77 of the score) played by the first trumpet solo, "which in Strauss's earlier works would never have been given to this instrument but to a wood-wind group."

But the main line of post-Wagnerian evolution, harmonic as well as orchestral, was continued not by Mahler but by his friend Schönberg. The difference between Schönberg's post-Wagnerism and Strauss's is roughly this: Strauss mainly developed the free diatonic polyphony of *Die Meistersinger*, Schönberg's evolution is essentially an intensification of the chromatic harmony and counterpoint of *Tristan*.[2] But Schönberg worked through his

[1] *Die neue Instrumentation.* Two vols. Berlin, 1928–29.
[2] Though diatonic elements play a part in his music even as late as the Second String Quartet (1908).

quasi-Wagnerian phase much more quickly than Strauss—
neither, of course, was ever a mere imitator of the master—
and changed his style in precisely the opposite direction from
Strauss. Whereas Strauss gave full rein to his innate lyrical
impulse and lapsed into fluent banality ("composing as the cow
gives milk," as he himself said of the writing of the *Alpensymphonie*), Schönberg took refuge in the intellectual world
of technical ingenuity that had obviously enticed him from the
beginning.

In this chapter I propose to discuss only the three important
early works of Schönberg written before this change in his style:
the string sextet, *Verklärte Nacht* (composed 1899), the *Gurrelieder* for soli, chorus and orchestra (composed and almost entirely
orchestrated in 1900–01, though completed only in 1911 and not
performed till 1913), and the symphonic poem *Pelleas und
Melisande* (comp. 1902–03). Wagnerian as these works are, study
of them is indispensable to the understanding of the mature
Schönberg for, although he writes in Wagnerian idiom, what he
has to say is almost purely Schönbergian. By grasping the nature
of his thoughts, the cast of his mind, while these are expressed
in familiar terms, it is much less difficult to understand them
when they are expressed in the strange terms of his highly
compressed later idiom.

Verklärte Nacht shows Schönberg at twenty-five taking over
the complete harmonic stock-in-trade of *Tristan* and expressing
himself in it with astounding ease and fluency. But it is characteristic of the composer that the form and content were new even
if the harmonic language was not strikingly so. (At any rate to
modern ears; contemporaries, who had not yet heard even
Salome, were worried by the presence of "last inversions of chords
of the ninth" and similar atrocities.) *Verklärte Nacht*, though
chamber music, is a symphonic poem in one movement, based on
a poem by Richard Dehmel, and falling into five sections corresponding with the sections of the poem; in short, a counterpart
of *Ein Heldenleben* carried out in a field hitherto practically
uninvaded by programme music.

The *Gurrelieder* and *Pelleas und Melisande* both suffer from
the elephantiasis that afflicted so much German music at this
period. Both are scored for colossal forces; the *Gurrelieder*
demand, among other things, four piccolos as well as four flutes,

seven clarinets, ten horns, six timpani, a vast mass of percussion including "a large iron chain," and strings so numerous that both first and second violins can be divided into ten parts, and violas and 'cellos each into eight—to say nothing of three four-part male choirs and an eight-part mixed choir. Needless to say, this enormous body of performers is not used simply to increase the volume of sound; it is used to produce effects of extra-ordinary subtlety and beauty of colour. But one often wonders whether, even so, the means are not disproportionate to the result. For instance, in Tove's first song, at the words "Abglanz nur der Gottesträume" (page 21 of both full score and vocal score) a canon between a solo first violin (and harp) and solo 'cello is accompanied by muted strings divided into no fewer than twenty-two parts (some pizzicato, some playing harmonics) as well as soft wind and brass. But Verdi had produced a very similar and even more striking effect in *Aïda* ("Vedi? di morte l'angelo" in the last scene) merely by sub-dividing an ordinary body of strings plus a flute and a couple of clarinets.

The *Gurrelieder* are particularly valuable for the light they throw on the emergence of Schönberg's personal style. The wide melodic leaps (e.g., Tove's "Nun sag ich dir zum ersten Mal: 'König Volmer, ich liebe Dich!' " page 40 of the vocal score) and the melodic angularity in general, the love of canon and imitation, the use in "The Wild Hunt of the Summer Wind" of a *speaker* whose part—pitch as well as rhythm—is indicated in musical notation: all these point to the mature Schönberg. The love of contrapuntal device, apparently for its own sake, is specially significant; Schönberg was a self-taught composer and the self-taught are generally as proud of their learning as the self-made man is of his wealth. Admittedly Schönberg had every reason to be proud; the imitations and so on are often—as in the accompaniment to Tove's first song—natural and beautiful. But in a composer who was soon to lay himself open to the charge of over-intellectualism and who, in his prose-writings, has always shown himself particularly sensitive to this charge, such pas-sages as the double canon of the final chorus are of more than ordinary significance.

In *Pelleas und Melisande* fresh bogies show their heads: whole-tone scales (Melisande's death), chords built up of fourths instead of thirds[1] (just before the first entry of the "Pelleas" theme), trombone *glissandi* (suggesting the gloom of the castle vaults). Schönberg asserts in his *Harmonielehre*[2] that when he first wrote whole-tone passages he was unacquainted with the use of the scale by either Liszt, the Russians or Debussy—or with any of the Oriental varieties of music in which the whole-tone mode is said (on what authority I do not know) to be employed. Not only that: obviously being uneasily aware of the artificiality of the scale, he asserts that he had already written a passage "pointing to the whole-tone scale" in a middle part in *Verklärte Nacht* without noticing it till it was pointed out to him. His whole-tone chords in *Pelleas*, too, he says, arose simply from the chromatic movement in contrary motion of augmented triads, the resultant chords being alternately augmented triads and whole-tone chords. Nor are they with him, as with Debussy, impressionistic colour-effects. "I have felt the chord more as a link with other chords, the scale as a peculiar alteration of melody. I have never over-valued either chord or scale." The gentleman doth protest too much. But he makes out a more convincing case for his chords built up of three superimposed perfect fourths, which occur only twice and are immediately resolved on to "normal" chords; as he points out, their ancestry is to be found in the opening of the finale of Beethoven's *Pastoral* Symphony and the distant hunting horns at the beginning of the second act of *Tristan*. However, within three or four years, in the first *Kammersinfonie* (comp. 1906), we find him using a melodic progression of perfect fourths as thematic material, as indeed Strauss had already done for the "Jochanaan" theme in *Salome*.

Schönberg has emphasized again and again in the *Harmonielehre* that "one must obey only one's ear, one's feeling for sound, one's creative impulse, fantasy; never mathematics or æsthetics" and, apropos of the whole-tone scale and other "new"

[1] At the beginning of the first movement of his E flat Symphony, Borodin makes considerable use of a chord which, owing to its layout:

F
C
A flat
E flat
B flat

sounds like a second inversion of a chord built up of four perfect fourths.

[2] Vienna, 3rd edition, 1922.

scales, that "one can compose freely in a tonality only when the feeling for this tonality is present in one's unconscious self." Which is perfectly true. But there is all too much evidence that Schönberg's practice in his later works does not square with these admirable axioms—which, indeed, sound suspiciously defensive.

But in *Pelleas* Schönberg's intellectualism had not yet turned to its drier forms. The piece as a whole is intensely romantic, perhaps the highest peak of post-Tristanesque romanticism. For the most part the intellectualism is apparent only in the extreme complexity of the polyphony: the incredible elaboration and multiplication of inner parts, the interweaving of themes in combination and imitation. The orchestral polyphony of *Pelleas* is, in fact, more complicated than that of *Ein Heldenleben* or the *Domestica*—and is moreover intensely chromatic. As Wellesz says,[1] "It is clear that after this work Schönberg could go no further in this direction. . . . He had to strike out in a new direction, which he found in his middle period through the employment of strict forms." In other words by a gradual return to severely classical principles of construction. As we shall see later, "return to classicism" soon became a very popular motto.

Just two months after the first performance of Schönberg's *Pelleas* (in January, 1905), the so-called "Third Symphony" of another very individual post-Wagnerian composer was given for the first time in Paris: Skryabin's *Poème divin*. The course of Skryabin's development was not dissimilar to Schönberg's. Beginning as a composer of beautifully polished piano miniatures, strongly Chopinesque in character, he soon came under the influence of Liszt and Wagner (very apparent in his Second Symphony (1903)) and quickly developed a highly individual harmonic idiom of his own. Like Schönberg's, it was essentially Chopinesque-Lisztian-Wagnerian in origin; like Schönberg he quickly developed a love of chords built up of fourths (see the second subject of the *allegro* of the Second Symphony for an early example of this).[2] But, unlike Schönberg, Skryabin failed

[1] *Arnold Schönberg.* Leipzig, 1921. An English translation by W. H. Kerridge was published by Dent in 1925.

[2] Even in the very early *Impromptu à la mazur*, Op. 2, No. 3, written in 1886, at the age of fourteen, a passing-note and a suspension combine to produce a fourths-chord—F,B,E,A—at bar 45. Chords of fourths also occur in the Preludes to Satie's *Le fils des étoiles* (1891).

to attract gifted young musical disciples. And the one really clever musician who might have continued his tradition—the Myaskovsky of the Second and Third Symphonies (1912 and 1915 respectively)—ultimately preferred to put his tongue in his cheek (or perhaps, indeed, to take it out) and write symphonies full of diatonic tunes that could be understood by the proletarian masses (e.g., Nos. 12, 14, 15 and 16 (written during the period 1932–36)).   Consequently the whole of the later development of Skryabinesque harmony is a mere side-track in the history of music as a whole.

Still, it is easy to follow Skryabin's evolution up to the Fifth Piano Sonata and the orchestral *Poème de l'extase* (both composed in 1907). And it is not difficult to see that he was far from being the genius his admirers took him to be; nearly as far as from being the Christ he took himself to be. His genuine talent for the lyrical and epigrammatic was soon exhausted, and his later works, the orchestral poem *Prometheus* (1911), the last piano sonatas and the rest, products of an incredible egomania, are essentially paper music, cunningly disguised elaborations of symmetrical harmonic schemes worked out beforehand bar by bar. His harmonic system itself—the foundation of each composition on a basic chord built up in fourths from notes selected from the natural harmonic series—is *a priori* no more sterile than the twelve-tone system of the later Schönberg, but it has been completely neglected by all later composers except a few minor Russians, and is therefore of little importance.

However, Skryabin is interesting in one other respect. He is the only artist who has not merely accepted Wagner's conception of an Art embracing all the arts but tried to extend it. As is well known, his *Prometheus* has a part for a "light keyboard" (*clavier à lumières*) controlling the play of coloured lights on a screen. But this was only a very mild experiment. Throughout the last ten years of his life (1905–15) his insane imagination brooded over a *Mystery* to be performed in a hemispherical temple in India (mirrored in a lake so as to produce a sphere, the perfect form), in which music, poetry, dancing, colours and scents would combine to produce in the participants "a supreme final ecstasy." "The physical plane of consciousness would disappear and a world cataclysm would begin."

Perhaps this, too, is the place to speak of the one important

English composer who came strongly under the direct influence of Wagner. Elgar, like the French composers of the Franck school with whom he has much in common, employed more or less Wagnerian harmony and Wagnerian methods of orchestra-tion as media for the expression of entirely individual, by no means German, musical thought.[1] And in *The Light of Life* (1896), *King Olaf* (1896), *Caractacus* (1898), *The Dream of Gerontius* (his most perfect large-scale work) (1900), *The Apostles* (1903) and *The Kingdom* (1906) he applied Wagnerian methods, including systematic use of leitmotives, to those favourite English forms, oratorio and cantata, and by the originality of his creative talent gave these moribund genres new life. Post-Wagnerian affinities are apparent in Elgar's purely orchestral works: for instance, the motto-theme and the Franckish transformation of themes in the First Symphony (1908) and a quite Straussian degree of musico-pictorial precision in the "symphonic study" *Falstaff* (1913). But in neither of these cases is the music itself either Franckish or Straussian. As for the earlier *Enigma Variations* (1899), they are remarkably free from "influence" of any kind, Wagnerian or any other. Elgar's melody, in particular, is strikingly individual. Indeed practically everything that he wrote, large work or small, bears the unmistakable cachet of a strongly marked personality—a fact which alone would suffice to place his work above that of any other British composer since Purcell. More than that it would be unwise to claim; his place is beside d'Indy and Dukas and Mahler, not with the Strausses and Debussys and Schönbergs.

[1] His sequences, for instance, owe more to Handel's than to Wagner's.

IV

THE MUSIC OF YESTERDAY AND TO-DAY

I. THE REACTION AGAINST ROMANTICISM: IMPRESSIONISM

In the music of Strauss, in early Schönberg and in Skryabin we have seen the romantic Wagnerian harmonic idiom turning over-ripe and then rotten, as we have seen the Wagnerian music-drama decaying in *Der Rosenkavalier* and the operas of Puccini. But before it died Wagnerism had done its work—or perhaps one should say, done the mischief. Ultra-romanticism had strained to breaking-point not only music's power of emotional expression but the very stuff of music as it had hitherto been known. *Tristan* and the later works of other composers which further exploited its idiom—such as Schönberg's *Pelleas*—had so enlarged the bounds of tonality that tonality seemed to have ceased to have any real meaning, and had accustomed the ear to accept so many text-book discords as normal and concordant that the old theoretical division of chords into consonant sheep and dissonant goats had become obviously ridiculous. Consonance and dissonance had become purely relative terms—as indeed they always have been. Similarly *Unendliche Melodie* had not only strained to pieces the metrical symmetry of pre-Wagnerian melody, but deprived rhythm of most of its primitive vitality. The tremendous power of Wagnerism had, so to speak, burst the boiler of romantic music. The time was ripe at the turn of the century for the making of a new music, non-romantic or at any rate non-emotional, a music that would naturally be based to some extent upon the shattered fragments of the old and that would also incorporate any new notions that were flying about.

The Russians alone, with their love of technical experiment for its own sake, had contributed a considerable number of such new notions: the whole-tone scale, Mussorgsky's empirical "expressionistic" harmony with its complete disregard of all precedent (revolutionary, whereas even that of *Tristan* is evolutionary), Korsakov's scale of alternate tones and semitones, another monkey-wrench in the machinery of tonality. In his orchestral *Fantasia on Finnish Themes* (perf. 1869), Dargomïzhsky at one point establishes the key of D major with a full close and gives the trombones a phrase unmistakably in D major too —accompanying it, however, with the dominant and tonic chords of E minor. Another passage in the same work presents the phenomenon of simultaneous major and minor. Polytonality became an accomplished fact then as early as the eighteen-sixties, though there is of course a very great difference between the occasional employment of such devices and the common use of them as a normal feature of a composer's style. Dargomïzhsky's brief experiments in whole-tone harmony have already been referred to.[1]

In his *Snowmaiden* (1882) Rimsky-Korsakov carried whole-tone harmony a step further; the *Leitharmonie* of the Wood Spirit in that work consists of a whole-tone chord—A flat, D, F sharp, B flat (resolved on to a G major triad' —and in one scene a chord is built up of all six notes of the whole-tone scale. Against an F sharp-D tremolo of the violins, the horns play in triplets an augmented triad, C-E-G sharp, to which the trombones enter on B flat; the chord is resolved on to an A major triad.

Nor were such experiments by any means peculiar to the Russians. The later works of Liszt—for instance, the melodrama, "Der traurige Mönch" (1860), the piano piece *Trübe Wolken* (1881), and *La lugubre gondola* for piano and violin (1882)—are full of daring harmonic chemistry and anticipations of expressionism and atonalism. And we find Verdi basing the "Ave Maria" of his *Quattro pezzi sacri* (1898) on an atonal *scala enigmatica*: C,D flat, E,F sharp, G sharp, A sharp, B,C in the ascending form. Then in his *Entwurf einer neuen Aesthetik der Tonkunst* (Leipzig, 1 07), that extraordinarily clever musician but very overrated composer, Ferruccio Busoni, suggested the subdivision of the whole tone into *six* equal parts and, more recently still, various composers (of whom the most important is Aloys Hába) have experimented with quarter-tones. Busoni also advocated the construction of a vast number of fresh scales based on fresh arrangements of tones and semitones. This putting the theoretical scale-abstraction before the living music,

[1] See page 147.

from which it should be deduced, is all too typical of the twentieth-century composer's attitude to his art.

On the other hand, even such a naïve composer as Dvořák, whom we are not accustomed to think of as a one-time revolutionary, seemed to his contemporaries dangerously like an anarchist. Hadow, writing in 1894,[1] regarded him as both an atonalist and a polytonalist. (Occasionally, of course; not as a rule.) "Dvořák is the one solitary instance of a composer who adopts the chromatic scale as unit, who regards all notes as equally related. His method is totally different from that of chromatic writers like Grieg and Chopin, for Grieg uses the effects as isolated points of colour, and Chopin embroiders them, mainly as appoggiaturas, on a basis of diatonic harmony. His 'equal temperament' is totally different from that of Bach, for Bach only showed that all the keys could be employed, not that they could be arranged in any chance order or sequence. But to Dvořák the chromatic passages are part of the essential texture, and the most extreme modulations follow as simply and easily as the most obvious. In a word, his work, from this standpoint, is truly a *nuova musica.* . . ." Or, as Hadow himself has pointed out elsewhere,[2] a realization of Liszt's dream of a *genre omnitonique.* Again: "We rather lose our bearings when, in the second of the *Legenden,* we find a phrase which has its treble in G and its tenor in D flat; or when, as in the fifth number of *The Spectre's Bride,* the music passes from one remote key to another with a continuous and facile display of resource that is apparently inexhaustible." Later, far more extreme developments have made us immune to any sense of bewilderment when confronted with Dvořák. Hadow himself qualified his opinion of that passage (at the return of the *Tempo primo* 24 bars before the end) in the *Legend,* Op. 59, No. 2 (composed in 1880), in a communication to the author of the article on "Atonality and Polytonality" in Cobbett's *Cyclopædic Survey of Chamber Music:*[3] "I do not think that Dvořák had any idea of polytonality. . . . Polytonality is not a part of his work, but I think it is a consequence." Precisely. These phenomena should be judged from a contemporary, not from a modern standpoint. If

---

[1] *Studies in Modern Music* (Second Series).
[2] *Music* (Home University Library). Williams and Norgate, N.D.
[3] O.U.P., 1929.

Dvořák was very far from being a whole-hogging polytonalist or atonalist, he was indisputably one of the pioneers of both polytonality and atonalism. And the same may be said of that unhappy might-have-been, Max Reger.

But these new elements and new possibilities were much less important than the new way of looking at music, the new musical mentality that began to use them as its materials. The new elements might have been used—as we have seen, they were actually used by Schönberg and others—as new means of romantic expression. The historic importance of Debussy is due not to his bold use of the new elements that had appeared in music—the whole-tone scale and the rest—but to his use of them, together with numerous relics of nineteenth-century methods, to make *a new music*. This new music, the result of an entirely fresh way of regarding music, sprang directly out of romanticism and still had a number of traits in common with it, but it was genuinely romantic no longer.

Ever since Beethoven, music had been largely concerned with non-musical values. It had drawn much closer to the other arts and its power of emotional expression had been enormously increased and at the same time made more precise. Even Brahms, the least literary of all the great nineteenth-century composers, the purest of all nineteenth-century thinkers-in-sound, was at least half a romantic. Even he had often been inattentive to the purely sensuous beauty of sound. And, broadly speaking, it is true to say that for the nineteenth-century romantic composer music was first and foremost a language; less a thing-in-itself than an audible symbol of ideas and emotions. The revolution begun by Debussy took the form of a return to intense interest in sound for sound's sake, in an acutely sensitive exploitation of timbres, of so-called "dissonances" (for their own sake as sound-colours instead of for their expressive values), and of such curious devices as the whole-tone scale. Nevertheless, Debussy's work was still for the most part far too closely linked with literature and painting and nature impressions to be absolute music. But it was a step in the direction of absolute music, a half-way house between romanticism and a new classicism, and Debussy himself actually arrived at pure neo-classicism in his last works, the three *Sonates pour divers instruments* written in 1915–17.

The new art of Debussy, generally called "musical impressionism" from its affinity with the work of the impressionist painters, was just as literary in origin as the romanticism of Berlioz sixty years earlier. Just as Berlioz's symphonies are obvious products of the age of *Hernani*, Debussy's most characteristic compositions could have been written only in a period that had absorbed Verlaine and Mallarmé. The French symbolist poets had derived from Poe, through Baudelaire, a purely sensuous conception of poetry.[1] They demanded that, as Verlaine put it, poetry should be "De la musique avant toute chose," a tissue of lovely word-sounds and verbal rhythms. The meaning of the words was of much less consequence; indeed, it was better that they should actually state nothing, should be merely evocative symbols. "I think there should be nothing but allusion," said Mallarmé. "The contemplation of objects, the fleeting image of the daydreams they excite—these are the song; the Parnassians take the thing as a whole and show it you; hence they are wanting in mystery; they deprive the mind of that delicious joy of believing that it is creating."

It was this sensuousness, this vagueness and this exquisite subtlety, this escape from thought in pure feeling—already half-musical—that Debussy transferred wholly to the sphere of music. A Debussy purely a musician, as Mozart and Haydn were purely musicians, is as unthinkable as a purely musical Berlioz. His music is always that of a man intensely in love with impressionist painting and Japanese prints and symbolist poetry. (And, in earlier days, at the end of the 'eighties, with the poems and paintings of Rossetti and the Pre-Raphaelites in general.) But these extra-musical influences alone would not have sufficed to make a musical revolutionary out of that young disciple of Massenet, the individuality of whose genius always lay in exquisite sensitiveness to circumambient influences rather than in any positive power of personality. Contemporary poetry and painting gave a general direction to his art, even to his technique. But if the youthful admirer and imitator of Lalo, Massenet and Saint-

[1] Poe's own definition of "the poetry of words," given in his essay on "The Poetic Principle," is "the rhythmical creation of beauty." "Its sole arbiter is taste. With the intellect or with the conscience, it has only collateral relations. Unless incidentally, it has no concern whatever either with duty or with truth."

Saëns had not been beset by numerous other musical loves—
from plainsong and Palestrina to Borodin, Mussorgsky and
Wagner (particularly the Wagners of *Tristan* and *Parsifal*[1])—
neither Mallarmé nor Monet and Renoir, nor (one fears) his
own musical personality, would have given him the materials to
build *Pelléas et Mélisande* or *La Mer*.

The hopeless inadequacy of the Massenet idiom for the expression of a vague and subtle mood, indeed of anything but sweet
sensuousness, is most completely demonstrated by the *Rêverie*
for piano written in 1890, though that, perhaps, is an extreme
instance of disparity between what Debussy wished to say and his
means of saying it, and in any case (as the composer himself
admitted) the piece is of little importance. The popular *Clair de
lune* from the *Suite bergamasque*, written at about the same time,
is another instance. In the earlier *Arabesques* and *Petite Suite*
and in some of the early songs the Massenet-Gounod idiom is
used to express ideas hardly distinguishable from those of
Massenet and Gounod themselves. Here and there this element
is tinctured by a slight flavour of Borodin. And, of the *Cinq
poèmes de Baudelaire* (1887–89), while one song, "Le Jet
d'eau," is still Borodinesque, the others are distinctly Wagnerian.

The nature of Debussy's evolution can be seen very easily in
his earliest important instrumental work, the String Quartet
(1893). As regards its external architecture the Quartet plainly
belongs to the school of Franck; it is in cyclic form, all four
movements being based on metamorphoses of a single theme,
and the broad traditional forms are no more modified than in the
works of d'Indy, Chausson and the other members of this school.
But in its internal organism it differs fundamentally from these.
The themes are not developed in the classical manner; they are
merely repeated in a sort of mosaic (in a manner that owes
something to the Russians) against delicately changing backgrounds. Edward Lockspeiser[2] has emphasized this quality by a
comparison with Beethoven's first quartet (Op. 18, No. 1), written
at nearly the same age: "That philosophic unity, that dignity,

---

[1] And possibly the curious *Sarabandes* (1887) and other compositions
of the eccentric café pianist, Erik Satie, with their progressions of unresolved ninths and other harmonic audacities. For that matter, there
are also consecutive ninths in Chabrier's *Le Roi malgré lui* (cf. the duet
for Alexina and Henri de Valois) which also appeared in 1887.

[2] *Debussy.*

that drama which Beethoven perceived" (and the Franckists, too, in their different way) "meant nothing to Debussy. As Beethoven's spacious structure is dependent on the growth of ideas, Debussy's mosaic-like form is made to convey a series of sensations."

Mosaic patterns conveying a series of sensations, or, rather, cumulatively conveying a single main impression with great intensity: that is the essence of Debussy's art and of impressionism in general. "As in painting so also in music," says Kurth,[1] "the most general characteristic of impressionism may be described as a dissolution of the old organic connections and a fresh lumping together [Zusammenballung] of the separate effects into a general effect of a new kind. . . . In impressionistic music the analogy with painting lies in the combination of tone-colours to a mood-conveying general colour-effect, often confused in sound, in which the separate elements are no longer to be grasped in a tonal sense. As in painting the objects are indicated only by the interweaving of separate shades of colour, the musical texture arises from the reflexes of fluid sound-shapes." Though, as Walter Niemann has pointed out,[2] the technique of musical impressionism has less in common with impressionistic painting than with the type of painting known as pointillisme, which produces its effects by the massing of an infinite number of tiny points of pure colour. In music the place of these points of colour is taken by tiny motives, thematic fragments, pregnant chords and subtle instrumental timbres.

Debussy's Quartet is very far from being a purely impressionistic work, of course. Tonality is loosened—the opening of the first movement is in the Phrygian mode—and it is very obvious that Debussy possessed nothing of the old classical sense of key-organization and its values; but his harmonies and melodic patterns have by no means lost all tonal significance and relationship; the call of the tonic is still felt. And although there is very little true organic connection, at least an outward show of it is kept up. The orchestral Prélude à L'Après-midi d'un faune (1894) is much nearer to pure impressionism, though there is a disconcerting lapse into the melodic idiom of Massenet in the D flat section (expressif et très soutenu). In this work a colour impressionism of subtle instrumentation intensifies the charm

[1] Romantische Harmonik.
[2] Die Musik seit Richard Wagner. Berlin, 1913.

of the impressionistic sound-patterns; tonality and organic connection are still further dissolved; only a certain amount of more
or less sustained melody and a drowsy, lifeless, but still definite
and more or less regular rhythmic pulse remain to hold the music
together in the old manner. The whole-tone scale, that very
potent agent of tonal disintegration, makes fleeting appearances
(see page 9, bars 1 and 2, of the miniature score), as it had
already done in the Quartet, though Debussy was yet a long
way from such complete whole-tone compositions as *Cloches à
travers les feuilles* (1907) and *Voiles* (1910).

In the orchestral *Nocturnes* (comp. 1897–99, perf. 1900–01)
and the opera *Pelléas et Mélisande* (perf. 1902) the process is
completed. Melody finally dissolves into motives or, at the most,
brief phrases. The back of metrical rhythm is finally broken, all-
through pulse being replaced by a series of disconnected throbs.

All these phenomena, it must be repeated, have their origin
in romantic music. We have already seen how romanticism
produced a slowing up, a devitalization of rhythm. And Debussy's
repetitions of phrases, and later of mere motives, due to intense
savouring of their sound-quality, remind one of Liszt's "wall-
paper patterns" and the general romantic delight in "the
dazzling idea as such." The repetitions are partly due in both
cases, the romantic and the impressionistic, to the fact that the
composers' imaginations are not functioning exclusively in
terms of absolute music, that their ideas are symbols suggesting
definite emotions or visual concepts. But with the impressionists the delight in mere sensuous sound is even more intense
than with the romantics. Nevertheless, even some of the very
same sensuous effects loved by Debussy were anticipated by
Liszt and Wagner. Debussy's very characteristic use of seconds
melted, as it were, into a single tone—as in *La lune descend sur
le temple qui fut* from the *Images* (1907), to take only one of
innumerable examples—may be found in Liszt's *Au bord d'une
source* (1836) and Wagner's song, "Im Treibhaus" (1857–58),
in both these cases suggesting the drip of water.

Indeed, Liszt's music is full of impressionistic traits.[1] Consider

[1] Individual traits of impressionism may be found in the music of
almost every age, from the Elizabethan keyboard writers to the five-
against-four effect for 'cellos and basses in the storm movement of
Beethoven's *Pastoral* Symphony.

such songs of his as the second setting of "Im Rhein, im schönen Strome" (1856) or the setting of Hebbel's "Blume und Duft" (1860). (His duet "O Meer im Abendstrahl" (1883) actually anticipates the still more modern musical "expressionism.") Schering[1] has contended with some reason that the *Sposalizio* of 1839 is in a sense impressionistic; *Au bord d'une source*, *Eglogue*, the end of *Les Cloches de Genève* (all from the first "year" of *Années de pèlerinage*), and the celebrated *Jeux d'eau à la Villa d'Este* of 1877 are all unmistakably so. The impressionistic elements in Wagner are less obvious, except in so far as such passages as the *Waldweben* are impressionistic, but *Tristan* contains a number of them: the answering horn-calls near the beginning of Act II (which seem to herald almost everything in modern music: impressionism, chords of fourths, polytonality), the very Debussyish opening of Act III,[2] the numerous pregnant silences of Act I, so like the silences and almost silences of *Pelléas*.

For the truth is, as Debussy himself probably knew in his heart, that *Pelléas* is a strangely Wagnerian work. Debussy had come so strongly under the influence of Wagner towards the end of the eighteen-eighties that he was obliged to struggle very consciously throughout the next two decades to escape that influence. Beginning his earliest stage-work, *Diane au bois*, in 1886, he wrote that it would be "ridiculous" to take Wagner as his model, but Vallas[3] tells us of *Rodrigue et Chimène* (1890–92) that beside the influences of Chabrier and Massenet, of Mussorgsky and the other Russian nationalists, that of Wagner is still very potent: "of *Tristan* when he had to interpret a mournful meditation or sing a love-duet (syncopations in the accompaniment, intervals of ninths in the voices), of *Götterdämmerung* when he wished to express some heroic sentiment, and of *Parsifal* (the flower-maidens' song)." Debussy wrote only three scenes of *Rodrigue* and then abandoned it, very conscious that he had not been true to himself. He was equally conscious of his own Wagnerism when he began work on *Pelléas*. Having completed the initial version of the fountain scene by September,

[1] "Über Liszts Persönlichkeit und Kunst" (*Peters Jahrbuch*, 1926).
[2] Wagner actually experimented with the whole-tone scale here (bars 6–10), and though he modified the passage afterwards it still retains a curious whole-tonal flavour.
[3] *Claude Debussy et son temps*. Paris, 1932.

1892, he was obliged to write to Chausson three or four weeks later that "it won't do at all. It resembles a *duo* by Mr. Thingumabob or no matter whom; above all, the ghost of old Klingsor, alias R. Wagner, kept peeping out." Debussy might assert as strongly as he liked that "the Wagnerian formula was suitable only to the particular case of Wagner's genius" and that one must try to be "*après Wagner* and not *d'après Wagner*." The very strength of his reaction shows how completely under the spell he was. And, for all his protests and all his striving, the direct influence is as evident as the indirect (the reaction). The ghost of old Klingsor is never in serious danger of being laid in *Pelléas et Mélisande*.

We may put it that *Pelléas* is a Wagnerian opera by a musician of strikingly original genius whose temperament was almost the perfect antithesis of Wagner's and whose essential technique was fundamentally different from Wagner's. *Pelléas* is a *Tristan* written not only in a more modern—not so very much more modern—vocabulary but with "endless" polyphonic melody replaced by the mosaics of impressionism, with passion and eloquence replaced by sensations and emotions barely hinted at and by a vocal language as simple as that of everyday life. These naturalistic vocal lines, so near to recitative, may have been suggested to Debussy by Mussorgsky or, more probably, by such old French masters as Rameau, Campra and Marc-Antoine Charpentier; they owe something too to plainsong.[1] But they are, in a sense, also an exquisite translation of Wagner into French. Not an imitation of Wagner's melodic line adapted to French words, such as one finds in Chabrier and Bruneau and d'Indy, but *the principle behind Wagner's line* applied in terms of the French language and French temperament: a fairly quick patter of even notes of short value, small intervals and narrow tessitura, absence of metrical stresses, everything very supple and subtle.

And although the orchestral background on which the dialogue rests is a scrappy, tenuous mosaic instead of a rich continuous

---

[1] As, of course, does Debussy's (and Ravel's) leaning to the old church modes. But the modes were much "in the air" at this period. All the composers who influenced Debussy and Ravel had experimented with them too: Liszt, Rimsky-Korsakov, Mussorgsky, Fauré, Satie, even Chabrier (cf. "Cher pays, pays du gai soleil" in *Le Roi malgré lui*).

polyphony, the mosaic like the polyphony is built up largely of leitmotives (associated, like those of *Tristan*, with moods and conceptions rather than with the characters as in the *Ring*) constantly disguised and transformed, just as "cyclic" themes had still been used with infinite subtlety in the orchestral *Nocturnes*. But, as d'Indy points out,[1] Debussy's use of leitmotives is quite different from Wagner's symphonic development of them: "His idea was to construct by means of these fragments" (i.e., the extremely simple, even rudimentary leitmotives) "a series of *pivot-themes*—if one may so express it —the function of which is to send out harmonic rays in all directions, rays that serve to present the musical speech in the ambience suited to it. . . . Thus the work consists of successions of melodic expositions of the *pivot-themes* with harmonic commentaries intended to create a peculiarly exquisite atmosphere about the declaimed text." Indeed, atmosphere is the be-all and end-all of *Pelléas*; not something that envelops the subject of the drama but the drama itself.

Debussy had every reason to be delighted with his discovery of Maeterlinck's play, for it might have been written expressly for the sort of music he wished to wrap about some drama. He never found such a subject again, though he spent the rest of his life looking for one and thought he had found it in Poe's *The Devil in the Belfry* and *The Fall of the House of Usher*, and again in Joseph Bédier's *Légende de Tristan*. But it is difficult to imagine Debussyan music mated with any play but this one of Maeterlinck's, and it is not surprising that *Pelléas* remained an isolated masterpiece.

The remainder of Debussy's creative career consisted for the most part of refinements of this impressionistic technique applied to two mediums: the piano and the orchestra. After *Pelléas* he wrote comparatively few songs, though he had been a prolific song-composer before, and one can easily trace in his songs his gradual evolution from the disciple of Massenet to the master of word-setting who could write such perfect essays in tone-speech as Geneviève's reading of the letter (Act I, Scene 2) on the one hand and the love-scene by the fountain (Act IV, Scene 4) on the other.

[1] *Richard Wagner et son influence sur l'art musical français.* Paris, 1930.

It is only in the orchestration that *Pelléas* owes nothing at all to Wagner. (Or to any other composer, even to Rimsky-Korsakov who sometimes appears to have given Debussy profitable hints.) The orchestra of *Pelléas* is absolutely individual. The ensemble is handled almost like a chamber orchestra (a combination that did not then exist), with extraordinary restraint and with remarkably little doubling. "In the whole score consisting of more than four hundred pages," as Wellesz points out,[1] "there are only a few pages of *tutti* and of these, again, only a few call for the full development of dynamic power. The instruments are written for throughout in the register in which they sound best; trumpets and trombones are used with the greatest economy. The orchestra is allowed to deploy its resources only in the entr'actes; when the voice enters, it is immediately damped down to the utmost extent possible." The point in Act II, Scene 1, where Mélisande loses the ring, is characteristic: a harp glissando, unsupported by any other instrument, is simply followed by an E held by the second violins and lightly intensified by a little throbbing rhythm on the harp. Wellesz also draws attention to the very characteristic scoring of the opening of Act I, Scene 3 (before the castle): the "Mélisande" motive is given to a solo oboe, *doux et expressif* (*un peu en dehors*); two low-lying flutes, a muted horn and half the 'cellos sustain the supporting harmonies, while violins and violas divided in six parts, and syncopated so that the oboe is not in the least covered, surround the whole with a light cloud of figuration. "This restraint is unnecessary in the purely orchestral works; nevertheless here too all unnecessary doubling for the sake of intensity is avoided and in quiet passages an 'openwork' [*durchbrochen*] chamber-music technique is employed."

In Debussy's later orchestral works, above all in the suite *La Mer* (1905) and the three *Images*—*Ibéria* (1908), *Rondes de Printemps* (1909) and *Gigues* (1913)—this technique of orchestral impressionism is developed perhaps to its *ne plus ultra*. Lightly held pedal notes, touches on tremolo strings (often muted and *divisi*), tiny piquant rhythmic motives, delicious little fragments of melody on a solo wind instrument, harp harmonics, glissando chords on the harp: these provide the tiny tiles with which Debussy builds up his mosaic patterns. At the same time it

[1] *Die neue Instrumentation.*

would be unfair to deny that there are more virile moments in his music, such as the famous passage for 'cellos in four parts (four players to each part—and Toscanini reinforces them with four solo violas an octave higher) in the first movement of *La Mer*, the brassy climax of the third movement, and a good many pages of *Ibéria*, particularly the almost banal third section, *Au matin d'un jour de fête*.

Ladislas Fábián has pointed out[1] that *La Mer* contains the first signs of a reaction on Debussy's part towards structural formalism and clearness of outline. This tendency is still more marked in the orchestral *Images*, above all in *Gigues*, and in the music to d'Annunzio's *Martyre de Saint Sébastien* (1911); and in the three chamber sonatas (1915–17) Debussy arrived at pure neo-classicism. But his technique remained impressionistic even after the spirit of his music had emerged from its sensuous day-dreams. *Les Rondes de Printemps*, for all its evolution from a single theme, its quasi-return to Franckist principles of structure, its rather acid dissonances, is absolutely *pointilliste* in the treatment of the orchestra; the opening pages of this movement, in particular, are as free from anything that could be called a "theme" as any music Debussy ever wrote.

Debussy's application of this impressionistic technique to the orchestra is rivalled in interest and importance by his use of it in his piano works. His piano compositions—especially those written after *Pelléas*: the *Estampes* (comp. 1903), the two books of *Images* (1905 and 1907), the *Children's Corner* (1908), the two books of *Préludes* (1910 and 1913) and the *Études* (1915) —are the most important contributions to the art of writing for the piano since Chopin and Liszt, and mark a most important stage in the history of piano literature. It is true the shadow of a younger French musician, Maurice Ravel, begins to fall on them from the *Estampes* onwards; the influence of Ravel's *Habanera* (composed in 1896 as a piece for two pianos; employed in 1907 as the third movement of the orchestral *Rapsodie espagnole*) on the second *Estampe* (*Soirée dans Grenade*) has often been pointed out. Not less noticeable is that of the pianistic writing in Ravel's *Jeux d'eau* (1901), itself heavily indebted to Liszt's *Jeux d'eau à la Villa d'Este*, on the third *Estampe* (*Jardins sous la pluie*) and *L'Isle joyeuse* (1904). In return, the first

[1] *Claude Debussy und sein Werk*. Munich, 1923.

Estampe (*Pagodes*) obviously suggested to Ravel the third movement, *Laideronette, Impératrice des Pagodes*, of his *Ma Mère
l'Oye* suite (comp. 1908), and the *Hommage à Rameau* from the
first set of *Images*, the opening of *Le Gibet* in Ravel's *Gaspard
de la Nuit* (1908). Indeed, the reciprocal technical influence of
these two French masters was so intimate and so constant as to
mislead even the most intelligent contemporary critics into finding close affinities in styles that were poles apart in spirit.

At the same time, whatever the debt of Debussy's keyboard-
writing to Ravel, it sprang first and foremost from his own
conception of music, his own technique of composition—and his
own technique of piano-playing. According to Vallas, Debussy
was "an original virtuoso, remarkable for the delicacy and
mellowness of his touch." (So delicate that, like Chopin, he was
accused of over-fondness for an almost inaudible *pianissimo*.)
"He made one forget that the piano has hammers—an effect
that he used to request his interpreters to aim at[1]—and he
achieved particularly characteristic effects by the use of both
pedals." There was no "bringing out" of melodies, no scale-
pyrotechnics—with Debussy scale-passages and the like were
soft washes of silvery colour—but a delicate play of sonorities
produced by the peculiar layout of chords, by contrasts and
minglings of register, by contrasts of touch, by giving a peculiar
transparent sonority to a detached note or chord here, by blurring
others with the sustaining pedal there. And Debussy exploits
to the full in his piano-works that "side-slipping" of chords in
the manner of the mediæval organum and *faux bourdon* which
we have already noticed in Verdi and Puccini. As early as the
Sarabande from *Pour le Piano* (1902, though the *Sarabande*
itself dates from 1896) he had not only used these side-slipped
chords but, as Puccini had done already in effect with his 6-5
chords in *Edgar*, applied this device to "added-note" chords,
i.e., chords that, despite their theoretical origin as inversions of
chords of the seventh and the like, produce the effect of ordinary
triads and inversions plus unresolved appoggiaturas. *Et la lune
descend*, from the second set of piano *Images*, is an excellent
example of the impressionistic use of the device, as the preceding

[1] In this respect his example has certainly not been followed by more
modern composers. Piano-writing since Debussy has tended more
and more to exploit the purely percussive nature of the instrument.

piece, *Cloches à travers les feuilles,* is of the impressionistic use
of the whole-tone scale. (Echoes of Liszt's *Au bord d'une source*
may also be noticed in *Cloches.*) And it would be difficult to find
a more perfect instance of impressionistic or *pointilliste* composition technique applied to the piano than the first piece of the
first book of *Images, Reflets dans l'eau.*

In the *Préludes* the method varies—as does the quality of the
inspiration. But, on the whole, like the orchestral *Images* and
other works of this period, they reveal Debussy's increasing preoccupation with clarity and simplicity of form and line and with
more or less "absolute" music. In turning thus to a form of
classicism towards the end of his life, he was not only following
the example of Berlioz, Schumann and the other great romanticists who had done the same; as with most of them, too, this final
classical phase seems to be marked by a falling-off in inspiration.
Few admirers of Debussy would claim that the *Sonates pour
divers instruments* are among his best compositions. Yet he was
right in claiming for the first—for 'cello and piano (1915)—
"proportions and form almost classical, in the good sense of the
word," and the second—for flute, viola and harp (1915)—is a
charming work, full of the most delicate line-drawing. Naturally
a good deal of the old impressionistic technique survives even
here, but the spirit is very far indeed from impressionism. And
in the first movement of the sonata for violin and piano (1917)
even the technique is marked by only the slightest surviving
traces of impressionism, though the fabric that is left is not
merely economical but disconcertingly etiolated.

One might almost put it that in Debussy's later works the
spirit of Ravel had triumphed over his own, for Ravel, with all
his impressionistic leanings and technique, was never an impressionist in spirit and outlook. Call him what you will—true
classicist or secret romanticist concealing his real feelings under
an ironic classical mask—he was never an impressionist in anything but occasional method. His musical ancestry differed considerably from Debussy's. In fact the only elements common to
both were the influences of Satie and the Russians, particularly
of Borodin—specially noticeable in Ravel's String Quartet (comp.
1903)—and of Rimsky-Korsakov, who left even more traces on
Ravel's orchestration than on Debussy's. The influence of Satie,
too, is often very obvious; the opening of *Les entretiens de la*

Belle et de la Bête in *Ma Mère l'Oye* is absurdly like the opening of Satie's first *Gymnopédie* (comp. 1888). But whereas Debussy sprang from Massenet on the one hand and Wagner and the French Wagnerians on the other, Ravel was always unmistakably the disciple of Fauré, greatest of Saint-Saëns's pupils, and the shadow of Saint-Saëns himself falls over Ravel's scores at times, even in such mature works as the Trio (1915), his masterpiece in the field of chamber music, the Rigaudon of *Le Tombeau de Couperin* (1917), and the Sonata for Violin and 'Cello (1922). Chabrier, too, meant much more to Ravel than to Debussy; not the Wagnerian Chabrier of *Gwendoline*, of course, but the robust, witty Chabrier of *Le Roi malgré lui* and the harmonic experimenter of the *Bourrée fantasque* for piano (1891). His influence is plain not only in the popular *Pavane pour une Infante défunte* (1899), where Ravel admitted it himself, but in such mature works as *Le Tombeau de Couperin* and *La Valse* (1919).

But it was Fauré, above all, who shaped Ravel, who (to compare lesser men with greater) played Haydn to his Beethoven. Fauré is at once one of the easiest and one of the most difficult composers to "place" in a few words. To say that he combined the technical skill and characteristically Latin polish and lucidity of his master Saint-Saëns with the lyrical sweetness of a Gounod, or that he came under such very different influences as plainsong and Chopin, is as misleading as it is true. Fauré's music has a gentle strength, a poetry, all its own. It invariably possesses those qualities that he himself considered most essentially French in art: "clarity of thought, sobriety and purity of form, sincerity and disdain of vulgar effect." His frankly romantic feeling was always held in check by an essentially classical mind. (It is significant that, although he loved Wagner, he evaded his influence more successfully than any other important French composer of the time.) And he had one curious weakness: he was comparatively insensitive to timbre[1] and was so little at home with the orchestra that on more than one occasion he entrusted the scoring of his music to a friend or a pupil. His music to *Pelléas et Mélisande* (1898), for instance, was

---

[1] See Koechlin's *Gabriel Fauré* (Paris, 1927): "Fauré's inspiration seems in general *to correspond to abstract sonorities*, from which the idea of timbre (paradoxical as this may be) has been dismissed."

orchestrated by Koechlin. So constituted, he naturally put the best of himself into songs and chamber music. But perhaps the most significant trait of Fauré's music is its ever increasing simplicity, its gradual reduction to absolute essentials; in this respect his influence on his younger compatriots and, through them, on modern music in general, has been incalculable. This simplification—this Hellenization, as Koechlin considers it—dates from the opera *Prométhée* (1900).

Fauré had to travel a long way from the fresh, lyrical romanticism of the early Piano Quartets in C minor (1879) and G minor (1886) to the bare simplicity of the D minor Trio (1923) and the String Quartet (1924). But, though no doubt he was following the course of a reaction that was not merely natural but inevitable, he was one of the leaders of that reaction. He did not merely follow the general trend; he helped to give it a certain direction.

Mainly, of course, through the work of his brilliant pupils: Ravel, Roger-Ducasse, Florent Schmitt, Koechlin and the rest. Above all, through Ravel. If any French composer has come closer to Fauré's ideals than Fauré himself, it is Ravel. And as with master, so with pupil: this constant striving for "clarity of thought, sobriety and purity of form" led in the end to the most severe economy of expression. Both reached it at nearly the same time; there is a curious kinship, underlying many obvious differences, between those last two chamber works of Fauré and Ravel's Sonata for Violin and 'Cello (completed in 1922) and Sonata for Violin and Piano (completed in 1927).

But Ravel was very much more than a brilliant disciple of Fauré. Above all, he absorbed the technique of Debussy's impressionism into his musical system. Ravel had a curious aptitude for such absorptions, e.g., of jazz in the foxtrot in *L'Enfant et les sortilèges* (1925) and of Spanish idioms in half a dozen works; and this is evidently connected with that love of pastiche and *tours de force* which reached its climax in the single interminable-seeming crescendo of the orchestral *Bolero* (1929) and the Piano Concerto for the Left Hand Only (1932). Examining Ravel's output piece by piece, one is tempted to say that it is practically all pastiche and *tours de force*, the solution of self-imposed problems—until one stands back and considers the whole as such and recognizes how completely and unmistakably

Ravelian it is from first to last. The impressionistic traits in his music—in its technique rather than in its essence—are no more Debussyish than *Le Tombeau de Couperin* is Couperinesque or *La Valse* a pastiche of Waldteufel or Johann Strauss.

So thoroughly eclectic was Ravel that impressionism, like the Spanish idiom that attracted him again and again throughout his career from the early *Habanera* to the late *Bolero*, is only one phase of his art. *Jeux d'eau*, written in 1901, is frankly impressionistic and, as we have seen, influenced Debussy himself. The String Quartet, composed in 1902–03, is not so at all. The *Miroirs* for piano (1905) were markedly influenced by Debussy; the *Sonatine* of the same year hardly in the least. But Ravel's most decidedly impressionistic works date from the years 1906–07: the *Introduction and Allegro* for harp with sextet accompaniment, the *Histoires naturelles*, the settings of de Regnier's "Les grands vents venus d'outre-mer" and Verlaine's "Sur l'herbe." Yet *L'Heure espagnole* also dates from 1907 and to reckon that as an impressionistic work would put a severe strain on an extremely useful term. After *Gaspard de la Nuit* (1908) Ravel turned back more and more to "clarity of thought and sobriety of form," though it is worth noting that what is probably his finest work, *Daphnis et Chloé* (comp. 1909–11) contains many pages (e.g., the daybreak movement) in which he most successfully applies a partly impressionistic technique to neo-classic ends.

But even in his most completely impressionistic works, Ravel always tended to preserve clear lines and clear structure. "Comme je me trouve mélodiste!" he is said to have exclaimed to Casella in 1908, and as Roland-Manuel[1] points out, at that date such a remark was not a boast but an admission, "for, round about 1908, melody was hardly more prized by the practitioners of chromatic polyphony than by the partisans of harmony for the sake of harmony." And not only was Ravel always essentially a melodist, or at any rate a line-drawer rather than a colourist, he was equally a formalist, showing an affection amounting almost to mania for the traditional first-movement form not only in such works as the piano *Sonatine* and the

[1] *Maurice Ravel et son œuvre dramatique*. Paris, 1928. This excellent book is by no means superseded by the same author's *À la gloire de Ravel* (Paris, 1938).

chamber compositions where one half-expects it but in things like *Jeux d'eau* where one decidedly does not. And he clung with equal tenacity to the "cyclic" principle beloved of Franck and his disciples.

There again, as in his harmony, he has something in common with Debussy. But the "melodist" and "formalist" has very little. Debussy seldom achieved anything more than fragments and torsos of melody, and he turned to formalism only towards the end of his life. Debussy at his most characteristic is vague, fluid, if not altogether formless in the conventional sense. But even in the work where Ravel's music seems to have come nearest to disintegration, the *Trois Poèmes de Mallarmé* (1913) for voice, piano, two flutes, two clarinets and string quartet, more Schönbergian or Stravinskian[1] than Debussyish, the second and third songs, "Placet futile" and "Surgi de la croupe," are thoroughly linear in feeling, and the work that immediately followed the *Trois Poèmes*, the A minor Trio, shows a marked reaction to firmer texture, a reaction that was continued and intensified in Ravel's later works. The *Trois Poèmes*, however, are symptomatic in another respect: economy of resource, in strong contrast with the instrumental lavishness of *Daphnis et Chloé*. This economy also becomes more marked in later works, from the Sonata for Violin and 'Cello on the one hand to *L'Enfant et les sortilèges* on the other. (See, for instance, the opening of *L'Enfant* with its two oboes moving in fifths and fourths, and the scene of the Princess, whose song is at first accompanied only by a flute playing mostly in its lowest register.)

Even before Ravel emerged into this severe neo-classical world of simple two-part counterpoints and while there was still some reason for considering him an impressionist, he was in reality only employing impressionistic means to classical ends. In that respect he was almost unique. True, few post-Debussyan composers have been genuine impressionists; it would almost be correct to say that Debussy himself was the only true impressionist, just as Wagner is the only composer who has written genuine Wagnerian music-drama; but of the innumerable musicians who have borrowed Debussy's methods or something

---

[1] Ravel wrote these *Poèmes* at a time when he was actually living with Stravinsky at Clarens and working with him at their rather unhappy "revision" of Mussorgsky's *Khovanshchina*.

like them, the great majority have applied them to express what Debussy abhorred: "romantic" emotion. There are exceptions —notably the Spaniard Falla, who brilliantly applied impressionistic technique in the treatment of strongly nationalistic material and to whom we shall return in the next chapter—but the irony of the general position is striking. Debussyism, a strong reaction against romanticism, the half-way stage to the neo-classicism that triumphed in the nineteen-twenties and early nineteen-thirties, also gave a new lease in life to dying romanticism.

Naturally these romantic impressionists are of all species. They range from the very robust Italian Respighi, who in such works as the popular *Fontane di Roma* (1918) combined quasi-impressionistic methods and a brilliant orchestral technique modelled on that of his master Rimsky-Korsakov with healthy Italian melodiousness and vulgarity, to the cosmopolitan dreamer Delius, one of the most individual composers of modern times. Delius owed even more to Grieg's bitter-sweet harmonies than to Debussy's impressionism and much of his work, e.g., the *Mass of Life* (comp. 1904–05), is frankly late romantic and not impressionistic at all. But such works as the orchestral fantasy *In a Summer Garden* (comp. 1908), the greater part of the opera *Fennimore and Gerda* (comp. 1908–10; perf. 1919), *Summer Night on the River* (comp. 1911), the *Song of the High Hills* for chorus and orchestra[1] (comp. 1912; perf. 1920), and the first two of the *North Country Sketches* (1913–14)—*Autumn* and *Winter Landscape*—are very beautiful examples of impressionistic technique applied to purely romantic expression. But it is characteristic of Delius that the third of the *North Country Sketches*, the *Dance*, is purely melodic and that the fourth, *The March of Spring*, for the most part purely impressionistic, finally solidifies into a square, marchlike melody. In *Summer Night on the River*, too, a perfectly clear melodic backbone holds the impressionistic harmonies together.

Although the principal charm of Delius's music lies in those strange, fascinating progressions of seemingly disconnected chromatic chords which emerged from his dreamy improvisation at the piano, he always showed a marked fondness for melody

[1] Or, rather, for an orchestra that includes a wordless chorus in its constitution.

which divides him, like the very different Ravel, from Debussy. In *Brigg Fair* (1907), the first *Dance Rhapsody* (1908) and *On hearing the first Cuckoo in Spring* (1912), three of his best and most characteristic works, he is content mainly to treat folk-tunes or a quasi-folk-tune with post-Griegish harmonies; here the influence of impressionism is very slight indeed.

Arnold Bax, also predominantly a melodist, was yet another late-romantic impressionist. Impressionistic traits are most marked in his piano music, and in such orchestral works as *The Garden of Fand* (1913), *Tintagel* (1917) and *November Woods* (1917).[1] In his piano sonatas, his chamber music and, above all, in his symphonies, of which the First dates from 1922, the Seventh from 1939, numerous débris of impressionism are mixed with quasi-Celtic folkish melodies and violent outbursts of gloomy, romantic emotion in a rather unsatisfactory amalgam.

But to group together the various composers who borrowed the devices of impressionism for their own ends would be even more difficult than to lump together all the musicians who are indebted in any way to Wagner. During the first two decades of the twentieth century, Debussy's influence was extraordinarily widespread. The fact that "Debussyism" was for a time a general term of abuse for everything new in music, as "Wagnerism" had been a generation or so earlier, is not as misleading as it might have been. Very few progressive composers did escape his influence altogether, though, as we have noticed in the case of Ravel and in a previous chapter in the case of Puccini, some of them had been in some details independently feeling their way in the same direction, though less boldly and confidently than Debussy.

II. LATER NATIONALIST TENDENCIES

One of the most curious symptoms of musical nationalist movements is their lack of enduring vitality. As sturdy yeoman

---

[1] Some of the best impressionistic piano music, other than Debussy's own, has been written by British composers. It would be difficult to find a better example of pure pianistic impressionism than John Ireland's *Island Spell* (1913). And the *Neptune* movement of Holst's *Planets* (comp. 1915) is perhaps the most remarkable piece of pure orchestral impressionism ever written.

families tend to get on in the world, losing all trace of their origin in a couple of generations and settling down into mediocre respectability, the pupils and artistic heirs of the most robust nationalist composers generally break away from the limitations of a folk-songish idiom and try to establish themselves as "universalists." That would matter less if they were something more than very talented mediocrities. But it would be stupid to pretend that Glazunov, Lyadov, Rakhmaninov and Arensky in Russia, or Suk and Novák among the Czechs, are anything but pale shadows of their masters and predecessors. Inferiority complex, the original cause of conscious artistic nationalism, is destroyed by the success of the movement it creates.

These epigones may have magnificent technique and streaks of genuine originality; most of them are gifted with an unfailing flow of pleasant lyrical melody. But they are not true personalities. It is evident that they write under no urgent pressure, have nothing really new or more than half vital to say.

The career of Glazunov, perhaps the most gifted of the Russian epigones, is more or less typical of them all. When his First Symphony, written at sixteen, appeared in 1882, it would have been natural to suppose that his rôle in Russian musical history would be that of a Brahms to Borodin's Schumann and Rimsky-Korsakov's Mendelssohn, a summing-up and surpassing of all that the "mighty handful" had contributed to music. The older men themselves thought so. But things turned out very differently. The environment was unfavourable and Glazunov, with all his gifts, was not the man to rise above his environment. The great artistic and intellectual fermentation from which Russian national music had been born was over by the eighteen-eighties. Rimsky-Korsakov himself had begun to lose interest in music that was essentially Russian and though it is true he often returned to his first love, he continued to the end of his life to make spasmodic attempts to write "universal" music, producing such dismal failures as the lifeless and colourless operas *Servilia* and *Pan Voevoda*. And he had completely surrendered to an academic, conservative view of music, so that Glazunov and his other pupils were taught to imitate only the superficial characteristics of the earlier nationalist movement, the use of folk-songs, folk-songish flavour generally, and colourful scoring, and to despise as "clumsy," "amateurish" and "eccentric" the qualities that now interest us most of all in the work of Mussorg-sky and his comrades.

Consequently Glazunov began by producing clever imitations of Borodin and Korsakov, such as his symphonic poem, *Stenka Razin* (comp. 1885), and then degenerated into a fluent, prolific, agreeable note-spinner whose music is neither very national nor very personal nor very significant in any respect whatever. His best works are perhaps the Fourth, Fifth and Sixth Symphonies (1894–96)—and all three curiously possess the same physiog-nomy. Indeed Glazunov himself must have been conscious that he was writing symphony after symphony without saying any-thing fresh, for his last, the Eighth, dates from 1904 when he still had thirty-two years of life before him.

Nevertheless, musical nationalism goes on. As one country, having pugnaciously asserted its musical individuality, settles down contentedly into the musical comity of nations, others, either excited by political oppression or a general sense of artistic inferiority, or merely stirred by the example of the rest, begin in the same self-conscious way to develop a specifically national art—usually based on folk-song. And then, too, even in the lands that have tired of national costume and taken to the musical lounge-suit common to all Europe, composers appear from time to time whose music seems to be completely impreg-nated with national characteristics and who are at the same time far too individual to be classed as mere epigones.

Such was the Moravian, Janáček, who, contending that "a fragment of national life is attached to every word uttered by the people; the melody of their speech should be studied in every detail," first evolved a type of vocal music with melodic inflec-tions derived from this Moravian peasant speech and then employed the same type of melodic line in his instrumental compositions as well. Even Janáček's early Compositions for Organ, Op. 12 (1884), are written in the laconic, ejaculatory, elliptical idiom peculiar to his most mature work, e.g., the opera *Jenůfa* (comp. 1902). And, unlike so many youthful revolu-tionaries, he did not turn conservative in middle age, though his operatic masterpiece *Katya Kabanova* (1921) shows more lyrical power. In 1926, at seventy-two, he remarked to a journalist, "I feel as if quite unsuspected new worlds were opening within me." And certainly the Sinfonietta and *Glagolitka* Mass, both dating from that year, are as typical of his bold, simple, utterly original, and sometimes naïvely dramatic, style as anything he wrote.

Stravinsky too—a much younger man than Janáček and a much more important European figure—must also be considered a latter-day nationalist. True, he followed his old master Rimsky-Korsakov and the general trend of Russian music by turning eclectic in mid-career but, paradoxically enough, this sort of change of course in middle life is itself a peculiarly Russian phenomenon.[1] Of the through-and-through Russianness of his early compositions there can be no question.

The early Symphony in E flat (comp. 1905–07) is a mere Glazunov-like imitation of Borodin and Rimsky-Korsakov; the finale introduces a folk-song theme used again in the *Three Little Songs* (*Memories of Childhood*) of 1913. But already in the orchestral piece *Fireworks* (comp. 1908) Stravinsky's own individuality begins to make itself apparent; though, paradoxically enough, this apparition is coincident with the impact of a fresh external influence. Both *Fireworks* and the *Fantastic Scherzo* that preceded it betray the impression made on Stravinsky by Dukas's *L'Apprenti sorcier*; so, for that matter, do several passages in his first big ballet, *The Fire-Bird* (1910), which (even if it had no other claim to attention) would be memorable as marking a new stage in the evolution of symphonic ballet. It was by far the most important ballet score since Tchaïkovsky's *Sleeping Beauty* and *Nutcracker*.

Before *The Fire-Bird*, Stravinsky had written the first act of another work not completed till 1914, the opera *The Nightingale*, and this first act—above all, the *larghetto* introduction—reveals yet another French influence: Debussy's. And this Debussyan influence persists also in the two Verlaine songs of 1910, "Un grand sommeil noir" and "La lune blanche," and in the cantata, *Zvezdolik* (*Le Roi des étoiles*) (1911). Nevertheless, the predominant strain in *The Fire-Bird* is still that of Rimsky-Korsakov. The orchestral virtuosity, the use of folk-melodies (e.g., in the *khorovod* of the princesses and the finale), the differentiation between the human (diatonic) and supernatural (chromatic)

[1] Compare the spiritual crises which had such disastrous effects on the creative careers of Gogol, Tolstoy and Balakirev. I have discussed the whole curious problem in an article in *The Contemporary Review* (reprinted in *On Russian Music*, London, 1939).

elements: all this is thoroughly Rimsky-Korsakovian,[1] just as the first fluttering dance of the Fire-Bird suggests Skryabin, her supplication Balakirev, and the "unholy dance" of Kashchey's subjects Borodin. The harmonic language is still mainly based on Rimsky-Korsakov's dry, "fantastic" chromaticism which reached its fullest development in his *Kashchey* and *Golden Cockerel*. Most significant of the mature Stravinsky, however, is the rhythmical power of the "unholy dance" (*Danse infernale*) where continual syncopation knocks the nominal 3-4 time into the most ingenious patterns. This tendency is still further developed in the composition that immediately followed *The Fire-Bird*, the piece written in 1910 which we now know as the final Sacrificial Dance of the Chosen Maiden in *The Rite of Spring*; here Stravinsky frankly abandons the pretence of a constant underlying metrical standard and writes time-signatures changing with practically every bar: 3-16, 5-16, 3-16, 4-16, 5-16, 3-16, 4-16, 3-16, etc.

The same tremendous rhythmic vitality pervades both of Stravinsky's next ballets, *Petrushka* (1911) and *The Rite of Spring* (completed only in 1913). And with these two works begins Stravinsky's individual harmonic evolution, of which the most striking symptom is the simultaneous use of arpeggios of C and F sharp to open the scene in Petrushka's compartment, probably the most frank acceptance of bi-tonality that had yet appeared in music. But even this procedure had near-precedents (e.g., the end of Strauss's *Zarathustra*) and practically all Stravinsky's other harmonic idiosyncrasies are little more than bold statements of what other composers had already hinted discreetly. The added-note chords of the last variation of the finale of *The Fire-Bird* and the "Russian dance" in *Petrushka* only repeat harshly what Debussy had expressed in the velvety tones of the *Sarabande* of *Pour le piano*. Again, Puccini, Debussy and others had played with what one is tempted to call the *novum organum*; Stravinsky does it here in the opening scene of *Petrushka* with a folk-tune thickened out into triads. But he does it with a difference. First the thickened-out tune is played against a quasi-pedal chord of G minor, and then this "pedal" itself comes to melodic life, so that we get a two-part

[1] Rimsky-Korsakov himself may have got this idea of diatonic-chromatic antithesis in opera originally from *Parsifal*.

counterpoint, thundered out by the full orchestra, in which each part is represented not by a single melodic strand but by triads or inversions. Yet the ear, as usual, easily accepts the violent clashes thus produced, for both contrapuntal strands are absurdly easy to follow. Mahler in his Sixth and Seventh Symphonies (1906 and 1908) had made much play with the close alternation of major and minor forms of a triad; indeed, Dargomïzhsky, as we have seen, had actually implied *simultaneous* major and minor in his *Finnish Fantasia* nearly half a century before *The Rite of Spring*; but it remained for Stravinsky (Circle Dance of the Young Maidens in *The Rite*, page 80 of the miniature score) actually to telescope the major and minor forms into a single chord. Similarly, plenty of other composers had written consecutive sevenths and ninths with the intervention of r ollifying thirds, even written them "naked" in moments of passionate excitement (c.f. the already mentioned passage in *Ein Helden-leben*); but it remained for Stravinsky to write bare, open sevenths for clarinets and ninths for violas, in cold blood as it were, as he does in this Circle Dance (page 81 of the miniature score). Aggregations of simultaneous appoggiaturas that never resolve; chords of no fewer than five piled-up perfect fifths (page 13) or perfect fourths (page 14): the Rite is full of such boxes on the listener's ear—and from this work onward Stravinsky's norm of consonance (or of tolerable dissonance) remained very considerably in advance of that of the musical man-in-the-street.

Stravinsky's style had from the first been either frankly melodic (with curiously static melodies such as one often finds in the older Russian composers) or based on motives that are no more developed, in the Beethovenian sense, than the opening theme of Borodin's B minor Symphony is developed. Nor do they follow with any suggestion of "logic." In *The Rite of Spring*, which is not held together as a whole by even the semblance of leitmotives as the two previous ballets had been, the handling of melodies[1] and motives is almost entirely mosaic-like and, in that respect, *impressionistic*. The break-up of the old underlying

---

[1] Still largely folkish in origin; the opening bassoon solo, for instance, is based on a Lithuanian melody (from Anton Juszkiewicz's *Litauische Volksweisen*, Cracow, 1900). Even the brilliant passage for piccolos on page 13 is only a variation of the very characteristic folk-theme given to the bassoons a few bars later.

regular metres also suggests impressionism. And Stravinsky's art has for the most part been as unemotional, as anti-romantic as Debussy's. But whereas impressionism dissolves rhythm into vague fluidity, Stravinsky breaks up the old regularity into new, strong patterns full of intense nervous vitality. And no one would dream of linking impressionism, and its subtle nuances and veiled suggestions, with Stravinsky's clear-cut, brutally percussive score. Stravinsky continued to use this quasi-impressionistic mosaic technique at least as late as *The Tale of the Runaway Soldier and the Devil* (1918) (usually known by its French title, *L'Histoire du Soldat*), but by that time his tastes and interests had begun to take that new orientation already referred to: towards experiments with problems of pure sound, towards neo-classicism and away from nationalism.

The three *Lyrics from the Japanese* (1913) for soprano, two flutes, two clarinets, piano and string quartet were straws indicating the composer's fresh leanings; like Ravel's *Trois Poèmes de Mallarmé*, written at the same place and time, they betray the influence of Schönberg's *Pierrot Lunaire* (1912)[1] in their remarkable compression and in the scoring, as well as harmonically. But both *The Fable of the Fox, the Cock and the Ram* (commonly called *Renard*) (comp. 1917; perf. 1922) and *The Wedding* (*Les Noces*) (comp. 1917; perf. 1923), as well as a whole series of short pieces dating from this period and based on popular Russian rhymes and songs (*Three Little Songs*, the *Pribautki* for voice and eight solo instruments, *The Cat's Lullabies, Four Russian Songs, Three Stories for Children, Twelfth Night Songs* for unaccompanied chorus), are—like all Stravinsky's earlier works from the E flat Symphony to the *Rite* —Russian not only in the superficial sense that they are largely based on folk-music and so on, but in the very essence of the musical thought. In *The Wedding*, for instance (and in other works, for that matter), instead of thematic development in the German manner we have that purely Russian type of development which consists of melodic repetition with constant changes including even the introduction of new elements into the melodic line.[2] Again, the clowning in these works of Stravinsky's

¹ See page 285.
² Borodin's employment of this device in *Prince Igor* has already been described on page 152.

is simply an exaggeration of that in *Igor, Sadko, Boris* and other Russian classics. Igor Glebov's remark in his *Kniga o Stravinskom*,[1] that a single line of organic development leads from Glinka's *Kamarinskaya* to Stravinsky's *Wedding*, is by no means such a rash generalization as it appears at first sight. Even in Stravinsky's later works the student of Russian music can still detect a good many symptoms of *essential* Russianness, but the superficial Russianness almost or quite disappears—there is very little of it in *The Tale of the Runaway Soldier*—though it breaks out again most delightfully in the one-act comic opera *Mavra* (1922), with its amusingly Glinka-like little overture.

In these three works—*The Wedding, Renard* and *The Tale of the Runaway Soldier*—Stravinsky experimented both with a new dramatic form and with new types of instrumentation. *The Wedding* is a choral ballet with the chorus off-stage in the orchestra; *Renard* is described by the composer himself as a "burlesque story sung and played, conceived for the stage . . . The piece is to be played by clowns, dancers and acrobats, preferably on a trestle-stage, the orchestra being placed behind. When the piece is given in a theatre, it must be played before the curtain. . . . The rôles are mute. The voices (two tenors and two basses) are in the orchestra"; *The Tale of the Soldier* is likewise to be played on a trestle stage, but the orchestra, instead of being placed behind, must be on a large "drum" at one side of the stage while on another "drum" on the opposite side sits a reader "before a little table with a pint of white wine." The music is increasingly formalized—*The Tale of the Soldier* consists of a chain of separate pieces: the soldier's march, *petit concert*, tango, waltz, ragtime, etc.—and at one time it seemed possible that with these experimental works Stravinsky had actually inaugurated a new musico-dramatic form that would supersede, or take its place beside, opera and ballet. The opera-oratorio *Œdipus Rex* (1927), with its speaker explaining the action, actors who move only their arms and heads, its male chorus on the stage more or less disguised as a bas-relief, and *Persephone* (1934), a "vision" in three acts with choral background and much recitative and spoken declamation, are so far Stravinsky's most important essays in this genre: less dramas than stage-concerts.

[1] Leningrad, 1929.

The instrumentation of the post-*Rite* works is also extremely interesting. *The Wedding*, originally conceived for a big chorus and orchestra, was finally scored for voices, four pianos (treated mainly as percussive instruments), xylophone, two side-drums, two tenor drums, tambourine, timpani, bass drum and cymbals, triangle, two *crotales* and a bell. *Renard* is laid out for a small orchestra of eighteen instruments, including cymbalom. *The Tale of the Runaway Soldier* demands a still smaller force: clarinet, bassoon, cornet, trombone, violin, double-bass and one percussion player who has to look after two side-drums, tenor drum, bass drum, cymbals and triangle. Here, in fact, was the first application of jazz (to which Stravinsky had been introduced by Ansermet a year or so before) to European art music. Jazz was bound to be unusually interesting to a musician with such leanings to both rhythmic vitality and percussive effects, and other consequences of this interest are apparent in the so-called "Ragtime" of *The Tale*, in the *Ragtime* for eleven solo instruments (also 1918) and the *Piano Rag-Music* (1919).

The peculiar constitution of the orchestra of *The Tale of the Runaway Soldier* had other consequences in the texture of the music. To write a balanced, even moderately homogeneous, chord for such a combination would be utterly impossible; naturally in selecting it Stravinsky had no intention of writing chords for it. Instead he gave full rein to the gift he had developed as early as *The Rite of Spring* for evolving melodic lines from the very nature of an instrument. The result is a music consisting mainly of horizontal lines drawn in sharply differentiated instrumental timbres, a counterpoint extraordinarily transparent and which, despite the apparent tautology, may justly be called *linear* (like the similar horizontal writing of the younger Germans) to distinguish it from the very chord-conscious polyphony of Wagner and Richard Strauss.

Increasing interest in the purely linear aspect of music quickly led Stravinsky towards a severe and rather dry neo-classicism which owed less to jazz than to the Bach of the less inspired concertos. For a time Stravinsky's anti-romanticism was so violent that he aimed at the complete exclusion of emotional expressiveness from his music. Experiments with the percussion were succeeded by experiments with the wind only—the *Symphonies of Wind Instruments* (1920), the Wind Octet (1923), and the Concerto for piano and wind (1924)—the strings being excluded as "too expressive." Stravinsky carried his affection for the early eighteenth century so far in *Œdipus Rex* as to provide Creon's "Respondit Deus" with a trumpet *obbligato* more or less in the manner of Bach and Handel.

Stravinsky's combination of strong nationalistic traits with advanced modernistic technical processes in *The Rite of Spring*, *The Wedding*, *Mavra* and other works and his deviations into a pure neo-classicism that is hardly nationalistic at all, are not peculiar to him. They are noticeable, for instance, in his brilliant young compatriot Prokofiev, and other composers of Soviet Russia, and in the Hungarian master, Bartók, to whom (with his friend Kodály) the musical world owes its introduction to true Hungarian folk-music, i.e., the music of the Magyars as distinct from the brilliant hybrid art of the Hungarian gypsies.

Bartók presents a most striking case of a composer evolving a highly individual style from a profoundly national one. Bartók's earlier works, such as the Rhapsody for piano and orchestra (1904) and the two Suites for orchestra (1905 and 1907), were nationalist in the purely superficial sense and, like so many compositions based on folk-melodies,[1] almost entirely impersonal. But Bartók's own very strong artistic personality quickly began to assert itself, as in the fine String Quartet No. 1 (1908). After the opera *Bluebeard's Castle* (comp. 1911), Bartók's nationalism became much less obvious, much more a matter of essential thought, though it was seldom completely suppressed (cf. the scherzo of the Second Quartet (1917), the finale of the First Violin Sonata (1921), the orchestral *Dance Suite* (1923) and the Piano Sonata (1926)). Above all, his saturation with the Magyar folk-scales completely deprived him of the diatonic sense of tonal values; not by an intellectual effort such as so many other atonalists have obviously had to make, but by a natural process. He acquired a tonal sense quite different from the normal; the notes of his melodies have quite other tonal functions than those the listener unconsciously tries to force on them.

And Bartók is essentially a melodist. He weaves his free, purely expressionistic melodies—no longer particularly folk-songish, but *set free* by folk-song—in counterpoints that sound intolerably

[1] Not all. Some composers (e.g., Vaughan Williams) have a curious gift for treating authentic folk-material in a quite personal way.

harsh only to those ears that cannot follow the unfamiliar logic
of the separate melodic lines. Harmony *per se* is to Bartók largely
a matter of colour, percussive colour—particularly in his piano-
writing. It must be admitted that his "norm of consonance" is
very advanced indeed, and that some of his middle-period works,
e.g., the Second Violin Sonata (1923) and the first Piano Concerto (1927), are tough nuts for the average listener to crack.
But his extraordinary sureness of touch, his perfect mastery of
form and medium, compelled the respect even of those who
were repelled by the harshness and austerity of the music as
pure sound, though the relative mellowness of such late works
as the Violin Concerto (1938) and the Sixth Quartet (1939) was
welcome even to his warmer admirers.

Sibelius and Falla are examples of nationalists still further
removed from folk-song than the later Bartók. Though each
made a few arrangements of Finnish and Spanish folk-melodies
respectively, neither introduced authentic folk-melodies into
his own music—with the exception of a few phrases associated
with the miller and his wife in Falla's ballet, *El Sombrero de
tres picos* (*The Three-Cornered Hat*) (1919), and a couple of
thematic scraps in the puppet opera, *El Retablo de Maese Pedro*
(1923). And whereas Falla's style is admittedly based essentially
on the very peculiar idioms of Spanish folk-music in general,
and that of Andalucía in particular, Sibelius's melodies are not
even cast in the mould of Finnish folk-song; the case of the
Violin Concerto (1903) to which Cecil Gray draws attention,[1]
where "some of the thematic material, notably the B flat minor
episode in the first movement and the second subject of the last,
with the characteristic falling fourth in both, is strikingly akin
in idiom to Finnish folk-songs of a certain type," is quite exceptional. Yet, for all that, his art is profoundly national, one of the
most striking instances of essential, as opposed to superficial,
nationalism in the whole history of music.

Falla once expressed his opinion[2] that "folk-music is most
satisfactorily cultivated by the cultivated musician, not when he
uses authentic tunes but when he 'feels' them, when he realizes
the foundations on which they rest and conveys the essence of

[1] *Sibelius.* O.U.P., 1931.
[2] See J. B. Trend's *Manuel de Falla and Spanish Music.* Allen and
Unwin, 2nd edition, 1925.

them in music that is all his own." That is what the great German masters of the past did quite unconsciously and what such composers as Brahms, Borodin, Bartók and Falla himself have done rather more deliberately. That is also what Sibelius has done, though in his case he has captured the spirit but sloughed off the tangible "body" much more completely than any other composer of such intensely national leanings. And for a very good reason: Finnish folk-music is not particularly beautiful.

Sibelius's intense Finnishness shows itself in other ways: in his frequent preoccupation with national legend; in the fine, harsh bleakness of his harmony; in his marvellous exploitation of the darker colours and lower registers of the orchestra[1]—he often writes for the wood-wind in their lowest registers, there are passages in his symphonies where trombones or bassoons are written so low that they cannot give the nuances the composer demands, and in *Aallottaret (The Oceanides)* (1914) he has even, as Gray points out, "applied the impressionist method of scoring to the bass instruments, thereby achieving effects of sonority hitherto unknown"; in fact, in his "granite"[2] method of orchestration in general. In this harsh forthrightness (though not in the degree of dissonance), in his masterly sureness of touch, Sibelius makes one think of Bartók. And, like Bartók's, his music is ultimately more interesting and more important as a personal manifestation than as a national one.

The whole of Sibelius that matters is summed up in his symphonies, probably the most important works in that form since Brahms's Fourth. But his earlier, more picturesque (but hardly more *romantic*)[3] orchestral pieces already contain the germs of

[1] Practically the only passage in earlier music that anticipates Sibelius's *colouring* is the end of the "Scène aux champs" in Berlioz's *Symphonie fantastique*.

[2] The phrase is Sibelius's own. Bengt de Törne, in his *Sibelius: a Close-up* (Faber and Faber, 1937), tells how he spoke to Sibelius of the impression produced by the first signs of Finland when returning to the country by sea, "low, reddish granite rocks emerging from the pale blue sea." Sibelius replied, "Yes, and when we see those granite rocks we know why we are able to treat the orchestra as we do."

[3] Even in the eighteen-nineties when romanticism was still in full bloom, Sibelius's music was singularly free from romantic traits. And, unlike practically all the nineteenth-century symphonists after Beethoven, he is not—except in his first two symphonies—a *lyrical* symphonist.

much that is most individual in his music. In *En Saga* (1892) one already notices the very characteristic sudden little melodic "knots," the long persistence of certain rhythms, the thickening out of melodies into quasi-faux-bourdon-like thirds, or sixths— an effect, curiously enough, as virile as the Italianate and Lisztian thirds and sixths in Richard Strauss are sensuous and feminine —and the altogether abnormal predominance of immensely long pedal-points (so different from Bruckner's whence Sibelius probably took the hint). In later works these organ-points are frequently elaborated into two alternating notes—e.g., the opening of the finale of the Second Symphony (1901) and the opening of the Fourth Symphony (1911)—or even into more extended *ostinato* figures that exercise an almost hypnotic influence on the mind. *Tuonelan Joutsen* (*The Swan of Tuonela*) (1893) is an early example of Sibelius's extraordinary gift for "continuous" melody and *Lemminkäinen palaa kotitienoille* (*The Return of Lemminkäinen*) (1895) is the earliest instance of his adoption of a method probably borrowed from Borodin but which Sibelius has since made entirely his own. "The thematic material," as Cecil Gray puts it, "consists of tiny scraps and fragments, tossed about from one group of instruments to another, which are gradually and progressively welded together into an organic whole as the work proceeds."

Many critics profess to see in Sibelius's First Symphony (1899) the influence of Tchaïkovsky, which seems to me entirely absent. Gray comes much nearer the mark when he points out that "the first subject of the initial movement is strikingly akin to that in the first movement of Borodin's Symphony in E flat, only sharpened and intensified," but he has quite failed to notice the influence exercised on Sibelius by Borodin's work in general and by the symphonic method of his E flat Symphony in particular. The identity of the dominating persistent rhythm of *En Saga* with the dominating persistent rhythm of the finale of the Borodin symphony, the rapid repeated notes and the drum figure of the scherzo of Sibelius's First Symphony (one feature derived from the scherzo of Borodin's Second, the other from the first movement of his First), the Borodinesque nature of the bustling scherzo of Sibelius's Second Symphony, and a good many other points of the same nature, might be individually dismissed as coincidences; collectively they present an impressive amount of evidence. The immediate repetition of the first *allegro* theme of Sibelius's First Symphony with a new initial motive is a borrowing of a very characteristic device of Borodin's; how far Sibelius developed it may be seen by his treatment of the flute theme in thirds just after letter B in the first movement of the Sixth Symphony (1923).[1] Far more important, however, is Sibelius's indebtedness to Borodin for the very basis of his symphonic method, that "gradual and progressive welding of tiny scraps into an organic whole" which we have already noticed in *Lemminkäinen*. Gray speaks of Sibelius's adoption of this method in the first movement of his Second Symphony and the first part of the finale of the Third (1907), and in still more subtle ways in later works, as "a veritable revolution . . . the introduction of an entirely new principle into symphonic form." But as we saw in an earlier chapter, Borodin had employed it forty years earlier in the first movement of his First Symphony,[2] where the thematic fragments of the *allegro* exposition are provisionally put together in the development section but finally and satisfactorily synthesized only in the coda.

On the other hand it must be said that Sibelius, a much more profound musical thinker than Borodin, has developed the symphony to heights that Borodin could never have reached. Above all, his later works—particularly the Fourth and Seventh Symphonies (1911 and 1924)—are the most remarkable examples that have so far appeared in the field of "absolute" symphonic music of a tendency, originating partly in Beethoven's last quartets, partly in Wagner's "endless stream" of thematic rather than genuinely melodic polyphony, partly in impressionism, to which Kurth draws attention in his *Romantische Harmonik*. Instead of the texture being evolved from themes, the themes such as they are—often mere scraps of motive or melody, even significant passage-work—arise as it were from the whole complex stream of musical thought and feeling. "So that," as Kurth puts it, "one often finds themes that taken by themselves appear insignificant or meaningless and have meaning only in connection with the whole complex." Here, in fact, in the actual

---

[1] See pages 6–7 of the miniature score. Readers unable to consult the score are referred to Cecil Gray's "Musical Pilgrim" booklet, *Sibelius: the Symphonies* (O.U.P., 1935), for music-type examples.

[2] See page 152.

texture of the music we have the spontaneous, unconscious aspect of the process deliberately employed by Borodin and Sibelius in the general architecture; there are close parallels in Bartók's quartets.

Equally striking is the conciseness of Sibelius's symphonic thinking from the Third Symphony onward. Not only conciseness of thematic language and economy of texture, but elision of everything inessential in architecture: repetitions, bridge-passages, introductions, conclusions and the like. Hardly any composer has equalled Sibelius in this faculty for beginning with a point, keeping to it, and finishing the moment he has nothing more to say. Here again the Fourth Symphony and still more the Seventh (in which all the elements of the classical symphony are compressed into one tightly knit organic movement) form the two highest peaks of Sibelius's art.

Sibelius's symphonies, in short, represent one extreme of the modern development of the symphony (from Beethoven's Fifth through Schumann's D minor), just as Mahler's represent the other (from Beethoven's Ninth through Berlioz's *Roméo et Juliette*). A piquant chance brought these two masters together in Helsingfors in November, 1907, and Sibelius's account of a conversation on this very point of difference has been recorded by Karl Ekman:[1] "When our conversation touched on the essence of symphony, I said that I admired its severity and style and the profound logic that created an inner connection between all the motives. This was the experience I had come to in composing. Mahler's opinion was just the reverse. 'Nein, die Symphonie muss sein wie die Welt. Sie muss alles umfassen.' ('No, symphony must be like the world. It must embrace everything.')"[2]

Mahler, himself essentially an Austrian nationalist despite his Jewish blood (which suggests that artistic nationalism may be a matter as much of environment as of descent), has certainly given us "worlds" in some of his symphonies, particularly the Second (1895), Third (completed 1898; performed 1902), Fourth (performed 1902) and Eighth (1910). In the Second, Mahler goes

[1] *Jean Sibelius: His Life and Personality.* (Translated by Edward Birse.) Alan Wilmer, 1936.

[2] Compare this with the similar definition of the symphony by Mahler on page 27.

no further than Beethoven had done in his Ninth except in length. After a big Brucknerian first movement, a Schubertian *andante con moto* and a *Ländler*, an alto soloist sings some consoling verses from Arnim and Brentano's famous anthology of German folk-song poetry, *Des Knaben Wunderhorn*; then, after a long orchestral episode, a Doomsday march in which Mahler tried to show "the great procession of the dead, rich and poor, kings and people, the *ecclesia militans* and the Popes" (to use his own words), the chorus sing Klopstock's hymn, "Aufersteh'n, ja aufersteh'n," to which Mahler added four stanzas of his own.

The Third Symphony is immensely long—it plays for two hours—compared with Sibelius's twenty-five-minute symphonies, yet the Fourth is so closely related to it as to seem almost a continuation; it certainly belongs to the same "world." No. 3 was originally to have been called *Meine fröhliche Wissenschaft*, apparently with reference to Nietzsche's book. After a huge first movement, "Pan's awakening; the entry of summer," come five shorter ones originally entitled: "What the meadow flowers tell me," "What the animals of the forest tell me," "What Man tells me," "What the Angels in Heaven tell me," and "What Eternal Love tells me." Man's message (alto solo) is Nietzsche's "Midnight Song" from *Zarathustra*; that of the angels is a choral setting of some naïve verses from the *Wunderhorn*. The finale of the Fourth Symphony really belongs to its predecessor; Mahler thought of it as "What the Child tells me" and it is yet another vision from the *Wunderhorn* of a heaven that can best be described as a German version of the negro heaven of *Green Pastures*. The three earlier movements of the symphony are, even thematically, little more than a prelude to it.

The Fifth, Sixth and Seventh Symphonies (1904–08) are purely instrumental—colossal works for colossal orchestras, with additional movements and with whole extended groups of themes instead of the old "first and second subjects"[1]—but in the Eighth (comp. 1907; perf. 1910), the so-called "Symphony of the Thousand," Mahler turned to words again. (He once significantly confessed to Arthur Seidl that when he conceived a great musical

---

[1] Sibelius, too, like most other modern symphonists, uses these groups, but compact groups of concise, interrelated themes; but that, after all, is not so far from the classical practice for even with Beethoven a "subject" may and often does embrace several "themes."

painting, he always came to a point where he was compelled to "use words as the vehicle of the musical idea.") Scored for soli, chorus and a gigantic orchestra that includes piano, harmonium, organ, mandoline and a force of four trumpets and three trombones posted apart from the main body, it consists of two huge movements: a setting of the "Veni creator spiritus" shaped in sonata-form, and a setting of the last scene of *Faust*, containing the elements of the normal slow movement, scherzo and finale.

Nothing could be in stronger contrast with Sibelius's brief pregnant motives than Mahler's long-drawn melodies. But that is in the true Austrian tradition. Like Schubert and Bruckner, Mahler was a lyrical symphonist whose musical roots were firmly planted in the soil of *Volkslieder* and popular soldiers' songs and military marches. There are even thematic links between Mahler's symphonies and his songs. The second of the *Lieder eines fahrenden Gesellen* (comp. 1884; appeared 1897), "Ging heut Morgens übers Feld," appears in the first movement and finale of the First Symphony (1889), and the trio of the funeral march of that work is based on the last song of the same song-cycle. His setting of "Die Fischpredigt des Heiligen Antonius" from *Des Knaben Wunderhorn* similarly turns up in the third movement of the Second Symphony, and another of the *Wunderhorn* songs—not in his set of twelve so-called *Wunderhorn-Lieder*, but No. 11 of the *Lieder aus der Jugendzeit* (1892)— "Ablösung im Sommer," is the basis of the third movement of the Third Symphony. And just as Mahler's first four symphonies are all connected with *Des Knaben Wunderhorn*, the next three are connected in spirit, if not in actual notes, with the *Kindertotenlieder* and the other five Rückert settings (all composed 1900–02; appeared 1905). It is not surprising that Mahler's greatest work, *Das Lied von der Erde* (comp. 1908; perf. 1911), is a hybrid composition that has equal claims to be considered a six-movement symphony with vocal *obbligati* or as a song-cycle with orchestral accompaniment.

But if Sibelius's Fourth Symphony can be compared, as Cecil Gray suggests, with "a species of star, which [physicists and astronomers] call a White Dwarf, the substance of which is so dense and compressed that a piece the size of a shilling may weigh as much as several tons," these titanic "worlds" of Mahler's have an unfortunate resemblance to the planet Jupiter, whose mean density is little greater than that of water. Moreover Mahler had the ill-luck to strike out in a direction that went out of fashion shortly after his death and long remained unpopular. With its pronounced reaction towards unemotional or very mildly emotional classicism, the music of the last forty-five years, of the most widely different schools, has consistently shown a strong tendency to economy: to terseness of expression as well as to economy of forces. Mahler is romantic, long-winded and spendthrift—completely out of tune with the art world of 1918 to 1945. Sibelius miraculously contrived, without making the least effort to be in the fashion, to be completely in tune with all that was best in its tendencies and at the same time to avoid its numerous sillinesses and superficialities. If any one composer can be said to sum up whatever is worthwhile in the music of the period between the wars it is Sibelius. To see how perfectly he expresses the spirit of the age one need only compare him with a composer from the extreme other end of Europe, a musician who superficially appears to have nothing in common with him: Manuel de Falla.

The similarity between Sibelius's relationship to folk-song and Falla's has already been referred to. But they are akin in other points than this: in their economy of expression (not only in texture, but in their habit of plunging directly into the matter in hand without preamble) and their freedom from romantic emotion. Neither went to that extreme of non-emotionalism which is the ideal of the later Schönberg and the Stravinsky of the *Symphonies of Wind Instruments*; but the emotion is latent in their music, as it is in Mozart's, not freely expressed as it was expressed in the music of practically every post-Beethovenian composer up to the first decade of the present century.

Admittedly Falla was by no means such an important figure in European music as Sibelius, but he put Spain back on the musical map of Europe as neither Pedrell, Albéniz nor Granados was able to do. Pedrell (1841–1922), with all his high ideals, his invaluable spadework in collecting Spanish folk-music, so fascinatingly mixed in origin,[1] was not a great enough creative

[1] "There are the powerful Oriental influences attendant on the Moorish invasion," says Eric Blom in his chapter on Pedrell in *Step-children of Music* (G. T. Foulis, N.D.), "the great Spanish school of church composers, who had an enormous hold on the populace; the

artist to secure general recognition. Granados produced a near-masterpiece in his set of *Goyescas* for piano (1911) but the bulk of his work is technically weak and rather superficial. Albéniz also produced one masterly set of piano-pieces, *Iberia* (1906–09), at the very end of his life, after coming under the influence of Debussy, but the majority of his numerous compositions are more or less conventionally "Spanish" salon-pieces. It remained for Falla to write music that is profoundly as well as superficially Spanish—and fine enough to be valued for something more than picturesque Spanishness.

Like Albéniz, Falla found artistic salvation through meeting Debussy. His first important work, the opera *La vida breve* (comp. 1904–05; perf. 1913), is nationalistic in the most obvious sense; good of its kind, but no more. But the impact of Debussy in 1907—and particularly (strangely enough) of Debussy's pseudo-Spanish piano-pieces: *La Soirée dans Grenade*, *La Puerta del Vino*, *La Sérénade interrompue*—gave Falla a new direction. The direct influence of Debussy is obvious in the four beautiful, atmospheric *Pièces espagnoles* for piano of 1909; then it passed, leaving Falla in command of a technique that is, after all, more akin to Ravel's than Debussy's and a musical language that is Spanish through and through, not merely on the surface, yet making practically no use of actual folk-material. He produced in comparatively quick succession three masterpieces: the orchestral *Noches en los jardines de España* (1916) and the two ballets, *El Amor brujo* (1915) and *El Sombrero de tres picos* (1919). In two later works, the puppet-opera *El retablo de Maese Pedro* (1923) and the Harpsichord Concerto (1926), Falla shed all but the last traces of superficial nationalism, though those best acquainted with Spanish music, such as Professor Trend, declare that *El retablo*, for instance, is "intensely Spanish in feeling,

---

narrative songs of the Catalan-Provençal minstrels, which are shot with Eastern elements dating from the Crusades; the ecclesiastical chant of Calvados, before the adoption of the Roman liturgy; the plainchant of the latter; Basque, Corsican, Italian, Arab, even Turkish influences; and much else beside." But it is the Oriental that dominates. Spanish folk-music is more nearly Oriental than that of any other European country, except perhaps Yugo-Slavia; far more than that of Hungary, for instance. As for Russia, commonly supposed to have Oriental affinities, the interest in Oriental music shown by Russian composers is mainly an interest in the exotic.

mainly owing to the vigour of the rhythms and the fact of those strongly conflicting rhythms being piled upon one another"[1] while the declamation catches "the exact tone and inflection of Spanish speech."[2] But if, like Bartók, Falla did not shed his national characteristics as completely as Stravinsky, his dropping of what is commonly called "Spanish idiom" is none the less significant.

One of the most curious features of Falla's music (and of that of Granados and Albéniz, to some extent), a national trait by no means as superficial as it may seem on first consideration, is the influence on its texture of the national instrument, the guitar. It is not only that the tone-quality of the guitar moulded Falla's harmony, his piano-style (as in the *Fantasía Bética* of 1919) and his string-writing (as in the miller's *farruca* in *The Three-Cornered Hat*, and dozens of other passages); guitar-technique is obviously the origin of the internal pedal-points of which Falla is so fond, just as the technique of the Norwegian "Hardanger violin" played a certain part in forming Grieg's later harmonic style. And it was doubtless the need for a clear, quasi-percussive—that is, guitar-like—element in everything he wrote that led Falla to include the piano in the scores of the *Noches, El Amor brujo* and *El Sombrero,* and the still more guitar-like harpsichord in that of *El Retablo*—occasionally *concertante,* as in the *Noches,* but generally as an ordinary orchestral instrument.

Falla, Stravinsky, Bartók, Kodály—all these composers are symptoms of what practically amounts to a second great out-break of musical nationalism, forty or fifty years after the first. And just as the first movement owed a good deal to Liszt and was a sort of offshoot of romanticism, this second one is at least dimly connected with Debussy and the decline and fall of romanticism. It was perhaps too sporadic to be spoken of as a "movement," but it was perceptible enough throughout the first two decades of the century and it has not yet entirely exhausted

---

[1] Glinka, who spent the winter of 1846–47 in Seville, was particularly struck by the rhythmic complication of Spanish dance music. He says he noticed at times three simultaneous rhythms: that of the singers, that of the guitar accompaniment, and that of the hand-clapping and feet of the dancers. (*Zapiski M. I. Glinki,* Moscow, 1930.)

[2] Trend: *Manuel de Falla and Spanish Music.*

itself. Moreover, it was sufficiently widespread to include the two most eclectic of all musical races: the English and the Jewish.[1]

The Jew's chameleon-like gift for adapting himself to his background has generally been fatal to any national quality in his art. Jewish composers—Mendelssohn, Meyerbeer, Rubinstein, Halévy, Schönberg and the rest—have nearly all been eclectics. Some, like Serov and Mahler, have even been more or less saturated by the musical atmosphere of the lands of their birth. But in many of Ernest Bloch's works—from the *Three Jewish Poems* (1913), *Three Psalms* (1912–14), *Schelomo* (1915), *Israel* Symphony (1915), and the First String Quartet (1916), through *Voice in the Wilderness* (1936) to the Second Quartet (1946)—the Jewish race has for the first time found its voice in modern art-music: a strange, half-Oriental voice, but one with a message of its own to deliver.

And at last, after more than two hundred years, England too has found again her own true musical accent, mainly in consequence of the discovery (it was nothing less than that) of English folk-music by Cecil Sharp and his predecessors and successors during the opening years of the present century. The unearthed treasures were treated in various ways. A great number were effectively "arranged" in various forms, from the simplest part-songs and solo songs with piano accompaniment to the high-spirited pieces of Percy Grainger—*Shepherd's Hey* (1913), *Country Gardens* (1918) and the rest—and such more elaborate compositions as Holst's *Somerset Rhapsody* (comp. 1906–07) and Vaughan Williams's three *Norfolk Rhapsodies* (comp. 1906–07).[2] One, "Brigg Fair," fell into the mind of a musician who was English by birth but not by blood, and, through his brooding on it, became the germ of a by no means folk-songish orchestral poem.

The evolution from folk-song of a rather consciously English idiom can be traced very easily in the work of Vaughan Williams;

[1] Even the African negro found a Europeanized voice in the music of Samuel Coleridge-Taylor (1875–1912).

[2] The Scots and Irish had anticipated the English to some extent, Mackenzie in his Scottish Piano Concerto (1897), Stanford in his *Irish* Symphony (1887) and the opera *Shamus O'Brien* (1896), and both in their Scottish and Irish Rhapsodies had employed native folk-themes —though only as the material for thoroughly Teutonic methods of working-out.

and most of the younger English composers whose music has a folk-songish accent seem to be almost as heavily indebted to Vaughan Williams as to the genuine, original article. In such works as *A Sea Symphony* (comp. 1910),[1] *Hugh the Drover* (perf. 1924) and *Sir John in Love* (1929), as in Holst's opera *At the Boar's Head* (1925), actual folk-songs are skilfully woven into more or less folk-songish original material. But, as A. E. F. Dickinson says of the references to "The Golden Vanity" and "The bold Princess Royal" in the scherzo of *A Sea Symphony*, "the interest of these interpolations is that one would scarcely notice them as such. So completely has Vaughan Williams mastered the secret of 'talking folk-song as to the manner born' that when he quotes a particular folk-tune, we feel he might have written it himself."[2] *A London Symphony* (1914) shows a curiously satisfactory fusion of folk-songish with other elements, and in the *Pastoral Symphony* (1922), *The Shepherds of the Delectable Mountains* (1922), *Sancta Civitas* (1925), *Job* (1931) and other works of this period Vaughan Williams evolved a modern-archaic musical speech, based mainly on folk-song and modal plainsong—though used with a very modern freedom that does not shy even at polytonality (e.g., bars 9–13 of the first movement of the *Pastoral Symphony*)—yet completely freed from the mere mannerisms of folk-song. The texture is a free, often modal polyphony, frequently a counterpoint of faux-bourdon-like chords, while such modern devices as the whole-tone scale are not excluded. At a later period, like so many nationalist composers, he seems to have realized the limitations of this austere but rather etiolated musical speech. The unsuccessful Piano Concerto (1933) and the Suite for Viola and Orchestra (1934) show him struggling to free himself, and the F minor Symphony (1935), like other British symphonies of the same period—Walton's and Bax's Sixth (both also 1935)—betrays a desire to emulate the symphonic methods of Sibelius. In the

[1] An interesting example of a genuine "choral symphony"; that is, not a symphony with choruses like Beethoven's Ninth or Mendelssohn's *Lobgesang*, but a normal symphony—and a more conventional one than Mahler's Eighth—scored throughout for chorus and orchestra. Almost the only comparable work is Holst's *Choral Symphony* (1925) on poems by Keats.

[2] *An Introduction to the Music of R. Vaughan Williams.* (Musical Pilgrim Series, O.U.P., 1928.)

Fifth (1943) he abandoned the struggle and returned, with new emotional warmth, to his earlier manner.

Side by side with the English folk-music revival, there was a wave of interest in Celtic folk-music. This also made a certain impression on modern British art-music, though no composer succeeded in "digesting" it as Vaughan Williams digested English folk-song. Boughton's opera *The Immortal Hour* (1914) is only partially successful, and in Bax's music the Celtic element —e.g., in the slow movement of the Piano Quintet (comp. 1915), the finale of the First String Quartet (comp. 1918), and the slow movements of the Third and Fourth Symphonies (1930 and 1932 respectively)—is only one of a number of heterogeneous ingredients, as the English folk-song element is in Holst.

At the same time it should be remembered that, beside the conscious and often merely superficial Englishness of the folk-song school, there is another, perhaps more essential kind of Englishness, perceptible even in the music of those composers who have been most dominated by Teutonic ways of musical thinking. Someone—I think Peter Warlock, but I have been unable to trace the passage—has drawn attention to the vein of "sensuous sweetness" that runs through all our best lyric poetry and through so much of our music even as early as "Sumer is icumen in" and from the Elizabethan madrigalists to Elgar, Delius, and the folk-song school. And then there is a wistful Elia-like tenderness that one finds particularly in Elgar (e.g., the first interlude in *Falstaff* and "Ysobel" in the *Enigma Variations*), but also in such younger composers as Britten (first movement of the *Serenade* for tenor, horn and strings (1943)) and Tippett (slow movement of the Concerto for double string orchestra (1939)), while the noble gravity common to such otherwise very different composers as Parry (e.g., Job's lamentation), Elgar (e.g., the "Nimrod" variation), and John Ireland (e.g., the slow movement of his Piano Sonata (1920)), if not peculiarly English, is profoundly true to the character of a nation that has produced a Milton and a Wordsworth.

And, finally, the individual qualities of Elgar's mind—often very English, despite its musical debt to Wagner and others— have left marks on composers totally different in outlook and thus, as it were, added new values to the stock of musical Englishness. Just as the technical influence of Vaughan Williams can be traced in Howells and Ireland and Moeran, and Delius's in Peter Warlock, Elgarian echoes can be detected not only in the later works of the one-time Stravinskyist, Arthur Bliss—e.g., the Clarinet Quintet (1933) and Music for Strings (1935)—but in passages of the Viola Concerto (1929) of William Walton, who in such early works as his First String Quartet (1923) had shown a leaning towards advanced modernism of the most uncompromising kind.

Naturally America, too, has felt the stirrings of artistic nationalism. Towards the end of the nineteenth century she produced one charming and individual tone-poet in Edward MacDowell, but MacDowell's art was fundamentally as Teutonic as Stanford's and he has had no important artistic posterity. The majority of American composers, like so many English ones, have been eclectic in the worst sense, colourless imitators of European masters. Nevertheless, many conscious efforts have been made to achieve genuine "American" music—music expressing "the modern American spirit" or music based on negro or American Indian or Spanish American or Anglo-Saxon folk-music—not only by American-born musicians such as Aaron Copland (*El Salón Mexico*, 1936), William Schuman (*American Festival Overture*, 1939), Roy Harris (*Folksong Symphony*, 1940), and Samuel Barber (*Excursions* for piano, pub. 1945), but by European composers who have temporarily settled in the United States, from Dvořák's *New World* Symphony (1893) to Ernest Bloch's orchestral rhapsody *America* (1926). Typical of the attempted expressions of industrial America—and of its period—is Converse's naïve symphonic poem, *Flivver Ten Million* (1927), which the composer described as "a joyous epic inspired by the familiar legend, 'The ten millionth Ford is now serving its owner'."

So far, America's most important contribution has been the new idioms of popular music: ragtime (about 1912) and jazz (about 1918). We have already noticed the impact of jazz on Stravinsky. In the country of its origin it has also penetrated into "serious" music in such works as Gershwin's *Rhapsody in Blue* (1923) and his opera *Porgy and Bess* (1935), and Gruenberg's *Daniel Jazz* (1924).

INTERLUDE: MUSIC IN THE NINETEEN-TWENTIES

Two features of the period immediately following the end of the 1914–18 War stand out unmistakably: the curious wave of sheer artistic silliness, of frantic desire for modernism-at-all-cost —closely associated with the decline of the Diaghilev Ballet— that swept both the victorious and the vanquished countries; and, far more important, the colossal development in mechanical reproduction of music.

The composers involved in this feverish "silly season" were by no means negligible. (Their work will be discussed in the next chapter.) There was a good deal of sense underlying their silliness, but something in the air of Europe—a high-spirited craziness, admirably expressed in popular music by the "hottest" type of jazz, that was in essence a reaction from the tense madness of the Great War—seemed to have turned the heads of all but the hidebound conservatives of art. Stravinsky was God and Diaghilev his Prophet, a prophet who solemnly proclaimed that *The Rite of Spring* was "greater than Beethoven." And the group of young French composers known as "Les Six"— Honegger, Milhaud, Poulenc, Auric, Tailleferre and Durey— who were Stravinsky's principal disciples, dragged out the veteran Satie to play John the Baptist for the second time in his eccentric life. To-day it is easy enough to see that Stravinsky is in the Meyerbeer class rather than among the Beethovens, that one or two of "Les Six" are really gifted and the rest comparative nonentities, and that Satie is merely what Sir Donald Tovey loved to describe as an Interesting Historical Figure.

Even the less extreme radicals of music were at that period very intolerant of the immediate past. They were not prepared, like their more callow comrades in art, to throw over not only Wagner and Brahms but Beethoven as well and to proclaim that music had ended with Bach or thereabouts and begun again with Stravinsky. But their general outlook is not unfairly exemplified by a statement by Arthur Bliss reported in the *Observer* of July 3rd, 1921: "Give me such works as *Le Sacre du Printemps*, *L'Histoire du soldat*, the *Sea Symphony* and *Savitri*, *The Eternal Rhythm*" (a recently produced orchestral piece by Goossens) "and *The Garden of Fand*, the Ravel Trio and Falla's *Vida breve*, *L'Heure espagnole* and the *Five Pieces* of Schönberg, and you can have all your Strauss *Domestic* and *Alpine* Symphonies, your Skryabin poems of earth, fire and water, your Schreker, your Bruckner and your Mahler." The anti-Teutonic bias of this statement, except as regards Schönberg, is very characteristic of those post-war years and Bliss's further denunciation of "the oratorio composed especially for the provincial festival on the lines laid down by the Canon and Chapter . . . the symphonic poem *à la* Strauss, with a soul sorely perplexed but finally achieving freedom, not without much perspiring pathos . . . the pseudo-intellectuality of the Brahms camp-followers, with their classical sonatas and concertos and variations, and other stock-in-trade . . . the overpowering grand operas, with their frothing Wotans and stupid King Marks" is wholly in keeping with the spirit of the age (not only of the nineteen-twenties but of the nineteen-thirties) in non-Germanic Europe, and to a great extent in Germany and Austria too.

The fermentation of post-war modernism in general, and a remarkable festival of contemporary music held at Salzburg in 1922 in particular, led to the foundation in 1923 of the International Society for Contemporary Music, whose annual festivals held in various countries in turn have sponsored an enormous quantity of the newest music. The Society adopted as its London headquarters the Contemporary Music Centre (founded 1920) of the British Music Society founded in 1918 in the ultra-patriotic flush induced by the War.

But these excitements were only temporary phenomena, though they have left a lasting memorial in the festivals of the International Society. The enormous strides in the mechanical reproduction of music, on the other hand, have brought about a permanent revolution of which the final consequences cannot yet be foreseen. Just as the public concert of the nineteenth century took the place of home music-making and the private concert of the royal or wealthy patron, mechanical reproduction in the home has begun to supplant the public concert. So far, it is true it has not done so; it has even *enlarged* the musical public and brought numerous recruits to the concert hall. But as mechanical reproduction gradually approaches perfection, it steadily becomes a more dangerous menace to the public concert.

It has produced revolutionary changes in the economics of the musical world; home music-making, and consequently the sale of instruments and sheet-music,[1] is very much less than in the days before the gramophone and before broadcasting. On the other hand, general knowledge of music of all kinds and periods is much more widely disseminated than formerly; musicians themselves are much better informed; high standards of performance are set;[2] and the musical culture of Britain, at any rate, is no longer confined to London, Edinburgh and a few great provincial cities.

The "mechanical reproduction" revolution, like most revolutions, has passed through various phases, each marking a bigger advance than the preceding one. We may call them the player-piano phase, the gramophone phase and the broadcasting phase. The player-piano phase was mainly pre-1920. At that period its superhuman capabilities attracted even composers; for instance in 1917 Stravinsky wrote an *Étude pour pianola* (afterwards orchestrated as *Madrid*, No. 4 of the *Four Studies* for orchestra of 1930). But as late as 1922 the player-piano was "far in front of the gramophone in its supply of the classics," and Hindemith's *Toccata* for it (Op. 40) dates from 1926. In an article in the *Observer* (October 29th, 1922) Percy Scholes wrote that "in player-piano roll form you can get, for instance, every one of the Beethoven piano sonatas, and every one of the piano concertos ('arranged,' i.e., with the orchestral part incorporated), all the nine symphonies, and much of the chamber music. Of Bach you have a considerable range, including the first twenty-four of the '48' and all the Inventions. Of Chopin you have a really enormous player-piano repertory. And in the more modern works you have a big collection, from nearly all Debussy . . . right down to Stravinsky's *Rite of Spring* complete, to perform. . . . The manufacturers of gramophone records have not as yet approached this comprehensiveness. Of complete big works they can sell you Beethoven's *Moonlight* and the *Kreutzer* Sonata, the

---

[1] One consequence of this is that composers now depend almost entirely on performing rights and mechanical-reproduction rights for their remuneration, instead of on sales royalties.

[2] In this respect the British musical competition festival movement, which developed enormously during the nineteen-twenties, also helped very materially.

Emperor Concerto, the Fifth Symphony, Dvořák's *New World*, and Skryabin's *Poem of Ecstasy*, but beyond these not much more than a very extensive and well-varied collection of odd 'movements'."

However, this position was before long handsomely rectified by the gramophone companies, and the introduction of electrical recording early in 1925 marked a big advance in the musical value of the instrument, reconciling to it the numerous musicians who had hitherto regarded it with a certain amount of contempt or suspicion.

Even before the gramophone had thus firmly established itself, another mechanical device appeared, quickly developed from its experimental, artistically unsatisfactory beginnings, and soon attained even wider popularity than the gramophone. The earliest transmissions of the British Broadcasting Company (now the British Broadcasting Corporation) began in 1922, and wireless concerts had been given from London for some months even before the formation of the Company. At first the programmes were curiously mixed. The first number of the *Radio Times* (September 28th, 1923) announced a London orchestral programme beginning with Elgar's first *Pomp and Circumstance* March and ending with a selection from Lionel Monckton's *Bric-à-Brac*, while in the middle a popular comedian was sandwiched between the *Meistersinger* Overture and Saint-Saëns's G minor Piano Concerto. And the Birmingham Station Orchestra's "Special Classical Programme of Tchaïkovsky's Music" a couple of days later was decidedly on the light side. But the Company's musical policy was in good hands and this state of affairs was soon changed for the better. Opera was broadcast . even in those early days: the garden scene from Gounod's *Faust* was relayed from the Old Vic in October, 1923, and excerpts from the British National Opera Company's winter season at Covent Garden were also broadcast.

Early in 1924 the B.B.C. embarked on a new policy, the organization of public concerts, and soon became one of the most important of London's concert-giving bodies. The first B.B.C. Symphony Concert was given at the Central Hall, Westminster, on February 22nd, 1924, when Percy Pitt conducted the Royal Albert Hall Orchestra. Five other concerts were given in that first series, the orchestras engaged being the Royal Philharmonic, the Royal Albert Hall and the London Symphony. The B.B.C.'s own Symphony Orchestra was not formed till 1930.

Nor was chamber music neglected by the B.B.C. A series of six public chamber concerts was given at the Chenil Galleries, Chelsea, in 1926. The following winter saw a series of six International Chamber Concerts at the Grotrian Hall, and these in turn led in 1927 to the first of those Concerts of Contemporary Music—orchestral as well as chamber—that are still among the most important means of introducing the newest music of all schools except the academic and reactionary not only to the London public but to listeners all over Britain.

The wide diffusion by broadcasting and the gramophone of music written in the most advanced contemporary idioms has done something to close that gulf between the modern composer and the average listener which was steadily widening since the early part of the present century, and given a healthy stimulus to the British composer. A composer can create naturally and spontaneously only in an idiom to which he is thoroughly accustomed, and the stodginess and conservatism that long afflicted British music was mainly due to the fact that for so many years the British composer had very little chance of saturating himself in the contemporary idiom even if he lived in London or one of the larger provincial cities, and none at all otherwise.

As I have written elsewhere:[1] "A man who has had the whole of *Tristan* as a familiar part of the musical furniture of his mind ever since he has been old enough to take any sort of intelligent interest in music is bound to have a different norm of consonance from the musician living in an English provincial town who, until the coming of wireless, has had no opportunity of knowing more about *Tristan* than can be gathered from one or two concert performances of the Prelude and 'Liebestod.' . . . We English as a musical nation have to pay the price of our provinciality. Possessing only one opera establishment of the first rank in the whole country (and that, until recently, beyond the financial reach of the musical masses) we cannot expect to keep up with the vanguard of musical thought as well as can the main body of 'ordinary listeners' in countries where every town of any size has long had a reasonably efficient opera-house, with

[1] *This Modern Stuff: An Introduction to Contemporary Music.* Duckworth, 3rd edition, 1946.

popular prices, and a more than reasonably efficient orchestra. . . . The German musical man-in-the-street has long had far better opportunities of getting used to Tristanesque harmony as a feature of everyday musical life than have the majority of British professional musicians.'' The ordinary British music-lover in the provinces was until the nineteen-twenties still living in the age of Brahms and Grieg, and the impact on his mind of the few separate manifestations of modern music that came his way was bound to be extraordinarily unpleasant. Even the keen concert-goer in thoroughly musical centres found it difficult enough to accustom his ear not merely to one or two fresh types of harmonic innovation, as his forefathers had to do, but to a whole host of innovations of the most varied kinds. The musical man-in-the-street found it quite impossible. But radio and the gramophone at least offered him a way out of the street if he cared to take it, and gave him the practically free *entrée* of the concert hall whenever he wanted it.

The consequences of the revolution produced by mechanical reproduction are therefore by no means limited to the economics of the musical world. They spread out in every direction, affecting the composer, the performer, the listener, in fact, the bases of the whole art of music as we know it.

III. TENDENCIES BETWEEN THE WARS: NEO-CLASSICISM AND THE TWELVE-TONE SYSTEM

We have already noticed in the music of the later Ravel, the later Stravinsky, Falla and other composers quite dissimilar in other respects a common tendency to what can only be called neo-classicism: avoidance of subjective emotion (in extreme cases, of emotion of any kind); abhorrence of rhetoric; abandonment of the technique of development in the Beethovenian sense; love of simplicity, terseness and economy in every means of expression; equal dislike of impressionism and of frank programme music; consideration of music as an affair of more or less abstract sound-patterns or sonorities, or at any rate as an absolute thing-in-itself, not as the symbol of certain feelings or ideas or definite objects. Their attitude, in short, was the perfect antithesis of romanticism and of the German metaphysical view of music closely bound up with it that had dominated the great bulk of European music since Beethoven. This second neo-classical reaction differed profoundly from the earlier one of the Leipzig school in the eighteen-forties, even in origin.

No doubt neo-classicism was a natural and inevitable reaction from extreme romanticism. As we have seen, impressionism was a first step towards it and numerous forebodings of it were apparent in many pre-1914 works, even German works, from Schönberg's *Five Orchestral Pieces* (1909) to Ravel's *Daphnis et Chloé* (1911). But the War of 1914–18, both by shutting off the influence of German contemporary music and by arousing chauvinistic feeling, greatly encouraged this neo-classical movement outside Germany. It almost became an anti-Teutonic movement. Latin clarity and frivolity and restraint, Slavonic naïveté and love of strong rhythms and bright, pure colours, combined to complete the overthrow of romanticism.

The qualities most fashionable in the music of the immediate post-war period are epitomized in the work of the young French group, "Les Six," and in such compositions as Prokofiev's *Love of the Three Oranges* (1921) and his piano concertos. Actually "Les Six" were no more a homogeneous band than the Russian "mighty handful" or any other such artistic clique recorded by history. The bond that held them together for a time was mainly accidental and time soon showed that they differed in their leanings as much as in their gifts. But they agreed in paying open homage to Stravinsky and Satie (and more discreet homage to Ravel) and in pursuing the anti-romantic ideals outlined above, ideals that were rather provocatively stated by their literary ally, Jean Cocteau. The texture of their music is essentially linear, and diatonic or modal if considered line by line (just as Debussy and Ravel are essentially diatonic or modal). And to emphasize this linear aspect of their music and obliterate possible harmonic implications they adopt, as Stravinsky had done, a style of instrumentation that makes it impossible for the separate lines to coalesce. The second of Milhaud's *Cinq Symphonies pour petit orchestre* (1917–22), for instance, is scored for flute, cor anglais, bassoon, violin, viola, 'cello and double-bass. And, with the same object, they make the fullest possible use of polytonality: usually two, or at most three, simultaneous keys, though in the third of Milhaud's *Cinq Symphonies* there are passages in five or even six simultaneous keys. A passage (pages 18–19 of the miniature score) from Milhaud's *Protée* (second suite) (pub. 1922) is typical of his orchestral texture; it is a piece of diatonic counterpoint in three real parts, two of them thickened out *organum*-wise:

(1) In E major, played by flutes, clarinets, horns and divided first violins, in perfect fourths (a revival of the most primitive form of *organum*).

(2) Essentially a fanfare based melodically on the arpeggio of the diminished seventh, E, G, B flat, D flat, but with each note thickened out into a massive opaque chord built up (or rather *down*) of the perfect fourth, minor sixth, diminished octave, and minor third—so that the E, for example, becomes the chord C sharp, E sharp, G sharp, B, E natural—played by oboes cor anglais, two bassoons, trumpets, trombones, divided second violins and divided violas.

(3) The bass—a single line in A major—played by bass clarinet, the other two bassoons, tuba, 'cellos and basses.

Milhaud is particularly fond of such chord agglomerations as the *organum* of the middle part here. They are carried to greater lengths in later works. In the nineteenth tableau, "Le Rédempteur," of his opera *Christophe Colomb* (1930), for instance, one orchestral "part" alone consists of no fewer than seven piled-up thirds; one of the two choruses is an independent four-part *organum* of its own, while another section of the orchestra moves chromatically in triad blocks—to say nothing of an independent part in octaves for the first chorus and a complicated independent *ostinato* figure for the rest of the orchestra. But with all this complication—in marked contrast with the extreme simplicity preached by "Les Six" in their early days—the music remains resolutely diatonic; except for the chromatically moving triads, the music is for a few bars absolutely free of accidentals. When Milhaud and the rest of "Les Six" occasionally attain what appears to be atonality, it is only through polytonal excesses. Their atonality, such as it is, has nothing whatever in common with the chromatic atonality of Schönberg.

For some time "Les Six" and other kindred spirits, such as Prokofiev and Lord Berners, found the best antidote to romanticism and impressionism in a cult of humour and parody. Ravel had shown the way in the grotesque instrumentation of the parodical passages in *L'Heure espagnole*; Stravinsky had followed it further. Satie, with characteristic love of the *outré*, introduced typewriters and sirens in the score of his ballet *Parade* (produced by Diaghilev in 1917), and Milhaud in a perfectly serious work, *Les Choéphores* (1927), used whips, hammers and whistles, together with the groanings of the chorus "to create an impression of foreboding and threatening disaster which" (according to one of his apologists)[1] "it would probably have been impossible to obtain by the use of purely musical means."[2] Eccentricity was also shown in the choice of words for musical setting; Milhaud abandoned poetry in favour of the catalogues of manufacturers of agricultural implements—*Machines agricoles* (1919)—and seedsmen—*Catalogue des fleurs* (1920). The most characteristic products of this phase were the series of ballets commissioned by Diaghilev, beginning with Satie's *Parade*: Prokofiev's *Chout* (1919), Poulenc's *Les Biches*, Auric's *Les Fâcheux*, Satie's *Mercure* and Milhaud's *Le Train bleu* (all 1924), Auric's *Les Matelots* (1925), Berners's *Triumph of Neptune* (1926), and Prokofiev's *Le Pas d'acier* (1927).

The ideals of "Les Six" were most faithfully embodied in the music of Poulenc and Auric. Poulenc was the arch-humorist, the most determined anti-romantic, of the group. He often showed delight in the comic songs of the Paris streets and in the idiom of popular dance music, but he was intensely sophisticated despite his apparent naïveté. In consequence of his desire for the utmost possible simplicity, he shows (like the later Ravel) a predilection for the simplest two-part writing and none of his works are more characteristic than the early sonatas for two clarinets and for clarinet and bassoon (1918 and 1922 respectively). The *Concert champêtre* for harpsichord and orchestra (1928) was the earliest proof that Poulenc was something more

[1] Rollo H. Myers: *Modern Music: Its Aims and Tendencies*. Kegan Paul, N.D.

[2] But even Milhaud was out-Milhaudé by the French-American composer Varèse in such works as *Hyperprism* (1923), in which flute, E flat clarinet, three horns, two trumpets and two trombones are pitted against a percussive mass of snare drum, Indian drum, mammoth bass drum, two cymbals, "crash" cymbals, gong, triangle, hammer and anvil, two Chinese blocks (high and low), "lion roar," large and small rattles, sleigh-bells and siren.

than the mere buffoon he once appeared to be. Like so many contemporary French composers, he showed himself a lyrical Ravelian at heart. So, too, did a younger champion of the ideals of "Les Six," Jean Françaix.

Neither Honegger nor Milhaud was completely faithful to the tenets of their group. Milhaud has always been something of a romanticist; his early Violin Sonata (composed in 1911) might almost have been written by one of the less gifted Franckists, and decidedly romantic passion is revealed again and again in his later works. As for Honegger, it is difficult to understand why he ever associated himself with "Les Six." The slow movement of his First String Quartet (comp. 1917) shows the influence of both Wagner and Debussy; he experimented with frankly realistic programme music in such orchestral pieces as *Pacific 231* (1924), a musical impression of a powerful locomotive which is a serious rival to the sheep in Strauss's *Don Quixote*, and *Rugby* (1928); and as early as 1921 he frankly avowed that he did not "seek a return to harmonic simplicity, as do some of the anti-impressionists." Honegger had in common with the rest of his group little more than a love of rather naïve, diatonic melodic material and free employment of polytonality. But he was one of the most eclectic of modern composers, a romanticist toying with neo-classicism, equally indebted to Stravinsky and to Schönberg, freely using any and every device past or present that happened to suit his purpose. Sometimes he achieved results of considerable beauty, as in the chorus "Alleluia" that concludes the second part of his "symphonic psalm" *Le Roi David* (1926, but originally conceived as incidental music to a play by René Morax in 1921). *Le Roi David* is the first of a series of cantatas and "dramatic oratorios" —such as *Le Cri du monde* (1931) and *Jeanne d'Arc au bûcher* (1937)—into which Honegger put some of his best work. There is at least a superficial affinity between these compositions and William Walton's oratorio *Belshazzar's Feast* (1931), for Walton too is an eclectic technician who uses the most diverse means to entirely personal ends.

Eclecticism in this sense—a sense in which Bach, Mozart and Beethoven may be said to have been eclectics—the use of any suitable technical means, without regard to its up-to-dateness or to *a priori* theories, is one of the healthiest tendencies in contemporary music. On the other hand, the most important contribution to the vocabulary of music between the wars was made by a composer who is almost universally regarded as the slave of a theory and who has certainly succeeded far better than Stravinsky in grasping the full implications of intellectual neo-classicism and evolving a style of music that embodies them. Whatever one may think of the æsthetic value of Schönberg's own music, it is hardly deniable that he and his school have given music the most striking new technical *idea* since Debussy devised the technique of impressionism.

But before we examine Schönberg's chromatic atonalism we must go back a little in time. We have seen in a previous chapter how in *Verklärte Nacht*, the *Gurrelieder* and *Pelleas und Melisande*, Schönberg had developed the romantic chromaticism of *Tristan* so far that he "could go no further in this direction. . . . He had to strike out in a new direction, which he found in his middle period through the employment of strict forms."[1] The word "forms" is to be understood here in two senses: broad architectural form and the details of the organic texture. As regards the latter, Wellesz claims that the D minor Quartet (1905), the first of the works conceived on these lines, playing for forty-five minutes, "does not contain a single inside part, a single figure, that is not thematic," and, although this may not be quite literally true, it is not a serious overstatement.   The infinite contrapuntal ingenuity displayed in the *Gurrelieder* is here applied to variations and transformations of a few generating themes on Franckish lines, but with a technique beside which Franck's appears childish. The use of the string quartet after the huge forces of the *Gurrelieder* and *Pelleas* was a severe discipline, symptomatic of Schönberg's new concentration on pure *line*.

Schönberg's architectural experiments both in this Quartet and in the *Kammersinfonie* No. 1 for fifteen solo instruments (perf. 1907) also owe something to Liszt and Franck and to Schumann's D minor Symphony, perhaps a little, too, to Strauss's *Domestica*. In each of these works he has taken the elements of first movement in sonata-form, slow movement, scherzo and finale, melted them down, and recast them in a single gigantic movement:

[1] See page 224.

Quartet in D minor	*Kammersinfonie*
First Section:	First Section:
Group of "first subject" themes	"First subject" group
Transition (*fugato*)	Transition
Group of "second subject" themes	"Second subject" group
First development	Reprise of "first subject"
Second Section:	Second Section:
Scherzo (with Trio)	Scherzo (with Trio)
Second (main) development	Third Section:
Reprise of "first subject" themes	Development
Third Section:	Fourth Section:
Adagio	Slow movement
Reprise of "second subject" themes	Fifth Section:
Transition	Brief review of themes from First Section
Fourth Section:	Conclusion
Rondo Finale	

It is interesting to compare these with the similar but less highly organized forms of the British chamber music "phantasy," called into being in the very year of the Schönberg Quartet by the first of W. W. Cobbett's chamber music competitions.[1] The *Kammersinfonie* is much more concise than the Quartet and is more "advanced" in every way, though it contains nothing as beautiful as the *adagio* of the earlier work.

The *Kammersinfonie* is a landmark in several respects. In 1906 when it was written, the chamber orchestra—in this case consisting of flute, oboe, cor anglais, clarinets in D and A, bass clarinet, bassoon, double bassoon, two horns and solo strings— had rarely been used; Wagner's *Siegfried Idyll* and the accompaniments to Mahler's *Wunderhorn-Lieder*, *Rückert-Lieder* and *Kindertotenlieder* were almost the only examples. (The first

[1] Cobbett stipulated only that the piece should be of short duration and without a break, though, if the composer desired, it might consist of "different sections varying in tempo and metre." But the result has generally been what Stanford described in his *Musical Composition* (Macmillan, 1911) as a "tabloid preparation of the three or four movements of a sonata, containing all the ingredients of the prescription and yet not exceeding the proportions of any one of them." Frank Bridge's Phantasy String Quartet (1905) and Phantasy Piano Quartet (1910), Vaughan Williams's Phantasy Quintet (1910), and Herbert Howells's Phantasy Quartet (1917) are excellent examples of the form.

composer to use the chamber orchestra in the theatre was Franz Schreker in his music to the pantomime *The Birthday of the Infanta* (1908); Strauss's *Ariadne* and Stravinsky's *Tale of the Runaway Soldier*, of course, came later still; after that the chamber orchestra became a favourite medium.) But from the *Sinfonie* onward Schönberg abandoned his earlier rich, Tristanesque scoring for a more purely linear style of orchestration. The big melodic leaps, the figuration and so on, suggest Brahms[1] and occasionally Mahler rather than Wagner. And although the harmony is still to a great extent deducible from *Tristan*, the free use of whole-tone themes, chords of fourths, and so on exorcises all but the last traces of romantic sensuousness and all but the last traces of tonality. But the work really faces both ways. The horn theme at the beginning, leaping up melodically in five perfect fourths, is absolutely modern and non-tonal; so is the important whole-tonish 'cello theme that follows. Yet the wind counter-theme in octaves is pure Wagner, and the viola melody at the beginning of the first transition passage (page 17 of the miniature score) even has the characteristic "Wagner turn."

In the Second Quartet in F sharp minor (1908) this duality is still more marked. The one-movement form is abandoned in favour of four short movements, of which the first and the scherzo are quite conventional in outline. But the third is at one and the same time slow movement and *development of the main themes of the preceding movements*. Moreover, Schönberg at this point follows the example of Mahler's symphonies and calls in the human voice: a dramatic soprano singing Stefan George's poem "Litanei." The voice is also used in the finale, which is absolutely free in form, and the words, again by George —"Ich fühle Luft von anderem Planeten" ("I feel the air of another planet")—tell the listener what he may expect. Whereas some of the material of the first three movements is still actually diatonic, this finale dispenses with a key-signature and is almost completely atonal, though F sharp major gradually emerges towards the end. Fourth-chords are now employed with chromatic alteration, and the melody that leaps over the surface of

[1] Schönberg's early unpublished songs and piano pieces are also said to be decidedly Brahmsian. A good case might be made out for Schönberg as the reconciler of Brahms and Wagner.

these harmonies, often in wide, dissonant intervals, is unlike anything that had hitherto been considered melodic.

The fifteen settings of poems from Stefan George's *Buch der hängenden Gärten*, written at about the same time as this Quartet, and which Schönberg himself described as the first embodiments of the ideal of form and expression that had been floating in his mind for years, are completely atonal. But for the words, they would be completely disintegrated as well, for the piano part is not only curiously independent of the voice but is not even coherent in itself, constantly introducing fresh figures and motives. This disintegration suggests impressionism, but its object is just the opposite: pure expression, unconditioned by architectural form and so concentrated that repetition is unnecessary.

In the works that immediately followed—the *Drei Klavierstücke* (Op. 11), the *Fünf Orchesterstücke* (Op. 16) and the curious "drama with one character," lasting just half an hour, *Erwartung* (all dating from 1909), the *Sechs kleine Klavierstücke*, Op. 19 (1911), and another highly concentrated drama *Die glückliche Hand* (comp. 1910–13),[1] all of them atonal—we see Schönberg grappling in various ways with the problems of this highly concentrated, purely expressionistic style. He too had arrived at a negation of romanticism, a neo-classicism of a kind equally different from that to which Debussy and Ravel were tending and from that to which Stravinsky was to turn later still. His attitude to emotion in music may be gathered from his remarks on Mahler's Ninth Symphony in 1913: "It conveys an almost passionless embodiment of beauty perceptible only to those who can renounce animal warmth and feel at home in the coolness of the spirit."

The first and second pieces of Op. 11 still retain traces of ternary form and their short melodic motives are still repeated and allowed to "grow"; but No. 3 is purely expressionistic: the only form is that produced by the expressive content and there is no repetition or development of motives. "Once stated," says Webern,[2] "the theme expresses all it has to say; it must be

---

[1] The characters are simply A Man (high baritone), A Lady and A Gentleman (both mimed parts only), with a chorus of six women and six men.

[2] Essay "Schönbergs Musik" in the symposium *Arnold Schönberg* (Munich, 1912).

followed by something fresh." The same may be said of *Erwartung*, but the *Five Orchestral Pieces* are less drastic in this respect. Each, however, embodies an experiment in instrumentation. The opening of No. 2, for instance, is an early instance of that "dissonance of scoring" afterwards so much employed by Stravinsky, "Les Six" and others. Played on a piano the effect would be of fourth-chord triads moving over a double pedal; but the notes of each "chord" are divided between a solo 'cello, an oboe and a muted trumpet so that one hears three-part polyphony instead of homogeneous chords,[1] while even the double pedal is shared by one bassoon and one muted trombone. In No. 3 (and in a similar passage in *Die glückliche Hand*) a strangely beautiful effect is produced simply by sounding a chord and imperceptibly changing its instrumental colouring. In No. 5, very typical of Schönberg's pointillistic polyphony, the composer introduced his now invariable system of indicating the principal part at each moment by a special sign.

The "decadent" literary element in *Erwartung* and *Die glückliche Hand* again predominates in the settings of "thrice seven poems" from Hartleben's translation of Giraud's *Pierrot Lunaire* for "speaking voice," piano, flute (doubling with piccolo), clarinet (doubling with bass clarinet), violin (doubling with viola), and 'cello (1912). The *Sprechstimme* has a part that carries to the utmost possible limit the declamatory method adumbrated in "Des Sommerwindes wilde Jagd" in the *Gurrelieder* and developed in *Die glückliche Hand*: rhythmically very precise, and *spoken* with as near an approximation as possible to an indicated pitch. Each piece is scored for voice and two or three of the instruments.

But perhaps the most significant feature of *Pierrot Lunaire* is the fresh reversion to "strict forms" in the second group. Schönberg, ever a formalist at heart, here tries to reduce his atonal chaos to order by casting the eighth piece, "Nacht," as a passacaglia, while the seventeenth and eighteenth are labyrinths of double canons, mirror-canons and canons *cancrizans* compared with which the final chorus of the *Gurrelieder* is as simple and spontaneous as a folk-song. "Nacht," however, is particularly significant, for the incessant repetitions of its main motive seem to

[1] In *Erwartung* there is an eleven-note chord with two notes doubled, divided between thirteen solo instruments.

have suggested to Schönberg the final solution to this problem of giving formal unity and cohesion to atonal,[1] expressionistic music.

Genuine atonal music is inevitably amorphous, backboneless; but Schönberg saw that it might be given a sort of artificial backbone by basing the contrapuntal parts on certain frequently recurrent patterns. This method is employed in the *Vier Orchesterlieder*, Op. 22 (comp. 1913–14) and in the first pieces composed after the long interim caused by the 1914–18 War:[2] the *Fünf Klavierstücke*, Op. 23 (comp. 1923), and the Serenade, Op. 24 (1923), for clarinet, bass clarinet, mandoline, guitar, violin, viola and 'cello (plus bass voice in the fourth movement, a setting of Petrarch decidedly more vocal than anything in *Pierrot Lunaire*). In the fifth piece of Op. 23 and the third and fourth movements of the Serenade, however, Schönberg went a step further, basing each piece not on ordinary motives recurring intermittently but on a "tone-row" (*Tonreihe*) of a peculiar nature used throughout: nothing less than the whole twelve notes of the chromatic scale[3] arranged in a certain arbitrary order. The particular *Tonreihe* used may be inverted, and both it and its inversion played backwards (and any of these may be transposed), but the whole piece is based on these four forms of the selected *Reihe*.

Apparently this system was not actually invented by Schönberg but by another Viennese atonalist, Josef Matthias Hauer, about 1914. Hauer[4] reckoned that the twelve notes of the duodecuple scale could be arranged in more than 479 million combinations, each susceptible of eleven transpositions; these he grouped according to interval relationships into forty-four *Tropen*—his *Tropen*

[1] In a very lengthy footnote to the third (1921) edition of his *Har-monielehre*, Schönberg denied that he is an atonalist: "I am a musician and have nothing to do with the atonal." But this is essentially a quibble about terms.

[2] These years were not entirely barren, for Schönberg worked at the poem and music of a colossal oratorio, *Die Jakobsleiter*, never finished.

[3] Or, as atonal composers logically prefer to call it, the duodecuple or twelve-tone scale—twopenny "chromatic" implying a penny-plain diatonic basis.

[4] Hauer afterwards explained his theories and practice in two pamphlets, *Vom Melos zur Pauke: Eine Einführung in die Zwölfton-musik* (dedicated to Schönberg) and *Zwölftontechnik: Die Lehre von den Tropen* (both Vienna, 1925), the first full of awful facetiousness, the second full of still more awful diagrams.

being essentially, though not in every respect, the same as Schönberg's *Tonreihen*. But Hauer is negligible as a composer and the twelve-tone method is now mainly associated with Schönberg, who incidentally in the 1921 edition of his *Harmonielehre* pays rather grudging tribute to Hauer, "whose theories, even where I find exaggerations, are deep and original and whose compositions, even those that I feel to be 'examples' rather than compositions, betray creative talent."

The function of the *Tonreihe* in atonal music is twofold. It is usually no longer a sort of *ostinato* motive, though that is how it originated and although it may still be used to some extent as such. It was employed thematically by Berg more than by Schönberg himself. But it roots up the last hard-dying traces of the old tonal functions and at the same time supplies a substitute for them, becoming what has been happily called[1] a "functional mode." (One thinks at once of the *Rāgs* of Indian music.) Even in the most completely atonal music before the introduction of the twelve-tone technique, too frequent recurrence of a certain note would invest it with a quasi-tonic importance to which the listener involuntarily related other notes in the old way. But Schönberg and Hauer, by insisting on the unbroken *Reihe*, ensure that no note shall be heard again till after the eleven others. Here, in short, we have melodic communism "of the most bigoted and persecuting type."

Still, all this is comprehensible enough—as is also the consequent emergence of what is practically a new modal system. But Schönberg's practice in such works as the Third Quartet, Op. 30 (1927), and the orchestral Variations, Op. 31 (1928), is very puzzling. He sounds notes of a *Reihe* simultaneously as a chord, distributes a *Reihe* between two or more parts and thus mixes it with inversions and transpositions of itself, completely destroying its significance as either motive or mode. But these extraordinarily dry and cerebral works were no doubt experimental and it is perhaps significant that whereas when Schönberg first turned back to the old dance forms—minuet, gavotte,

---

[1] By Richard S. Hill, whose essay, "Schönberg's Tone-Rows and the Tonal System of the Future" in *The Musical Quarterly* for January, 1936, is the earliest thorough examination of the system, and of Schönberg's application of it, in any non-German publication.

musette, etc.—in his *Suite für Klavier*, Op. 25 (1925), he based all
the pieces on the same *Tonreihe*, he published a similar *Suite for
String Orchestra* in 1935 in which the *Reihen* are abandoned
altogether and there are extraordinary reversions to sequences
and diatonic outlines. In the Piano Concerto (1944) he uses the
twelve-tone technique for purposes of frankly romantic expression.

Among Schönberg's pupils two—the two earliest—are outstanding: Anton von Webern and Alban Berg. Despite their
common allegiance, they have little else in common. Webern
was an extremist. As we have seen from the pronouncement
quoted on page 284, he always particularly admired the intensely
concentrated expressiveness of Schönberg's music and his own
work consists largely of attempts to carry that concentration even
further. The average length of his *Six Bagatelles* for string
quartet, Op. 9 (1913), is less than ten bars and as Erwin Stein[1]
says, "almost every note of a melody is given to a different
instrument, and each one is in a different tone-colour." The
third *Bagatelle*, just nine bars long, all muted and mostly harmonics, is a miniature museum of *Am Steg* and *Am Griffbrett*
markings, alternate *arco* and *pizzicato*, etc. The *Bagatelles* may
be extreme instances but they are by no means untypical of
Webern's highly compressed style. He sometimes uses a large
orchestra for pieces nearly as brief.

Berg's *Four Pieces for Clarinet and Piano*, Op. 5 (1913), are
essays in the same sort of intense concentration. But Berg is
a more easily approachable figure than Webern and such
austerities are rare in his music. Much more moderate in his
tendencies, much more lyrical and spontaneous than either his
master or his fellow-pupil, he followed Schönberg faithfully in
adopting the twelve-tone system and strict forms. In the *adagio*
of the *Kammerkonzert* for violin, piano and thirteen wind instruments (1925) and the third movement of the *Lyrische Suite*
for string quartet (1926) the material of the expositions appears
inverted in the reprises. But even when Berg indulges in the
most ingenious scholastic devices he seems to breathe into them
that quickening breath of genuine life which so often seems to be
lacking in Schönberg, despite his repeated assertions that he wrote

[1] Quoted by Edwin Evans in his article on Webern in *Cobbett's
Cyclopedic Survey of Chamber Music.*

in a sort of creative frenzy. Berg's *Sieben frühe Lieder* (1907)—including the beautiful setting of Rilke's "Traumgekrönt"—are full of quite Straussian lyricism; one detects the influences of Wagner and Mahler, even of Brahms. And Wagnerian echoes are still perceptible not only in the otherwise very Schönbergian String Quartet, Op. 3 (1910), with its unrepentant sequences, but even in the finale of the mature twelve-tone *Lyrische Suite*.

Berg's remarkable gifts are seen at their best in his two operas, both settings of decadent, or rather psychopathic, tragedies—*Wozzeck* (completed 1920; produced 1925) and *Lulu* (practically completed in 1934, though the scoring was not quite finished at the composer's death in 1935)—his concert aria *Der Wein* for soprano and orchestra (1929) and his Violin Concerto (comp. 1935). In *Wozzeck* and the *Kammerkonzert* Berg had not yet begun to employ the twelve-tone system; in the *Lyrische Suite* and still more in *Der Wein* the richness, plasticity and suppleness of the music he wrings from it are astonishing; and in the Violin Concerto—being very much more artist than doctrinaire—he achieves a remarkable reconciliation between the twelve-tone idiom and such diatonic elements as a Carinthian folk-song and Bach's *Choral* "Es ist genug" (from the Church Cantata, *O Ewigkeit, du Donnerwort*) which are woven into the score.[1]

Berg in fact uses the twelve-tone system only as far as it suits him. Thus practically the whole of the thematic material of *Lulu* is derived from a single *Tonreihe*, but the twelve-tone "law" of note-recurrence is much more loosely applied than in Schönberg and Hauer. Similarly Berg adopted Schönberg's harmony, his chamber-music-like orchestral technique, his system of indicating principal and secondary orchestral parts, his *Sprechstimme* (in parts of *Wozzeck*), his strict architectural forms, his mirror-canons and canons *cancrizans*, but he never made a fetish of any one of them. Technically, his relation to Schönberg is not unlike that of Bach to a school-contrapuntist such as Fux.

Much has been said, for instance, about the strictly musical (i.e., instrumental) forms Berg has imposed on the dramatic action of *Wozzeck*. (On that of *Lulu*, too, to some extent, but in this

[1] The *Tonreihe* on which the Concerto is built—G, B flat, D, F sharp, A, C, E, G sharp, B, C sharp, E flat, F, E natural—contains diatonic "cells," as it were.

opera there is a tendency to "vocal" forms: arias, duets, and so on.)
Actually these "strict forms" have more in common with those
that Alfred Lorenz has detected in Wagner than with those in the
second part of *Pierrot Lunaire*. Each scene is not only a dramatic entity but a musical entity, though naturally the whole
texture is organic and continuous as with Wagner's "periods."

The three five-scene acts consist musically of five character
sketches, a five-movement symphony, and five "inventions"
respectively. In the first act, showing the wretched Wozzeck's
relation to his environment, each scene is grouped about one
protagonist in relation to the hero; thus in Scene 1 we see the
Captain being shaved by Wozzeck (Suite consisting of prelude,
pavane, gigue, gavotte, and reprise of prelude) while in Scene 4
the pedantic Doctor's examination of him takes the form of a
passacaglia. The five scenes of Act II, in which Wozzeck
gradually discovers his mistress's unfaithfulness, are cast in the
forms of a more or less orthodox symphonic first movement, a
fantasia and fugue, a *largo*, a scherzo (with *Ländler* and waltz
elements), and a rondo (preceded by a slow introduction). Each
scene of the third act (Wozzeck's murder of his mistress, and
suicide) is musically based on one special feature: a theme, a
note, a rhythm. Thus the scene of Marie's remorse takes the
form of a theme with seven variations and a final fugue; the
music of the murder scene is entirely centred on the note B as
a pedal-point; the scene in the low dance-hall where Wozzeck
seeks escape from his thoughts is dominated by a polka rhythm.
Similarly in *Lulu* the whole scene of Schwarz's suicide is based
on the 5-4 rhythm

But despite this structural rigidity, it is fairly evident—and
the Violin Concerto is conclusive proof—that Berg was always
essentially a romantic. Indeed, romanticism seems to be now
deeply rooted in the German nature. It is apparent even in the
later works of Hindemith: beginning with the symphony *Mathis
der Maler* (1934) and the opera on the same subject, and the
viola concerto on fifteenth-century folk-song themes, *Der
Schwanendreher* (1935). Yet of all German composers it was
Hindemith who appeared for a time most wholeheartedly to
have embraced neo-classicism in the Stravinskian sense.

We can see already that Hindemith's neo-classicism was only a passing phase. His early works—for instance, the two Quartets, Op. 10 (1919) and Op. 16 (1920), and the opera *Mörder, Hoffnung der Frauen* (1920)—are full of romantic, Wagnerian echoes, echoes too of Brahms, Richard Strauss and Max Reger (who in some ways anticipated Schönberg and Berg in pouring fundamentally romantic sentiment into the old strict forms). At the same time, in all these works one notices the composer's trend towards harmonic simplicity and clear-cut rhythmic patterns and by 1922 Hindemith emerged as a sort of German Milhaud, all spiky "linear counterpoint" and percussion effects. (The fashionable cant of the day called this sort of thing "back to Bach," though the only point of contact with Bach was through the latter's least inspired concertos with their incessant, more or less mechanical rhythmic bustle.) But whereas Milhaud was a polytonalist, Hindemith leaned to atonality.

This neo-classical Hindemith emerged fully in 1922 in the somewhat Schönbergian Third String Quartet, Op. 22, and the *Kammermusik No. 1* (two pieces: a *concerto grosso* for chamber orchestra and a wind quintet). The song-cycle *Das Marienleben*, Op. 27 (1924), suggests the second section of *Pierrot Lunaire* in its employment of the strict forms of passacaglia, *basso ostinato*, and so on. During the next seven or eight years Hindemith produced an enormous quantity of music in this style, the most important works being the opera *Cardillac* (1926) and a series of *concerti grossi* for various combinations, usually styled either *Kammermusik* or *Konzertmusik*. The oratorio *Das Unaufhörliche* (1931) showed unobtrusive traces of a return to a less dry and cerebral manner, and even earlier the variations on "Prinz Eugen" in the *Konzertmusik* for wind, Op. 41 (1927), had revealed Hindemith's interest in German folk-song. In *Mathis, Der Schwanendreher* and all the later works both these tendencies are much more marked. In Hindemith then, as in Bartók, Berg, Walton and other representative musicians, a distinct swing back from the arid neo-classicism of the nineteen-twenties is perceptible in the mid-nineteen-thirties; a swing back not, of course, to full-blooded romanticism but to a saner balance between the tendencies we call classical and romantic.

Two other features are noticeable in Hindemith's music: the influence of the modern dance formulas, particularly jazz, and

A HUNDRED YEARS OF MUSIC

the cultivation of a genre that flourished exceedingly in post-1918 Germany: *Gebrauchsmusik* (utility music). Admittedly Hindemith's intellectualized, almost non-sensuous jazz (for instance, the finale of the concerto, *Kammermusik, No. 1*) is much less attractive than such "jazz operas" of the period as Křenek's *Jonny spielt auf*[1] (1927), and Weill's *Mahagonny* (1927) and *Dreigroschenoper* (1930), and far inferior to Constant Lambert's brilliant *The Rio Grande* for chorus and orchestra (1928). Yet his dry, bracing physical vigour is in pleasant contrast with the decadent spirit of the Weill works.

Gebrauchsmusik was partly a phase of the "no-romantic-metaphysical-nonsense" attitude to music, partly a recognition of that gulf between the modern composer and the average listener mentioned in the previous chapter, and an attempt to close it. Even if he can "appreciate" contemporary music, the average amateur cannot play it; it is technically far too difficult. Such works as Hindemith's *Sing- und Spielmusiken für Liebhaber und Musikfreunde*, Op. 45 (1927), and Weill's *Der Jasager* (1930), an opera for schoolchildren to perform, are attempts to supply "domestic and community music" (*Haus- und Gemeinschaftsmusiken*), things that any very moderately gifted amateur singer or player can take part in. Even Hindemith's *Kammermusik* works are also "utilitarian" in another sense: that is to say, each (like Bach's cantatas and Haydn's and Mozart's *divertimenti*) has been written for a special player or players or for a special occasion.

A still more interesting form of *Gebrauchsmusik* is that written for the films. Hindemith was a pioneer in this field, writing music for *Felix the Cat* in 1927, i.e., even in the days before the sound-film. Since then music has been written for films by distinguished composers in every country: Honegger, Prokofiev,

---

[1] Křenek is an ex-pupil of Franz Schreker, whose operas—curious hotch-potches of Strauss, Schönberg and Puccini, of impressionism and decadent romanticism—enjoyed considerable popularity in Germany after the War of 1914–18. But Schreker left little mark on his clever pupil. Křenek is mainly a brilliant exponent of linear polyphony, and *Jonny spielt auf* was only an amusing aberration. Perhaps his best works are the expressionistic song-cycle, *Reisebuch aus den Oesterreichischen Alpen* (1929), and the twelve-tone opera *Karl V* (1936). His book *Studies in Counterpoint* (New York, 1940) is a good practical introduction to twelve-tone composition.

Bliss, Walton, Vaughan Williams and many others. The most successful English practitioner of yet another form of *Gebrauchsmusik*—music for radio plays and features—is Benjamin Britten, who possesses clever, facile technique and a remarkable gift for evoking mood or atmosphere with a very few notes; his music to Edward Sackville-West's *The Rescue* (1943) and Louis MacNeice's *The Dark Tower* (1946) should be models for radio- and film-composers, in the same way that Walton's *Macbeth* music (1942) is a model of modern incidental music for the stage. (In not one of these three cases would it be possible for the composer to put together anything so substantial as a concert suite from his pregnant fragments.) Britten shows the same evocative power in many passages of his more important works: for instance, in the memorable setting of "The splendour falls on castle walls" in the *Serenade* for tenor, horn and string orchestra (1943) and the opening of Act I of his second opera *Peter Grimes* (1945). (The first, *Paul Bunyan* (1941), has been written off as a failure.) His technical facility, like Ravel's, seeks problems to solve: the problems of setting difficult French (*Les Illuminations*, 1939) or Italian (*Seven Sonnets of Michelangelo*, 1940), of writing for treble voices and harp (*A Ceremony of Carols*, 1942), of writing a Prelude and Fugue for 18-part string orchestra (1943)—the string orchestra, with its limitations, seems to be his favourite medium—of composing a whole suite for solo tenor, solo horn and string orchestra (the *Serenade*), of devising chamber opera as in *The Rape of Lucretia* (1946) and *Albert Herring* (1947) or an opera without female parts as is *Billy Budd* (1951). His creativeness is obviously stimulated by such technical problems. When he lacks their stimulus or the stimulus of some particular virtuoso performer, when he has no atmosphere to evoke or dramatic characters to create, when (in short) he has to write an extended piece of pure music, as in his concertos and quartets, he is less successful.

Britten's music, of course, sounds much less "modern" than most of that which was being written in the early nineteen twenties. But so does the music written by nearly everyone else towards the end of the nineteen-forties. Even towards the end of the nineteen-thirties the extreme rigours of "Central Europeanism" were being noticeably relaxed. Emotion and even euphony began to sneak back into fashionable musical society.

Berg's Violin Concerto and Bartók's, Hindemith's three Piano
Sonatas (1936), Stravinsky's *Persephone* sound positively reactionary by comparison with the music these composers had been
writing ten years earlier. As we have seen in an earlier chapter,
one-time English revolutionaries like Bliss and Walton began
to betray affinities with such a conservative as Elgar.

This tendency to conservatism was sharply accelerated by the
jackboot of authority in the totalitarian states. In Nazi Germany
modern tendencies in music and the other arts were regarded
as decadent and anarchistic; in Russia as "formalistic," out of
touch with life, and (above all) bad because incomprehensible
to the proletarian masses—the old Tolstoyan test. In Germany
both Schönberg and Hindemith were banned in favour of dull
late-romantic, conservative nonentities such as Pfitzner. In
Russia the clever, if superficial, operas of Shostakovich—*The Nose*
(1929) and *The Lady Macbeth of Mtsensk* (1934)—were first
praised, then looked upon with disfavour, while Dzerzhinsky's
Quiet Flows the Don (1935), dull, straightforward, and technically barely competent, was held up as a model. To get his work
published and performed, the Soviet composer must, unless he
is a very dull dog indeed, compromise his artistic integrity and
write music acceptable to the authorities—must, in fact, write
Gebrauchsmusik and *Gemeinschaftsmusik* whether he wants to
or not. Such composers as Myaskovsky, Prokofiev and Shostakovich himself have done so. And if the means is wholly bad, the
end—the closing of that fatal gulf between composer and
listener—is not. The rôle of Marcus Curtius is not wholly un-
heroic. But it is terribly unrewarding. The Soviet composer
may faithfully strive after "socialist realism," may dutifully
write heroic "monumental" works when the Soviet Government
feels that patriotic sentiment needs to be stirred or bolstered up
(Prokofiev's *Alexander Nevsky*, a cantata expanded from earlier
film music (1939); Shostakovich's Seventh (*Leningrad*) and
Eighth Symphonies (1942 and 1943)); he may be proclaimed to
the rest of the world as one of the cultural glories of the Soviet
Union. All this avails him nothing when ever a wave of artistic
Puritanism or backwoodsmanship sweeps over the Kremlin.
There is no harm in writing to order, but the orders of the
eighteenth-century aristocrat, even sometimes those of the
twentieth-century film- or radio-producer, were and are often
given by men of taste and liberal culture.

IV. MUSIC SINCE 1945

Composers outside the U.S.S.R., too, are now far more willing to write to order. The old ideal of craftsmanship with a small "c" has returned to supplant the essentially romantic, nineteenth-century ideal of Art with a capital "A." The commissioned work is no longer despised; the page from the composer's musical autobiography no longer seems so vitally important to the rest of the world. Partly because of this new attitude of less self-conscious individualism, partly in simple reaction against the extremism and experimentalism of the period that drew to an end in the middle of the nineteen-thirties, many composers after the Second World War became relatively conservative; they even once more acquired something very like a common language. It was an eclectic language, embodying many of the results of earlier experiment, a language that does not violently repel or puzzle the average intelligent concertgoer even if it does not violently attract him: melodically rather angular, predominantly linear in texture, continually crossing the frontier between tonality and atonality, unsentimental but not without restrained or ironically masked emotion and sometimes opening up real depths.

This is the language generally employed, with innumerable personal variations of harmonic acerbity, melodiousness and tonal reference, by Bliss and Walton, Britten and Tippett, Rawsthorne and Berkeley in Britain and by composers all over the world from William Schuman, Roy Harris, Barber and Copland in the United States to Prokofiev and Shostakovich in the Soviet Union. But it is a conservative language; progressive and would-be progressive composers have sought either to establish a new common language or to create new kinds of music.

One of the latter, *musique concrète*, which attracted considerable notice in the early nineteen-fifties, was the invention of a Frenchman—Pierre Schaeffer—and aroused the attention of his compatriots Messiaen (b. 1908) and Boulez (b. 1926); it consists essentially of the organization of recorded natural or musical sounds, often in ingeniously distorted forms. At about the same period German radio-engineers began to experiment with a more promising idea: electrophonic music. The idea of producing musical tone purely by electromagnetic vibrations had been explored between the wars by such inventors as the Russian Lev Theremin, the German Friedrich Trautwein, and the Frenchman Maurice Martenot, who produced instruments named after themselves—*theremin, trautonium, ondes Martenot*—as well as by manufacturers who used similar means to imitate existing instruments such as the organ. Of these only the *ondes Martenot* attracted much attention from serious composers, chiefly as a new voice in the orchestra, as in Messiaen's *Turangalîla-Symphony* (1948), or with piano as Milhaud had used it as early as 1932. It is true that *ondes Martenot* had been employed alone —for instance, by Messiaen in his *Fête des belles eaux* for six such instruments (1937) and his incidental music to *Œdipus Rex* (1942) and by Honegger in his *Sortilèges* (1946)—but even here they had been treated in the manner of normal instruments, whereas the electronic music of the nineteen-fifties begins *de novo*, treating electronically produced sound as a basis for *montage* in the manner of *musique concrète* and often employing 'spatial' effects of sound coming from various directions. This last device has been specially exploited by Karlheinz Stockhausen (b. 1928) whose *Studie I* has been claimed to be the earliest electronic composition with sinus-tones.

Much more important than these experiments was the belated flowering of the twelve-tone method after the war not only in the hands of young German composers such as Stockhausen, Hans Werner Henze (b. 1926), and Giselher Klebe (b. 1925) who had been cut off from such 'decadent' forms of music under the Nazi *régime* but, more surprisingly, in the Latin countries (largely owing to the advocacy of René Leibowitz and his brilliant pupil Pierre Boulez) and, most surprisingly of all, in the music of the septuagenarian Stravinsky (*Canticum sacrum* (1955), *Agon* (1957) and *Movements* (1959)). The idol of this generation of twelve-tone composers was not, however, Schönberg himself but Webern who captivated them largely by the fragmented, pointillistic textures that had resulted from his strivings after intense compression. Such scores as Boulez's *Le marteau sans maître* (1954) and Luigi Nono's *Il canto sospeso* (1956) are outstanding works of this post-Webern school. Both Boulez and Nono also exemplify another post-1945 tendency: the exploitation of melodic percussion instruments (notably including the marimbaphone and vibraphone) which can perhaps be traced from the

Turangalîla-Symphony of Messiaen, with whom Boulez studied for a time.

The concept of composing with twelve-note series has interested many other composers than the true and avowed exponents of the method. As early as 1938 Bartók had introduced twelve-tone passages in the first movement of his Violin Concerto and thus pointed the way to a compromise with tonal music quite different from Berg's in *his* Violin Concerto, but no important composer attempted to follow this lead until the twelve-note revival after 1945. Since then such compromises, of every kind and degree, have become highly popular. One finds the basically serial composer modifying his principles as Dallapiccola does in his opera *Il Prigionero* (comp. 1944–48) and his oratorio *Job* (1950), and Henze in his *König Hirsch* (1956), *Prinz von Homburg* (1960) and other operas, and on the other hand the essentially diatonic musician making serial gestures like Britten's in *The Turn of the Screw* (1954), *A Midsummer Night's Dream* (1960) and *Cantata Academica* (1960); the results are of course totally different. Roger Sessions's Piano Concerto (1956) and Aaron Copland's Piano Fantasy (1957), to take only two examples, are much more advanced essays in serialism by essentially tonal composers.

The principle of serialization has even been applied to the other elements of music. 'Rhythmic rows' seem to have originated with Messiaen and 'serial' metres based on mathematical proportions or progressions with Boris Blacher. Nono's *Canto sospeso* has serialized note-values, and in Křenek's *Quaestio Temporis* for chamber orchestra (1960) everything is serially predetermined: pitch of each note, duration of pitch, structural sections, and so on. In the opposite direction from 'predetermined' serial music, we now have music that admits not only the element of improvisation—long lost to serious music, and preserved in jazz more vitally than in the meanderings of the organ-loft—but the element of sheer chance: the so-called "aleatory" technique. Thus Stockhausen, notably in his *Klavierstück XI* (1956) and his *Zyklus* for percussion (1959), leaves the performer to decide in which order component sections are to be played, while Boulez in *Pli selon pli* (*Portrait de Mallarmé*) (begun in 1957 with two "Improvisations" on Mallarmé sonnets, and still a "work in progress") gives us controlled improvisation, "a planned succession of predefined chance procedures". In some of the works of the Pole Witold Lutoslawski, the Belgian Henri Pousseur and the American Earle Brown the succession is less planned and the chance procedures are less closely predefined.

These wide-ranging experiments with new physical media and new ways of handling both old and new methods of sound-production may open up ways to a new music or they may be mere exploration of blind-alleys. At present one can only comment that composers, like the human race generally, have acquired technical powers out of all proportion to their ability to apply them to any spiritual end (using the word "spiritual" in its widest sense). It may be a good thing that musicians should play with the basic elements of sound, naïvely or intellectually, should build a new music either on the ruins of the old or begin again *de novo*. Peri's *Euridice* must have seemed very childish, as music, to people accustomed to the great polyphony of the sixteenth century; it sounds childish to us; but it was a symptom of great things that were to come. One cannot exclude the possibility that the seemingly most absurd "aleatory" experiment may be a precursor of future masterpieces.

CHRONOLOGY

(Dates of first performance unless otherwise stated)

1827 Beethoven died.

1828 *Masaniello*. Marschner's *Vampyr*. Schubert died.

1829 *William Tell*. Marschner's *Templer und Jüdin*. Schumann's *Papillons* begun.

1830 Berlioz's *Symphonie fantastique*. *Fra Diavolo*. Mendelssohn's *Fingal's Cave* comp.

1831 *La Sonnambula*. *Norma*. *Zampa*. *Robert le Diable*.

1832 Spohr's *Weihe der Töne*. *L'elisir d'amore*. Chopin's first Mazurkas pub.

1833 *Lucrezia Borgia*. *Hans Heiling*. Mendelssohn's *Italian* Symphony. Chopin's first Nocturnes and Studies pub.

1834 *Harold in Italy*. Chopin's first Valse pub. Boieldieu died.

1835 *Lucia di Lammermoor*. *La Juive*. Schumann's *Carnaval* fin. Chopin's first Scherzo pub. Bellini died.

1836 *Les Huguenots*. *A Life for the Tsar*. *Das Liebesverbot*. Chopin's Second Concerto, first Ballade and first Polonaises pub. Liszt's *Années de pèlerinage (première année)* pub. *St. Paul* comp.

1837 Berlioz's *Requiem*. Lortzing's *Zar und Zimmermann*. Field died.

1838 *Benvenuto Cellini*. Schumann's *Kreisleriana* and *Novelletten* comp.

1839 Berlioz's *Roméo et Juliette*. Schubert's C major Symphony. Chopin's *24 Preludes* pub.

1840 Bulk of Schumann's songs comp. Wagner's *Faust* Overture comp. Chopin's B flat minor Sonata pub. Mendelssohn's *Hymn of Praise* comp.

1841 Schumann's First and Fourth Symphonies. Chopin's F minor Fantaisie pub.

1842 *Rienzi*. *Ruslan and Lyudmila*. Mendelssohn's *Scottish* Symphony. Schumann's Piano Quintet and Quartet comp. Cherubini died.

1843 *The Flying Dutchman*. *Paradise and the Peri*. *Don Pasquale*. *The Bohemian Girl*. Franz's first songs pub.

1844 *Ernani*. David's *Le Désert*.

1845 *Tannhäuser*. Chopin's *Berceuse* and B minor Sonata pub.

1846 *La Damnation de Faust*. Schumann's Piano Concerto and Second Symphony. *Elijah* comp.

1847 *Martha*. Verdi's *Macbeth*. Mendelssohn died.

1848 Glinka's *Kamarinskaya*. Donizetti died.

299

1849 *Le Prophète.* Nicolai's *Merry Wives of Windsor.* Schumann's *Faust.* Liszt's *Tasso.* Berlioz's *Te Deum* fin. Chopin died.

1850 *Lohengrin.* Schumann's *Genoveva.* Liszt's *Prometheus.*

1851 *Rigoletto.* Schumann's *Rhenish* Symphony. Liszt's first two Hungarian Rhapsodies pub. Spontini and Lortzing died.

1852 Schumann's *Manfred* Overture. Brahms's C major Piano Sonata.

1853 *La Traviata. Il Trovatore.* Liszt's *Hungarian Fantasia. Das Rheingold* begun.

1854 *L'Enfance du Christ.* Liszt's Piano Sonata pub., and *Les Préludes* and *Orpheus* perf.

1855 *I Vespri Siciliani.* Liszt's E flat Concerto.

1856 *Die Walküre* completed. *Siegfried* begun. Schumann died.

1857 Liszt's *Faust* and *Dante* Symphonies, *Die Ideale* and *Hunnenschlacht. Simone Boccanegra.* Glinka died.

1858 Liszt's *Hamlet. Der Barbier von Bagdad.*

1859 *Tristan* completed. Gounod's *Faust. Un ballo in maschera.* Brahms's D minor Piano Concerto. Spohr died.

1860 Vincent Wallace's *Lurline.*

1861 Liszt's first *Mephisto Waltz.* Balakirev's *King Lear* music. Marschner died.

1862 *La forza del destino. Béatrice et Bénédict.* Halévy died.

1863 *Les Troyens.* Bizet's *Pêcheurs de perles.*

1864 Brahms's F minor Piano Quintet. Balakirev's *Russia. La belle Hélène.* Meyerbeer died.

1865 *Tristan* perf. Schubert's *Unfinished* Symphony. Liszt's *Totentanz* and *St. Elisabeth. L'Africaine.*

1866 *The Bartered Bride. Mignon.*

1867 Gounod's *Roméo et Juliette.* Verdi's *Don Carlo.* Tchaïkovsky's First Symphony. Borodin's First Symphony finished.

1868 *Die Meistersinger. Ein Deutsches Requiem.* Boito's *Mefistofele.* Grieg's Piano Concerto comp. Rossini died.

1869 First version of *Boris Godunov* comp. *Prince Igor* begun. Brahms's first set of Hungarian Dances. Berlioz and Dargomïzhsky died.

1870 Tchaïkovsky's *Romeo and Juliet.* Franck's *Béatitudes* comp. Balfe died.

1871 *Aïda. Siegfried* finished. Auber died.

1872 *The Stone Guest.*

1873 Brahms's *Haydn Variations.* Tchaïkovsky's *Tempest* and Second Symphony. *The Maid of Pskov.*

1874 *Götterdämmerung* fin. *Boris Godunov* perf. Goetz's *Taming of the Shrew. Die Fledermaus.*

1875 *Carmen.* Dvořák's "Third" Symphony. Saint-Saëns's *Danse macabre.* Tchaïkovsky's Third Symphony and B flat minor Concerto.

1876 *The Ring* at Bayreuth. Grieg's *Peer Gynt* music. Brahms's First Symphony.

1877 Verdi's *Otello*. Brahms's Second Symphony. Borodin's Second Symphony. Tchaïkovsky's Fourth Symphony.
1878 Brahms's Violin Concerto. Dvořák's first set of Slavonic Dances.
1879 *Eugene Onegin*. Fauré's C minor Piano Quartet.
1880 Brahms's Academic Festival Overture. Dvořák's "First" Symphony. Franck's Piano Quintet.
1881 Brahms's B flat Piano Concerto. Tchaïkovsky's Violin Concerto. *Tales of Hoffmann*. Mussorgsky died.
1882 *Parsifal*. *Snowmaiden*. Raff died.
1883 Brahms's Third Symphony. Franck's *Chasseur Maudit*. Last book of Liszt's *Années de pèlerinage* pub. Wagner died.
1884 Massenet's *Manon*. Mahler's *Lieder eines fahrenden Gesellen* comp. Smetana died.
1885 Brahms's Fourth Symphony. Dvořák's "Second" Symphony. Franck's *Variations symphoniques*.
1886 Bruckner's Seventh Symphony. Saint-Saëns's Symphony in C minor. *Gwendoline*. *Khovanshchina*. Franck's Violin Sonata comp. Liszt died.
1887 Strauss's *Aus Italien*. *Le Roi malgré lui*. Borodin died.
1888 *Le Roi d'Ys*. Rimsky-Korsakov's *Scheherazade*. Strauss's *Don Juan*. Tchaïkovsky's Fifth Symphony. Wolf's first songs pub. and *Mörike-Lieder* comp.
1889 Dvořák's Fourth Symphony. Franck's Symphony and String Quartet. Mahler's First Symphony.
1890 *Prince Igor*. *Cavalleria rusticana*. Tchaïkovsky's *Queen of Spades* and *Sleeping Beauty*. *Tod und Verklärung*. Wolf's *Spanisches Liederbuch* fin. Franck died.
1891 Brahms's Clarinet Quintet. Wolf's *Italienisches Liederbuch*.
1892 *I Pagliacci*. Sibelius's *En Saga* comp. Lalo and Robert Franz died.
1893 *Falstaff*. *Hänsel und Gretel*. Tchaïkovsky's *Pathétique* Symphony. Dvořák's *New World* Symphony. Debussy's String Quartet. Tchaïkovsky and Gounod died.
1894 *Prélude à l'Après-midi d'un faune*. Strauss's *Guntram*. Chabrier and Rubinstein died.
1895 *Till Eulenspiegel* and *Also sprach Zarathustra*. Mahler's Second Symphony.
1896 *La Bohème*. *Der Corregidor*. Dukas's Symphony. Bruckner died.
1897 *Fervaal*. Strauss's *Don Quixote*. Skryabin's Piano Concerto. *L'Apprenti sorcier*. Brahms died.
1898 *Ein Heldenleben*. *Sadko*. *Hiawatha's Wedding Feast*.
1899 *Enigma Variations*. *Verklärte Nacht* and Sibelius's First Symphony comp. Chausson and Johann Strauss died.
1900 *Louise*. *Tosca*. *The Dream of Gerontius*. Debussy's *Nocturnes*. Rakhmaninov's C minor Piano Concerto. *Gurrelieder* begun. Sullivan died.
1901 *Feuersnot*. Skryabin's First Symphony. Sibelius's Second Symphony comp. Verdi died.

1902 *Pelléas et Mélisande.* Mahler's Third and Fourth Symphonies.
1903 Skryabin's Second Symphony. *The Apostles.* Ravel's Quartet and Sibelius's Violin Concerto comp. Wolf died.
1904 *Madam Butterfly. Symphonia domestica.* Mahler's Fifth Symphony. Delius's *Appalachia.* Dvořák died.
1905 *Salome. Le Poème divin.* Schönberg's *Pelleas und Melisande. La Mer.* Ravel's *Miroirs* comp.
1906 *The Kingdom.* Mahler's Sixth Symphony. *Sea-Drift.* Schönberg's *Kammersinfonie* comp.
1907 *Kitezh. .The Golden Cockerel* comp. *Brigg Fair. Ariane et Barbe-Bleue.* Sibelius's Third Symphony comp. Grieg died.
1908 *Poème de l'extase.* Mahler's Seventh Symphony. Debussy's *Ibéria.* Stravinsky's Symphony in E flat. Elgar's First Symphony. Rimsky-Korsakov died.
1909 *Elektra. A Mass of Life.* Schönberg's *Fünf Orchesterstücke.* Albeniz died.
1910 *The Fire-Bird.* Elgar's Violin Concerto. Mahler's Eighth Symphony. Debussy's *Préludes* begun. Balakirev died.
1911 *Der Rosenkavalier. Petrushka.* Skryabin's *Prometheus. Das Lied von der Erde. L'Heure espagnole.* Bartók's *Bluebeard's Castle.* Elgar's Second Symphony. Sibelius's Fourth Symphony comp.
1912 *Ariadne auf Naxos. Pierrot Lunaire. Daphnis et Chloé.* Mahler's Ninth Symphony. Massenet and Coleridge-Taylor died.
1913 *The Rite of Spring. Gurrelieder.* Elgar's *Falstaff.*
1914 *Josephslegende.* Stravinsky's *Nightingale. The Immortal Hour.* Vaughan Williams's *London* Symphony.
1915 *El amor brujo.* Strauss's *Alpensymphonie.* Debussy's 'Cello Sonata, Ravel's Trio and Sibelius's Fifth Symphony comp. Skryabin died.
1916 Falla's *Noches en los jardines de España* comp. Reger and Granados died.
1917 *Les Noces. Le Tombeau de Couperin* and Bartók's Second Quartet comp. Prokofiev's *Classical Symphony* and Third Piano Concerto.
1918 *The Planets. Gianni Schicchi.* Stravinsky's *Tale of the Soldier.* Boito, Cui, Debussy, Leoncavallo and Parry died.
1919 Delius's Violin Concerto. Elgar's 'Cello Concerto. *Hymn of Jesus. El Sombrero de tres picos.*
1920 *Pulcinella. Song of the High, Hills. Wozzeck* comp.
1921 *Love of the Three Oranges* prod. Honegger's *Le Roi David* (original form). Ravel's Sonata for violin and 'cello. Humperdinck died.
1922 Stravinsky's *Renard* and *Mavra.* Bliss's *Colour Symphony.* Saint-Saëns died.
1923 *Façade.* Bartók's Second Violin Sonata and Sibelius's Sixth Symphony comp.
1924 Strauss's *Intermezzo. Pacific 231.* Sibelius's Seventh Symphony comp. Busoni, Fauré, Puccini and Stanford died.

1925 *L'Enfant et les sortilèges*. Holst's Choral Symphony. Hindemith's Piano Concerto, Op. 36. Bartók's Fourth Quintet. Satie died.

1926 *Portsmouth Point*. *Cardillac*. Janáček's *Glagolitika Mass*.

1927 *Doktor Faust*. *Schwanda the Bagpiper*. *Œdipus Rex* and *Apollo Musagetes*. Shostakovich's First Symphony. Walton's *Sinfonia Concertante*. Berg's *Lyrische Suite*.

1928 *Die ägyptische Helena*. *Neues vom Tage*. *The Rio Grande*. Schönberg's *Variationen für Orchester* comp.

1929 Walton's Viola Concerto. Ravel's *Bolero*. *Sir John in Love*.

1930 Milhaud's *Christophe Colomb*. *Symphonie des Psaumes*. *Morning Heroes*. *Dreigroschenoper*. Copland's Piano Variations. Warlock died.

1931 *Belshazzar's Feast*. Vaughan Williams's *Job*. Stravinsky's Violin Concerto. Ravel's Piano Concerto. Barber's *Dover Beach*.

1932 Prokofiev's Fifth Piano Concerto. Ravel's Concerto for Left Hand Only.

1933 *Arabella*. Bliss's Clarinet Quintet and Viola Sonata. Vaughan Williams's Piano Concerto.

1934 *Mathis der Maler*. *Persephone*. *The Lady Macbeth of Mtsensk*. *Lulu* comp. Elgar, Holst, Delius and Bruneau died.

1935 *Die schweigsame Frau*. *Der Schwanendreher*. Walton's First Symphony. Vaughan Williams's F minor Symphony. Bax's Sixth Symphony. Berg and Dukas died.

1936 *Summer's Last Will and Testament*. *Peter and the Wolf*. Berg's Violin Concerto. Bartók's Fifth Quartet. Glazunov, Respighi and Van Dieren died.

1937 Schönberg's Fourth Quartet. Stravinsky's *Jeu de cartes*. *Checkmate*. Orff's *Carmina burana*. Ravel, Szymanowski and Roussel died.

1938 Strauss's *Friedenstag* and *Daphne*. Bartók's Violin Concerto comp. Britten's Piano Concerto (first version). Rawsthorne's *Symphonic Studies*. Prokofiev's *Alexander Nevsky*.

1939 Bartók's *Divertimento* and Sixth String Quartet comp. Bliss's Piano Concerto. *Les Illuminations* comp. Walton's Violin Concerto comp.

1940 Britten's *Sinfonia da Requiem*. Stravinsky's Symphony in C. Rubbra's Third Symphony.

1941 Strauss's *Capriccio* comp. Bliss's String Quartet. Britten's First Quartet. *A Child of our Time*.

1942 Stravinsky's *Danses concertantes* comp. Shostakovich's Seventh (*Leningrad*) Symphony. Hindemith's *Ludus Tonalis*. Schönberg's Piano Concerto.

1943 Bartók's Concerto for Orchestra comp. Britten's *Serenade* comp. Vaughan Williams's Fifth Symphony. Shostakovich's Eighth Symphony.

1944 Stravinsky's *Scènes de ballet* comp. *Miracle in the Gorbals*. Copland's *Appalachian Spring*. Prokofiev's Fifth Symphony and *War and Peace*.

1945 Strauss's *Metamorphosen* comp. Bartók's Third Piano Concerto comp. Stravinsky's Symphony in Three Movements. Bartók and Webern died. *Peter Grimes*. Britten's Second Quartet comp. Tippett's First Symphony.

1946 Strauss's Oboe Concerto. *The Rape of Lucretia*.

1947 Walton's String Quartet No. 2, in A minor. *Albert Herring*. Falla died. Henze's Violin Concerto. Seiber's *Ulysses*. *Dantons Tod*.

1948 Vaughan Williams's Sixth Symphony. Stravinsky's Mass. Messiaen's *Turangalîla-Symphonie*.

1949 Rubbra's Fifth Symphony. Richard Strauss died. Britten's *Spring Symphony* comp. Bliss's *The Olympians*. Fricker's First Symphony.

1950 Dallapiccola's *Il prigionero* prod. Fricker's Violin Sonata. Menotti's *The Consul*.

1951 *Billy Budd*. *The Rake's Progress*. Vaughan Williams's *The Pilgrim's Progress*. Elliott Carter's String Quartet. Fricker's Second Symphony. Searle's *The Riverrun*. Hindemith's *Harmonie der Welt* Symphony. Schönberg died.

1952 Henze's *Boulevard Solitude*. Fricker's Viola Concerto.

1953 *Gloriana*. Stockhausen's *Kontra-Punkte* and *Klavierstücke I–IV*. Prokofiev and Bax died.

1954 *The Turn of the Screw*. Copland's *The Tender Land*. Walton's *Troilus and Cressida*. *Le Marteau sans maître*.

1955 Tippett's *The Midsummer Marriage* prod. Shostakovich's Tenth Symphony. Stravinsky's *Canticum sacrum*. Honegger died.

1956 Vaughan Williams's Eighth Symphony. Shostakovich's Violin Concerto. Henze's *König Hirsch*. Walton's Cello Concerto. Nono's *Il canto sospeso*.

1957 *Agon*. Hindemith's opera, *Harmonie der Welt*. Poulenc's *Dialogues des Carmélites*. Copland's Piano Fantasy. Boulez's *Pli selon pli* begun. Stockhausen's *Gruppen für drei Orchester*. Sibelius died.

1958 Stravinsky's *Threni*. Shostakovich's Eleventh Symphony. Vaughan Williams's Ninth Symphony. Boulez's *Le Soleil des eaux*. Fricker's *Vision of Judgment*. Vaughan Williams died.

1959 Stravinsky's *Movements*. Shostakovich's 'Cello Concerto. Stockhausen's *Zyklus für einen Schlagzeuger*. Blomdahl's *Aniara*. *Moses und Aron* prod.

1960 Britten's *Midsummer Night's Dream*. Fricker's Third Symphony. Křenek's *Quaestio Temporis*. Messiaen's *Chronochromie*. Nono's *Intolleranza 1960*. Henze's *Der Prinz von Homburg*.

1961 Elliott Carter's *Double Concerto*. Lutoslawski's *Jeux vénitiens*. Henze's *Elegy for Young Lovers*.

1962 *King Priam*. Britten's *War Requiem*.

1963 Poulenc died.

BIBLIOGRAPHY

OWING to the vast literature of the subject, it is impossible to give more than a selected bibliography. Preference has been given to books on the music rather than on the composers and purely biographical studies have been omitted altogether. The date given is that of the first edition, unless otherwise stated. Much valuable information will be found in such periodicals as *Music and Letters*, *The Music Review*, the New York *Musical Quarterly*, *La Revue musicale*, *Zeitschrift für Musikwissenschaft*, the *Jahrbuch der Bibliothek Peters*, etc.

A—BOOKS ON INDIVIDUAL COMPOSERS

ALBENIZ   Collet, Henri: *Albéniz et Granados*, 1926.

AUBER   Malherbe, Charles: *Auber*, N.D.

BALAKIREV   Grodzky, B.: *M. I. Balakirev*, 1910.

BARTÓK   Stevens, Halsey: *The Life and Music of Béla Bartók*, 1953.

   Seiber, Matyas: *The String Quartets of Béla Bartók*, 1945.

BAX   Hull, Robert: *Handbook on Arnold Bax's Symphonies*, 1932.

BERG   Redlich, H. F.: *Alban Berg*, 1957.

BERLIOZ   Barzun, Jacques: *Berlioz and the Romantic Century*, 1950.

   Berlioz, Hector: *Mémoires*, 1870 (*Eng. ed.* 1884).

   Coquard, Arthur: *Berlioz*, 1909.

   Elliot, J. H. *Berlioz*, 1938.

   Hippeau, Edmond: *Berlioz et son temps*, 1890.

   Wotton, Tom S.: *Four Works of Berlioz* ("*Musical Pilgrim*"), 1929. *Hector Berlioz*, 1935.

BIZET   Cooper, Martin: *Bizet*, 1938.

   Dean, Winton: *Bizet*, 1948.

   Gauthier-Villars, Henry: *Bizet*, N.D.

   Landormy, Paul: *Bizet*, 1929.

   Parker, D. C.: *Georges Bizet*, 1926.

BLOCH   Chiesa, M. T.: *Ernest Bloch*, 1932.

BORODIN   Dianin, S.: *Borodin* (*Eng. ed.* 1963).

   Khubov, G.: *Borodin*, 1933.

BRAHMS   Browne, P. A.: *Brahms: The Symphonies* ("*Musical Pilgrim*"), 1933.

   Colles, H. C.: *Brahms* (2nd ed. 1920). *The Chamber Music of Brahms* ("*Musical Pilgrim*"), 1933.

BRAHMS
Evans, Edwin (Sen.): *Handbook to the Chamber and Orchestral Works of Brahms*, 1933–35. *Handbook to the Pianoforte Works of Brahms*, 1936. *Handbook to the Vocal Works of Brahms*, 1912.

Friedländer, Max: *Brahms's Lieder* (*Eng. ed.* 1928).

Geiringer, Karl: *Johannes Brahms*, 1935 (*Eng. ed.* 1936).

Kalbeck, Max: *Johannes Brahms*, 1904–15.

Latham, Peter: *Brahms*, 1948.

Mason, D. G.: *The Chamber Music of Brahms*, 1933.

Murdoch, William: *Brahms*, 1933.

Niemann, Walter: *Brahms*, 1920 (*Eng. ed.* 1929).

BRITTEN
Mitchell, D., and Keller, Hans, *ed.*: *Benjamin Britten: a Commentary*, 1953.

White, E. W.: *Benjamin Britten*, 1948.

BRUCKNER
Decsey, Ernst: *Bruckner*, 1930.

Halm, A.: *Die Symphonien Anton Bruckners*, 1914.

Kurth, Ernst: *Anton Bruckner*, 1925.

Newlin, Dika: *Bruckner, Mahler, Schoenberg*, 1947.

Wickenhauser, Richard: *Anton Bruckners Symphonien*, N.D.

BRUNEAU
Hervey, Arthur: *Alfred Bruneau*, 1907.

BUSONI
Dent, E. J.: *Ferruccio Busoni*, 1933.

Nadel, Siegfried: *Ferruccio Busoni*, 1931.

CHABRIER
Martineau, René: *Emmanuel Chabrier*, 1911.

CHARPENTIER
Delmas, Marc: *Gustave Charpentier et le lyrisme français*, 1931.

CHOPIN
Abraham, Gerald: *Chopin's Musical Style*, 1939.

Hedley, Arthur: *Chopin*, 1947.

Huneker, James: *Chopin: the Man and his Music*, 1901.

Leichtentritt, Hugo: *Analyse der Chopin'sche Klavierwerke*, 1921.

Niecks, Frederick: *Frederick Chopin as Man and Musician*, 1888.

DARGOMÏZHSKY
Findeisen, N.: *A. S. Dargomïzhsky*, 1904.

DAVID
Brancour, René: *Félicien David*, N.D.

DEBUSSY
Boucher, Maurice: *Claude Debussy*, 1930.

Fábián, Ladislas: *Claude Debussy und sein Werk*, 1923.

Koechlin, Charles: *Debussy*, 1927.

Liebich, Mrs. Franz: *Claude-Achille Debussy*, 1908.

Liess, Andreas: *Claude Debussy: Das Werk im Zeitbild*, 1936.

Lockspeiser, Edward: *Debussy*, 1936.

Shera, F. H.: *Debussy and Ravel* ("*Musical Pilgrim*"), 1927.

Vallas, Léon: *Claude Debussy*, 1932 (*Eng. ed.* 1933).

DELIBES   de Curzon, Henri: *Léo Delibes*, 1926.

DELIUS   Fenby, Eric: *Delius as I knew him*, 1936.

Heseltine, Philip: *Frederick Delius*, 1923.

Hutchings, Arthur: *Delius*, 1948.

DUKAS   *Paul Dukas: Special number of* "*La Revue musicale*" (May, 1936).

Samazeuilh, Gustave: *Paul Dukas*, 1913.

DVOŘÁK   Fischl, V. ed.: *Antonin Dvořák: His Achievement*, 1942.

Hoffmeister, Karel: *Antonin Dvořák* (*Eng. ed.* 1928).

Robertson, Alec: *Dvořák*, 1945.

Sourek, O., and Paul Stefan: *Dvořák: Leben und Werk*, N.D.

ELGAR   Dunhill, Thomas: *Sir Edward Elgar*, 1938.

Maine, Basil: *Elgar: His Life and Works*, 1933.

Newman, Ernest: *Elgar* (2nd ed. 1920).

Reed, W. H.: *Elgar as I knew him*, 1936. *Elgar*, 1939.

Shera, F. H.: *Elgar: Instrumental Works* ("*Musical Pilgrim*"), 1931.

FALLA   Roland-Manuel: *Manuel de Falla*, 1930.

Trend, J. B.: *Manuel de Falla and Spanish Music*, 1929.

FAURÉ   Fauré-Fremiet, Philippe: *Gabriel Fauré*, 1929.

Koechlin, Charles: *Gabriel Fauré*, 1927 (*Eng. ed.* 1946).

Suckling, Norman: *Fauré*, 1946.

FRANCK   Demuth, Norman: *César Franck*, 1949.

Grace, Harvey: *The Organ Works of César Franck*, 1948.

Horton, John: *César Franck*, ("*Musical Pilgrim*"), 1948.

d'Indy, Vincent: *César Franck* (*Eng. ed.* 1909).

GLINKA   Calvocoressi, M. D.: *Glinka*, 1911.

Findeisen, N. F.: *Glinka*, 1896.

GOUNOD   Bellaigue, Camille: *Gounod*, 1919.

Hillemacher, P. L.: *Gounod*, 1906.

GRANADOS   (See Albéniz).

GRIEG   Abraham, Gerald, ed.: *Grieg*, 1948.

Fellerer, K. G.: *Edvard Grieg*, 1942.

GRIEG   Fischer, Kurt von: *Griegs Harmonik und die nordländische Folklore*, 1938.

Monrad-Johansen, D.: *Edward Grieg*, 1934 (*Am. ed.* 1938)

Rokseth, Yvonne: *Grieg*, 1933.

Schjelderup and Niemann: *Edward Grieg*, 1908.

Stein, Richard: *Grieg*, 1921.

de Stoecklin, Paul: *Grieg*, 1926.

HÉROLD   Pougin, Arthur: *Hérold*, N.D.

HINDEMITH   Hindemith, Paul: *A Composer's World*, 1952.

Strobel, Heinrich: *Paul Hindemith*, 1931 (*revised and greatly enlarged edition*, 1948).

HONEGGER   George, André: *Arthur Honegger*, 1926.

Tappolet, Willy: *Arthur Honegger*, 1933.

D'INDY   Landormy, Paul: *Vincent d'Indy*, 1932.

JANÁČEK   Hollander, Hans: *Janáček*, 1963.

LALO   Servières, Georges: *Edouard Lalo*, 1925.

LISZT   Bergfeld, Joachim; *Die formale Struktur der symphonischen Dichtungen Franz Liszts*, 1931.

Calvocoressi, M. D.: *Liszt*, N.D.

Chantavoine, Jean: *Liszt* (4th ed. 1920).

Kókai, Rudolf: *Franz Liszt in seinen frühen Klavierwerken*, 1933.

Pohl, Richard: *Franz Liszt: Studien und Erinnerungen*, 1883.

Raabe, Peter: *Liszts Schaffen*, 1931.

Searle, Humphrey: *The Music of Liszt*, 1954.

MAHLER   Bekker, Paul: *Gustav Mahlers Sinfonien*, 1921.

Mitchell, Donald: *Gustav Mahler: The Early Years*, 1958.

Specht, Richard: *Gustav Mahler*, 1920.

Stefan, Paul: *Gustav Mahler*, 1925.

MASSENET   Brancour, René: *Massenet*, 1922.

MENDELSSOHN   Armstrong, Thomas: *Mendelssohn's "Elijah"* (*"Musical Pilgrim"*), 1931.

Dahms, Walter: *Mendelssohn*, 1919.

Horton, John: *Mendelssohn's Chamber Music* (*"Musical Pilgrim"*), 1946.

MEYERBEER   de Curzon, Henri: *Meyerbeer*, N.D.

Dauriac, Lionel: *Meyerbeer*, 1930.

MUSSORGSKY   Belaiev, Victor: *Mussorgsky's "Boris Godunov"* (*Eng. ed.* 1928).

Calvocoressi, M. D.: *Mussorgsky*, 1946.

Fedorov, Vladimir: *Moussorgsky*, 1935.

PARRY   Maitland, J. A. Fuller: *The Music of Parry and Stanford*, 1934.

PIZZETTI   Tebaldini, Giovanni: *Ildebrando Pizzetti*, 1931.

PROKOFIEV   Nestyev, I.: *Prokofiev* (*Eng. ed.*, 1961).

PUCCINI — Carner, Mosco: *Puccini*, 1958.

Puccini, Giacomo: *Letters* (*Eng. ed.* 1931).

Specht, Richard: *Giacomo Puccini*, 1932 (*Eng. ed.* 1933).

RAKHMANINOV — Lyle, Watson: *Rachmaninoff*, 1938.

RAVEL — Demuth, Norman: *Ravel*, 1947.

Jankélévich, Vladimir: *Maurice Ravel*, 1938.

Myers, Rollo: *Ravel: Life and Works*, 1960.

Roland-Manuel: *À la gloire de Ravel*, 1938 (*Eng. ed.* 1947). *Maurice Ravel et son œuvre*, 1914. *Maurice Ravel et son œuvre dramatique*, 1928.

(See also under Debussy.)

REGER — Lindner, Adalbert: *Max Reger*, 1923.

Rahner, H. E.: *Max Regers Choralfantasien für die Orgel*, 1936.

RIMSKY-KORSAKOV — Rimsky-Korsakov, N. A.: *Letopis moey muzïkalnoy zhizni*, 1909 (*Eng. ed.* 1924).

van der Pals, N. van Gilse: *N. A. Rimsky-Korssakow: Opernschaffen*, 1929.

Yastrebtsev, V. V.: *My Recollections of Rimsky-Korsakov*, 1917.

ROGER-DUCASSE — Ceillier, Laurent: *Roger-Ducasse*, 1920.

ROUSSEL — Deane, Basil: *Albert Roussel*, 1961.

Demuth, Norman: *Albert Roussel*, 1947.

SAINT-SAËNS — Hervey, Arthur: *Saint-Saëns*, 1921.

Lyle, Watson: *Camille Saint-Saëns*, 1923.

Neitzel, Otto: *Camille Saint-Saëns*, 1899.

SATIE — Myers, Rollo: *Erik Satie*, 1948.

Templier, P. D.: *Erik Satie*, 1932.

SCHÖNBERG — Rufer, Josef: *The Works of Arnold Schoenberg*, 1962.

Schönberg, Arnold: *Style and Idea*, 1951.

Stefan, Paul: *Arnold Schönberg*, 1924.

Stuckenschmidt, H. H.: *Arnold Schoenberg*, 1959.

Wellesz, Egon: *Arnold Schönberg*, 1921 (*Eng. ed.* N.D.).

Various authors: *Arnold Schönberg und seine Orchesterwerke* (*Pult und Takstock*, March, 1927). *Arnold Schönberg*, 1912. *Arnold Schönberg zum 50sten Geburtstage*, 1924. *Arnold Schönberg zum 60 Geburtstage*, 1934.

SCHUMANN — Abert, H.: *Robert Schumann*, 1903.

Abraham, Gerald, *ed.*: *Schumann: a Symposium*, 1952.

Bötticher, W.: *Robert Schumann: Einführung in Persönlichkeit und Werk*, 1941.

Chissell, Joan: *Schumann*, 1948.

SCHUMANN Gertler Wolfgang: *Robert Schumann in seinen frühen Klavierwerken*, 1931.
Korte, Werner: *Robert Schumann*, 1937.
Maitland, J. A. Fuller: *Schumann's Concerted Chamber Music* ("*Musical Pilgrim*"), 1929. *Schumann's Pianoforte Works* ("*Musical Pilgrim*"), 1927.
Niecks, Frederick: *Robert Schumann*, 1925.
von Wasielewski, W. J.: *Robert Schumann* (4th ed. 1906).

SHOSTAKOVICH Rabinovich, D.: *Dmitry Shostakovich* (*Eng. ed.*, 1959).

SIBELIUS Abraham, Gerald, ed.: *Sibelius*, 1947.
Gray, Cecil: *Sibelius*, 1931. *Sibelius: the Symphonies* ("*Musical Pilgrim*"), 1935.
Krohn, Ilmari: *Der Formenbau in den Symphonien von Jean Sibelius*, 1942.
Niemann, Walter: *Jean Sibelius*, 1917.
Roiha, Eino: *Die Symphonien von Jean Sibelius*, 1941.
de Törne, Bengt: *Sibelius—a Close-up*, 1937.

SKRYABIN Dickenmann, Paul: *Die Entwicklung der Harmonik bei A. Skrjabin*, 1935.
Sabaneev, L. L.: *Skryabin* (2nd ed. 1923).
Swan, A. J.: *Scriabin*, 1923.

SMETANA Nejedlý, Zdeněk: *Frederick Smetana* (*Eng. ed.* 1924).
Ritter, William: *Smetana*, 1907.
Tiersot, Julien: *Smetana*, 1926.

STANFORD (See Parry.)

STOCKHAUSEN Wörner, K. H.: *Karlheinz Stockhausen*, 1963.

STRAUSS, RICHARD Armstrong, Thomas: *Strauss's Tone-poems* ("*Musical Pilgrim*"), 1931.
Blom, Eric: *Strauss's "Rose Cavalier"* ("*Musical Pilgrim*"), 1930.
Del Mar, Norman: *Richard Strauss: a Critical Commentary*, I, 1962
Muschler, R. C.: *Richard Strauss*, N.D.
Newman, Ernest: *Richard Strauss*, 1908.
Röttger, Heinz: *Das Formproblem bei Richard Strauss*, 1937.
Schuh, Willi: *Über Opern von Richard Strauss*, 1947.
Specht, Richard: *Richard Strauss und sein Werk*, 1921.
Strauss, Richard: *Correspondence with Hugo von Hofmannsthal* (*complete Eng. ed.* 1961).

STRAVINSKY Belaiev, Victor: *Igor Stravinsky's "Les Noces"* (*Eng. ed.* 1928).

Evans, Edwin: *Stravinsky's "Fire Bird" and "Petrushka"* ("*Musical Pilgrim*"), 1933.

Glebov, Igor: *Kniga o Stravinskom*, 1929.

Schaeffner, André: *Igor Stravinsky*, 1931.

Stravinsky, Igor: *Chronicle of My Life* (*Eng. ed.* 1936).

Stravinsky and Robert Craft: *Conversations with Igor Stravinsky*, 1959. *Memories and Commentaries*, 1960. *Expositions and Developments*, 1962.

Vlad, Roman: *Stravinsky*, 1960.

White, E. W.: *Stravinsky's Sacrifice to Apollo*, 1930. *Stravinsky*, 1947.

TCHAÏKOVSKY

Abraham, Gerald, *ed.*: *Tchaïkovsky*, 1946.

Blom, Eric: *Tchaïkovsky's Orchestral Works* ("*Musical Pilgrim*"), 1927.

Evans, Edwin: *Tchaïkovsky* (2nd ed. 1935).

Knorr, Ivan: *Peter Tschaïkowsky*, 1900.

VAUGHAN WILLIAMS

Day, James: *Vaughan Williams*, 1961.

Dickinson, A. E. F.: *Vaughan Williams*, 1963.

Howes, Frank: *The Dramatic Works of Ralph Vaughan Williams* ("*Musical Pilgrim*"), 1937. *The Later Works of R. Vaughan Williams* ("*Musical Pilgrim*"), 1937.

VERDI

Bellaigue, Camille: *Verdi*, N.D.

Bonavia, Ferruccio: *Verdi*, 1930.

Hussey, Dyneley: *Verdi*, 1940.

Roncaglia, Gino: *L'Ascensione creatrice di Giuseppe Verdi*, 1940.

Toye, Francis: *Giuseppe Verdi*, 1931.

Weissmann, Adolf: *Verdi*, 1922.

WAGNER

Adler, Guido: *Richard Wagner*, 1904.

Bekker, Paul: *Richard Wagner*, 1924 (*Eng. ed.* 1931).

Donington, Robert: *Wagner's "Ring" and its Symbols*, 1963.

Ergo, Emil: *Uber Wagners Harmonik und Melodik*, 1914.

d'Indy, Vincent: *Richard Wagner et son influence sur l'art musical français*, 1930.

Jacobs, R. L.: *Wagner*, 1935.

Lorenz, Alfred: *Das Geheimnis der Form bei Richard Wagner*, 1924–33.

Newman, Ernest: *A Study of Wagner*, 1899. *Wagner as Man and Artist* (3rd ed. 1963).

Stein, Herbert von: *Dichtung und Musik im Werk Richard Wagner*, 1962.

Thomas, Eugen: *Die Instrumentation der "Meistersinger" von Richard Wagner*, N.D.

WAGNER   Wagner, Richard: *Gesammelte Schriften* (*Eng. ed.* 1895–99). *On Conducting* (*Eng. ed.* 1897). *Opera and Drama* (*Eng. ed.* N.D.).

WALTON   Howes, Frank: *The Music of William Walton* ("*Musical Pilgrim*," two vols., 1942).

WEBERN   Kolneder, W.: *Anton Webern*, 1961.

WOLF   Bieri, Georg: *Die Lieder von Hugo Wolf*, 1935.
                Decsey, Ernst: *Hugo Wolf* (new ed., 1921).
                Newman, Ernest: *Hugo Wolf*, 1907.
                Sams, Eric: *The Songs of Hugo Wolf*, 1961.

B—GENERAL BOOKS ON THE PERIOD

Abraham, Gerald: *Studies in Russian Music*, 1935.
   On Russian Music, 1939.
   Eight Soviet Composers, 1943.
   This Modern Music (3rd ed. 1955).
Adler, Guido, ed.: *Handbuch der Musikgeschichte* (2nd ed. 1929).
Bacharach, A. L., ed.: *British Music of our Time*, 1946.
Bartók, Béla: *Das ungarische Volkslied*, 1925 (*Eng. ed.* 1931).
Bauer, Marian: *Twentieth Century Music*, 1933.
Bekker, Paul: *The Changing Opera* (*Eng. ed.* 1935).
Bennett, Joseph: *Forty Years of Music*, 1908.
Berlioz, Hector: *Traité de l'instrumentation*, 1841 (*Eng. ed.* 1882; enlarged German ed. by Richard Strauss, 1904).
Blom, Eric: *Stepchildren of Music*, N.D.
Botstiber, Hugo: *Geschichte der Ouverture und freien Orchesterformen*, 1913.
Bücken, Ernst: *Die Musik des 19ten Jahrhunderts bis zur Moderne*, 1929.
Busoni, Ferruccio: *Entwurf einer neuen Ästhetik der Tonkunst*, N.D. (*Eng. ed.* N.D.).
   Von der Einheit der Musik, 1922.
Carner, Mosco: *A Study of Twentieth-century Harmony*, 1942.
Carse, Adam: *The Orchestra from Beethoven to Berlioz*, 1948.
Chase, Gilbert: *The Music of Spain*, 1941.
Cheshikin, Vsevolod: *History of Russian Opera*, 1905.
Cobbett, W. W., ed.: *Cyclopedic Survey of Chamber Music*, 1929.
Coeuroy, André: *La Musique française moderne*, 1924.
   Panorama de la musique contemporaine, 1928.
Colles, H. C.: *Symphony and Drama, 1850–1900* (*Oxford History of Music, Vol. VII*), 1934.
Cortot, Alfred: *French Piano Music* (*Eng. ed.* 1932).
Cowell, Henry, ed.: *American Composers on American Music*, 1933.
Dannreuther, Edward: *The Romantic Period* (*Oxford History of Music, Vol. VI*), 1905.
Davison, Henry: *From Mendelssohn to Wagner*, 1912.
Dumesnil, René: *La Musique contemporaine en France*, 1930.

Dunhill, T. F.: *Chamber Music*, 1913.

Dyson, George: *The New Music*, 1924.

Einstein, Alfred: *Music in the Romantic Era*, 1947.

Foster, Myles Birket: *History of the Philharmonic Society of London* (1813–1912), 1912.

Gray, Cecil: *A Survey of Contemporary Music*, 1924.
Predicaments, 1936.
The History of Music, 1928.

Grove, Sir George, ed.: *Dictionary of Music and Musicians* (4th ed.— Eric Blom, 1954, supp. vol. 1961).

Hadow, Sir Henry: *Studies in Modern Music*, 1892.

Hartog, Howard, ed.: *European Music in the Twentieth Century*, 1957.

Hauer, J. M.: *Vom Melos zur Pauke*, 1925.
Zwölftontechnik, 1925.

Hervey, Arthur: *French Music in the 19th Century*, 1903.

Hindemith, Paul: *Unterweisung in Tonsatz*, 1937 (*Eng. ed.* 1941).

Hueffer, Francis: *Half a Century of Music in England*, 1889.

Hull, A. Eaglefield: *Modern Harmony*, 1918.
Ed.: Dictionary of Modern Music and Musicians, 1924.

Huneker, James: *Mezzotints in Modern Music*, 1899.

Istel, Edgar: *Die Blütezeit der musikalischen Romantik in Deutschland*, 1909.

Jean-Aubry, G.: *French Music of To-day*, 1919.

Kilburn, N.: *Chamber Music and its Masters* (2nd ed. 1932).

Klauwell, Otto: *Geschichte der Programmmusik*, 1910.

Koechlin, Charles: *Traité de l'Harmonie*, 1925–30.

Křenek, Ernst: *Uber neue Musik*, 1937.
Studies in Counterpoint, 1940.

Kurth, Ernst: *Romantische Harmonik und ihre Krise in Wagners "Tristan,"* 1920.

Lambert, Constant: *Music Ho!*, 1934.

Lavignac, A., ed.: *Encyclopédie de la Musique et Dictionnaire du Conservatoire*, 1913–31.

Liszt, Franz: *Gesammelte Schriften*, 1880–83.

Locke, A. W.: *Music and the Romantic Movement in France*, 1920.

Maitland, J. A. Fuller: *English Music in the 19th Century*, 1902.

Matthews, W. S. B., ed.: *A Hundred Years of Music in America*, 1906.

McNaught, W. S.: *A Short Account of Modern Music and Musicians*, 1937.

Mellers, W. H.: *Studies in Contemporary Music*, 1948.

Mersmann, Hans: *Die moderne Musik seit der Romantik*, 1929.
Musik der Gegenwart, N.D.

Mitchell, Donald: *The Language of Modern Music*, 1963.

Myers, Rollo H.: *Modern Music*, 1923.
Music in the Modern World, 1939.

Newman, Ernest: *Musical Studies*, 1905.

Niecks, Frederick: *Programme Music*, 1906.

Niemann, Walter: *Die Musik seit Richard Wagner*, 1913.
  Die Musik Skandinaviens, 1906.
  Die Nordische Klaviermusik, 1917.
Pannain, Guido: *Modern Composers*, 1932 (*Eng. ed.* 1932).
Parry, Sir Hubert: *The Art of Music*, 1893.
Perle, George: *Serial Composition and Atonality*, 1962.
Riemann, Hugo: *Geschichte der Musik seit Beethoven*, 1901.
Riesmann, Oskar von: *Monographien zur Russischen Musik* (*Vol. I, Glinka, Serov and Dargomïzhsky*), 1923.
Rietsch, Heinrich: *Die Tonkunst in der zweiten Hälfte des 19 Jahrhunderts*, 1900.
Rimsky-Korsakov, N. A.: *Principles of Orchestration* (*Eng. ed.* N.D.).
Rohozinski, L.: *Cinquante ans de musique française*, 1925–26.
Rolland, Romain: *Musiciens d'aujourd'hui*, 1908 (*Eng. ed.* 1915).
Salazar, A.: *La música contemporanéa en España*, 1930.
  Music in Our Time, 1946.
Scholes, Percy A.: *The Mirror of Music*, 1947.
Schönberg, Arnold: *Harmonielehre*, 1911.
Schuh, Willi: *Zeitgenössische Musik*, 1947.
Schumann, Robert: *Gesammelte Schriften* (3rd ed. 1883; *Eng. ed.* N.D.).
Searle, Humphrey: *Twentieth Century Counterpoint*, 1954.
Slonimsky, Nicolas: *Music since 1900*, 1937.
  Music of Latin America, 1945.
Stein, Erwin: *Orpheus in New Guises*, 1953.
Tiersot, Julien: *Un demi-siécle de musique française*, 1924.
Tovey, Sir Donald: *Essays in Musical Analysis*, 1935–37.
Vaughan Williams, Ralph: *National Music*, 1934.
Walker, Ernest: *A History of Music in England*, 1907 (3rd ed., rev. by J. A. Westrup, 1952).
Weissmann, Adolf: *The Problems of Modern Music* (*Eng. ed.* 1925).
Wellesz, Egon: *Die neue Instrumentation*, 1928.

INDEX OF COMPOSERS AND WORKS